Computer Engineering

Computer Engineering

Edited by **Dewayne Hopper**

Willford Press

New York

Published by Willford Press,
118-35 Queens Blvd., Suite 400,
Forest Hills, NY 11375, USA
www.willfordpress.com

Computer Engineering
Edited by Dewayne Hopper

International Standard Book Number: 978-1-68285-100-5 (Hardback)

Printed in the United States of America.

Contents

Preface

This book has been a concerted effort by a group of academicians, researchers and scientists, who have contributed their research works for the realization of the book. This book has materialized in the wake of emerging advancements and innovations in this field. Therefore, the need of the hour was to compile all the required researches and disseminate the knowledge to a broad spectrum of people comprising of students, researchers and specialists of the field.

Computer engineering is a rapidly evolving field that integrates computer science and electrical engineering. Some of the diverse topics covered in this book address the varied branches that fall within the scope of this subject by discussing concepts like multimedia, embedded systems, computer networking and language programming, microprocessors, etc. It is a compilation of valuable researches and case-studies by eminent experts from around the world that aim to explain the most significant concepts and advancements in the above mentioned fields. It will help the readers in keeping pace with the rapid changes in this discipline.

At the end of the preface, I would like to thank the authors for their brilliant chapters and the publisher for guiding us all-through the making of the book till its final stage. Also, I would like to thank my family for providing the support and encouragement throughout my academic career and research projects.

Editor

1

Using the OOPP method to analyze complex industrial systems

Mohamed Najeh Lakhoua[1]* and Taieb Ben Jouida[2]

[1]High Institute of Applied Sciences and Technology (ISSAT), Laboratory ACS (Analysis and Command of Systems), Route de Tabarka 7030, Mateur, Tunisia.
[2]High Institute of Applied Sciences and Technology (ISSAT), SEPE (Systemic, Energetic, Productique and Environnement), Route de Tabarka 7030, Mateur, Tunisia.

The aim of this paper is to propose a methodology for the analysis and modeling of complex industrial systems and to validate it through a case study. In fact, an effective management of a complex industrial system can be only in systems whose activities are synchronized and enabling a good traceability. The development of a reliable information system (IS) is primordial. The methodology is divided into five steps and it is based on the use of OOPP (objectives oriented project planning) method. In this research, a case study of a grain silo in Tunisia is presented.

Key words: Analysis and modeling, information system, planning, OOPP method, grain silo.

INTRODUCTION

As a result of the evolution of the socio-economic context of the country after the process of globalization and of the partnership particularly with the European Union, the managers have inscribed in their priorities the upgrading of grain silo in Tunisia. The model developed was a general one; in order to validate this model, it was applied to a situation of a grain silo located in Tunis, considered like a pilot application. This choice was taken in consideration of the importance of this unit (the most big storage capacity in Tunisia: 54000 tonnes) (Annabi, 2004) because of its strategic position and the diversity of its activities. We respected also the culture and the historic of the enterprise.

In order to establish a model for upgrading a grain silo, we proceeded at first to the instruction of the situation close to the managers according to a brain-storming approach; secondly, we exploited an analysis of the existing one done by the supporting comity constituted. This analysis was achieved according to a participate approach associating the diverse structures of the office of cereals directly concerned by the activities of a grain silo and adopting an environment of quality comity.

After a proposition to adopt a systemic approach, exploiting notably the OOPP (objectives oriented project planning) method in analysing the activities of a grain silo according to the Office of Cereals Policy, a Total Quality Comity was constituted. Its purpose was to upgrade according to a total quality management (TQM) approach that was confided. A series of production workshops are organised. These workshops are either collectively organised, implicating all that are concerned by the diverse assigned functions of the grain silo or are dedicated to a specific function.

This paper can be loosely divided into five parts. First, we present participative methods literature. Second, we present the design methodology of the OOPP method. The next section presents a methodology of analysis of complex industrial systems. Next, the results of the application of the OOPP method are presented. The last section concludes this article giving some advantages of the method used.

PARTICIPATIVE METHODS LITERATURE

There are many methods that have been used to enhance participation in Information System (IS) planning and requirements analysis (Cavelery, 1994; Jackson, 1995; Lakhoua, 2006). We review some methods here because we think them to be fairly representative of the general kinds of methods in use. The methods include Delphi, focus groups, SADT (Structured Analysis Design Technique), OOPP method, multiple criteria decision-making (MCDM), and total quality management (TQM).

The objective of the Delphi method is to acquire and aggregate knowledge from multiple experts so that participants can find a

*Corresponding author. E-mail: Lakhoua@enit.rnu.tn.

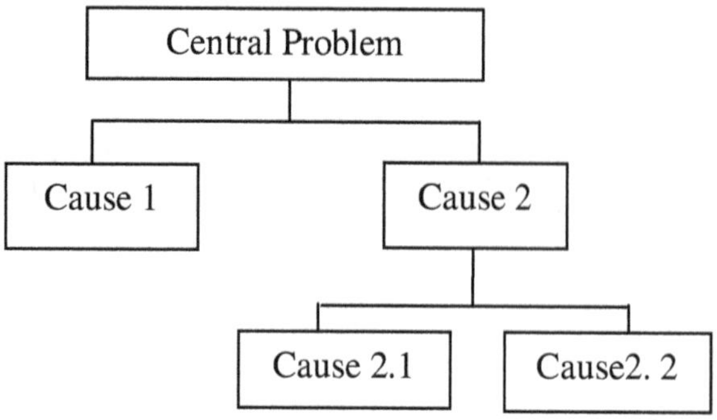

Figure 1. Problem tree.

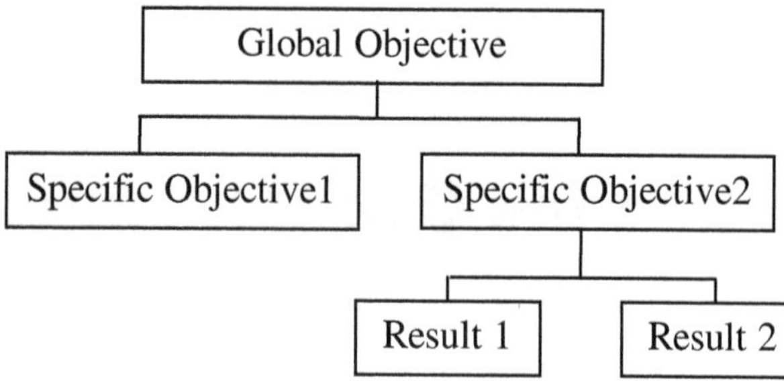

Figure 2. Objective tree.

consensus solution to a problem (Roth, 1990).

A second distinct method is focus groups (or focused group interviews). This method relies on team or group dynamics to generate as many ideas as possible. Focus groups have been used for decades by marketing researchers to understand customer product preferences (Parent, 2000).

MCDM views requirements of gathering and analysis as a problem requiring individual interviews (Jain, 1991). Analysts using MCDM focus primarily on analysis of the collected data to reveal users' requirements, rather than on resolving or negotiating ambiguities. The objective is to find an optimal solution for the problem of conflicting values and objectives, where the problem is modelled as a set of quantitative values requiring optimization.

TQM is a way to include the customer in development process, to improve product quality. In a TQM project, data gathering for customers needs, that is requirements elicitation may be done with QFD (Stylianou, 1997).

The SADT method represents attempts to apply the concept of focus groups specifically to information systems planning, eliciting data from groups of stakeholders or organizational teams (Marca, 1988; Jaulent 1989, 1992). They are characterized by their use of predetermined roles for group/team members and the use of graphically structured diagrams. SADT enables capturing of a proposed system's functions and data flow among the functions.

The OOPP method (AGCD, 1991; Killich, 2002), also referred to as Logical Framework Approach (LFA), is a structured meeting process. This approach seeks to identify the major current problems using cause-effect analysis and search for the best strategy to alleviate those identified problems. OOPP method has become the standard for the International Development Project Design. Team Technologies have continued to refine the approach into TeamUP.

DESIGN METHODOLOGY OF THE OOPP METHOD

The design methodology of the OOPP method (Annabi, 2003) is a rigorous process, which if used as intended by the creators, will impose a logical discipline on the project design team. If the process is used with integrity the result will be a high quality project design. The method is not without its limitations, but most of these can be avoided with careful use of ancillary techniques. Many things can go wrong in the implementation phase of a project, but if the design is flawed, implementation starts with a severe handicap.

The first few steps of the LFA are: situation analysis; stakeholder analysis; problems analysis (Walter, 1998; McLean, 1988).

The document of "Situation Analysis" describes the situation surrounding the problem. The source could be a feasibility study, a pre-appraisal report, or be a compilation done specifically for the project design workshop. Typically, the document describes the problem situation in detail, identifies the stakeholders and describes the effects of the problems on them.

The stage of "Stakeholder or Participation Analysis" is an analysis of the people, groups, or organizations that may influence or be influenced by the problem or a potential solution to the problem. This is the first step to understanding the problem. We might say, without people or interest groups there would be no problem. So to understand the problem, we must first understand the stakeholders. The objectives of this step are to reveal and discuss the interest and expectations of persons and groups that are important to the success of the project.

If there is no agreement between participants on the statement of the problem, it is unlikely there will be agreement on the solution. This stage of "Problem Analysis" therefore seeks to get consensus on the detailed aspects of the problem. The first procedure in problem analysis is brainstorming. All participants are invited to write their problem ideas on small cards. The participants may write as many cards as they wish. The participants group the cards or look for cause-effect relationship between the themes on the cards by arranging the cards to form a problem tree (Figure 1).

In the step of "Objectives Analysis" the problem statements are converted into objective statements and if possible into an objective tree (Figure 2). Just as the problem tree shows cause-effect relationships, the objective tree shows means-end relationships. The means-end relationships show the means by which the project can achieve the desired ends or future desirable conditions. Frequently, there are many possible areas that could be the focus of an "intervention" or development project. The next step addresses those choices.

The objective tree usually shows the large number of possible strategies or means-end links that could contribute to a solution to the problem. Since there will be a limit to the resources that can be applied to the project, it is necessary for the participants to examine these alternatives and select the most promising strategy. This step is called "Alternatives Analysis". After selection of the decision criteria, these are applied in order to select one or more means-end chains to become the set of objectives that will form the project strategy.

After defining the objectives and specifying how they will be measured (OVIs) and where and how that information will be found (MOVs), we get to the detailed planning phase: "Activities Planning". We determine what activities are required to achieve each objective. It is tempting to say: "always start at the situation analysis stage and from there determine who the stakeholders are".

We present some studies of the OOPP method in IS planning that has been presented in various researches.

Gu et al. (1994) presented an object-oriented approach to the development of a generative process planning system. The system consists of three functional modules: object-oriented product model, object-oriented manufacturing facility model module, and object-oriented process planner.

Peter (2000) questioned the appropriateness of highly structured strategic planning approaches in situations of complexity and change, using the Cambodian-German Health Project as a case study. He has demonstrated the limitations of these planning processes in complex situations of high uncertainty, with little reliable information and a rapidly changing environment.

Peffers et al. (2005) used information theory to justify the use of a method to help managers better understand why and what new IT (Information Technology) applications and features will be most valued by users, and how to apply this method in a case study involving the development of financial service applications for mobile devices.

METHODOLOGY OF ANALYSIS OF COMPLEX INDUSTRIAL SYSTEMS

After proposition to adopt a systemic approach, exploiting notably the OOPP method to analysis the activities of a grain silo (Lakhoua, 2008), we organised a series of production workshops. These workshops are either collectively organised, implicating all that are concerned by the diverse assigned functions of the grain silo or are dedicated to a specific function.

In fact, the technique of work group through the organization of workshops proved to be very efficient since through the stake in common of the appraisals of people resources, a synergy of group creates it and an adherence to the project of upgrading operates itself.

A various workshops have been organized to make the diagnosis and to identify the various functions of a grain silo. In fact, in addition to classic functions (exploitation, maintenance, management of stock, quality produces, common services), the function "Insurance Quality and System of information" has been instituted.

The first workshop identified began the basic functions, defined participants of the dedicated workshops and established a first planning. Then, during these workshops diverse validations and adjustments are done. This is because of the synergy phenomenon of the group and of the complement of the functions. The dedicated workshops caused the exploit of the expertise of the resource persons for the description with logic and in a hierarchy manner the diverse activities of functions.

The different steps of the methodology of the upgrading of a grain silo and their chronological events are:

Step 1: initialisation of the process of the upgrading of the grain silo by conversion of the results of the supporting comities according to OOPP formalism.
Step 2: preliminary definition of different functions of the grain silo and constitution of the commissions according to the defined functions. The participants at a commission are been chosen by speciality. The results of works of each commission are presented in a workshop and preliminary validation was done.
Step 3: coherence of the works of the dedicated workshops by a Total Quality Cell.
Step 4: presentation of the dedicated functions and global validation of the activities of each function.
Step 5: determination of the operational parameters of the analysis, particularly the delimitation of the responsibilities of the diverse activities.

The OOPP method constitutes a tool of a global systemic modelling enabling the analysis of a complex situation by a hierarchically decomposition until it reaches an elementary level that allows an operational planning. This method, widely used in the planning of complex projects, involves many operators and partners.

In Tunisia, this method was used in Development projects financed by bilateral or multilateral co-operation mechanism (with Germany, Belgium, Canada, World bank), in upgrading different structures (Training and Employment through MANFORME project, Organization of the Tunis Mediterranean Games 2001...) and in restructuring private and public enterprises.

An effort has been provided in order to bring improvements to this method (Annabi, 2003). The OOPP method has been spread and a new MISDIP denomination (Method of Specification, Development and Implementation of Project) was adopted. The MISDIP method adopts the OOPP analysis which is meant to complete it, to specify the system of organization, to specify the system of information, and to contribute to its development and implementation.

Analysis of the information

The identification and the analysis of the information exchanged by the activities indicate the dynamics and the communication between the elements of the system that we propose to study or to manage (Annabi, 2003).

So, an information matrix was defined. This matrix establishes a correlation between activities and their information. The information concerning an activity can be classified in two categories: (1) Imported information by an activity is supposed to be available: it is either produced by other activity of the system, or it comes from outside; (2) The produced information by an activity reflects the state of this activity. This last information may be exploited by other activities of the project.

In fact, the information produced by an activity can be considered like a transformation of imported information by this activity.

Information matrix

In order to specify this information, we define an information matrix (Table 2) that is associated with OOPP analysis which determines the relations between the activities or the concerned structures, and also identifies the information sources, determines the manner in which the information is exploited (Annabi, 2003).

To make sure of the quality of information system, we define some logic-functional rules reflecting the coherence, the reliability and the comprehensiveness of the analysis by an information matrix in which the lines are related to activities and the columns, to information. This matrix is constituted like this: (1) The first line is reserved to the first activity A1; (2) The first column is reserved to the first information If1 linked to this activity; (3) If If1 is imported by A1, we inscribe « 0 » in the correspondent box; if it is produced by A1, we inscribe « 1 » ; (4) We pass after that to the second information If2 and we associate the correspondent binary character « 0 » if the information is imported by the activity A1 and « 1 » if it is produced by the same activity; (5) We proceed in the same way until all the information concerning A1 is exhausted; (6) We pass after that to the second line that is correspondent to the second activity A2; (7) If If1 concerns A2, we inscribe the correspondent binary number (0 or 1 according to this information is imported or produced), otherwise, we leave a blank in the correspondent box, then we add the new information that concerns the current activity and (8) We follow the same step as far as exhausting of all activities and of all correspondent information.

We finally construct progressively a matrix of big dimension if the system is complex; it is constituted of « 0 », « 1 » and « blank ».

The information matrix defined enables us to establish a correlation between the activities and their information. This matrix was used in order to specify the information exchanged between the different elements of a system.

RESULTS OF THE OOPP ANALYSIS OF A GRAIN SILO

The production of the enterprise is often based on a technical process that cannot be taken as good knowledge

Table 1. Information matrix associated to the OOPP analysis.

N°	Code	Activity	If_1	If_2	If_3	if_4	If_5	If_6	If_7	If_8	If_9
1		A_1	0	0	1	1					
2		A_2		0	0		1	0			
3		A_3	1	0	0	0		0	0	1	
4		A_n									

Table 2. Analysis of the different functions of a grain silo using the OOPP method.

N°	Code	Designation
1	GO	Functions of the grain silo defined
2	SO1	Exploitation of the grain silo assured
3	*R1.1*	Planning of the exploitation of the grain silo assured
4	R1.2	Realisation of the operations assured
5	SO2	Maintenance of the grain silo assured
6	R2.1	Planning of the maintenance of the grain silo assured
7	R2.2	Intervention assured
8	R2.3	Management of the material resources assured
9	SO3	Management of the stock assured
10	R3.1	Programme of the movement of the cereals established
11	R3.2	Movement of the cereals recorded
12	R3.3	Reporting elaborated
13	SO4	Function of cereals quality management assured
14	R4.1	Evaluation of cereal quality assured
15	R4.2	Preservation of cereal quality assured
16	R4.3	Amelioration of cereal quality assured
17	SO5	Function of common services management assured
18	R5.1	Administrative management of the personnel assured
19	R5.2	Formation management assured
20	R5.3	Financial and book-keeping management assured
21	SO6	Function of assurance quality and Information System defined
22	R6.1	Function of assurance quality defined
23	R6.2	Information system efficient

knowledge only if other functions of support are led as well. So the enterprise, in addition to the technical functions of basis, is called to assure various functions of different natures: Human resource management, accountant, financial, communication, management of stock, maintenance, formation etc.

The achievement of every function requires the realization of various activities. Because functions bound some to others, and that activities are interdependent, there is a place to assure a function of co-ordination, allowing the enterprise to evolve previously of a coherent manner according to its definite objectives. The function "Assurance quality and Information System" is determinant to assure a system of communication and co-ordination of activities of an enterprise.

After the OOPP analysis, six specific objectives are identified corresponding to the basic functions of a grain silo (exploitation, maintenance, quality product management, management of the common services, TQM and Information System). The analysis of the Specific Objectives (SO) enables us to identify 14 Results (R) and more than 1700 activities. The Table 1 presents results of the OOPP analysis of a grain silo.

In order to design the responsibility of each activity, we adopt the structured analysis elaborated using the two methods SADT and OOPP after a validation and we proceed to identify the responsibility of the activities and their collaborators for the diverse functions of a grain silo.

The final production of the application of the OOPP method enabled us to answer clearly the questions: "what?" and "who?" and allowed the establishment of the record post and the elaboration of the chart of a grain silo notably the specification of the responsible of the activities and their collaborators. The answer to the question "how?" led to the elaboration of the work procedures, but the answer to the question "when?" made

Table 3. Sample of the OOPP analysis of a grading system of cereals.

N°	Code of activity	Activity	Imp.Inf	Prod.Inf
179	SO4	Evaluation of cereals assured	N°AT	N°PT
180	R4.1	Identification of the grading scale assured	NatCer, N°LtCer, VPA, BPQI	
184	R4.2	Improvements and reductions determined		
185	A4.1.1	Identify the improvements to add to basic price		
186	S4.1.1.1	Identify the codes of improvements		CdImp
190	S4.1.1.2	Identify the improvements values		VImp
194	A4.1.2	Identify the reductions to reduce from price base		
195	S4.1.2.1	Identify the codes of reductions		CdRed
199	S4.1.2.2	Identify the reductions values		VRed
203	R4.3	Payment ticket established		
204	A4.3.1	Cereal price determined		
205	S4.1.3.1	Determine the total of improvements		TotImp
209	S4.1.3.2	Determine the total of reductions		TolRed
213	S4.1.3.3	Determine the gross price		GP
217	S4.1.3.4	Determine the deduction		Ded
221	S4.1.3.5	Determine the net price		NP

made for the establishing of the planning of the actions. And finally by answering to the question " where?" we were able to determine the frontiers post. The most important function that exists in the new structure, compared to that in the application, is the TQM function and Information System.

In order to present a sample, an information matrix connected to the OOPP analysis, we present the case study of the grading system of cereals that allows us to determine the price of transactions of cereals (Durum wheat, Soft wheat, Barley, etc).

In fact, we consider every element of the grading system of cereals (Grading Parameters, Cereal variety, Reception ticket, demand of analysis, Analysis ticket, Payment ticket, Cereal sampling ticket,...) like an information that can be expressed according to other information (Number of order, date, quantity, etc).

By exploiting the information matrix defined, we constitute an "information matrix of cereal grading system" (IMGSC) where we give in the last column the different relations excising this system.

The information matrix connected to the grading system of cereals allows firstly to determine the relations between the activities defined in the descriptive table of tree of objectives, and secondly to identify and to exploit the information sources that constitute the different parameters of the model.

The complete OOPP analysis of grading system of cereals released 263 activities, giving 279 information. We can identify various types of information source: declarative (name, N° Lot...), measure (specific weight, percentage of impurities, time...), data base (Grading scale, sample protocol, homogenisation protocol, basic price, etc), valorisation (improvement value, reduction value, net price, etc).

Table 3 presents, in a linear form, some parts of the analysis and precise the information field concerning activities and specifying the imported information (Imp.Inf) and the produced information (Prod.Inf). We present in Table 4 a part of the IMGSC.

Every imported or produced information by an activity is codified: N°AT (number of analysis ticket), N°PT (N° of the payment ticket), NatCer (nature of the cereals), N°LtCer (number of lot of cereals), VAP (value of a grading parameter), BPQI (basic price per quintal)...

Conclusion

In most situations, an industrial system such as a grain silo already existing, conditioned by its history, its culture and its context are in difficulty facing the necessity to restructure itself in an organizational and technological environment in perpetual evolution. This is how all operation of upgrading first of all requires a diagnosis based on a various function analysis.

The global analysis exploits the various available documents (legal texts, balances, reports...) on the one hand and takes on the other hand in consideration of various testimonies through investigations, the interviews or the collective workshops; otherwise, it also takes observations through visits as a basis and even of the specific operations. The exploitation of this diagnosis enables for the elaboration of the project, restructuring thereafter.

In this paper, a methodology of analysis and modelling for the upgrading of industrial systems has been presented. A participative method (OOPP) has been used and a practical case of a grain silo has been used to verify the model developed. This analysis enables to identify the different activities in a grain silo. It enables then to implant a process of the tractability of flux movements

Table 4. Part of the IMGSC associated to the OOPP analysis.

N°	Code \Inf	223	224	225	227	228	229	235	236	237	239	240	241	Relation
1	T4.1.3.1.1	1												$TotImp_1 = VImp_{1.1} + VImp_{1.2} + ... + VImp_{1.14}$
2	T4.1.3.1.2		1											$TotImp_2 = VImp_{2.1} + VImp_{2.2} + ... + VImp_{2.12}$
3	T4.1.3.1.3			1										$TotImp_3 = VImp_{3.1} + VImp_{3.2} + VImp_{3.3} + VImp_{3.4}$
4	T4.1.3.2.1				1									$TolRed_1 = VRed_{1.1} + VRed_{1.2} + ... + VRed_{1.14}$
5	T4.1.3.2.2					1								$TolRed_2 = VRed_{2.1} + VRed_{2.2} + ... + VRed_{2.12}$
6	T4.1.3.2.3						1							$TolRed_3 = VRed_{3.1} + VRed_{3.2} + VRed_{3.3} + VRed_{3.4}$
7	T4.1.3.5.1	0			0			0			1			$NP_1 = GP_1 + TotImp_1 - TolRed_1 - Ded_1$
8	T4.1.3.5.2		0			0			0			1		$NP_2 = GP_2 + TotImp_2 - TolRed_2 - Ded_2$
9	T4.1.3.5.3			0			0			0			1	$NP_3 = GP_3 + TotImp_3 - TolRed_3 - Ded_3$

movements with the knowledge of the handling circuits and the actions of the maintenance of the equipment.

REFERENCES

AGCD (1991). Manuel pour l'application de la «Planification des Interventions Par Objectifs (PIPO). 2ème Edition, Bruxelles, Belgique.

Annabi M (2003). PIPO étendue : Méthode Intégrée de Spécification, de Développement et d'Implémentation de Projet (MISDIP). STA'2003, Sousse, 21-23 déc.

Annabi M, Bel Hadj MT (2004). Partenariat Université-Entreprise dans le processus de mise à niveau : Cas de l'Office des Céréales. Forum Scientifique: Medelec, 25-26 Nov.

Cavelery P (1994). Soft Systems Thinking: A Pre-condition for Organizational Learning, Human Systems Management. Pages 259-267.

Gu P, Zhang Y (1994). OOPPS: an object-oriented process planning system. Comput. Ind Engr, 26(4): 709-731.

GTZ (1991). Methods and Instruments for Project Planning and Implementation. Germany.Provide page and site in the work.

Jackson MC (1995).Beyond the Fads: Systems Thinking for Managers. Systems Research, pp.25-42.

Jain HK, Tanniru MR, Fazlollahi B (1991). MCDM approach for generating and evaluating alternatives in requirement analysis. Inf. Syst. Res. 2(3): 223-239.

Jaulent P (1989). SADT un langage pour communiquer. IGL Technol, Eyrolles, Paris.

Jaulent P (1992). Génie logiciel les méthodes : SADT, SA, E-A, SA-RT, SYS-P-O, OOD, HOOD. Armand Colin, Paris.

Killich S (2002). TeamUp, a software-technical support-tool, businesses of the future. Aachen, 2002.

Lakhoua MN (2008). Analyse systémique d'un environnement de production en vue d'implanter un système d'information. Thèse de doctorat, ENIT, Tunisie.

Lakhoua MN, Ben Jouida T, Annabi M (2006). State of the art of Strategic Planning. ICTTA'06, IEEE, Damascus, Syria, 1: 453-458.

Marca DA, McGowan CL (1988). SADT: structured analysis and design technique. New York: McGraw-Hill Book.

McLean D (1988). Logical Framework in Res. Planning and Evaluation. Int. Serv. of Natl. Agric.Res. Working, Washington.

Parent M, Gallupe RB, Salisbury WD, Handelman JM (2000). Knowledge creation in focus groups: can group technologies help? Inf. Manag.38 (1): 47-58.

Peffers K, Tunanen T (2005). Planning for IS applications: a practical, information theoretical method and case study in mobile financial services. Inf. Manag, 42, 3, 483-501.

Peter SH (2000). Planning and change: a Cambodian public health case study. Soc. Sci. Med. 51: 1711-1722.

Roth RM, Wood WCI, Delphi A (1990). Approach to acquiring knowledge from single and multiple experts. Conference on Trends and Directions in Expert Systems.

Stylianou AC, Kumar RL, Khouja MJ (1997). A Total Quality Management-based systems development process. The DATA BASE for Advances in Inf. Syst. 28 (3): 59-71.

Walter EM (1998). Introduction à la méthode de Planification des Projets par Objectifs. Rapport de l'atelier de formation REFA,

2

Optimized mask selection for person identification and camera distance measurement based on interocular distance

Khandaker Abir Rahman[1*], Shafaeat Hossain[1], Al-Amin Bhuiyan[2], Tao Zhang[3], Md. Hasanuzzaman[1] and H. Ueno[4]

[1]Department of Computer Science and Engineering, University of Dhaka, Dhaka-1000, Bangladesh.
[2]Department of Electronics and Computer Science, Jahangirnagar University, Savar, Bangladesh.
[3]Department of Automation, Tsinghua University, Beijing, China.
[4]National Institute of Informatics (NII), Tokyo, Japan.

This paper presents a multi-resolution masks based pattern matching method for person identification. The system is commenced with the construction of multi-resolution mask cluster pyramid, where the mask size is chosen depending on the distance between two eyes, computed from the detected face. Experimental results show the effectiveness of the system with significantly higher precision, recall rates and matching probability comparing with conventional single resolution mask based person identification systems. This paper also presents a novel person to camera distance measuring system based on eye-distance. The distance between centers of two eyes (interocular distance) is used for measuring the person to camera distance. The variation in eye-distance (in pixels) with the changes in camera to person distance (in inches) is used to formulate the distance measuring system. Experimental results show the effectiveness of the distance measurement system with an average accuracy of 94.11%.

Key words: Single resolution mask, multi-resolution masks, person to camera distance, person identification.

INTRODUCTION

Many algorithms have been proposed for person identification (Valentin, 1994; Chellappa, 1995; Zhao, 2002), creating a new industry (Hansen, 2005). Scientists working with these systems know that some persons are harder to recognize than are others. Consequently, research on person identification remain in the center of attention to the researchers because of its' versatile application. These researches are diversified in two methods (Brunelli, 1983), geometric feature-based methods and template-based ones. The basic method of template matching uses a convolution mask (template), tailored to a specific feature of the search image, which we want to detect. Other sophisticated methods involve extensive pre-processing and transformation of the extracted grey-level intensity values. Turk and Pentland (Turk, 1991) used principal component analysis (PCA), to pre-process the gray-levels of the image. The other implementation of template matching method is using a deformable mask (Yuille, 1992; Black, 2007). Instead of using several fixed size masks, a deformable mask is used and there by changed the size of the mask hoping to detect a face in an image. Hasanuzzaman et al. (2005) proposed a system that first detects the face and identifies the user to learn skin-color information of the person (Hasanuzzaman, 2005; Hasanuzzaman, 2007). It uses face templates pyramid with different resolutions and orientations where two eyes on the upper part of the probable face are located to make sure of the presence of the face (Bhuiyan, 2004).

For measuring object to camera distance, two widely used approaches are: contact and non-contact approaches (Chen, 2007). In contact-based approach, various methods can be used, such as ultrasonic distance measurement (Carullo, 1996; Carullo, 2001), laser reflection methods (Osugi, 1999; Shin, 2000). These two methods use the theory of reflection. If the

*Corresponding author. E-mail: abir.bd@gmail.com.

reflection surface is not uniform, the measuring system generally performs poorly or not at all. On the other hand, image-based measuring systems based on pattern recognition or image analysis techniques (Kanade, 1995; Tanaka, 1998) generally demand huge amount of storage capacity and high-speed processors. The proposed distance measurement method in this paper is quite different from other existing image processing based person to camera distance measuring techniques which requires additional CCD cameras (Sid-Ahmed, 1990; Liguori, 2001), laser projectors, etc. during the measurements. The distance between two eyes (in pixels) of a person in an image reduces as the person moves away from the camera and vice versa. This property is used to measure the person to camera distance based on a certain eye-distance in real time.

To overcome the problems and difficulties encountered by the existing person identification techniques caused by mainly huge computational necessity, an eye-distance based mask selection for person identification method is presented in this paper. Based on an established relationship between the eye-distance and face size (both in pixels), the mask dimension is selected for further processing by computing the minimum distance qualifier (Manhattan Distance). The proposed method in this paper is quite different from other existing template matching based person identification systems which uses single resolution mask. This method improves the mask selection procedure thus saving computational cost significantly by simply discarding masks of unnecessary dimensions at the very beginning.

The partial work of this paper has been presented in MUE, 09 (Rahman, 2009a, b). Thus the complete work is presented in this paper.

PROPOSED SYSTEM

Eye distance measurement

This system forms an image pyramid of the input images and uses a template matching approach for face and eye detection (Chen, 2007). An image pyramid is a set of copies of the original image at different scales, thus representing a set of different resolutions. To locate the face a mask is moved pixel-wise over each image in the pyramid, and at each position the image section under the mask is passed to a function that assesses the similarity of the image section to a face. If the similarity value is high enough (with respect to some threshold), the presence of a face at that position is assumed. From that position, the position and size of the face in the original image is generated. This eye detection is identical to face detection system which forms an image pyramid of the detected face images and uses a template matching approach for eye detection. The Euclidian distance between two eyes is computed using the following:

$$d_{ep} = \sqrt{(E_{LX} - E_{RX})^2 + (E_{LY} - E_{RY})^2} \quad (1)$$

Where (E_{LX}, E_{LY}) and (E_{RX}, E_{RY}) are the coordinates of the left and right eyes respectively and d_{ep} is the distance between two eyes in terms of pixels.

Formulation of person to camera distance measurement equation

After a comprehensive study conducted over 35 people of both sexes and from different height ranges, it is found that a relation exists between eye distance (in pixels) and person to camera distance (in inches). A sample square of eye distance versus person to camera distance graph of several persons is presented in Figure 1. From the figure it is noticeable that the square of eye distance versus person to camera distance graph is significantly identical thus it can be generalized for persons of different physical identities. Table 1 presents collected measured data of three persons on different predefined camera to person distances (in inches).

Equations (2) and (3) are formulated after a thorough study of the nature of Eye Distance^2 versus Person to Camera Distance graphs of 35 people, which simulates the graphs in real-time.

$$d_{ep}^{\ 2} = \frac{MAX_{ed}}{(1 + \frac{d_c - Mid_G}{Mid_G})(\sqrt{d_c - MIN_{ed}} - 1)} \quad (2)$$

$$d_c' = d_c \pm V(2 - \frac{d_{ep}}{MAX_{ed}}) \quad (3)$$

where d_{ep} is the distance between two eyes, MAX_{ed} is the maximum eye distance point, MIN_{ed} is the minimum camera distance point, Mid_G is the mid point of square of eye distance Vs person to camera distance graph , d_c is the primary camera to person distance (with error), d_c' is the corrected camera to person distance and V is the correction weight. Positions of MAX_{ed}, MIN_{ed}, Mid_G points are shown in Figure 2. These values are generalized considering the data collected of 35 people.

Before measuring the person to camera distance, the person is trained with different predefined distances from the camera starting from 7 inches and increased up-to 31

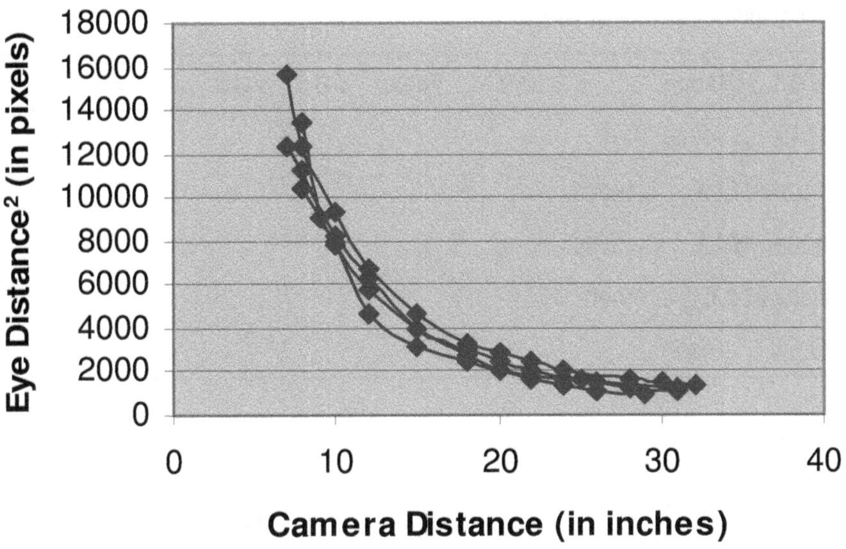

Figure 1. Sample relation between eye-distance and person to camera distance.

Table 1. Sample measured data.

Square of eye distance (in pixels)			Person to camera distance (in inches)
Person 1 (Abir)	Person 2 (Wahid)	Person 3 (Robin)	
1228	1150	1225	31
1350	1329	1370	28
1580	1450	1685	25
1900	1959	2034	22
2226	2145	2501	20
2720	2890	3000	18
4000	3986	4005	15
5800	6120	6277	12
7800	7980	8200	10
10400	10350	11211	8
14500	13500	12400	7

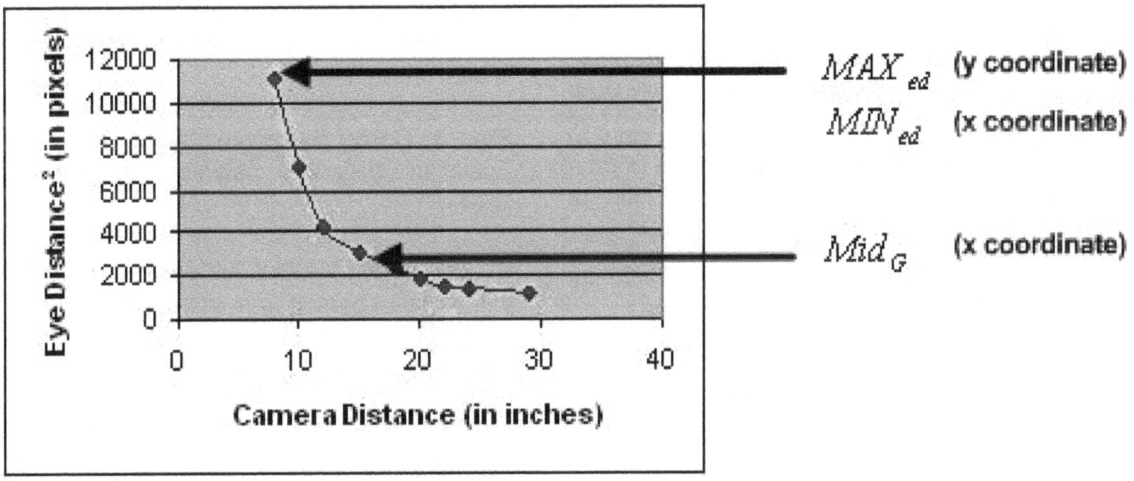

Figure 2. Relation between eye distance and object to camera distance.

Table 2. Intrinsic parameter table.

MAX_{ed} Range	MIN_{ed} Value	Mid_G Value	Value of V	Sign
MAX_{ed} >16000	8	23	8	+
13000< MAX_{ed} <=16000	8	20	6	+
11000< MAX_{ed} <=13000	8	18	4	+
9500< MAX_{ed} <=11000	8	15	0	N/A
MAX_{ed} <=9500	7	15	4	-

Table 3. Relation between eye distance, face size and height.

No. of persons	Height range	Actual camera to object distance (in inches)	Average eye distance (in pixels)	Average face dimension
5	5' 8" and over	32	34.33	58 × 58
		30	36.07	65 × 65
		28	38.19	68 × 68
		24	43.32	78 × 78
		22	47.09	85 × 85
		20	50.38	90 × 90
		18	55.31	100 × 100
		15	65.11	115 × 115
		12	80.46	145 × 145
		10	93.43	168 × 168
		8	107.90	190 × 190
		7	129.29	213 × 213

inches. During the training session corresponding person to camera distances (in inches) and eye distances are mapped and the MAX_{ed} value of that person (when the person is in the highest distance from the camera) is set by the system. It is also found that there are generally 5 categories of MAX_{ed} values ranging from 16000 - 9500 in which the persons tested have been categorized.

Depending on the MAX_{ed} value, the other parameters of (2) and (3) are set according to Table 2. Figure 3 shows the different square of eye distance versus person to camera distance graphs depending on different MAX_{ed} value. The values of Table 3 are set after analyzing the characteristics of square of eye distance versus person to camera distance graphs of Figure 3.

Person to camera distance measurement

Person to camera distance measurement is accomplished by calculating the eye distance and then mapping the corresponding person to camera distance from the generalized (2) and (3) with the values of the parameters from Table 2 after identifying the person along with corresponding MAX_{ed} value of that person. If the person is not identified then the default parameters values are chosen. Figure 4 shows the complete architecture of the proposed distance measuring system. The person to camera distance measurement algorithm is described bellow:

Step 1: Detect the center of the two eyes and find the Euclidian distance between them (Hasanuzzaman, 2007).

Step 2: If the person is identified then retrieve the MAX_{ed} value of that person from the database.

Step 3: Set the values of MIN_{ed}, Mid_G, V from Table 2 according to MAX_{ed}, where MAX_{ed} is the maximum eye distance point, MIN_{ed} is the minimum camera distance point, Mid_G is the mid point of Eye Distance^2-

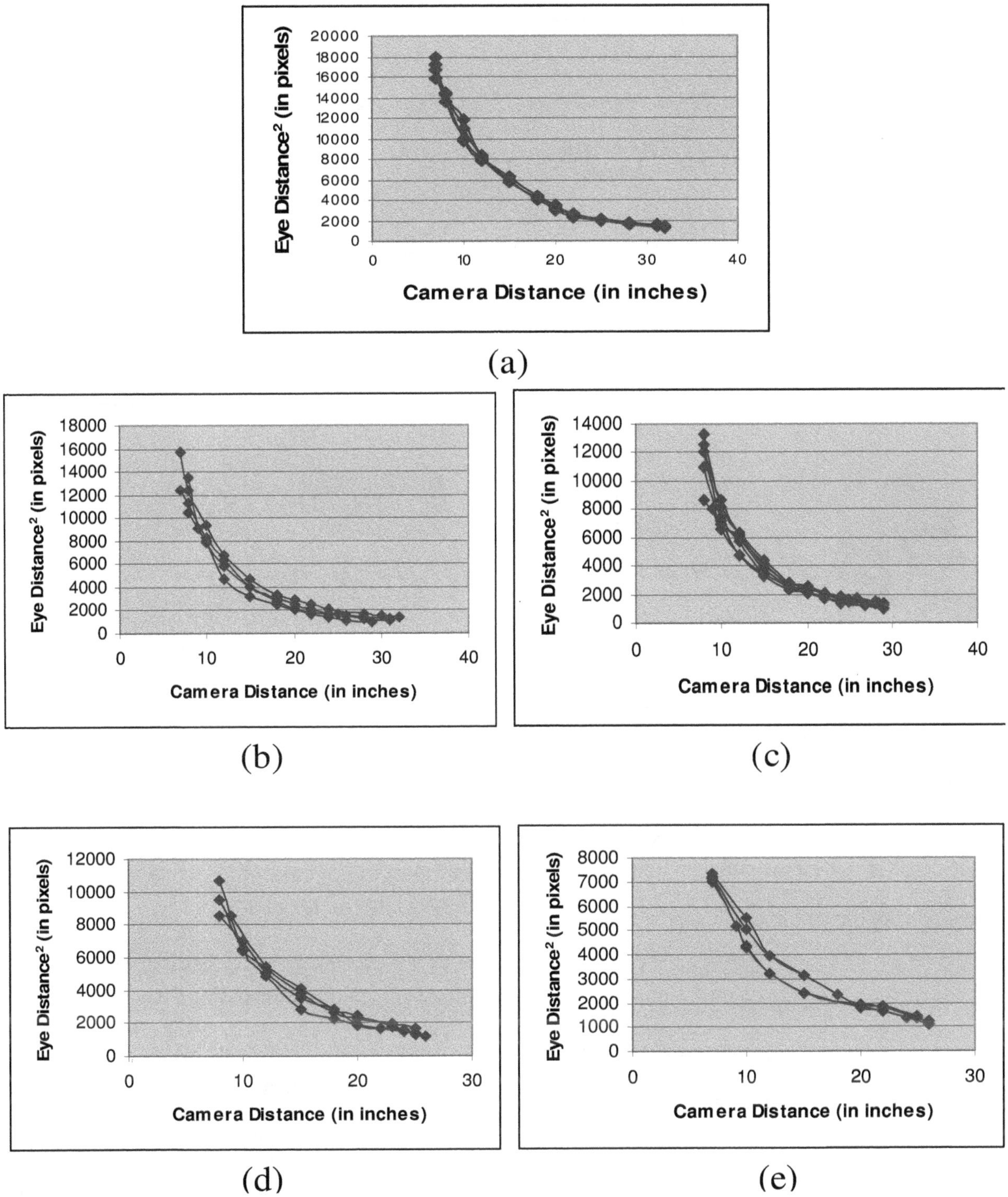

Figure 3. Square of eye distance versus person to camera distance graph (a) where MAX_{ed} >16000 (b) for 13000< MAX_{ed} <=16000, (c) for 11000< MAX_{ed} <=13000, (d) for 9500< MAX_{ed} <=11000 and (e) MAX_{ed} <=950.

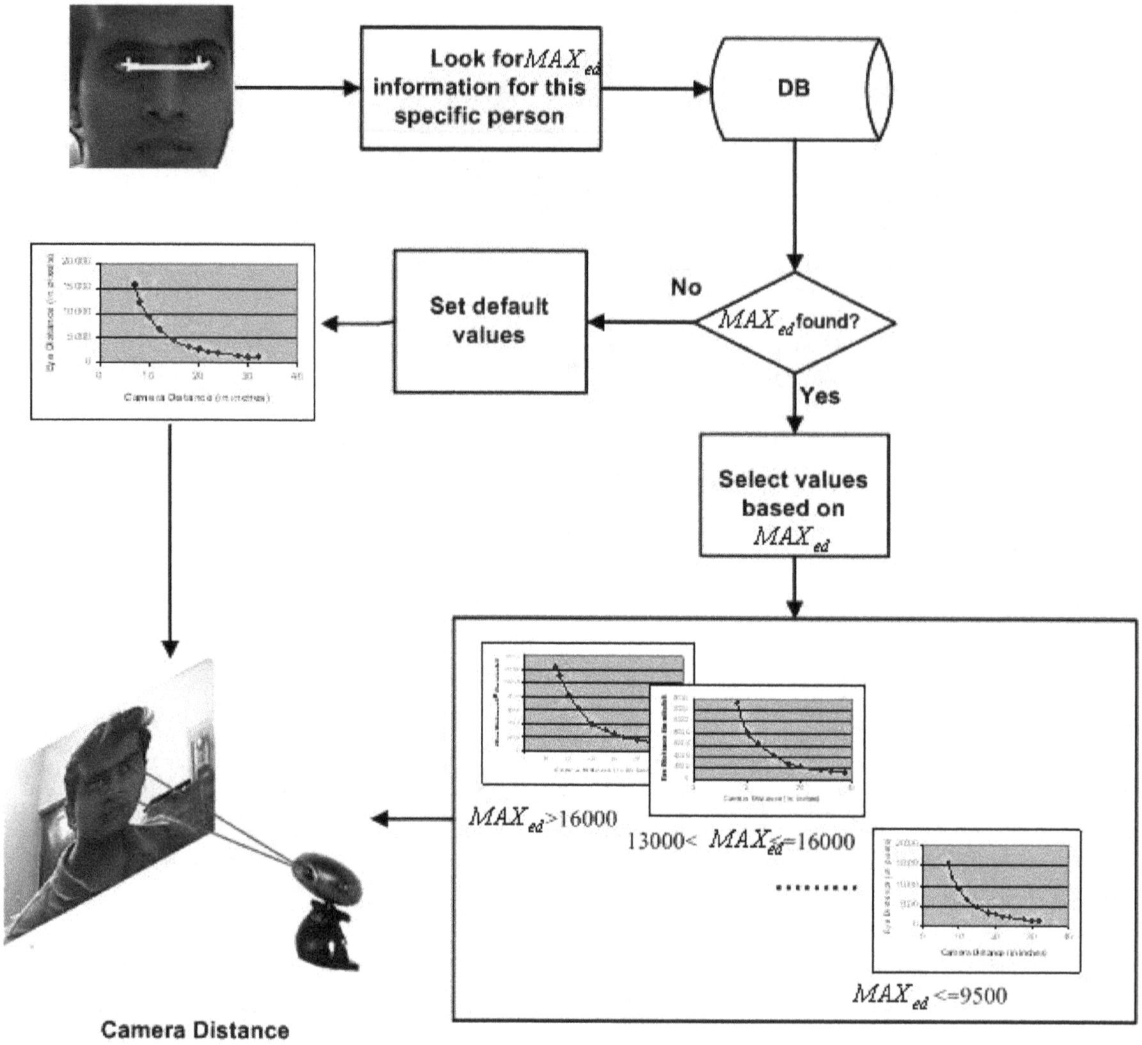

Figure 4. Person to camera distance measurement system architecture.

Camera Distance graph and V is the correction weight.

Step 4: Calculate primary camera to person distance, d_c from the (4)

$$d_c^{2} (d_c - MIN_{ed} - 1) = \left(\frac{MAX_{ed} \times MID_G}{d_{ep}^{2}}\right)^2 \quad (4)$$

Where d_{ep} is the distance between two eyes.

Step 5: Make correction to the camera to person distance by the following equation:

$$d_c' = d_c \pm V\left(2 - \frac{d_{ep}}{MAX_{ed}}\right)$$

Where d_c is the primary camera to person distance (with error), d_c' is the corrected person to camera distance and V is the correction weight and return d_c'.

Step 6: If the person is not identified, set the default value as MAX_{ed} = 11000 and goto Step 2.

Normalization and training

After face is detected, the face area is normalized before passing to the face recognition and person identification module as shown in Figure 5. Detected face is converted to grayscale using (5) and scaled to nearest dimension using (6) and saved as a gray bmp Image;

$$Gr_i = \frac{R_i + G_i + B_i}{3}, i = 1, 2, 3, \ldots\ldots, M \times N \quad (5)$$

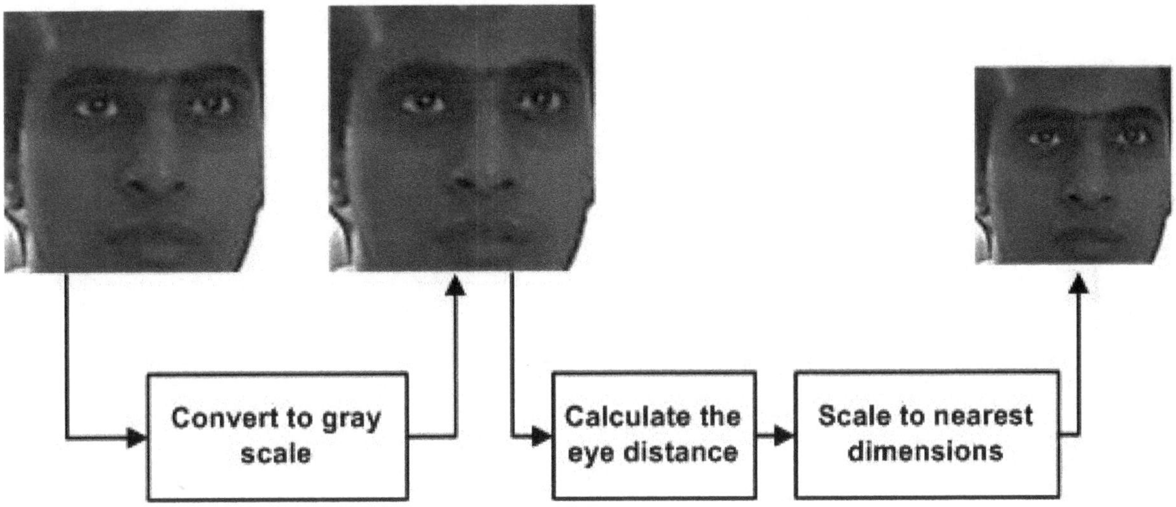

Figure 5. Normalization method.

Where, Gr_i is the gray level value of ith pixel of the gray image. *R_i, G_i, and B_i* corresponds to red, green and blue components of the ith pixel in the color image. Suppose $M \times N$ is the initial image dimension, it is scaled to $M' \times N'$ dimension. The scaling is done as follows. Suppose, we have a segment of square $P[(x^l, y^l)-(x^h, y^h)]$ we sample it to dimension $Q[(0,0)-(M' \times N')]$ using following expression,

$$Q(x^q, y^q) = P(x^l + \frac{(x^k - x^l)}{M' \times N'} x^q, y^l + \frac{(y^k - y^l)}{M' \times N'} y^q) \quad (6)$$

The training module is invoked when a new face is encountered. The person must be trained before he/she can be identified in future encounter. This module takes face samples and creates a face cluster for a new person, P_i. The face cluster is normalized and rescaled to different dimensions (50 × 50, 60 × 60, 70 × 70, 80 × 80, 90 × 90 and 100 × 100) and inserts in the training database.

Relation between eye distance and face size

After a comprehensive study over twenty four persons, it is found that both eye distance and face dimension are largely interdependent. Table 3 shows the relation of person height, eye distance and face dimension. Figure 6 shows the relation between eye distance and face size for the persons with different height ranges. From the collected data it is noticeable that relation between eye distance and face dimension is linear regardless of height of a person. It is also found that, the average face dimension is approximately 1.8 times of average eye distances.

Person identification

In the person identification system, multi-resolution masks are used to make the system robust against face size. The Person Identification module of the system has a training face database containing K images (I_t) with different resolutions. The person identification system takes input test image, I_{ts} one by one generated from face detection and normalizes to nearest mask size depending on the eye distance. The mask size is selected for matching with the previously saved templates with different dimensions by the following (7),

$$M' \times N' = M_s \times d_{ep} \quad (7)$$

where, $M' \times N'$ is the mask size, M_s is mask factor which is determined empirically to 1.8, as found in Subsection C and d_{ep} is the eye distance in pixels. Figure 7 shows the relation between M_s and d_{ep}.

The system generates Boolean decision regarding whether the input image(s) are recognized or not. The eye-distance based mask selection process is shown in Figure 8. This person identification method is described using following steps.

Step 1: Calculate the eye distance, d_{ep}

Step 2: Set the value of Mask Size Factor, M_s =

Step 3: Normalize and set the dimension of the face size,

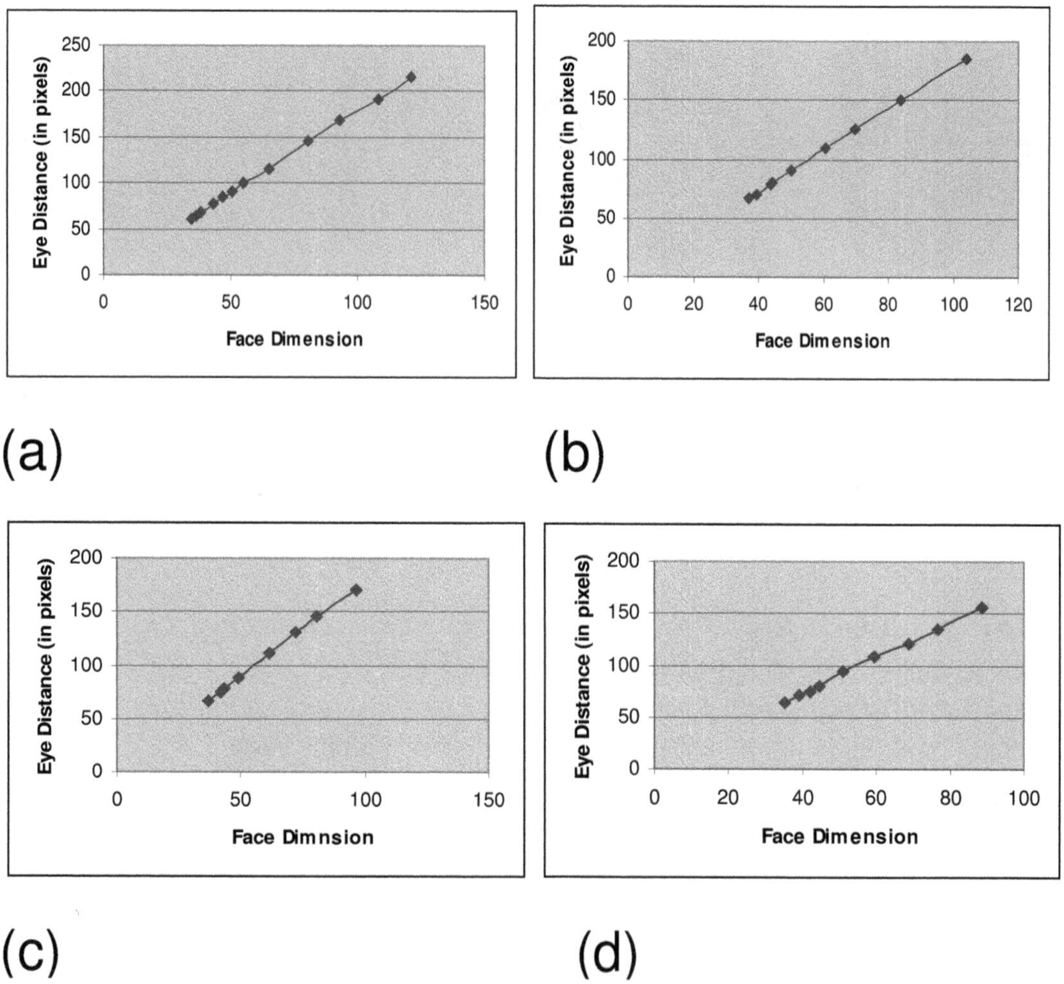

Figure 6. Relation between eye distance and face size, (a) height ranging over 5' 8'', (b) height ranging between 5' 4'' and 5' 7'', (c) height ranging between 5' and 5' 3'', (d) height ranging bellow 5'.

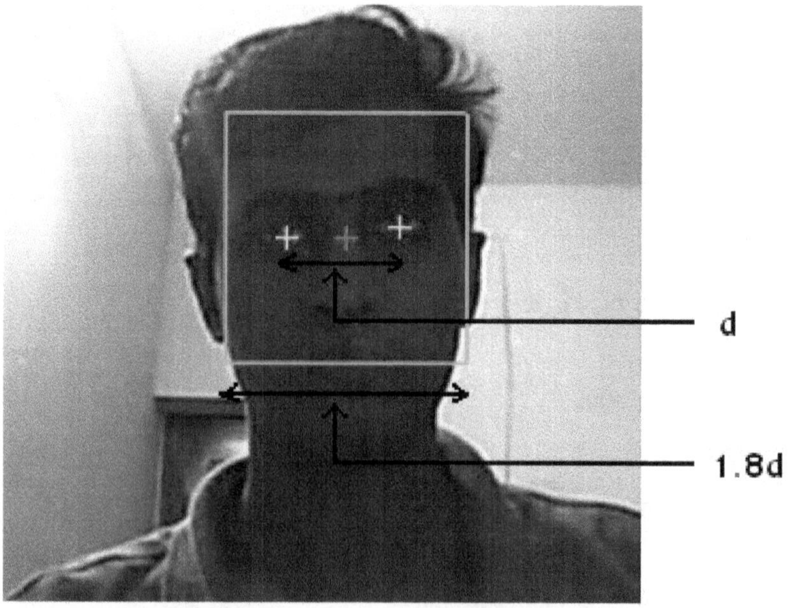

Figure 7. Relation between eye distance and mask size.

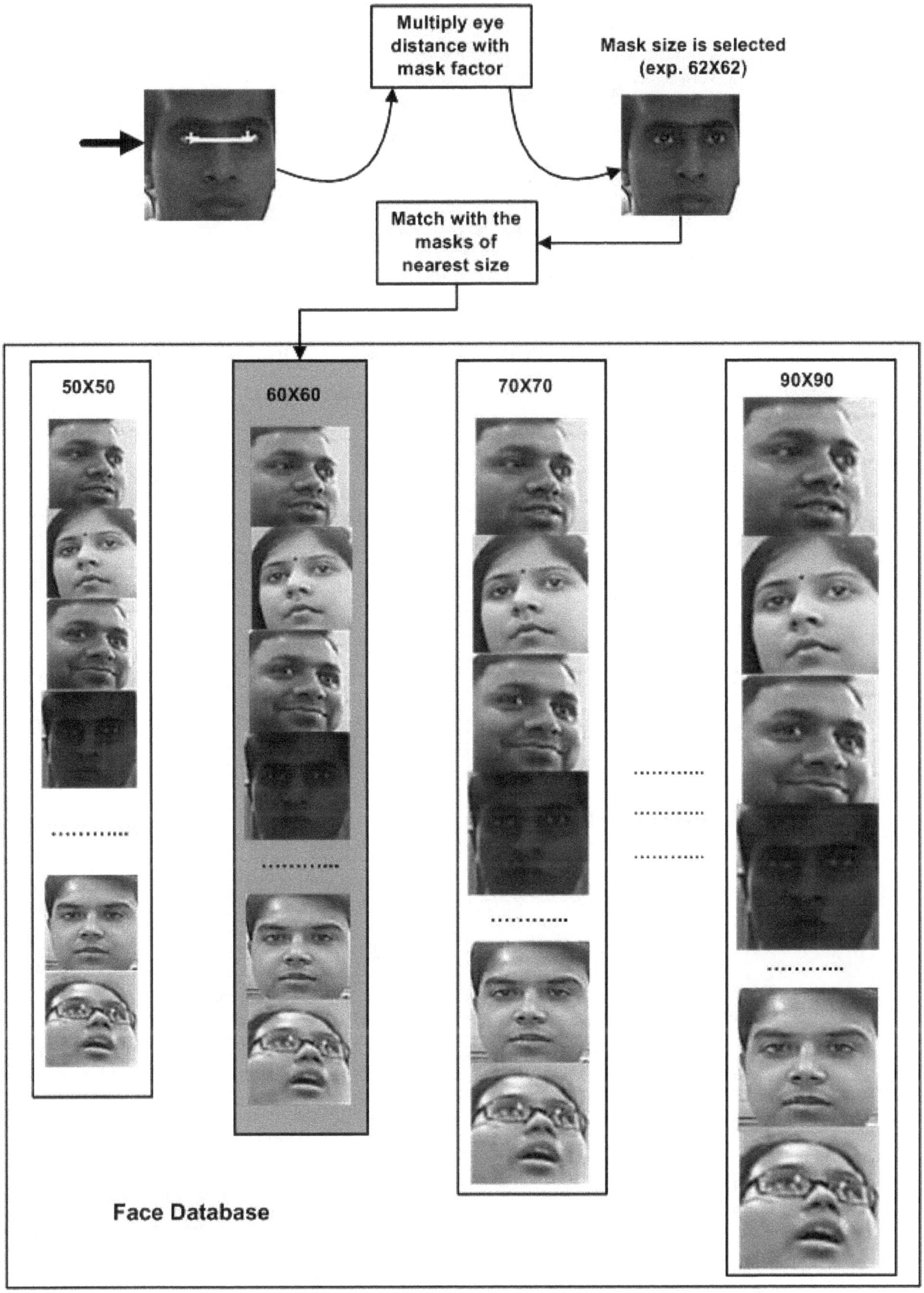

Figure 8. Person identification.

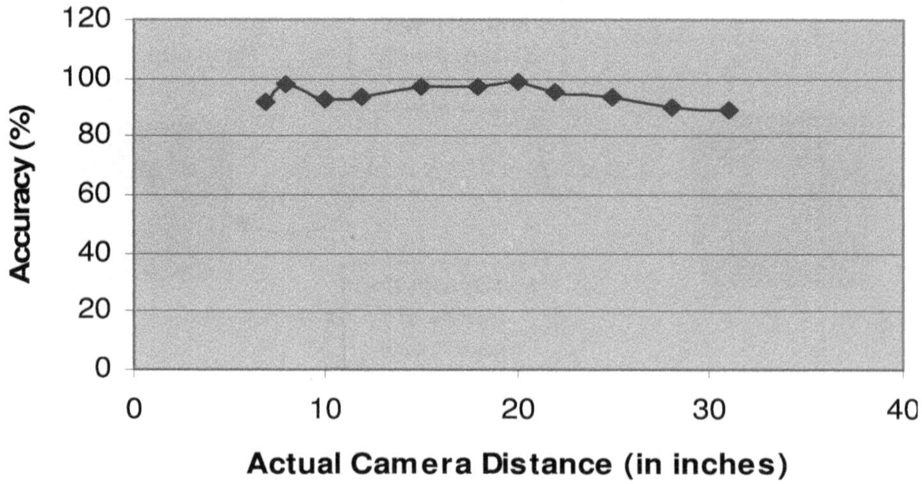

Figure 9. Accuracy (%) of the measured distance with the actual distance.

$M' \times N' = M_s \times d_{ep}$ where M_s is the Mask Size Factor and d_{ep} is the eye distance.

Step 4: For i = 1 to K, calculate Manhattan Distance, δ^i between I_{ts} and all the training images with nearest dimension by the following equation,

$$\delta^i = \sum_{j=1}^{M' \times N'} \left| I_{ij} - I_{ts} \right| ,$$

Where I_{ts} is the test image I_{ij} is the jth pixel of ith training image and K is the number of images in the face database.

Step 5: Calculate the minimum Manhattan Distance, η_M from Step 4 by the equation
η_M = Min (δ^i),

Where δ^i is the ith Manhattan Distance

Step 6: If minimum Manhattan distance, $\eta_M \leq T$ for a test image and threshold value, T then person is identified

Step 7: Else person is not identified and should be adapted and trained for future identification.

EXPERIMENTAL RESULTS

This system uses *A4 Tech PK-336MB* CCD camera for image acquisition (a4tech.com, 2009). Each captured image is digitized into a 320 × 320 matrix with 24 bit color. The system captures 30 image frames per second. The system considers every 5th frame captured by camera for further processing. Thus the system processes 6 image frames per second for face area and eye detection (FaceVACS SDK). Accuracy of person to camera distance measurement results using the proposed method are shown in Table 4, where real distances, measured distances, and accuracy (for distances from 7 - 31 inches) of 35 persons are recorded. Figure 9 shows the accuracy (%) of the proposed system at different predefined distances. The average accuracy of 94.11% is obtained. Though other conventional measuring results shows slight accurate where error rates range from 1 - 8% (Wang, 2006; Lu, 2006), the proposed system validated its' superiority in terms of simplicity and cost effectiveness.

Comparison between single and eye-distance based multi-resolution masks has been done by analyzing precision and recall rates over twenty three persons. The accuracy (%) which is compared on thirty five persons with different eye distances. The precision and recall rates for both single resolution mask and eye-distance based multi-resolution masks is presented in Table 5.

It can be inferred from Table 5 that, both precision and recall rates are significantly higher for eye-distance based multi-resolution mask than single resolution mask based person identification and thus outperforms the single resolution mask counterpart. Figure 10 and 11 show the comparison between precision and recall rates with multi-resolution and single resolution mask respectively. Figure 12 shows the sample matching probability of the system for both single mask and multi-resolution masks. Table 6 shows the performance comparison in terms of matching probability. Figure 13 shows the matching probability comparison graph of single resolution mask and eye-distance based multi-resolution mask for person identification. It is noticeable from the above figure that,

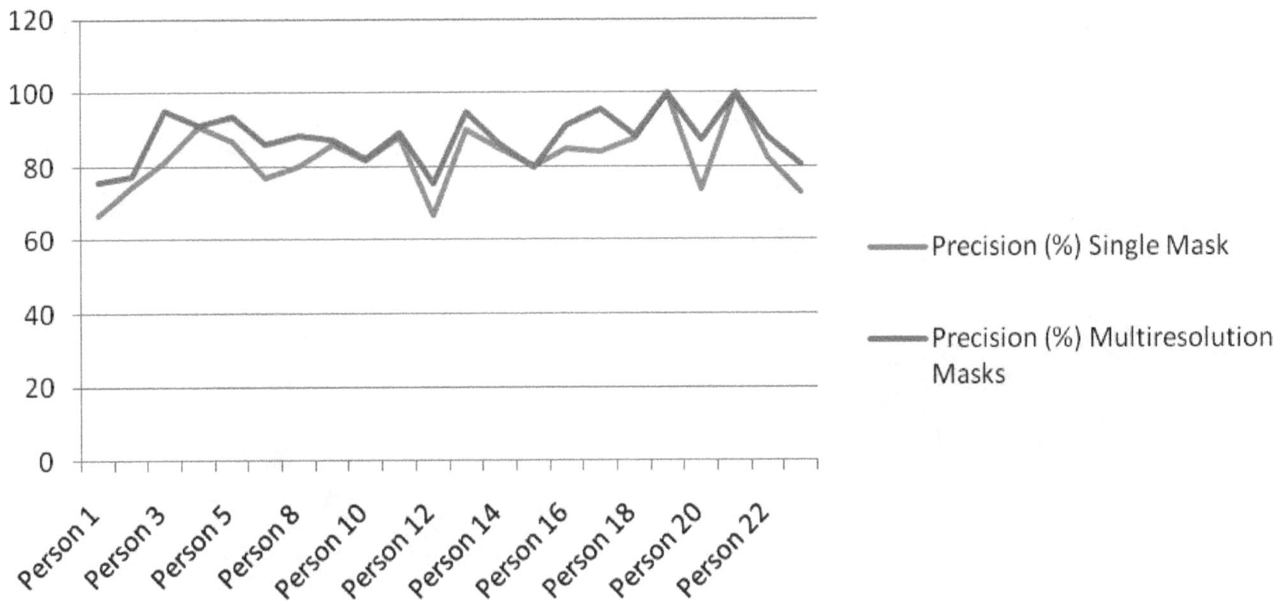

Figure 10. Performance comparison between multi-resolution masks and single resolution mask in terms of precision rates.

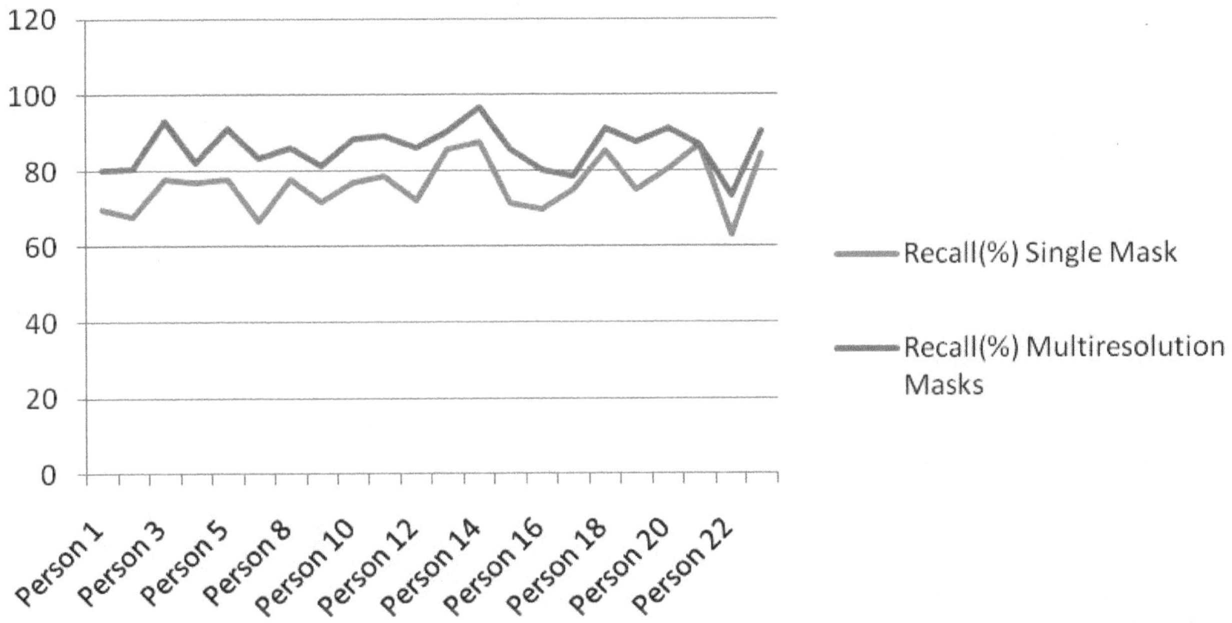

Figure 11. Performance comparison between multi-resolution masks and single resolution mask in terms of recall rates

accuracy is declining with the increment of eye-distance.

CONCLUSION

In this paper, an improved mask selection criterion from multi-resolution masks is proposed for person identification thus making a major contribution in areas of face recognition and person identification. There are several systems for choosing the mask size for person identification but the proposed eye-distance based mask selection is more robust and reliable as it reduces the computation time drastically. The system can now easily predict the best possible size of the mask and ignore other sizes at the very beginning. The proposed system has an average precision rate of 88.25% and average

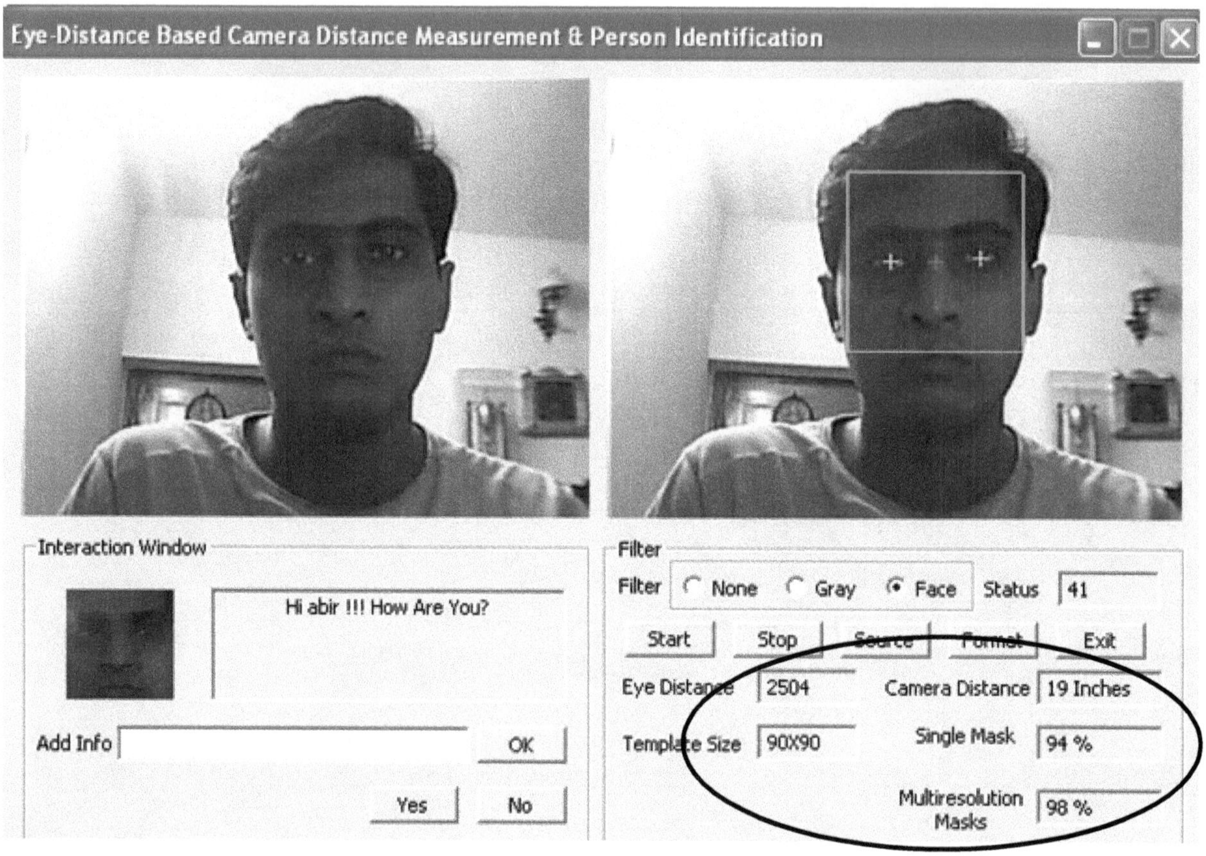

Figure 12. Matching probability of person identification for both single resolution mask and multi-resolution masks (eye distance = 50 pixels).

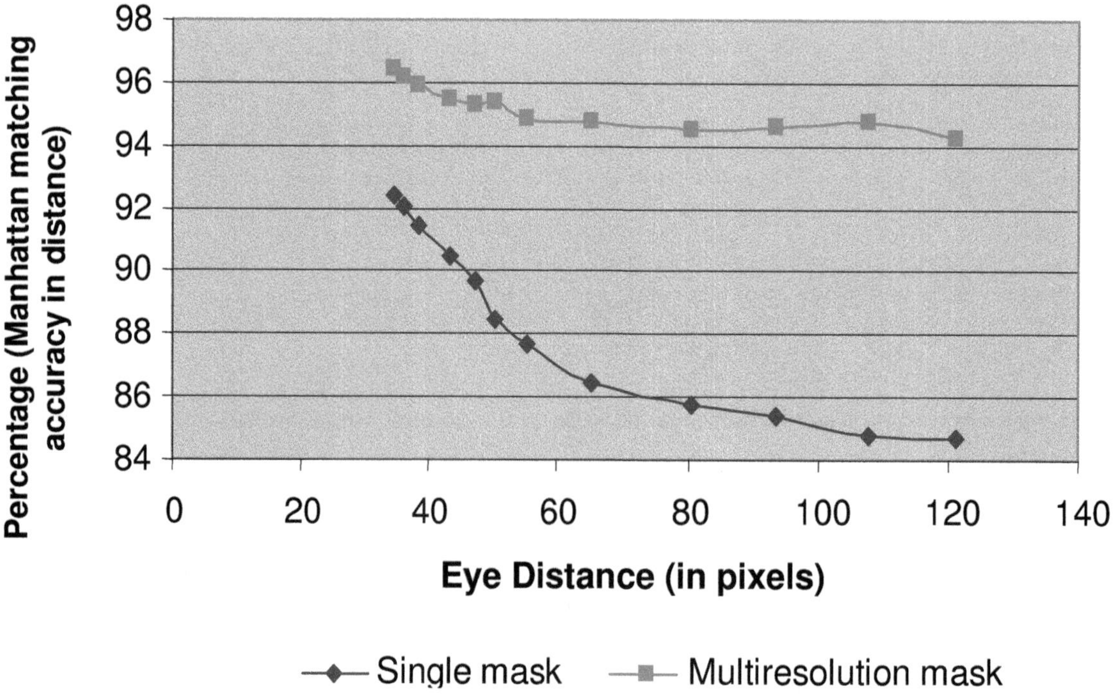

Figure 13. Matching probability comparison of single resolution mask and eye-distance based multi-resolution masks for person identification.

Table 4. Accuracy of the distance measurement method.

Actual person to camera distance (in inches)	System person to camera distance (in inches)	Accuracy (%)
31	33.8	88.96
28	31	90.25
25	26.7	93.2
22	23	95.45
20	20.3	98.5
18	18.2	96.88
15	14.5	96.66
12	10.71	93.25
10	9.24	92.4
8	8	97.55
7	7.76	92.14

Table 5. Performance comparison of single resolution mask and eye-distance based multi-resolution masks.

Person	Single resolution mask		Multi-resolution mask (based on eye-distance)	
	Precision (%)	Recall (%)	Precision (%)	Recall (%)
Person 1	66.66	70	76.19	80
Person 2	74.5	67.85	77.58	80.35
Person 3	81.39	77.77	95.45	93.33
Person 4	90.9	76.92	91.42	82.05
Person 5	86.88	77.94	93.54	91.17
Person 6	76.92	66.66	86.2	83.33
Person 8	80	77.77	88.57	86.11
Person 9	86.11	72.09	87.5	81.39
Person 10	81.63	76.92	82.14	88.46
Person 11	88	78.57	89.28	89.28
Person 12	66.67	72.22	75.6	86.11
Person 13	90	85.71	95	90.47
Person 14	84.85	87.5	86.11	96.87
Person 15	80	71.42	80	85.71
Person 16	84.85	70	91.42	80
Person 17	84	75	95.65	78.57
Person 18	87.88	85.29	88.57	91.17
Person 19	100	75	100	87.5
Person 20	74	80.43	87.5	91.3
Person 21	100	86.84	100	86.84
Person 22	82.6	63.33	88	73.33
Person 23	72.97	84.37	80.55	90.62

recall rate of 86.05%, which is much higher comparing with the single resolution mask based person identification (Rahman, 2009). The matching probability of the system which is near to approximately 90%, is also significantly higer than single resolution mask based person identification. This paper also presents a simple image-based person to camera distance measuring system. The proposed method has significant importance because of its lower cost and simpler algorithm for real-time implementation. Because of the simplicity of the proposed approach, hardware-intensive techniques, such as echo detection, additional CCD cameras, laser projector (Rahman, 2009; Wang, 2007), flash lights etc. are no longer required for obtaining a satisfactory person to camera distance measurement. One of the major limitations of this system is that, the system requires more secondary memory space for storing masks with different dimensions than single resolution mask based

Table 6. Comparison of matching probability between single resolution mask and multi-resolution masks.

Average eye distance (in pixels)	Matching probability(%) with single resolution mask	Matching probability (%) with multi-resolution masks
34.33	90.42	96.39
36.07	92.07	96.15
38.19	91.43	95.87
43.32	90.47	95.48
47.09	89.7	95.27
50.38	88.49	95.34
55.31	87.68	94.89
65.11	86.44	94.72
80.46	85.77	94.5
93.43	85.43	94.6
107.90	84.79	94.78
121.29	84.72	94.2

person identification approach because it scales the training images to different dimensions. The ultimate goal of this research is to implement the proposed person identification system in the field of robotics, biometric devices and other related fields.

REFERENCES

Bhuiyan MA, Ampornaramveth V, Muto S, Ueno H (2004). On Tracking of Eye For Human-Robot Interface, Int. J. Robot. Automat. 19(1): 42-54.

Black J, Tim E (2007). Multi Camera Image Measurement and Correspondence, Proceedings of the 7th WSEAS Int. Conf. on Signal Processing, omputational Geometry and Artificial Vision, Athens, Greece 1: 107-115.

Brunelli R, Poggio T (1983). Face recognition: Features versus templates, IEEE Trans. PAMI 15(10): 1042- 1062.

Carullo A, Ferraris F, Graziani S (1996). Ultrasonic Distance Sensor Improvement Using a Two-Level Neural Network, IEEE Transactions on Instrumentation and Measurement 45(2): 677-681.

Carullo A, Parvis M (2001). An ultrasonic sensor for distance measurement in automotive applications, IEEE Sensors J. 1(2): 143-147.

Chellappa R, Wilson CL, Sirohey S (1995). Human and machine recognition of faces: A survey. Proceedings of the IEEE 83(5): 705-740.

Chen CC, Hsu T, Wang C, Huang (2007). Three –Dimensional Measuremnt of a Remote Object with a Single CCD Camera, Proceedings of the 7th Int. Conf. on Signal Processing, Computaional Geometry and Artificial Vision, Athens, Greece, August, 2007 7(2): 141-146.

FaceVACS-SDK, Version 1.9.9. Cognitec Systems GmbH, [Online] URL: www.cognitec.com.

Hansen DM, Mortensen BK, Duizer PT, Andersen JR, Moeslund TB (2005). Automatic Annotation of Humans in Surveillance Video, Int. J. Compt. Vision 63(2): 103-115.

Hasanuzzaman M, Zhang T, Ampornaramveth V, Gotoda H, Shirai Y, Ueno H (2005). Knowledge-Based Person-Centric Human-Robot Interaction by Means of Gestures, Int. J. Info. Tech. 4(4): 496-507.

Hasanuzzaman M, Zhang T, Ampornaramveth V, Gotoda D, Shirai Y, Ueno H (2007). Adaptive visual gesture recognition for human–robot interaction using a knowledge-based software platform, Robotics and Autonomous Systems, Elsevier 55: 643-657.

Kanade T, Kano H, Kimuram S (1995). Development of a Video-Rate
Stereo Machine, Proc 1995 IEEE/RSJ Int. Conf. on Intelligent Robots and Systems, Pittsburgh, USA, August, 1995 3: 95-100.

Liguori C, Pietrosanto A, Paolillo (2001). An on-line stereo vision system for dimensional measurements on rubber extrusions, in Proc. 11th IMEKO TC4 Int. Sym., Lisbon, Portugal 13/14: 15-19.

Lu Ming-Chih, Wang Wei-Yen, Chu Chun-Yen (2006). Image-Based Distance and Area Measuring Systems, IEEE Sensors J. 6(2): 495-503, April.

Osugi K, Miyauchi K, Furui N, Miyakoshi H (1999). Development of the scanning laser radar for ACC system, JSAE Rev. 20: 579-554.

Rahman KA, Hossain MS, Bhuiyan M, A-A, Zhang T, Hasanuzzaman M, Ueno H (2009). Person to Camera Distance Measurement based on Eye Distance, Proceedings of the 3rd International Conference on Multimedia and Ubiquitous Engineering (MUE).

Rahman KA, Hossain MS, Bhuiyan M, A-A, Zhang T, Hasanuzzaman M, Ueno H (2009). Eye Distance Based Mask Selection for Person Identification, Proceedings of the 3rd International Conference on Multimedia and Ubiquitous Engineering (MUE).

Shin HT (2000). Vehicles Crashproof Laser Radar, M.S. thesis, Opt. Sci. Center, National Central Univ., Chung Li City, Taiwan, R.O.C.

Sid-Ahmed MA, Boraie MT (1990). Dual camera calibration for 3-D machine vision metrology, IEEE Trans. Instrum. Meas. 39(3): 512-516.

Tanaka Y, Gofuku A, Nagai I, Mohamed A (1998). Development of a Compact Video-rate Range finder and its application, Proc. 3rd Int. Conf. on Advanced Mechatronics, Okayama, Japan, August pp. 97-102.

Turk M, Pentland (1991). Eigenfaces for recognition, J. Cogn. Neurosci. 3(1): 71-86.

Valentin D, Abdi H, O'Toole AJ, Cottrell GW (1994). Connectionist models of face processing: A survey Pattern Recognition 27(9): 1209.

www.a4tech.com, last visited on 01/03/2009.

Wang Ti-Ho, Lu Ming-Chih, Hsu Chen-Chien, Wang Wei-Yen, Tsai Cheng-Pei, Chen Cheng-chuan (2006). A Method of Distance Measurement by Digital Camera, Proceedings of 2006 CACS Automatic Control Conference, St. John's University, Tamsui, Taiwan, Nov. 10-11, pp.1065-1069.

Wang T, Lu M, Wang W, Tsai C (2007). Distance Measurement Using Non-metric CCD Camera, Proceedings of the 7th Int. Conf. on Signal Processing, Computaional Geometry and Artificial Vision, Athens, Greece, August, 2007 7(1): 1-6.

Yuille P, Hallinan P, Cohen D (1992). Feature Extraction from Faces Using Deformable Templates, Int. J. Computer Vision 8(2): 99-111.

Zhao W, Chellappa R, Rosenfeld A, Phillips J (2002). Face Recognition: A Literature Survey. Technical Report CSTR4167R, Univ. of Maryland, 2000. Revised.

3

Quality of service constrained task mapping and scheduling algorithm for wireless sensor networks

Medhat H. A. Awadalla[1]* and Rania R. Darwish[2]

[1]Department of Communication, Electronics and Computers, Faculty of Engineering, University of Helwan, Egypt.
[2]Department of Mechatronics, Faculty of Engineering, University of Helwan, Egypt.

Efficient task mapping and scheduling is a crucial factor for achieving high performance in multimedia wireless sensor networks. This paper presents Quality of Service (QoS) - constrained task mapping and scheduling algorithm for multi-hop clustered wireless sensor networks. With the objective of meeting high performance and providing real-time guarantees, the algorithm simultaneously schedules the computation tasks and associated communication events of real time applications. The proposed scheduling algorithm exploits linear task clustering, augmented with task duplication and migration approach. Thus, reduces inter-task communication costs. Meanwhile, mitigates local communication overhead incurred due to communication medium contention. Experimental results and comparisons, based on both randomly generated application graphs, as well as graphs of some real-world applications, demonstrate that the proposed task mapping and scheduling scheme significantly surpasses previous approaches in terms of both quality and cost of schedules, which are mainly presented with deadline missing ratio, schedule length, and total application energy consumption.

Key words: Multimedia wireless sensor networks, task mapping and scheduling, linear clustering, real time applications.

INTRODUCTION

The availability of inexpensive hardware such as low cost small-scale imaging sensors, CMOS cameras, and microphones, has immensely funneled the emergence of a new class of wireless sensor networks, known as Multimedia Wireless Sensor Networks (MWSN). These sensor networks apart from boosting the existing applications of WSNs will create a new wave of applications that interface with the real world environment. For example, multimedia surveillance sensor networks, traffic monitoring and environmental monitoring (Dai and Akyildiz, 2009; Dimokas et al., 2008; Campbell et al., 2005; Holman, 2003). For most of these applications, it might be beneficial for the sensor network paradigm to be rethought in view of the need for energy efficient multimedia algorithms with tight quality of service (QoS) expectations (Akyilidiz, 2007). Real-time, collaborative in-network processing gains recognition as a viable solution for balancing the performance and consumption in MWSN (Wang and Wang, 2007). These algorithms allow the extraction of semantically relevant information at the edge of the sensor network. Applying these algorithms assists at increasing the system scalability by reducing the transmission of redundant information, along with merging data originated from multiple views, on different media and with multiple resolutions (Akyilidiz, 2007; Yick et al., 2008).

Collaborative in network processing partitions applications into smaller tasks executed in parallel on different sensor nodes. Dependencies between tasks are maintained through the exchange of intermediate results between sensor nodes (Tian and Ekici, 2007). Therefore, task mapping and scheduling plays an essential role in collaborative in-network processing by solving the following problems. First, assigning tasks into sensors. Second, determining the execution sequence of tasks on sensors. Finally, scheduling communication transactions

*Corresponding author. E-mail: awadalla_medhat@yahoo.co.uk.

between sensor nodes (Gu et al., 2007; Tian et al., 2007).

This paper proposes a Quality of Service (QoS)-constrained task mapping and scheduling algorithm resilient for real-time multimedia application in MWSN. The proposed approach simultaneously exploits linear clustering algorithm augmented with task duplication and migration approach. The proposed approach aimed at increasing network lifetime, meanwhile guarantee meeting application deadline. Furthermore, task scheduling and communication scheduling in the proposed approach are carried out in parallel. Thus, resulting in a realistic schedule due to the incorporation of communication contention awareness in the task scheduling, which is critical in real time multimedia applications.

The rest of the paper is organized as follows: Discussion of most related work; details of underlying system architecture; Introduction of the proposed task mapping and scheduling algorithm; the performance evaluation results; and finally, conclusion.

BACKGROUND

Collaborative in-network processing has been widely pursued by the research community in order to achieve energy saving and network scalability objectives. Giannecchini et al. (2004) proposed an online task scheduling mechanism (CoRAl) to allocate the network resources between the tasks of periodic applications in wireless sensor networks in an iterative manner: The upper-bound frequencies of applications are first evaluated according to the bandwidth and communication requirements between sensors. The frequencies of the tasks on each sensor are then optimized subject to the upper-bound execution frequencies. However, CoRAl assumes that the tasks are already assigned to sensors without addressing the task mapping problem. Furthermore, energy consumption is not explicitly discussed in (Wang and Chandrakasan, 2002). Wang et al. (2002) proposed a Distributed Computing Architecture (DCA) which executes low-level tasks on sensing sensors and offloads all other high-level processing tasks to cluster heads. However, processing high-level tasks can still exceed the capacity of the cluster heads' computation power. Furthermore, the application-specific design of DCA limits its implementation for generic applications. Yu et al. (2005) proposed an Energy-balance Task Allocation (EbTA) onto a single-hop cluster of homogenous sensor nodes connected with multiple wireless channels. In this work, communication over multiple wireless channels are first modeled as additional linear constraints of an Integer Linear Programming (ILP) problem. Then, a heuristic algorithm is presented to provide a practical solution. However, the communication scheduling model in Yu and Prasanna (2005) does not exploit the overhearing property of wireless communication, which can conserve energy and reduce schedule length. Furthermore, the small number of available orthogonal channels can not satisfy the requirement of multiple wireless channels assigned in every cluster, especially in densely deployed networks. Zhu et al. (2007) exploited divide-and conquer technique in order to allocate tasks for heterogeneous sensor networks. The tasks are first grouped into task partitions, and then optimal execution schedule based on the optimal schedules of the tasks partitions is generated. Kumar et al. (2003) presented a data fusion task mapping mechanism for wireless sensor network. The proposed mechanism in Kumar et al. (2003) comprises data fusion API and a distributed algorithm for energy aware role assignment. The data fusion API enables an application to be specified as a coarse-grained dataflow graph. While, the role assignment algorithm maps the graph onto the network, and optimally adapts the mapping at run-time using role migration. Zhu et al. (2007) and Kumar et al. (2003) assumed an existing underlying communication model. Tian et al. (2007) proposed EcoMapS algorithm for energy constrained applications in single-hop clustered wireless sensor networks. EcoMapS aimed at mapping and scheduling communication and computation simultaneously. EcoMapS aims to schedule tasks with minimum schedule length subject to energy consumption constrains. However, EcoMapS does not provide execution deadline guarantees for applications. Tian et al. (2007) presented Multi Hop Task Mapping and Scheduling (MTMS) for multi-hop clustered wireless sensor networks. This work simultaneously addressed computation and communication scheduling. Further, the task mapping is maintained through adopting Min-Min task scheduling algorithm. However, MTMS shows a very low capacity to meet strict applications deadline.

Apart from all these efforts, this work is motivated for addressing all the above mentioned drawbacks and developing a QoS constrained task Happing and sche@uling algorithm for multi-hop cHustered multime@ia wireless senRor networks. Th@ main idea behiJd the proposed algorithm is to group tasks that are heavily communicate with each other to be processed on the same sensor. Thereby, reducing the number of inter-task communication operations. Furthermore, the proposed algorithm tries to redundantly allocate some of the application tasks on which other tasks critically depend. Which in turn yields at significant reduction in the start times of waiting tasks and eventually improves the overall schedule length of the application? Thus, guarantee meeting very strict application deadlines.

PRELIMINARIES

Network and interference model

The proposed task mapping and scheduling strategy targets multi-hop cluster-based network architectures, the following discusses the assumed network and the interference model.

i.) All sensor nodes are grouped into k-hop clusters, where k is the hop count of the longest path connecting any two nodes.
ii.) Each cluster is assumed to execute a specific application, which is either assigned during the network set up time or remotely distributed by the base station during the network operation.
iii.) Cluster heads are responsible for creating the applications' schedules within the clusters.
iv.) Location information is locally available within clusters.
v.) Intra-cluster communication is assumed to be handled over a single common channel, which results in further constrains on the scheduling problem arises from the contention taking place in the shared communication channel, because of sensor competing on the shared communication channel.
vi.) Inter-cluster communication is assumed to be isolated from other clusters through time division or multiple wireless channels assignment mechanisms.

INTERFERENCE MODEL

This works assumes that communication within each cluster is handled over a single common channel. In other words, the communication channel is shared by all sensors within each cluster. Thus, one of the major problems that will arise is the reduction of capacity due to the interference caused by simultaneous transmissions. So, in order to achieve robust and collision free communication a careful interference-aware communication schedule should be constructed.

In this paper, we assume that the time is slotted and synchronized, and to schedule two communication links at the same time slot, we must ensure that the schedule will avoid the interference. Two different types of interference have been studied in the literature, namely, primary interference and secondary interference. Primary interference occurs when a node transmits and receives packets at the same time. Secondary interference occurs when a node receives two or more separate transmissions. Here, all transmissions could be intended for this node, or only one transmission is intended for this node. Thus, all other transmissions are interference to this node. Several different interference models have been used to model the interferences in wireless networks. However RTS/CTS interference model is adopted through out this work. In this model, all nodes within the interference range of every pair of either the transmitter or the receiver cannot transmit. Thus, for every pair of simultaneous communication links, say m_{ij} and m_{pq}, it should satisfy that they are four distinct four nodes, that is., $s_i \neq s_j \neq s_p \neq s_q$, and s_i and s_j are not in the interference ranges of s_p and s_q, and vice versa [16].

APPLICATION MODEL

Directed Acyclic Graph (DAG) can represent applications executed within each cluster. A DAG T = (V, E) consists of a set of vertices V representing the tasks to be executed and a set of directed edges E representing communication dependencies among tasks. The edge set E contains directed edges e_{ij} for each task $v_i \in V$ that task $v_j \in V$ depends on. The computation weight of a task is represented by the number of CPU clock cycles to execute the task. Given an edge e_{ij}, v_i is called the immediate predecessor of v_j and v_j is called the immediate successor of v_i. An immediate successor v_j depends on its immediate predecessors such that v_j cannot start execution before it receives results from all of its immediate predecessors. A task without immediate predecessors is called an entry-task and a task without immediate successors is called an exit-task. A DAG may have multiple entry tasks and one exit-task. If there are more than one exit-tasks, they will be connected to a pseudo-exit-task with computation cost equal to zero (Yu and Prasanna, 2005; Zhu et al., 2007).

ENERGY CONSUMPTION MODEL

The energy consumption of transmitting and receiving *l* bit data over a distance *d* that is less than a threshold d_0 are defined as $E_{tx}(l,d)$ and $E_{rx}(l)$, respectively (Tian and Ekici, 2007).

$$E_{tx}(l,d) = E_{elec} \cdot l + \varepsilon_{amp} \cdot l \cdot d^2 \qquad (1)$$
$$E_{rx}(l) = E_{elec} . l$$

Where E_{ele} is the energy dissipated to run the transmit or receive electronics, and ε_{amp} is the energy dissipated by the transmit power amplifier. In the proposed communication scheduling algorithm, the energy consumption incurred due to sending and receiving a data packet can be expressed as (1) and (2) respectively. Also the energy consumption of executing *N* clock cycles with CPU clock frequency *f* is given as (Tian and Ekici, 2007),

$$E_{comp}(V_{dd}, f) = NCV_{dd}^2 + V_{dd}(I_o e^{\frac{v_{dd}}{nV_T}})(\frac{N}{f}), \qquad (2)$$
$$f \cong K(V_{dd} - c)$$

Where V_T is the thermal voltage, V_{dd} is the supply voltage, and C, I_o, n, K, c are processor-dependent parameters (Wang, 2008; Shih et al., 2001).

The proposed task mapping and scheduling algorithm

This section presents the proposed task mapping and allocation algorithm. The proposed algorithm comprises of two mechanisms. Linear task clustering algorithm, and sensor assignment mechanism based on a task duplication and migration scheme.

```
1. Initially mark all edges as
   unexamined
2. WHILE there is an edge
   unexamined DO
3. Determine the critical path
   composed of unexamined
   edges only.
4. Create a cluster by putting
   the communication load
   equal to zero on all the
   edges on the critical path.
5. Mark the entire edges
   incident on the critical
   path and the entire edges
   incident to the nodes in
   the cluster as examined.
6. ENDWHILE
```

Figure 1. Linear clustering sequence.

TASK CLUSTERING

This work adopted linear clustering algorithm (Kwok and Ahmed, 1999) for mapping tasks onto distinct clusters. The rational behind this mapping is to reduce the overall energy consumption, as well as the schedule length of the application, since communication between tasks within the same cluster costs negligible time and energy.

This phase assumes an unlimited number of sensors, implying that the number of clusters is also unlimited. Linear Clustering first determines the set of nodes constituting the critical path, then assign all the critical path nodes to a single cluster at once. These nodes and all edges incident on them are then removed from the directed acyclic graph. The linear clustering algorithm is outlined in Figure 1.

SENSOR ASSIGNMENT MECHANISM

The obtained task clusters from the previous step are scheduled on the actual sensors through the following steps:

i.) Map the obtained μ task clusters into the p physical sensors.
ii.) Determine the execution sequence of the computation tasks on sensors.
iii.) Schedule the Communication between the sensor nodes.

CLUSTER MAPPING

In this phase, the obtained task clusters from the previous step are mapped into the actual sensor nodes. As the main concern in this paper is proposing an energy-aware scheduling algorithm, this mapping takes into account the remaining energy level of the sensor nodes. This means that, the sensor node with higher remaining energy level will be assigned more working load than that having less remaining energy. It worth to be noted that multiple task clusters can be mapped to the same sensor node. First the load of each task cluster is computed. Then the normalized load of each sensor node is computed which can be expressed as (5). In which the sum of all loads of all task clusters assigned to the sensor is normalized by the sensor remaining energy.

$$L_k = \frac{\sum_i C_i}{E_k} \qquad (5)$$

Where, C_i is the energy needed to execute task cluster i, and E_k is the remaining energy of sensor k.

Figure 2 depicts the pseudo code of this phase. Initially, all task clusters are sorted in non-increasing order of their load. Then for each cluster, the normalized load of each sensor node is calculated as if it is assign to it. Then the cluster would be assigned to the sensor node that gives the minimal normalized load.

TASK SCHEDULING

In this step, determining the execution sequence for the tasks on the sensors is carried out. This step comprises two components: task scheduling with duplication, and global task migration. Figures 3 and 4 outline the pseudo code and the flow chart for the proposed scheduling algorithm. Initially, all tasks are sorted into a list L. in which tasks are ordered according to the bottom level priority and precedence constrain. Without any duplication, the algorithm first attempts to schedule the previous phase. Obviously, to calculate the task starting time on its assigned sensor ts(v_j,S), all the receiving communication transactions from v_j parents should be

```
1. Sort the list Π containing all unmapped task
   clusters
2. WHILE Π is not empty DO
3. Select the first element π in Π
4. Calculate the normalized load for each
   sensor node
5. Assign π to the sensor node that gives the
   minimal normalized load
6. Update the normalized load of the sensor
7. Remove π from Π
8. ENDWHILE
```

Figure 2. Cluster mapping sequence.

```
1.  Traverse the application graph V downwards and compute Latest Finishing Time (LFT) for
    every task.
2.  Sort tasks v ∈ V into list L according to precedence constrains.
3.  For every vj ∈ V DO
// Calculate the Earliest Starting Time of vj on its assigned sensor s ts(vj, s).
4.  For each vi ∈ pred(vj) DO
5.  IF SEN(vi) ≠ s THEN
6   Determine route M=<m1,m2,.........mn> from SEN(vi) to s
7.  Process links from m1 to mn and assign to each mk the earliest free interval on
        the communication channel not causing any interference.

8.  ENDIF
1.  ENDFOR
2.  Calculate ts(vj, s)
//  Check the duplication condition
3.  If duplication condition is satisfied THEN
4.          Duplicate vcp on s
5.          Schedule vj on s
6.          ELSE
7.               IF tf(vj, s) < LFT(vj) THEN
8.               Schedule vj on s
9.             Else
10.               Migrate vj to s(vcp)
11.               Schedule vj on s(vcp)
12.              ENDIF
13.     ENDIF
14. ENDFOR
```

Duplication Conditions:

$$t_f(v_i,s)_{with\ duplication} < LFT(v_i)$$

$$t_s(v_i,s)_{with\ duplication} < t_s(v_i,s)_{with\ no\ duplication}$$

$$Cost(v_i)_{duplication} < Cost(v_i)_{with\ no\ duplication}$$

Figure 3. Task scheduling scheme.

scheduled on the wireless channel. The task critical parent v_{cp} which has the heaviest communication and the latest arrival time is identified. Then duplicating the task critical parent v_{cp} is investigated. If this duplication helps in advancing the task starting $ts(v_j)$ time, reducing the consumed energy, and meanwhile preserves the task deadline, this phase is accepted. Otherwise, it is rejected.

In some cases, the duplication mechanism fails at satisfying the task deadline constrain. In such cases, the algorithm employs a global migration process for the task, where the task under consideration began to be migrated to other sensor. To reduce this migration impact on the

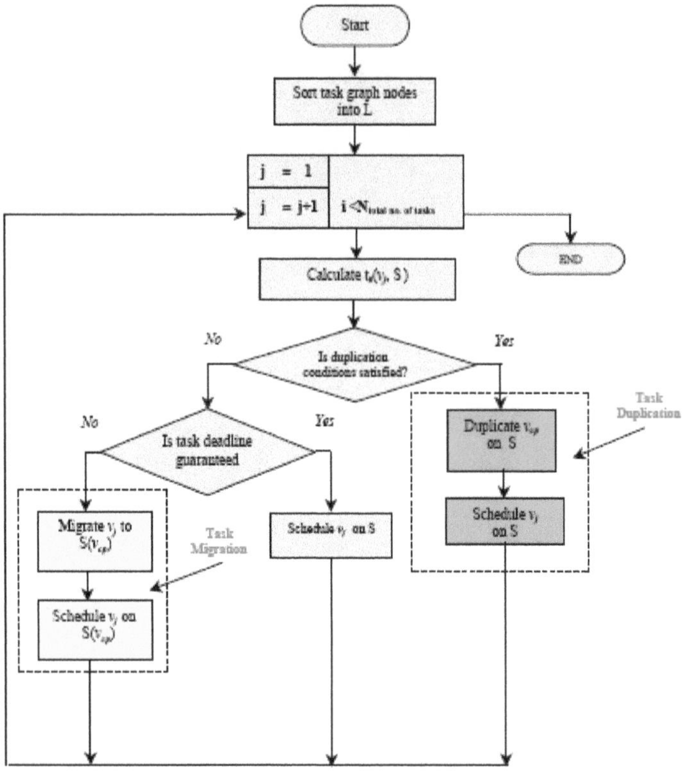

Figure 4. Task scheduling flow chart.

energy increase, the destination sensor is selected as the sensor that holds its critical parent.

SCHEDULING COMMUNICATION BETWEEN SENSOR NODES UNDER THE RTS/CTS MODEL

In order to satisfy dependencies between tasks, scheduling a task should include scheduling all its entering edges on the shared communication wireless channel. Figure 3, steps 4 - 9 stand for scheduling communication scheduler mechanism. As previously mentioned, this work concerned with multi-hop clustered wireless sensor networks. So, the sender and the receiver of a communication transaction may be one or more hops away, moreover, multiple communication transmissions could occur simultaneously. Thus, First a routing algorithm should be employed in order to determine the appropriate route $<m_1, m_2, \ldots\ldots, m_n>$ for each entering edge $e_{ij} \in$ pred (v_j) of task v_j. The basic idea here is after determining the appropriate route for all entering edges for the considered task, all these routes are sorted according to their length and the communication volume. Then, every link m_{xy} of the generated path is scheduled on the earliest free interval on the communication channel. Here, the adopted communication scheduler is interference-aware mechanism, in which scheduling a transmission between sensor x and sensor y on the interval [A, B] is valid, if and only if it will not result in a collision at either node x or node y (or any other node).

Moreover, the proposed communication scheduler makes use of the overhearing, which is a unique characteristic of wireless communication. That is, when a communication transaction generated from a certain task requested by several destinations. The sender only sends one transmission to one destination, and all other transaction destinations lying in its transmission range will receive it. Thus, prune out superfluous transmission from the source, as multiple destination can hear the same transmission with only one transmission from the source. Thus yields in shortening the communication latency, and results in significant reduction in the consumed energy.

SIMULATION RESULTS

This section presents the results of the conduced experiments analyzing many aspects of the proposed scheduling. The objective is to investigate the energy efficiency, and applications deadline guarantees of the proposed model compared to recently proposed models. For this purpose, an experimental evaluation on real world applications, along with randomly generated application graphs is carried out.

In the evaluation experiments, the schedule length, the energy consumption and the deadline missing ratio are

Table 1. Simulation parameters.

Attribute	Value
Channel bandwidth	1Mb/s
Transmission range *r*	10 m
E_{elec}	50 nJ/b
ε_{amp}	10 pJ/b/m^2
V_T	26 mV
C	0.67 nF
I_o	1.196 mA
n	21.26
K	239.28 MHz/V
C	0.5V

observed. The schedule length is defined as the finish time of the exit task of an application. The energy consumption includes the communication and computation expenses of all sensors. The deadline missing ratio is defined as the number of schedules with schedule lengths larger than the application deadline. For the sake of comparison the same parameters as in MTMS (Tian and Ekici, 2007) have been adopted. Table 1 summarizes these simulation parameters.

RANDOMLY GENERATED APPLICATION GRAPHS

In order to evaluate the effectiveness of the proposed scheduling mechanism, simulations were first conducted on randomly generated application graphs. The randomly generated application graphs were scheduled on randomly created multihop clusters. For the sake of parameters as that used while evaluating MTMS (Tian and Ekici, 2007).

EFFECT OF NUMBER OF TASKS

In order to investigate the effect of varying the number of the application tasks on the total energy consumption, and deadline missing ratio, experiments were conducted on three sets of randomly generated applications with 40, 45, 50 tasks. Figure 5 shows a comparison between the proposed scheduling mechanism, and MTMS in terms of energy consumption. It can be seen that, as the number of tasks of the application increases, the energy consumption increase in both the MTMS and the proposed scheduling. Whereas, the proposed scheduling scheme shows lower energy consumption compared to that of MTMS. On the other hand, Figure 6 depicts the deadline missing ratio of the proposed scheduling scheme and MTMS with respect to different deadlines for different number of tasks. It can be seen, that MTMS is dramatically affected by increasing the number of tasks while, the proposed scheduling scheme shows better capacity to meet application deadline even in very strict ones. Thus, the proposed scheduling scheme shows better scalability than MTMS in terms of energy consumption and application deadline.

EFFECT OF COMMUNICATION LOAD

In order to investigate the effect of varying the communication load on the proposed scheme performance, experiments were conducted on randomly generated application graphs with 40 tasks. Three different setting for application graphs were considered. Communication load uniformly distributed in [600 bit, ±10%], [800 bit, ±10%], [1,000 bit, ±10%] with fixed computation load equal to [300 KCC, ±10%] on the performance of the proposed scheduling scheme. As shown in Figure 7, the performance of MTMS is highly affected by varying the communication load. As the communication load increases the deadline missing ratio of MTMS increases. Whereas, the proposed scheduling scheme is less likely to be affected by varying the communication load.

REAL WORLD APPLICATIONS

In addition to randomly generated application graphs, this study also has considered application graphs of three real world problems: Gauss Jordan elimination (Jin et al., 2008), LU factorization, (Jin et al., 2008) and Real-life distributed visual surveillance example (Tian and Ekici, 2007).

For the experiments of Gauss Jordan elimination, Figure 8 gives the schedule length of both MTMS and the proposed scheduling scheme at various numbers of tasks. The smallest size graph in this experiment has 15 tasks and the largest one has 45 tasks. In both algorithms, the obtained schedule length increases, as the number of tasks increases. However, in all cases the proposed scheduling scheme results in shorter schedule length. As in Gauss Jordan elimination, Figure 9 presents the schedule length for LU factorization of both the proposed scheduling mechanism and MTMS. Different number of tasks are used in this experiment. The number of tasks varies between 14 tasks and 43 tasks. It could be seen that the proposed scheduling outperforms MTMS in terms of the schedule length.

Also, in order to demonstrate the effectiveness of the proposed scheduling algorithm, the same distributed visual surveillance example used in Tian and Ekici (2007) is considered. In this experiment, the performance of the proposed scheduling is compared to MTMS (Tian and Ekici, 2007), DCA (Giannecchini et al., 2004) and EbTA (Wang and Chandrakasan, 2002). Table 2 summarizes this comparison. In this set of experiments the performance of the proposed scheduling is evaluated in terms of schedule length, energy consumption, and the

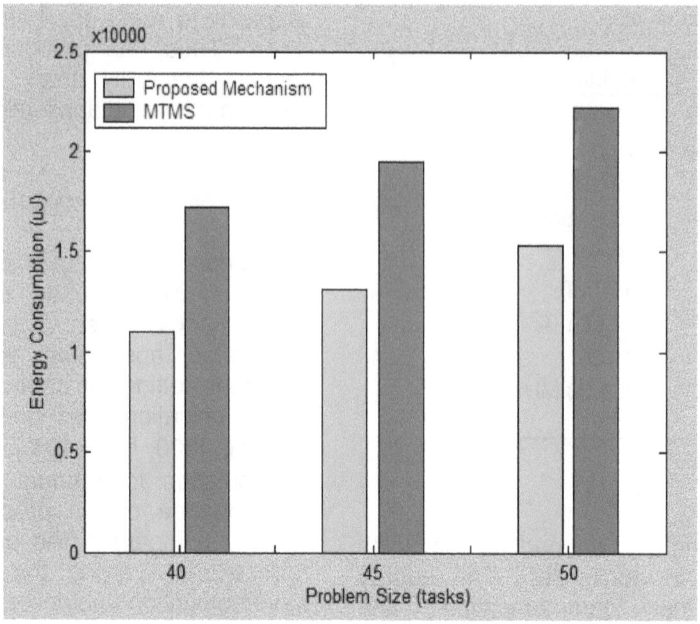

Figure 5. Energy consumption versus number of tasks.

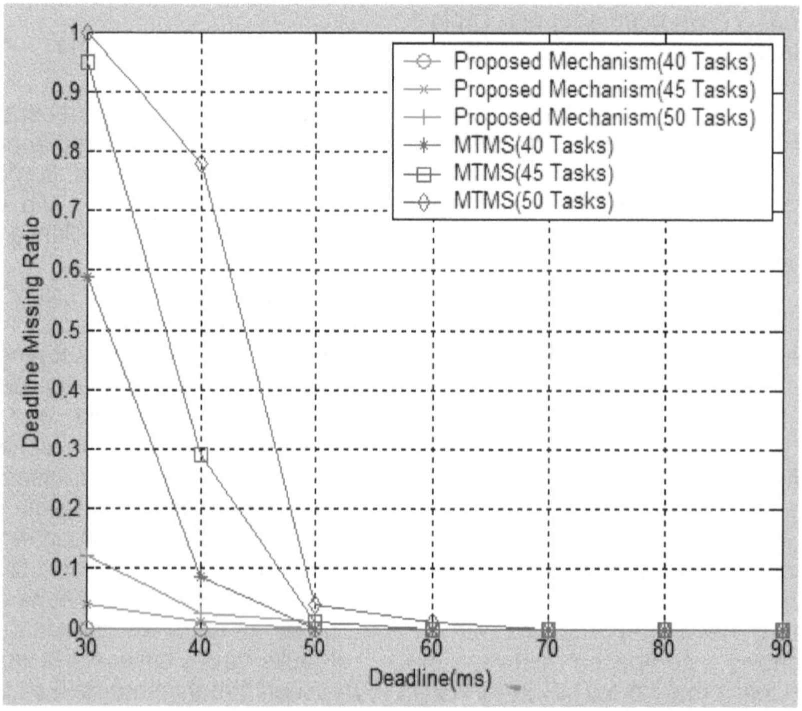

Figure 6. Deadline missing ratio versus the deadline of different number of tasks.

maximum energy consumption per-node. Regarding the schedule length, it could be seen that the proposed scheduling results in the shortest schedule length among all other algorithms MTMS, EbTA, and DCA. This is because the proposed scheduling mitigates channel contention through redundantly duplicating some of the graph tasks in which other tasks critical depend. Thus, resulting in shorter schedule lengths, which in turn enables the proposed scheduling scheme to satisfy very strict application deadlines? For energy consumption, the proposed schedule also produces the smallest application energy consumption between MTMS, EbTA, and DCA.

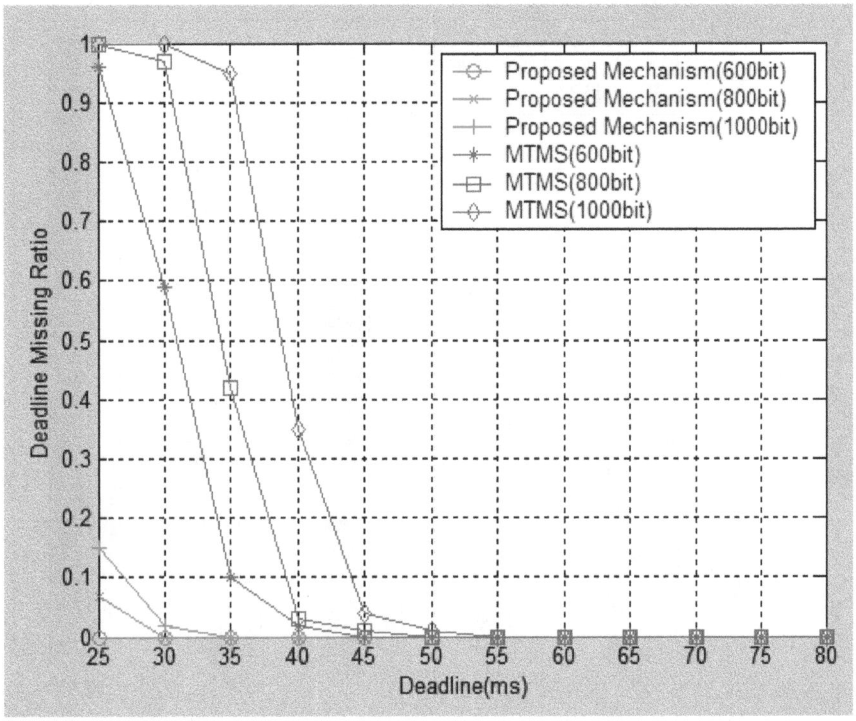

Figure 7. Deadline missing ratio versus deadline for different communication load.

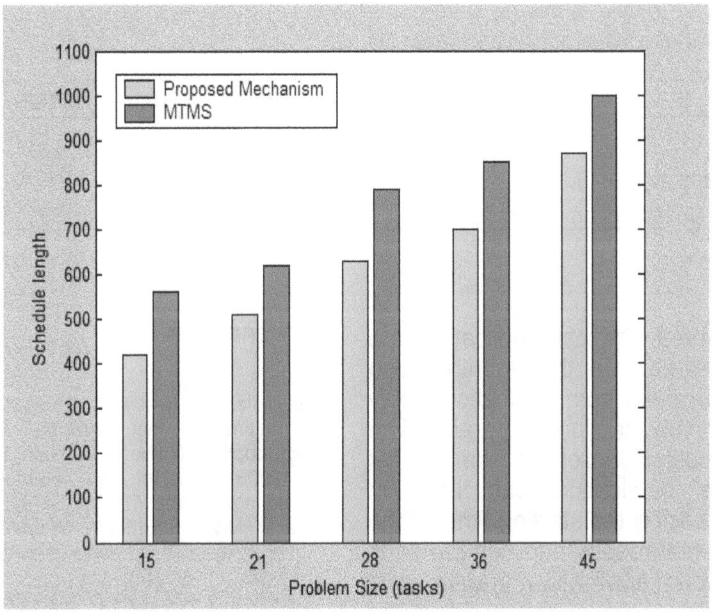

Figure 8. Scheduling length for Gauss Jordan elimination problem versus number of tasks.

Finally, the proposed scheduling results in the smallest maximum energy consumption per node. Thus, employing our proposed scheduling algorithm yields in a fair energy consumption balance across the cluster sensor nodes.

Conclusions

This paper proposes Quality of Service (QoS)-constrained task mapping and scheduling algorithm for multimedia wireless sensor networks. The proposed algorithm adopted

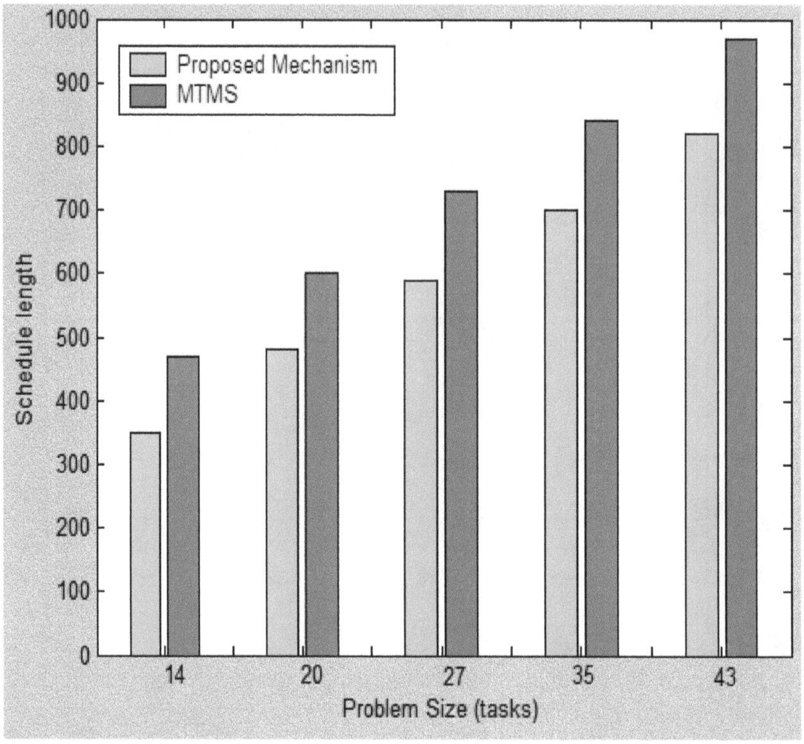

Figure 9. Scheduling length for LU factorization problem versus number of tasks.

Table 2. Simulation with the visual surveillance example.

Metrics	Proposed scheme	MTMS	EBTA	DCA
Schedule Length(ms)	2.11	3.00	3.00	5.64
Overall Energy Consumption(µJ)	1170	2194	2743	2238
Maximum Energy Consumption per node (µJ)	284	592	298	1139

linear task mapping, augmented with task duplication and migration approach. At the same time, the algorithm also takes into consideration the exact communication delay by scheduling communication transactions in parallel. The proposed algorithm judiciously duplicated the critical predecessors only if the duplication can help in conserving energy, and advancing the starting time of the succeeding tasks. Experimental results and comparisons conducted on both real–world application graphs, and randomly generated application graphs, revealed that the proposed scheduling algorithm outperforms previous scheduling algorithms in terms of schedule length, energy consumption, and deadline missing ratio.

In our future work, recovering functionality from sensors failure will be handled. Also, since in large-scale networks cluster heads are not in direct range of the sink, thus, our future work will investigate developing non-interfering inter-cluster multi-hop routing algorithm. Furthermore, varying the network parameters will be addressed to study its effect on the performance of the overall system.

REFERENCES

Akyilidiz IF, Melodia T, Chowdhury K (2007). "A survey on wireless multimedia sensor networks". J. Comput. Netw., 51(4): 921-960.

Campbell J, Gibbons P, Nath S, Pillai P, Seshan S, Sukthankar R (2005). "IrisNet: an internet-scale architecture for multimedia sensors," Proc. Of the ACM Multimedia Conference, pp. 1230-1236.

Dai D, Akyildiz IF (2009). "A spatial correlation model visual information in wireless multimedia sensor networks". IEEE Trans. Multimed., 11(6): 1148-1159.

Dimokas N, Katsaros D, Manolopoulos Y (2008). "Cooperative caching in wireless multimedia sensor networks". J. Mob. Netw. Appl., 13(4): 345-356.

Giannecchini S, Caccamo M, Shih CS (2004). "Collaborative Resource Allocation in Wireless Sensor Networks," Proc. Euromicro Conf. Real-Time Syst. (ECRTS '04), pp. 35-44.

Gu Y, Tian Y, Ekici E (2007). "Real-time multimedia processing in video sensor networks". J. Image Commun., 22: 237-251.

Holman R, Stanely J, Ozkan T (2003). "Applying video sensor networks to near shore environmental monitoring". IEEE Trans. Distributed Comput., 2(4): 765-779.

Jin S, Schiavone G, Turgut D (2008). "A performance study of multiprocessor task scheduling algorithms". J. Supercomput., (48): 77-97.

Kumar R, Wolenetz M, Agarwalla B, Shin J (2003). "Dfuse: A framework for distributed data fusion". Proc. Of ACM Conference on Embedded Networked Sensor Systems (SenSys'03), pp. 114-125.

Kwok Y, Ahmed I (1999). "Static scheduling algorithms for allocating directed task graphs to multiprocessors". ACM Comput. Surv. (CSUR), 31(4): 406- 471.

Shih EC, Ickes N, Min R, Sinha A, Wang A, Chandraksan A (2001). "Physical layer driven protocol and algorithm design for energy-efficient wireless sensor networks", Proc. of ACM MobiCom'01, pp. 272-286.

Tian Y, Ekici E (2007). "Cross-layer collaborative in-network processing in multihop wireless sensor networks". IEEE Trans. Parallel and Distributed Syst., 6(3):297-310.

Tian Y, Ekici E, Ozguner F (2007). "Cluster-based information processing in wireless sensor networks: an energy-aware approach," J. Wireless Commun. Mob. Comput., (7): 894-907.

Wang A, Chandrakasan A (2002). "Energy-efficient DSP's for wireless sensor networks". IEEE Signal Process. Mag., pp. 68-78.

Wang A, Chandrakasan A (2002). "Energy-Efficient DSPs for Wireless Sensor Networks," IEEE Signal Process. Mag., pp. 68-78.

Wang X, Wang S (2007). "Collaborative signal processing for target tracking in distributed wireless sensor networks. J. Parallel and Distributed Comput., (67):501-515.

Wang Y. Wang W. Yang X, Song W (2008). "Interference-aware joint routing and TDMA link scheduling for static wireless networks". IEEE Trans. Parallel and Distributed Syst., 19(12):1709-1724.

Yick J, Mukherjee B, Ghosal D (2008). "Wireless sensor network survey." J.Comp. Netw., (52): 2292-2330.

Yu Y, Prasanna V (2005). "Energy-balanced task allocation for collaborative processing in wireless sensor networks." ACM/Kluwer J. Mob. Netw. Appl., 10(1-2): 115-131.

Zhu J, Li J, Gao H (2007). "Tasks allocation for real-time application in heterogeneous sensor networks for energy minimization" Proc. Of 8th ACIS International Conference on Software Engineering, Artificial Intelligence, Networking, and parallel/Distributed Computing.

A survey of agent-oriented software engineering paradigm: Towards its industrial acceptance

O. Zohreh Akbari

Department of Information and Communication Technology, Faculty of Engineering, Payame Noor University, Tehran, Iran. E-mail: z.o.akbari@gmail.com.

Agent-oriented software engineering (AOSE) paradigm represents an interesting means of analyzing, designing and building complex software systems quite suitable to new software development requirements. Many scientific researches have been focused on this paradigm, yet its current state still reports relative lack of industrial acceptance compared to others. As a survey of AOSE paradigm, this paper outlines the overall state of this paradigm; and by identifying its weaknesses in detail, leads to a proposal solution to such shortcoming. This solution, in keeping with the existing approaches that aim to use situational method engineering (SME) in collaborative manner between agent-oriented methodology designers, suggests the use of a methodology evaluation framework in the process as well. This framework is a means to collect the best method fragment and evaluate consecutively the methodology during the development process for possible methodology improvements. The proposed solution is then readjusted to help software development organizations to reach the fifth level of Capability Maturity Model (CMM).

Key words: Agent-oriented software engineering (AOSE), capability maturity model (CMM), evaluation framework, methodology, project-specific, situational method engineering (SME).

INTRODUCTION

The complexity of software development process had caused the development of increasingly powerful and natural abstraction with which to model and develop complex systems. Procedural abstraction, abstract data types, and objects are all examples of such abstractions (Wooldridge et al., 1999). During the past two decades, with the increase in complexity of projects associated with software engineering, agent concepts that originated from Artificial Intelligence (AI) have been considered to devise a new paradigm for handling complex systems (Genesereth and Ketchpel, 1994; Jennings and Wooldridge, 1996, 2000; Shoham, 1990, 1993; Wooldridge, 1997).

Agent-oriented software engineering (AOSE) paradigm represents an interesting means of analyzing, designing and building complex software systems and it is quite suitable to the new software development requirements (agent-oriented methodologies strengths). But although many scientific researches have been fo-cused on this paradigm (existing agent-oriented software engineering), its current state still reports relative lack of industrial acceptance compared to others.

This paper aims to outline the current standing of AOSE paradigm (a survey of agent-oriented software engineering paradigm) and propose a solution to its relative lack of industrial acceptance compared to others, which is then readjusted to present a plan for software development organizations to reach the fifth level of CMM (proposal solution to agent-orientation promotion). Key building blocks of the proposed approach are an evaluation framework for agent-oriented software engineering methodologies (existing approaches for evaluating agent-oriented methodologies) and a project-specific methodology building framework (existing approaches for evaluating agent-oriented methodologies), which both have suitable instances but have never been merged. A practical instance of the proposal plan (agent open method) is also presented in this paper using these suitable frameworks.

A SURVEY OF AGENT-ORIENTED SOFTWARE ENGINEERING PARADIGM

In order to outline the current state of agent-oriented software engineering paradigm, this section starts with defining AOSE methodologies (The definition of agent-oriented software engineering methodology), then briefly goes over its history (the history of agent-oriented software engineering paradigm), lists existing AOSE methodologies (existing agent-oriented software engineering methodologies) and states their strengths and weaknesses (strengths and weaknesses of agent-oriented methodologies).

The definition of agent-oriented software engineering methodology

To define AOSE methodology, it is first necessary to have a precise definition of methodology itself. Regarding (Brinkkemper, 1996; CMS, 2008; Firesmith, 2002; Lyytinen, 1987; IEEE, 1990; Sturm and Shehory, 2003; Sudeikat et al., 2004) the definition considered for a software engineering methodology in this paper is as follows: A business process equipped with distinct concepts and modeling tools for developing software (Akbari and Faraahi, 2008).

The methodology definition merged with software engineering paradigm concept constitutes the AOSE methodology definition. An agent-based system is a system in which the key abstraction used is that of an agent (Jennings and Wooldridge, 2000; Wooldridge, 1997) and (Wooldridge and Jennings, 1995). Thus by agent-oriented software engineering we mean a software engineering paradigm in which the key abstraction used is that of an agent. Considering this description and the mentioned definition for methodology, an agent-oriented software engineering methodology can be defined as follows: An agent-oriented software engineering methodology is a business process of developing software, equipped with distinct concepts and modeling tools, in which the key abstraction used in its concepts is that of an agent.

The history of agent-oriented software engineering paradigm

AOSE Paradigm, which was first proposed by Yoav Shoham in 1990, is based on a societal view of computation (Shoham, 1990 and 1993). The main source of this paradigm is AI (Debenham and Henderson-Sellers, 2002; Wooldridge, 1997) or precisely, Distributed Artificial Intelligence (DAI) (Bond and Gasser, 1998; Henderson-Sellers and Gorton, 2003). Nevertheless, in agent-orientated software engineering, agents are about computer science and software engineering more than they are about AI (See Wooldridge, 1997 for more description).

Agent-oriented paradigm has multiplied a lot during the past two decades, and although it was first limited to academic researches, it has interested the industry within the last years as well (Debenham and Henderson-Sellers, 2002; Henderson-Sellers and Gorton, 2003). It should be pointed out that after almost a decade of its introduction, the progress of this paradigm has faced a great transformation, which some researches refer to as the entrance to the new generation of software engineering methodologies (Dam and Winikoff, 2003; Henderson-Sellers and Gorton, 2003) (Figure 1) shows the effect of this transition on the number of AOSE methodologies designed per year. The main idea of this transition is based on SME (Harmsen, 1997) and the unification strategy of existing issue (AOSE TFG, 2004), to build a framework for designing project-specific methodologies. The mentioned approach is the researchers' solution to eliminate the relative industry rejection of this paradigm, or eliminate its weaknesses (AOSE TFG, 2004; Henderson-Sellers and Gorton, 2003; Henderson-Sellers et al., 2004). Such issues can be found in (Cossentino and Seidita, 2004), (Henderson-Sellers and Gorton, 2003) and (Juan et al., 2002), which will be described later.

EXISTING AGENT-ORIENTED SOFTWARE ENGINEERING METHODOLOGIES

This section goes through the identification of existing AOSE methodologies. Having the complete list of these methodologies can be a good base to distinguish the current state of AOSE paradigm, yet despite this standing, this list may also be used as a resource reference for the existing project-specific methodology building frameworks to complete their repositories (existing approaches for creating agent-oriented project-specific). The number of existing agent-oriented software engineering methodologies is very high despite their newness. Due to the limited space, examples of existing AOSE methodologies are presented in two separate tables in order of the year of presentation: Table 1 lists the AOSE methodologies introduced before year 2000, and Table 2 lists the AOSE methodologies introduced after year 2000. It should be pointed out that items presented at rows number 37, 43 and 57 are more than just simple methodologies, and are frameworks for creating agent-oriented project-specific methodologies, which will be described in (existing approaches for creating agent-oriented project-specific).

Figure 1 shows the number of AOSE methodologies designed each year from 1990, when AOSE paradigm was first introduced. As it is shown, the number of designed AOSE methodologies has a significant increase in year 2002, but has dropped again the year after. This could have several meanings:

1. AOSE paradigm had dramatically improved till year 2002 that has interested many methodology designers and users at the time: despite some exceptions, the number of methodologies designed has increased each

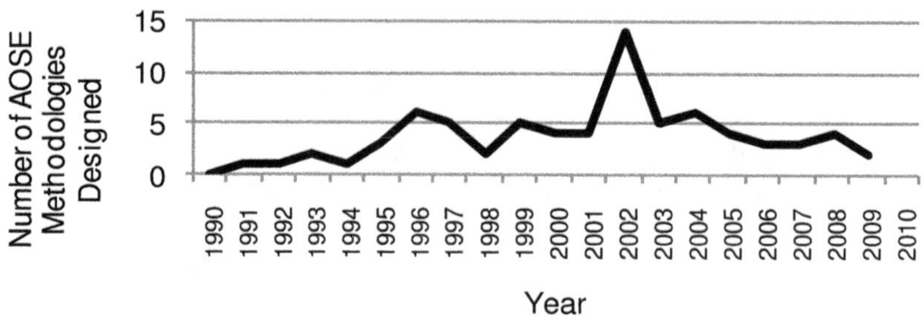

Figure 1. The number of AO methodologies designed each year.

Table 1. List of AOSE methodologies introduced before year 2000.

#	Methodology	Year	Reference(s)
1	ARCHON	1991	(Cockburn and Jennings, 1996)
2	MADE	1992	(O'Hare and Wooldridge, 1992)
3	DRM	1993	(Singh et al., 1993)
4	TOGA	1993	(Gadomski, 1993)
5	CIAD	1994	(Verharen and Weigard, 1994; Verharen, 1997)
6	Agent Factory	1995	(Collier, 1996, 2002; Collier and O'Hare, 1999; O'Hare and Collier, 1998)
7	AOMfEM	1995	(Kendall et al., 1996)
8	Cassiopeia	1995	(Collinot and Drogoul; 1998, Collinot et al., 1996)
9	AAII (KGR)	1996	(Kinny and Georgeff, 1996; Kinny et al., 1996)
10	AOAD	1996	(Burmeister, 1996)
11	AWIC	1996	(Muller, 1996)
12	CoMoMas	1996	(Glaser, 1996)
13	MASB	1996	(Moulin and Brassard, 1996)
14	MAS-CommonKADS	1996	(Iglesias et al., 1998)
15	AALAADIN	1997	(Ferber, 1997; Ferber and Gutknecht, 1998)
16	AMBSA	1997	(Neal Reilly, 1997)
17	AOIM	1997	(Kindler et al., 1997)
18	CaseLP	1997	(Martelli et al., 1997)
19	DESIRE	1997	(Brazier et al., 1997)
20	Adept	1998	(Jennings et al., 1998)
21	AMBIA	1998	(Gao and Sterling, 1998)
22	AOAaD	1999	(Wooldridge, 1999)
23	HIM	1999	(Elammari, 1999)
24	MaSE	1999	(Deloach, 1999, 2005)
25	MASSIVE	1999	(Lind, 1999, 2001)
26	ZEUS	1999	(Nwana et al., 1999)
27	ASEfIA	2000	(Zamboneli et al., 2000)
28	Gaia	2000	(Wooldridge et al., 2000; Zamboneli et al., 2005)
29	MESSAGE/UML	2000	(Caire et al., 2000; Evans et al., 2001)
30	SODA	2000	(Omicini, 2000)

year and about 14 methodologies were introduced in year 2002.

2. AOSE paradigm has provided the necessary conditions for creating project-specific methodology building frameworks: two project-specific methodology building frameworks were defined in year 2002, and also one in year 2004.

3. The introduction of project-specific methodology building frameworks has relevantly answered the user willingness to setup project-specific methodology, yet there is still room for improvements: the number of methodologies designed per year has significantly decreased since year 2002, yet there are still some methodologies designed independent from project-specific

Table 2. List of AOSE methodologies introduced after year 2000.

#	Methodology	Year	Reference(s)
31	Agent-SE	2001	(Far, 2001)
32	AOSM	2001	(Shi, 2001)
33	Styx	2001	(Bush, 2001)
34	Tropos	2001	(Bresciani et al., 2001, 2004; Castro et al., 2001, 2002; Mylopoulos et al., 2001)
35	ADELFE	2002	(Bernon et al., 2002)
36	ALCCIG	2002	(Zhang et al., 2002)
37	CAOMF	2002	(Juan et al., 2002a; Juan et al., 2003; Taveter and Sterling, 2008)
38	IEBPM	2002	(Taveter and Wagner, 2002)
39	INGENIAS	2002	(Pavon and Gomez-Sanz, 2003, 2005)
40	MESMA	2002	(Cuesta et al., 2002)
41	Nemo	2002	(Huget, 2002)
42	ODAC	2002	(Gervais, 2002)
43	Agent OPEN	2002	(Debenham and Henderson-Sellers, 2002; Henderson-Sellers and Gorton, 2003; Henderson-Sellers et al., 2005)
44	PASSI	2002	(Cossentino and Potts, 2002; Cossentino, 2005)
45	Prometheus	2002	(Cervenka, 2003; Padgham and Winikoff, 2002a,b)
46	ROADMAP	2002	(Juan et al., 2002b)
47	SABPO	2002	(Dikenelli and Erdur, 2002)
48	SADDE	2002	(Sierra et al., 2002)
49	MAGE	2003	(Shi et al., 2003, Shi et al., 2004)
50	OPM/MAS	2003	(Sturm et al., 2003)
51	RAP/AOR	2003	(Taveter and Wagner, 2005; Wagner, 2003)
52	RoMAS	2003	(Yan et al., 2003)
53	SONIA	2003	(Alonso et al., 2005)
54	AMBTA	2004	(Sardinha et al., 2004)
55	AODM	2004	(Tian et al., 2004)
56	CAMLE	2004	(Shan and Zhu, 2004)
57	FIPA	2004	(Cossentino and Seidita, 2004; Garro et al., 2004)
58	MAOSEM	2004	(Wang and Guo, 2004)
59	RAOM	2004	(Giret and Botti, 2004)
60	MAHIS	2005	(Li and Liu, 2005)
61	MAMfHMS	2005	(Giret, 2005)
62	OMASM	2005	(Villaplana, 2005)
63	OWL-P	2005	(Desai et al., 2005)
64	ADMuJADE	2006	(Nikraz et al., 2006)
65	MOBMAS	2006	(Tran et al., 2007; Tran and Low, 2008)
66	WAiWS	2006	(Lu and Chhabra, 2006)
67	ADEM	2007	(Cervenka and Trencansky, 2007; Whitestein technologies, 2008)
68	ASPECS	2007	(Cossentino et al., 2007)
69	ForMAAD	2007	(Hadj-Kacem et al., 2007)
70	ANEMONA	2008	(Giret, 2008)
71	MASD	2008	(Abdelaziz et al., 2008)
72	MASIM	2008	(Clancey et al., 2008)
73	PerMet	2008	(Grislin-Le Strugeon et al., 2008)
74	AOMEIS	2009	(Athanasiadis and Mitkas; 2009)
75	ODAM	2009	(Mao et al., 2009)

methodology building frameworks.

Strengths and weaknesses of agent-oriented methodologies

In this section the necessity of agent-orientation usage is discussed as the agent-oriented methodologies strengths and its weaknesses, in terms of its relative industrial rejection.

Agent-oriented methodologies strengths

Agent-oriented methodologies strengths can be considered in two different aspects:

1. Inclusion of other paradigms' capabilities and presentation of more abilities: AOSE paradigm includes all the capabilities of other paradigms (e.g. object-oriented, knowledge engineering and service-oriented) and even more abilities.

a) Agent-oriented methodologies versus object-oriented metho-dologies: As stated by Shoham (Shoham, 1993), agents can be considered as active objects with mental states (Iglesias et al., 1999) which means despite the common characteristics between objects and agents they are not just simple objects but they present more capabilities (Iglesias et al., 1999).
b) Agent-oriented methodologies versus knowledge engineering methodologies: Most of the problems subject to knowledge engineering methodologies are also present in designing Multi-Agent Systems (MAS) as knowledge acquisition, modeling, and reuse. Furthermore, these methodologies conceive a knowledge-based system as a centralized one, thus they do not address the distri-buted or social aspects of the agents, or their reflective and goal- oriented attitudes (Iglesias et al., 1999).
c) Agent-oriented methodologies versus service-oriented methodo-logies: Regarding service-oriented methodologies, it should be pointed out that service is only one of the several concepts presented by an agent, and that agents may not be just service performers, but also predictives – they may volunteer information or services to a user, without being explicitly asked, whenever it is deemed appropriate (Jennings and Wooldridge, 1996).

2. Suitability with new software development requirements: As mentioned before, due to the complexity of software development process, wide range of software engineering paradigms has been devised (e.g. structured programming, object-oriented programming, procedural programming and declarative programming) (Jennings and Wooldridge, 2000). But recently, with the high rate of increase in complexity of projects associated with software engi-neering, agent concepts, which originated from artificial intelligence, have been considered to devise a new paradigm for handling complex systems (Genesereth and Ketchpel, 1994; Jennings and Wooldridge, 1996, 2000; Shoham, 1990, 1993; Wooldridge, 1997). Some special applications of this paradigm are presented in (Wooldridge and Ciancarini, 2001).

Agent-oriented methodologies weaknesses

Agent-oriented methodologies weaknesses can be considered in two different aspects:

1. The lack of attraction for methodology user to use the agent-oriented paradigm:
a) Lack of agent-oriented programming languages: Although programming languages are only part of the development story, industry is reticent to adopt a new paradigm at the conceptual level if it is impossible to implement these ideas in a currently acceptable, commercially viable programming language (Henderson-Sellers and Gorton, 2003).
b) Lack of explicit statement of agent-orientation advantages: The benefits of agent technology must be declared by introducing the cases where AOSE paradigm succeeds and other existing paradigms fail (Henderson-Sellers and Gorton, 2003).
c) Relative difficulty of learning concept related to agent-oriented paradigm (AI): As an example the usage of Gaia agent-oriented methodology (Wooldridge et al., 2000) requires learning logic, which decreases the adoption of this methodology, since usually methodology users are not familiar with logic and do not tend to learn it (Sturm and Shehory, 2003).
d) High cost of AO acquisition: The acquisition of this paradigm by software development organizations requires a high cost for training the development team (Henderson-Sellers and Gorton, 2003).

2. The lack of attraction for methodology user to use existing agent-oriented methodologies:

a) Relative immaturity: The AO paradigm immaturity, which is a relative matter compared to other paradigms (Dam and Winikoff, 2003), is clearly because of it newness.
b) Marketing of multiple AO methodologies: As long as the availability and marketing of multiple agent-oriented methodologies are in competitive manner, this feature is an obstacle to their widespread industrial adoption, since it leads to confusion of methodology users (Henderson-Sellers and Gorton, 2003).
c) Lack of confrontation with wrong expectation of one-size-fits-all methodology: No unique specific methodology

can be general enough to be useful to every project without some level of personalization (AOSE TFG, 2004). Users usually think a unique methodology has general usage and ignore the fact that each methodology is designed for some specific goals (e.g. specific domain or different parts of life cycle). Thus when a specific methodology does not fit their requirements and leads to project failure they conceive the problem from the side of methodology whereas the problem is with the wrong methodology selection (Henderson-Sellers and Giorgini, 2005). Agent-oriented paradigm should support its user with the awareness and facilities to find the proper methodology for his project from existing methodologies or to change the existing instances in order to fit the project.

d) Lack of confrontation with user willingness to setup an owned project-specific methodology: The high number of existing AO methodologies can be seen as a proof that methodology users, often prefer to setup an owned methodology specially tailored for their needs instead of reusing existing ones (AOSE TFG, 2004). AO paradigm should support its user with the awareness and facilities to avoid setting up his methodology from the scratch, but to change the existing instances in order to fit the project.

PROPOSAL SOLUTION TO AGENT-ORIENTATION PROMOTION

The progress of AOSE paradigm is dependent to the elimination of its weaknesses as mentioned above. Clearly, when the software development organization becomes justified for using agent-orientation, by its strengths, it will accept its cost and learning effort much easier, since it knows that in long-term this paradigm will not just pay back this cost but that its benefits would be more than others.

With the emergence of industry willingness for agent-orientation, the next problem to be eliminated would be the lack of attraction for agent-oriented methodologies. It is obvious that identifying the strengths and weaknesses of each methodology can be the first step to its progress and wide industrial acceptance as well (Akbari and Faraahi, 2008; Aose TFG, 2004; Dam and Winikoff, 2003). In addition, the availability and marketing of multiple methodologies which is an obstacle to the ease of selection, lack of the presence of a one-size-fits-all methodology and the need of project-specific methodologies, shows the necessity for exploitation of a project-specific building framework.

Thus it is suggested that software development organizations use an evaluation framework for agent-oriented methodologies such as the one described in existing approaches for evaluating agent-oriented methodologies in order to choose the best for their project, and in case of finding no fitting match to exploit the evaluation results for building effective project-specific methodologies. This might be done by completing and thus improving existing methodologies by replacing their weak parts with strong parts from other methodologies, using one of the frameworks for creating agent-oriented project-specific methodologies described in (existing approaches for creating agent-oriented project-specific methodologies). Thus a consolidated approach as also expressed in (Henderson-Sellers and Gorton, 2003) could give a better signal to the industry. With this regard, it is suggested that instead of competing, agent-oriented methodology designers collaborate with each other by evaluating their own methodologies using an appropriate evaluation framework, to collect the method fragments with their rankings in order to use these information for method engineering. This is quite feasible since most of the agent-oriented methodologies are academic and not commercial products.

This approach would: (i) help to improve existing methodologies by identifying their weaknesses, (ii) make the availability of multiple methodologies an advantage (having wide range of method fragment options), (iii) do away with the wrong expectation on one-size-fits-all methodology, and (iv) answer to user willingness to setup an owned project-specific methodology. Clearly this approach will attract methodology users to use agent-oriented methodologies, and in other words results to industrial acceptance of AOSE paradigm. In addition the usage of the frameworks for creating agent-oriented project-specific methodologies will not only make it possible to use programming languages from other paradigms which are suitable for agent-orientation, but the industry willingness for this paradigm will encourage language designers as well.

This solution to AOSE weaknesses may also be readjusted to propose a plan for development organizations to reach the fifth level of CMM. Figure 2 explains this plan. In CMM organizational maturity framework (Humphery, 1990; Paulk et al., 1993), 5 maturity levels are distinguished (Harmsen, 1997): Initial, Repeatable, Defined, Managed and Optimizing. Since the proposed plan exploits the SME in order to build project-specific methodologies, it is clear that it satisfies the third level of CMM. In addition, since the evaluation framework assesses the methodologies for management plans and thus the management plans' method fragments are constructed to methodology, both process and products are regularly evaluated by the project management team to satiate the forth level of CMM. The feedback that is given by the organization while employing the methodology using the evaluation framework causes the methodology correction to take place continuously and concurrent with its exploitation, and satisfies the 5th level of CMM.

What has taken place by now is the growth of repository by adding all the AOSE methodology's components without considering any evaluation (Henderson-Sellers et

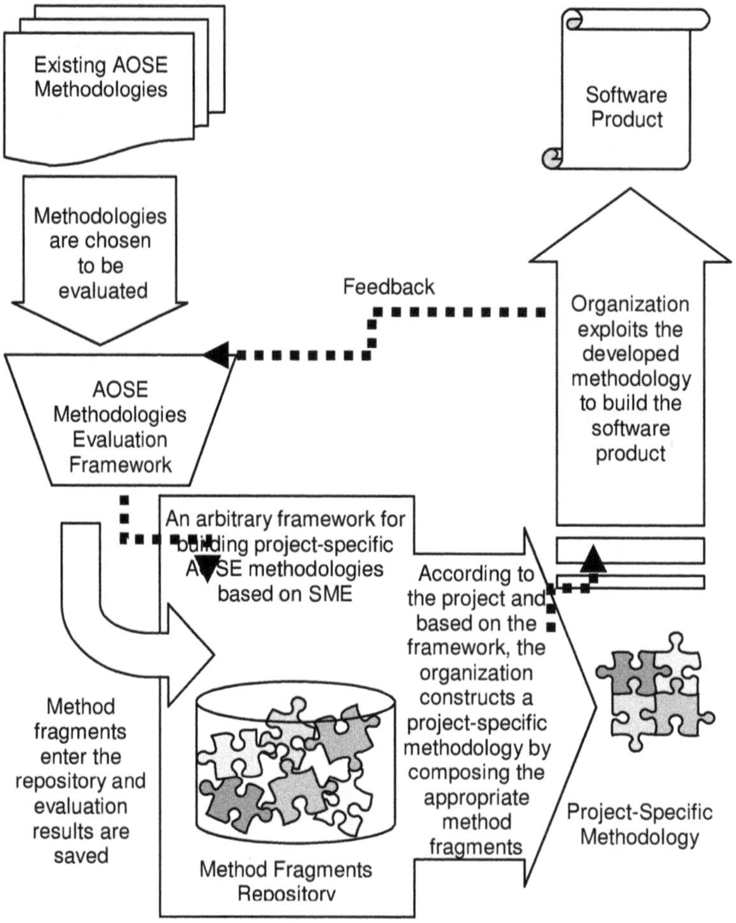

Figure 2. Proposal plan for agent-oriented software development organizations to reach the fifth level of CMM.

al., 2003; Henderson-Sellers et al., 2004; Henderson-Sellers et al., 2006). But the approach presented here is the usage of an evaluation framework and a project-specific methodology building framework simultaneously together. So, each methodology would first be evaluated, and the method fragments with their grades entered in the repository. This makes possible the selection of method fragments with desired grades at the methodology building stage which better implements SME approach. To implement this plan, an evaluation framework and a project-specific methodology building framework are needed. Existing approaches for evaluating agent-oriented methodologies and existing approaches for creating agent-oriented project-specific methodologies describes existing approaches of each of the frameworks.

EXISTING APPROACHES FOR EVALUATING AGENT-ORIENTED METHODOLOGIES

Researches considering the evaluation of agent-oriented methodologies are limited to (Akbari and Faraahi, 2008, 2009; Cernuzzi and Rossi, 2002; Dam and Winikoff, 2003; Henderson-Sellers and Giorgini, 2005; Kumar, 2002; Lin et al., 2007; Sabas et al., 2002; Shehory and Sturm, 2001; Sturm and Shehory, 2003; Sudeikat et al., 2004; Yu and Cysneiros, 2002) and some other studies that compare two or three methodologies, only with respect to the expressiveness and the concepts supported by the methodology (Sturm and Shehory, 2003). Most of the mentioned evaluation frameworks suffer from one or both of the following shortcomings: (1) Lack of coverage for all of the methodology aspects, (2) Lack of definition of a precise evaluation metric. As mentioned above, methodology is referred to as an economical process of developing software, equipped with distinct concepts and modeling tools (Akbari and Faraahi, 2008, 2009). In this regard methodologies can be considered in six major aspects: concepts, notation, process, pragmatics, support for software engineering and marketability. In addition, evaluation metric should be able to present different levels of methodology support for each criterion. The framework presented in (Akbari and Faraahi, 2008) and completed in (Akbari and Faraahi, 2009) evaluates methodologies from all aspects men-tioned and defines a metric with 7 levels of support; thus it perfectly overcomes the mentioned shortcomings of most evaluation frameworks.

As stated in (Akbari, 2010) the most important difference between the mentioned evaluation framework with existing approaches is that this framework is multi-layered (Figure 3); meaning that methodologies are first considered in the six mentioned aspects and in detailed layers base on the criteria and sub-criteria. Actually, each criterion refer to its sub-criteria, thus it increases the preciseness and clarity of the evaluation and helps the evaluator through the process. Furthermore, users will use the evaluation results accordingly to their required level. For example, for software development organization customer, the overall grade of methodology is important; thus average of methodology rating are presented to him (according to the metric of the framework, resulting average should be rounded in each level of evaluation, to fit one of the 7 levels). But on the contrary, for software developer the grade obtained for most detailed criteria are important.

EXISTING APPROACHES FOR CREATING AGENT-ORIENTED PROJECT-SPECIFIC METHODOLOGIES

Existing approaches for creating agent-oriented project-specific methodologies are based on situational method Engineering (SME). The term method engineering (ME) goes back to Maynard, who introduced it as the research area in mechanical engineering, addressing the definition of methods to industrial engineering (Maynard, 1939). In definition, ME approaches do not necessarily take into account the project or situation in which a method will be applied (Harmsen, 1997). SME is the sub-area of ME directed towards the controlled, formal and computer-assisted construction of situational (project-specific) methods out of method fragments (a description of an Information System (IS) engineering method, or any coherent part thereof) (Harmsen, 1997). A well-known synonym for SME is Methodology Engineering, which was first introduced in (Kumar and Walke, 1992).

Despite the strengths of existing approaches for creating agent-oriented project-specific methodologies, they also have some weak points:

1. Lack of methodology evaluation and result saving while storing a methodology in method fragments repository.
2. Lack of consideration of method fragment capability while creating a project-specific methodology

To eliminate mentioned shortcomings, two different approaches may be considered:

1. Screening the method fragments at storing stage, by evaluation and storing strong method fragments with high grades.

2. Evaluating and storing all the method fragments with their corresponding evaluation results, and postponing the selection of method fragments with desired grade to methodology building stage.

Clearly, the second approach is the best one and follows the SME goals. Since SME is not always seeking to assemble the method fragments with high grades, but more precisely, it seeks to assemble the proper method fragments (with proper capabilities). For example, a software development organization that works on large, complex, and business-critical projects, must consider management plans in its methodology (Firesmith and Henderson-Sellers, 2002), and as much as the project is larger, more complex and more business-critical, the management plans method fragments should be stronger with higher grades of evaluation. Yet in opposite way software development organization that works on small, simple, and non-critical projects does not need restricted management plans. In this case, restricted management plans would not even help the progress of software development, but would be an overload to development team by defining unnecessary fruitless tasks. Thus, in such cases, method fragments with average or even low grades would be sufficient for the project-specific methodology.

As a result, weaknesses of existing approaches for creating agent-oriented project-specific methodologies also show the necessity of joining these frameworks with evaluation frameworks in order to build project-specific methodologies and thus improve agent-oriented methodologies acceptance. The existing project-specific methodology building frameworks are briefly introduced in the following sections.

Agent OPEN method

OPEN, which stands for Object-oriented Process, Environment and Notation, was first outlined in (Henderson-Sellers and Graham, 1996) and was published in (Graham et al., 1997) as a full life cycle methodology (Firesmith and Henderson-Sellers, 2002). OPEN Process Framework (OPF) consists of: (i) a process metamodel of framework from which can be generated an organizationally specific process, (instance) created using a method engineering approach from (ii) a repository and (iii) a set of construction guidelines. The major elements in OPF metamodel are Work Units (Activities, Tasks and Techniques), Work Products, Producers and two auxiliary ones (Stages and Languages) (Henderson-Sellers et al., 2003).

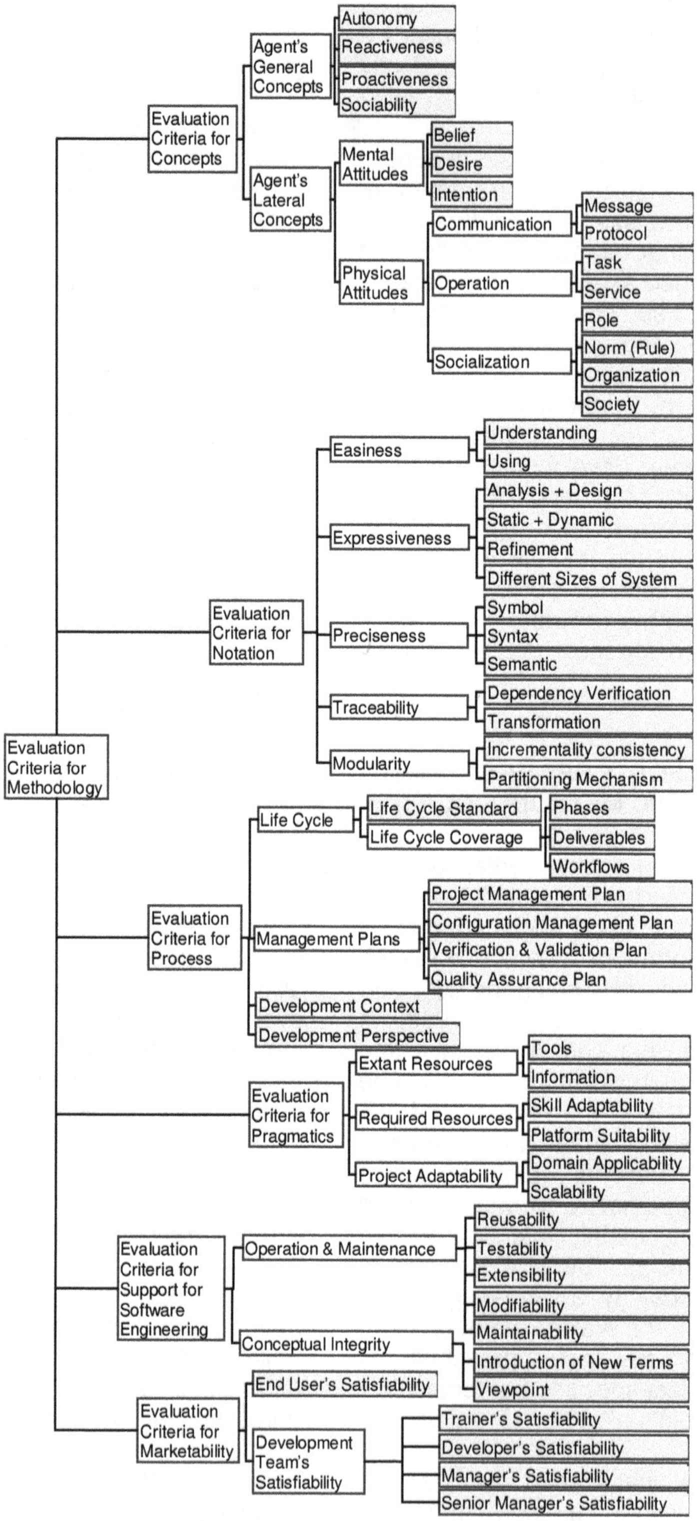

Figure 3. Different levels of criteria in evaluation framework introduced in (Akbari, 2010).

To extend this approach to support agent-oriented information systems, (Debenham and Henderson-Sellers, 2003) analyzes the differences between agent-oriented and object-oriented approaches in order to be able to itemize and outline the necessary additions to the OPF's repository in the standard format provided in (Henderson-

Sellers et al., 1998). A list of method fragments added to OPF from existing agent-oriented methodologies can be found in (Henderson-Sellers, 2005, 2004, 2006 and 2003).

Feature-based method

In (Juan et al., 2002) is proposed a modular approach enabling developers to build customized project-specific methodologies from AOSE features. An AOSE feature is defined in (Juan et al., 2003) to encapsulate software engineering techniques, models, supporting Computer-Aided Software Engineering (CASE) tools and development knowledge such as design patterns. It is considered a stand-alone unit to perform part of a development phase, such as analysis or prototyping, while achieving a quality attribute such as privacy. Comparing to Agent OPEN method, an AOSE feature can be defined in terms of these notions as a Work Unit performed by one or more Producers in support of a specific software engineering stage resulting in one or more Work Products represented in the respective Languages (Taveter and Sterling, 2008). Differing from Agent OPEN approach, this method does not regard it necessary to rely on the formal metamodel of method fragments and has demonstrated in (Juan and Sterling, 2003; Juan et al., 2002, 2003; Sterling and Taveter, 2009) that informal approach to methodology composition works equally well and is more likely to be adopted in industry.

This method identifies and standardizes the common elements of the existing methodologies. The common elements could form a generic agent model on which specialized features might be based. The remaining parts of the methodologies would represent added-value that the methodologies bring to the common elements, and should be componentized into modular features. The small granularity of features allows them to be combined into the common models in a flexible manner. By conforming to the generic agent model in the common elements, it is expected that the semantics of the optional features remain consistent (Juan et al., 2002).

FIPA methodology technical committee method

This work refers to the FIPA Methodology Technical Committee activity and it consists in a quite open approach that allows the composition of elements coming from a repository of fragments of existing design processes that could be expressed in terms of a standard notation. Specifically dealing with the methods integration problem in this contribution, two different approaches have been considered to obtain methods integration: (i) guided by a MAS meta-model; (ii) guided by a development process. In the first approach, while building his own methodology, the designer has to preliminary identify the elements that compose the meta-model of the MAS he is going to build; then he has to choose the method fragments that are able to produce the identified meta-model elements. The second approach focuses on the instantiation of some software development process that completely cover the development of MAS. Given a specific problem and/or an application domain, the process will be instantiated by selection, for each phase, suitable method fragments, chosen from agent-oriented methodologies proposed in the literature or ad-hoc defined (AOSE TFG, 2004; Cossentino and Seidita, 2004; Garro et al., 2004).

A PRACTICAL INSTANCE OF PROPOSAL PLAN

As mentioned, to implement the plan proposed in proposal solution to agent-orientation promotion, an evaluation framework and a project-specific methodology building framework are needed. Existing approaches for evaluating agent-oriented methodologies shows that the evaluation framework presented in (Akbari, 2010) perfectly overcomes the shortcoming of most of the existing evaluation frameworks. In addition, since this framework is a feature-based framework, it has the following advantages as well:

1. Previous success (Sturm et al., 2004).
2. The possibility of implementation independent from external resources (e.g. industrial partners) (Sturm et al., 2004).
3. Lack of need of empirical information (Siau and Rossi, 1998)
4. The possibility of direct and detailed identification of methodologies' weaknesses in order to improve them by SME, with stressing on features.

Among existing project-specific methodology building frameworks, Agent OPEN matches the proposed plan best, since:

1. It is more complete and mature compared to others.
2. It has more existing resources compared to others, which facilitates the current research.
3. Method fragment repository of this method is richer compared to others.
4. It is also approved by FIPA (FIPA has some suggestions on merging its own method with Agent OPEN method).

Conclusion

The study of AOSE paradigm strengths shows the necessity of its usage; yet its current state reports relative lack of industrial acceptance compared to others. This paper proposes a solution to this problem which aims to eliminate the weaknesses of this paradigm by the usage of an evaluation framework and a project-specific methodology building framework, simultaneously in a software development organization. The usage of SME, considerations for project management plans, and continuous improvements in the methodology through a wise combination of these frameworks may also lead the organization to reach the fifth level of CMM. In this regard, following future works are suggested:

1. Activities towards implementation and exploitation of the proposal plan:

a) Enriching the method fragment repository: The list of AOSE methodologies presented in existing agent-oriented software engineering methodologies may be used as a reference of methodologies, in order to extract their method fragments and complete the repositories of project-specific methodology building frameworks.
b) Storing the methodologies' evaluation results: The information stored may be used as a means to select suitable method fragments for building a project-specific methodology.

2. Activities towards completion of proposal plan details:

a) Enforcing the identification of the method fragments related to each criterion while storing a methodology: This will facilitate the selection of suitable method fragments with desired grades (level of property implementation) while building a project-specific methodology.
b) Defining a change management plan for continuous changes that occur in proposal plan structure and data: These changes may occur towards improving the evaluation framework, and/or the methodology in use.
3. Activities towards adding more capabilities to the proposal plan:

a) Preparing possibilities to design Domain-Specific Languages (DSL): The availability of project-specific methodologies is useless if no proper programming languages assure the software implementation. Thus, it is suggested to establish the facilities for designing DSLs along with the building project-specific methodologies as well.
b) Preparing possibilities to determine the proper paradigm for the project and change dominant paradigm of the proposal plan: As the software development organization needs to exploit a project-specific methodology, in case of wide range of projects handled by the organization, there may be the need for different paradigms as well. Thus the proposal plan may be equipped with a framework to select the proper paradigm to handle the project and follow the software development process with this paradigm, which needs suitable evaluation framework and project-specific methodology building framework as well.

REFERENCES

Abdelaziz T, Elammari M, Branki C (2008). MASD: towards a comprehensive multi-agent system development methodology, Meersman R, Tari Z, Herrero P. (Eds.), OTM Workshops, LNCS 5333: 108–117.

Akbari ZO, Faraahi A (2008). Evaluation Framework for Agent-Oriented Methodologies, Proceedings of World Academy of Science, Engineering and Technology, WCSET Paris, France, 35: 419-424, ISSN 2070-3740.

Akbari ZO, Faraahi A (2009). A Feature-Based Framework for Agent-Oriented Methodologies Evaluation, In Proceedings of CCSR, Tehran, Iran, pp 125-133.

Akbari ZO (2010). An Evaluation Framework for Agent-Oriented Methodologies and Its Utilization in Creating an Efficient Agent-Oriented Methodology, M. Sc Thesis, Payame Noor University, Tehran, Iran.

Alonso F, Frutos S, Martinez L, Montes C, Sonia (2004). a methodology for natural agent development, In Gleizes M.P., Omicini A, Zambonelli F (Eds.): ESAW. LNCS 3451, Springer-Verlag Berlin Heidelberg, (2005), pp 245-260.

AOSE Technical Forum Group (2004). AL3-TF1 Report, The first AgentLink III Technical Forum (AL3-TF1), Rome, Italy.

Athanasiadis IN, Mitkas PA (2009). A methodology for developing Environmental Information Systems with Software Agents, Whitestein Series in Software Agent Technologies and Autonomic Computing, Birkhauser Verlag Basel/Switzerland, pp. 119-137.

Bernon C, Gleizes MP, Picard G, Glize P (2002). The ADELFE methodology for an intranet system design, In Giorgini P, Lespérance Y, Wagner G and Yu E (Eds.). Proceedings of Agent-Oriented Information Systems (AOIS). pp. 1-15.

Bond AH, Gasser L (1988). A Survey of Distributed Artificial Intelligence, Readings in Distributed Artificial Intelligence, Morgan Kaufmann Publishers: San Mateo, CA.

Brazier FMT, Dunin-Keplicz BM, Jennings NR, Treur J (1997). DESIRE: modelling multi-agent systems in a compositional formal framework, Int J. Cooperative Inf. Syst. 6(1), 67-94.

Bresciani P, Giorgini P, Giunchiglia F, Mylopolous J, Perini A, (2004). Tropos: An agent-oriented software development methodology, Auton. Agents Multi Agent Syst. 8(3): 203-236.

Bresciani P, Perini A, Giorgini P, Giunchiglia F, Mylopoulos J, (2001). A Knowledge Level Software Engineering Methodology for Agent-Oriented Programming, Proceedings of the 5th International Conference on Autonomous Agents, Agents'01, Montreal, Canada, pp. 648-655.

Brinkkemper S (1996). Method engineering: engineering of information systems development methods and tools, Inf. Software Technol. 38: 275-280.

Burmeister B (1996). Models and methodology for agent-oriented analysis and design, In Fischer K. editor, Working Notes of the KI'96 Workshop on Agent Oriented Programming and Distributed Artificial Intelligence, Dresden.

Bush G, Cranefield S, Purvis M (2001). The Styx agent methodology, The Information Science Discussion Paper Series, Number (2001/02).ISSN 1172-6024, Department of Information Science, University of Otago, Dunedin, New Zealand.

Caire G, Leal F, Chainho P, Evans R, Garijo F, Gomez J, Pavon J, Kearney P, Stark J, Massonet P (2000). Agent Oriented Analysis using MESSAGE/UML, In Wooldridge M., Weiss G, Ciancarini P, (Eds.). AOSE II, 119-135, LNCS 2222, Berlin: Springer-Verlag.

Castro J, Kolp M, Mylopoulos J (2001). A Requirements-Driven Development Methodology, In: Proceedings of the 13th International Conference on Advanced Information Systems Engineering (CAiSE'01) pp. 108-123.

Castro J, Kolp M, Mylopoulos J (2002). Towards requirements-driven information systems engineering: The Tropos project, Inf. Syst. 27(6): 365-389.

Cernuzzi L, Rossi G (2002). On the Evaluation of Agent Oriented Methodologies, in Proc. of the OOPSLA (2002) Workshop on Agent-Oriented Methodologies.

Cervenka R, Trencansky I (2007). The Agent Modeling Language – AML, A Comprehensive Approach to Modeling Multi-Agent Systems, Whitestein Series in Software Agent Technologies and Autonomic Computing, ISBN: 978-3-7643-8395-4.

Cervenka R (2003). Modeling Notation Source: Prometheus, Version: 03-04-02, Foundation for Intelligent Physical Agents.

Clancey WJ, Sierhuis M, Seah C, Buckley C, Reynolds F, Hall T, Scott M (2007). Multi-agent simulation to implementation: a practical engineering methodology for designing space flight operations, In Artikis A et al. (Eds.): ESAW. LNCS 4995, Springer-Verlag Berlin Heidelberg, (2008) pp. 108-123.

CMS (2008), Selecting a development approach, Centers for Medicare and Medicaid Services (CMS), Original Issuance: February (2005). Revalidated: March.

Cockburn D, Jennings NR (1996). ARCHON: A distributed artificial intelligence system for industrial applications, In O'Hare GMP, Jennings NR, (editors), Foundations of Distributed Artificial Intelligence, pp. 319–344, JohnWiley & Sons.

Collier R (1996). The Realisation of Agent Factory: An Environment for the Rapid Prototyping of Intelligent Agents, M. Phil Thesis, UMIST, UK.

Collier RW (2002). Agent Factory: a framework for the engineering of agent-oriented applications, PHD Thesis, National University of Ireland.

Collier RW, O'Hare GMP (1999). Agent Factory: A Revised Agent Prototyping Environment, in 10th Irish Conference on Artificial Intelligence and Cognitive Science (AICS).

Collinot A, Drogoul A (1998). Using the Cassiopeia method to design a soccer robot team, Appl. Artif. Intell. (AAI) J. 12(2-3): 127-147.

Collinot A, Drogoul A, Benhamou P (1996). Agent-oriented design of a soccer robot team, In Proceedings of the Second International Conference on Multi-Agent Systems (ICMAS'96), 41-57, Menlo Park, CA: American Association for Artificial Intelligence.

Cossentino M, Potts C (2002). A CASE tool supported methodology for the design of multi-agent systems. In Ababnia HR and Mun Y (Eds.), Proceedings of the International Conference on Software Engineering Research and Practice (SERP'02), Las Vegas pp. 315-321.

Cossentino M, Seidita V (2004). Composition of a New Process to Meet Agile Needs Using Method Engineering, Software Engineering for Large Multi-Agent Systems, vol. III, LNCS Series, Elsivier Ed.

Cossentino M (2005). From requirements to code with the PASSI methodology, In Henderson-Sellers B, Giorgini P (Eds.), Agent-oriented methodologies (Chapter 4). Hershey, PA: Idea Group.

Cossentino M, Gaud N, Hilaire V, Galland S, Koukam A (2007), ASPECS: an Agent-oriented Software Process for Engineering Complex Systems, In Proc. of the Fifth Agent Oriented Software Engineering Technical Forum (AOSE-TF5), Hammameth, Tunisia.

Cuesta P, Gomez A, Gonzalez JC, Rodriguez FJ (2002). The MESMA approach for AOSE, 4th Iberoamerican Workshop on Multi-Agent Systems (Iberagents'2002). a workshop of IBERAMIA'2002, The VIII Iberoamerican Conference on Artificial Intelligence.

Dam KH, Winikoff M (2003). Comparing agent-oriented methodologies, Proceedings of the 5th Int Bi-Conference Workshop on Agent-Oriented Information Systems (AOIS), Melbourne, Australia.

Debenham J, Henderson-Sellers B (2003). Designing agent-based process systems - Extending the OPEN process framework, In Plekhanova V (Ed.), Intelligent agent software engineering, Chapter VIII pp. 160-190, Hershey, PA: Idea Group Publishing.

Debenham JK, Henderson-Sellers B (2002). Full lifecycle methodologies for agent-oriented systems – the extended OPEN process framework, In Proceedings of Agent-Oriented Information Systems (Eds. Giorini P, Lespreance Y, Wagner G, Yu E), Toronto pp. 87-101.

DeLoach SA (1999). Multiagent systems engineering: A methodology and language for designing agent systems, In Proceedings of the First International Bi-conference Workshop on Agent-Oriented Information Systems (AOIS '99), In the Third International Conference on Autonomous Agents, Seattle, USA.

DeLoach SA (2005). Multi-Agent Systems Engineering: An Overview and Case Study, In Henderson-Sellers B, Giorgini P (Eds.), Agent-oriented methodologies (Chapter 11), Hershey, PA: Idea Group.

Desai N, Mallya AU, Chopra AK, Singh MP (2005). OWL-P: a methodology for business process development, Kolp M, Bresciani P, Henderson-Sellers B, Winikoff M (Eds.), Agent-Oriented Information Systems III, 7th International Bi-Conference Workshop, AOIS. pp. 79-94.

Dikenelli O, Erdur RC (2002). SABPO: A Standards Based and Pattern Oriented Multi-agent Development Methodology, ESAW, 213-226.

Elammari M, Lalonde W (1999). An agent-oriented methodology: high-level and intermediate models, In the proceedings of AOIS (Agent-Oriented Information Systems), In the Third International Conference on Autonomous Agents, Seattle, USA.

Evans R, Kearney P, Stark J, Caire G, Garijo F , Gomez Sanz J, Pavon J, Leal F, Chainho P, Massonet P (2001). MESSAGE: Methodology for engineering systems of software agents, EURESCOM Technical Information.

Far BH (2001). Agent-SE: A Methodology for Agent Oriented Software Engineering, In Jin Q, Li J, Zhang N, Cheng J, Yu C, Noguchi S, (Eds.), Enabling Society with Information Technology, Springer pp. 357-366.

Ferber J, Gutknecht O (1997). Aalaadin: a meta-model for the analysis and design of organizations in multi-agent systems, rapport de recherche, Lirmm, univ. de Montpellier.

Ferber J, Gutknecht O (1998). A Meta-Model for the Analysis and Design of Organizations in Multi-Agent Systems, In Proceedings of the Third International Conference on Multi Agent Systems (ICMAS98), Paris, France.

Firesmith DG, Henderson-Sellers B (2002). The OPEN Process Framework: An Introduction, Addison-Wesley, UK, ISBN 0-201-67510-2.

Gadomski AM (1993). TOGA: A Methodological and Conceptual Pattern for modeling of Abstract Intelligent Agent, Proceedings of the First International Round-Table on Abstract Intelligent Agent, Gadomski AM, (editor) pp. 25-27.

Gao X, Sterling L (1998). A Methodology for Building Information Agents, In Yang Y, Li M, Ellis A, (editors), Web Technologies and Applications, Chapter 5, pp. 43-52, International Academic Pulishers.

Garro A, Fortino G, Russo W (2004). Using Method Engineering for the Construction of Agent-Oriented Methodologies, In Proc. of WOA 04 – Dagli Oggetti Agli Agenti, Sistemi Complessi e Agenti razionali, pp. 51-54, Torino, Italy.

Genesereth MR, Ketchpel SP (1994). Software agents, Communications of the ACM, 37, 7, pp. 48-53.

Gervais MP (2002). ODAC: An Agent-Oriented Methodology Based on ODP, J. Auton. Agents Multi Agent Syst. 7: 199-228.

Giret A, Botti V (2004). Towards a Recursive Agent Oriented Methodology for Large-Scale MAS, In Giorgini P, Muller JP, Odell J, (Eds.): AOSE (2003). LNCS 2935, 25–35, Springer-Verlag, Berlin, Heidelberg.

Giret A (2008). ANEMONA: a multi-agent methodology for holonic manufacturing systems, Springer Series in Advanced Manufacturing, First edition, ISBN-13: 978-1848003095,

Giret A, Botti V, Valero S (2005). MAS methodology for HMS, In Marik V, Brennan RW, Pechoucek M (Eds.): HoloMAS. LNCS 3593, Springer-Verlag Berlin Heidelberg pp. 39-49.

Glaser N (1996). The CoMoMAS methodology and environment for multiagent system development, In Zhang C, Lukose D (Eds.), Multi-agent systems methodologies and applications, pp. 1-16, Second Australian Workshop on Distributed Artificial Intelligence, LNAI 1286, Berlin: Springer-Verlag.

Graham I, Henderson-Sellers B, Younessi H (1997). The OPEN Process Specification, Addison-Wesley.

Grislin-Le Strugeon E, Anli A, Adam E (2006). A methodology to bring MAS to information systems, In Kolp M et al. (Eds.): AOIS. LNCS 4898, Springer-Verlag Berlin Heidelberg, (2008) pp. 90-104.

Hadj-Kacem A, Regayeg A, Jmaiel M (2007). ForMAAD: a formal method for agent-oriented application design, Web Intell. Agent Syst. 5(4): 435-454, IOS Press, Amesterdam, Netherland, ISSN: 1570-1263.
Harmsen AF (1997). Situational Method Engineering, Doctoral dissertation University of Twente, With ref., index and summary in Dutch, ISBN: 90-75498-10-1.
Henderson-Sellers B, Giorgini P (2005). Agent-Oriented Methodologies, Idea Group Publishing, ISBN 1-59140-587-4.
Henderson-Sellers B, Gorton I (2003). Agent-based Software Development Methodologies, White Paper on OOPSLA 2002 Workshop on Agent-Oriented Methodologies, COTAR, Sydney.
Henderson-Sellers B, Graham IM (1996). OPEN: Toward Method Convergence, IEEE Comput. 29(4): 86–89.
Henderson-Sellers B (2005). Evaluating the Feasibility of Method Engineering for the Creating of Agent-Oriented Methodologies, In Pechoucek M, Petta P, Varga LZ, (Eds.), CEEMAS pp. 142–152.
Henderson-Sellers B, Debenham J, Tran QNN (2004). Adding agent-oriented concepts derived from GAIA to Agent OPEN, In Advanced Information Systems Engineering: 16th International Conference, CAiSE. Riga, Latvia pp. 98-111, Berlin: Springer-Verlag.
Henderson-Sellers B, Debenham J, Tran QN, Cossentino M, Low G (2006). Identification of Reusable Method Fragments from the PASSI Agent-Oriented Methodology, In Agent Oriented Information Systems III, Lecture Notes in Computer Science, 3529, Springer-Verlag GmbH, 95-110.
Henderson-Sellers B, Giorgini P, Bresciani P (2003). Enhancing Agent OPEN with concepts used in the Tropos methodology, in Proceedings of the Fourth International Workshop Engineering Societies in the Agents World, Imperial College London, UK.
Henderson-Sellers B, Simons AJH, Younessi H (1998). The OPEN Toolbox of Techniques, Addison-Wesley, UK, 426 pp.
Henderson-Sellers B, Tran Q, Debenham J, Gonzalez-Perez C (2005). Agent-oriented information systems development using OPEN and the agent factory, Information Systems Development Advances in Theory, Practice and Education: 13th International Conference on Information Systems Development, ISD (2004). Vilnius, Lithuania, 149-160, New York: Kluwer Acadmic / Plenum Publishers.
Huget M (2002). Nemo: an agent-oriented software engineering methodology, In Proceedings of OOPSLA Workshop on Agent-Oriented Methodologies, Debenham J, Henderson-Sellers B, Jennings NR, Odell J, Seattle, USA.
Iglesias CA, Garijo M, Gonzalez JC (1999). A Survey of Agent-Oriented Methodologies, in Intelligents Agents IV: Agent Theories, Architectures, and Languages, 1555 of LNAI, Springer-Verlag pp. 317-330.
Iglesias CA, Garijo M, Gonzalez JC, Velasco JR (1998). Analysis and design of multiagent systems using MAS-CommonKADS. In Singh, MP, Rao A, Wooldridge MJ (eds.), Intelligent Agents IV (LNAI 1365), Springer-Verlag: Berlin Germany pp. 313-326.
Jennings N, Wooldridge M (1996). Software Agents, IEEE Rev. 17-20.
Jennings NR, Wooldridge M (2000). Agent-Oriented Software Engineering, In Handbook of Agent Technology (ed. Bradshaw J.), AAAI/MIT Press.
Jennings NR, Norman TJ, Faratin P (1998).ADEPT: An agent-based approach to business process management, SIGMOD Record 27(4): 32-39,
Juan T, Sterling L (2003). The ROADMAP meta-model for intelligent adaptive multiagent systems in open environments, In Giorgini P, Muller J, Odell J, (Eds.), Agent-Oriented Software Engineering IV, 4th International Workshop, AOSE. Melbourne, Australia, Revised Papers (LNCS 2935, 53–68), Berlin, Germany: Springer-Verlag.
Juan T, Pearce A, Sterling L (2002).ROADMAP: Extending the Gaia methodology for Complex Open Systems, Proceedings of the First International Joint Conference on Autonomous Agents and Multi-Agent Systems (AAMAS), Bologna, Italy.
Juan T, Sterling L, Winikoff M (2002). Assembling agent oriented software engineering methodologies from features, In Giunchiglia F, Odel J, Weiss G, (Eds.), Agent-Oriented Software Engineering III, Third International Workshop, AOSE. Bologna, Italy, Revised Papers and Invited Contributions (LNCS 2585, 198–209). Berlin, Germany: Springer-Verlag.
Juan T, Sterling L, Martelli M, Mascardi V (2003). Customizing AOSE methodologies by reusing AOSE features, In Rosenschein JS, Sandholm T, Wooldridge M, Yokoo M, (Eds.), Proceedings of the Second International Joint Conference on Autonomous Agents and Multiagent Systems (AAMAS), Melbourne, Australia, 113–120.
Kendall EA, Malkoun MT, Jiang C (1996). A methodology for developing agent based systems for enterprise integration. In Lukose D, Zhang C, (editors), Distributed Artificial Intelligence Architecture and Modelling: Proceedings of the First Australian Workshop on DAI, LNCS 1087, Springer-Verlag: Heidelberg, Germany pp. 85-99.
Kindler C, DeLuke R, Rhea J, Kunz JC (1997). Development and Demonstration of an Agent-Oriented Integration Methodology, Kaman Sciences Corporation, Rome, NY, Contract Number F30602-94-C-0216.
Kinny D, Georgeff M (1996). Modelling and design of multi-agent systems, In Intelligent Agents III: Proceedings of the Third International Workshop on Agent Theories, Architectures, and Languages (ATAL-96), LNAI 1193, Berlin: Springer-Verlag.
Kinny D, Georgeff M, Rao A (1996). A methodology and modelling technique for systems of BDI agents, In Proceedings of the Seventh European Workshop on Modelling Autonomous Agents in a Multi-Agent World (MAAMAW-96), Eindhoven, The Netherlands, pp. 56-71, Springer.
Kumar K, Welke RJ (1992). Method Engineering, a Proposal for Situation-Specific Methodology Construction, In Systems Analysis and Design: A Research Agenda, Cotterman and Senn (Eds.), Wiley pp. 257-268.
Kumar M (2002). Contrast and comparison of five major Agent Oriented Software Engineering (AOSE) methodologies, Available at http://students.jmc.ksu.edu/grad/madhukar/www/professional /aose paper.pdf.
Li C, Liu L (2005). MAHIS: An Agent-Oriented Methodology for Constructing Dynamic Platform-Based HIS, Australian Conference on Artificial Intelligence, 705-714.
Lin C, Kavi KM, Sheldon FT, Daley KM, Abercrombie RK, (2007). A Methodology to Evaluate Agent Oriented Software Engineering Techniques, Software Agents and Semantic Web Technologies Minitrack, IEEE Proc. HICSS-40, Big Island HI.
Lind J (1999). MASSIVE: Software Engineering for Multiagent Systems, PhD Thesis, University of Saarland, Saarbrucken.
Lind J (2001). Iterative software engineering for multiagent systems, The MASSIVE Method, (LNAI 1994), Berlin: Springer-Verlag.
Lu H, Chhabra M (2006). A methodology for agent oriented web service engineering, In Shi Z, Sadananda R (Eds.): PRIMA LNCS 4088, Springer-Verlag Berlin Heidelberg, 2006 pp. 650-655.
Lyytinen K (1987). A Taxonomic Perspective of Information Systems Development: Theoretical Constructs and Recommendations, In Critical Issues in Information Systems Research, Jr, R J B, Hirschheim RA, (eds.) John Wiley & Sons Ltd., 3-41.
Mao X, Zhao J, Wang J(2009). Engineering adaptive multi-agent systems with ODAM methodology, In Ghose A, Governatori G, Sadananda R, (Eds.): PRIMA 2007, LNCS 5044, Springer-Verlag Berlin Heidelberg pp. 380-385.
Martelli M, Mascardi V, Zini F (1997). CaseLP: a Complex Application Specification Environment based on Logic Programming, In Proc. of ICLP'97 Post Conference Workshop on Logic Programming and Multi-Agents pp. 35-50.
Maynard HB, Stegemerten GJ (1939). Operation Analysis, McGraw-Hill, New York.
Moulin B, Brassard M (1996). A Scenario-Based Design Method and an Environment for the Development of Multiagent systems, In Lukose D, Zhang C, (editors), Proceedings of the First Australian workshop on Distributed Artificial Intelligence, Lecture Notes in Artificial Intelligence, No. 1087, pp. 216-231, Springer-Verlag.
Muller HJ (1996). Towards agent systems engineering, , Special Issue on Distributed Expertise, Int. J. Data Knowledge Eng. (23): 217–245.
Mylopoulos J, Kolp M, Castro J (2001). UML for agent-oriented software development: The Tropos proposal, Proceedings of the 4th

International Conference on the Unified Modeling Language, UML'01, Toronto, Canada, October 1-5, Springer pp. 422-442.
Neal Reilly WS (1997). A Methodology for Building Believable Social Agents, Proceedings of the First International Conference on Autonomous Agents (Agents '97), Marina del Rey, CA, USA, 114-121, ACM Press, New York, ISBN 0-89791-877-0, ACM Order Number 605971.
Nikraz M, Caire G, Bahri PA (2006). A methodology for the development of multi-agent systems using the JADE platform, Computer Systems Science and Engineering, 21(2), 99–116.
Nwana H, Ndumu D, Lee L, Collis J (1999). ZEUS: A Tool-Kit for Building Distributed Multi-Agent Systems, Appl. Artif. Intell. J. 13(1): 129-186.
O'Hare GMP, Wooldridge MJ (1992). A software engineering perspective on multi-agent system design: Experience in the development of MADE, In Avouris NM, Gasser L, (Eds), Distributed Artificial Intelligence: Theory and Praxis pp. 109–127, Kluwer Academic Publishers: Boston, MA.
O'Hare GMP, Collier RW, Conlon J, Abbas S (1998). Agent Factory: An Environment for Constructing and Visualising Agent Communities, 9th Irish Conference on Artificial Intelligence and Cognitive Science (AICS).
Omicini A (2000). SODA: societies and infrastructures in the analysis and design of agent-based systems, In Agent-Oriented Software Engineering, LNCS, 1957 pp. 185-193, Berlin: Springer-Verlag.
Padgham L, Winikoff M (2002). Prometheus: A methodology for developing intelligent agents, In Giunchiglia F, Odell J, Weiß G, (Eds.), Agent-Oriented Software Engineering III Proceedings of the Third International Workshop on Agent-Oriented Software Engineering (AAMAS'02) pp. 174-185, LNCS 2585.
Padgham L, Winikoff M (2002). Prometheus: A pragmatic methodology for engineering intelligent agents, In Debenham J, Henderson-Sellers B, Jennings N, Odell JJ, (Eds.), Agent-oriented Software Engineering III Proceedings of the Workshop on Agent-oriented Methodologies at OOPSLA. Seattle pp. 97-108, Sydney: Centre for Object Technology Applications and Research.
Pavon J, Gomez-Sanz J (2003). Agent Oriented Software Engineering with INGENIAS, Proc. 3rd International Central and Eastern European Conference on Multi-Agent Systems (CEEMAS). Marik V, Muller J, Pechoucek M, (Eds.), Multi-Agent Systems and Applications II, LNAI 2691, Spring-Verlag pp. 394-403.
Pavon J, Gomez-Sanz JJ, Fuentes R (2005). The INGENIAS methodology and tools, In Henderson-Sellers B, Giorgini P, (Eds.), Agent-oriented methodologies (Chapter 9), Hershey, PA: Idea Group.
Sabas A, Badri M, Delisle S (2002). A Multidimentional Framework for the Evaluation of Multiagent System Methodologies, 6th World MultiConf on Systemics, Cybernetics and Informatics (SCI) pp. 211-216.
Sardinha J, Milidiu R, Lucena C, Paranhos P (2004). A Methodology for Building Trading Agents in Electronic Markets, Technical Report, Computer Science Department, PUC-Rio, Brazil, PUC-RioInf.MCC36/04.
Shan L, Zhu H (2004). Software engineering for multi-agent systems III: Research issues and practical applications, In Choren R, Garcia A, Lucena C, Romanovsky A, (Eds.), Proceedings of the Third International Workshop on Software Engineering for Large-Scale Multi-Agent Systems pp. 144-161, Berlin: Springer-Verlag.
Shehory O, Sturm A (2001). Evaluation of modeling techniques for agent-based systems, Agents pp. 624-631.
Shi Z, Jiao W, Sheng Q (2001). Agent-oriented software methodology, CEEMAS Cracow, Poland.
Shi Z, Zhang H, Cheng Y, Jiang Y, Sheng Q, Zhao Z (2004). MAGE: An Agent-Oriented Programming Environment, IEEE ICCI pp. 250-257.
Shi Z, Zhang H, Dong M, Zhao Z (2003). MAGE: Multi-Agent Environment, Proc. of the Int. Conference on Compt. Networks and Mobile Computing (ICCNMC'03) pp. 181-188.
Shoham Y (1990). Agent-Oriented Programming, Technical Report STAN-CS-1335-90, Computer Science Department, Stanford University, Stanford, CA 94305.
Shoham Y (1993).Agent-Oriented Programming, Artif. Intell. 60(1):51-92
Siau K, Rossi M (1998).Evaluation of Information Modeling Methods – A Review, In Proc. 31 Annual Hawaii International Conference on System Science pp. 314-322.
Sierra C, Sabater J, Agusti J, Garcia P (2002). Evolutionary Programming in SADDE, AAMAS'02, ACM, Bologna, Italy pp. 1270-1271.
Singh MP, Huhns MN, Stephens LM, (1993). Declarative representations of multiagent systems, IEEE Trans. Knowledge Data Eng. 5(5): 721–739.
Standards Coordinating Committee of the Computer Society of the IEEE, (1990). IEEE Standard Glossary of Software Engineering Terminology, IEEE Standards Board, IEEE Std 610.12.
Sterling L, Taveter K (2009). The art of agentoriented modeling, Cambridge, MA, London, England: The MIT Press.
Sturm A, Shehory O (2003). A Framework for evaluating agent-oriented methodologies, In Giorgini P, Winikoff M (Eds.), Proceedings of the Fifth Int. Bi-Conference Workshop on Agent-Oriented Information Systems pp. 60-67, Melbourne, Australia.
Sturm A, Dori D, Shehory O (2003). Single-Model Method for Specifying Multi-Agent Systems, Proceeding of Second Int. Joint Conference on Autonomous Agents and Multi Agent Systems pp. 121-128.
Sturm A, Shehory O, Dori D (2004). Evaluation of Agent-Oriented Methodologies, In AgentLink AOSE TFG1.
Sudeikat J, Braubach L, Pokahr A, Lamersdorf W (2004). Evaluation of agent-oriented software methodologies: Examination of the gap between modeling and platform, Proceedings of the Workshop on Agent-Oriented Software Engineering (AOSE), New York, USA.
Taveter K, Wagner G, (2005). Towards radical agent-oriented software engineering processes based on AOR modelling, In Henderson-Sellers B, Giorgini P, (Eds.), Agent-oriented methodologies (Chapter 10), Hershey PA: Idea Group.
Taveter K, Wagner G (2002). A multi-perspective methodology for modelling inter-enterprise business processes, In Arisawa H, Kambayashi Y, (Eds.): ER (2001). Workshops, LNCS 2465, Springer-Verlag Berlin Heidelberg pp. 403-416.
Taveter K, Sterling L (2008), Features as Loosely Defined Method Fragments, AOSE TFG08.
Tian J, Foley R, Tianfield H (2004). A new agent-oriented development methodology, Proceedings of the Intelligent Agent Tech., IEEE/WIC/ACM Int. Conference pp. 373–376.
Tran QN, Low G (2008). MOBMAS: A Methodology for Ontology-Based Multi-Agent Systems Development, Inf. Software Technol. 50: 697–722.
Tran QNN, Beydoun G, Low G (2007). Design of a peer-to-peer information sharing MAS using MOBMAS (ontology-centric agent-oriented methodology, In Advances in Information Systems Development, Springer pp. 63-76.
Verharen E, Weigard H (1994). Agent-Oriented Information Systems Design, In Ras Z, Zemankova M, editors, Poster Proceedings of the International Symposium on Methodologies for Intelligent Systems (ISMIS'94), Amsterdam, 378- 392.
Verharen EM (1997). A Language-Action Perspective on the Design of Cooperative Information Agents, PhD thesis, Katholieke Universieit Brabant, the Netherlands.
Villaplana EA (2005). Proposal for an organizational MAS methodology, AAMAS'05, 1370.
Wagner G (2003). The agent-object-relationship meta-model: Towards a unified view of state and behavior, Inf. Syst. 28(5): 475-504.
Wang L, Guo Q (2004). Mobile Agent Oriented Software Engineering (MAOSE), In Karmouch A, Korba L, Madeira E (Eds.): MATA LNCS 3284, Springer-Verlag Berlin Heidelberg pp. 168-177.
Whitestein Technologies (2008). LS/TS Product Brochure, Available at http://www.whitestein.com/library/Whitestein Technologies_LS-TS_ProductBrochure.pdf.
Wooldridge M, Ciancarini P (2001). Agent-Oriented Software Engineering: The State of the Art, In Ciancarini P. and Wooldridge M. (editors), Agent-Oriented Software Engineering, Springer-Verlag Lecture Notes in AI (1957).
Wooldridge M (1997). Agent-based software engineering, IEE Proc. Software Eng. 144(1): 26–37.

Wooldridge M, Jennings NR, Kinny D (1999). A methodology for agent-oriented analysis and design, In Proceedings of the Third International Conference on Autonomous Agents (Agents 99), 69–76, Seattle, WA.

Wooldridge M, Jennings NR, Kinny D (2000). The Gaia methodology for agent-oriented analysis and design, J. Autonomous Agents Multi Agent Syst. 3(3): 285-312.

Wooldridge M, Jennings NR (1995). Intelligent agents: theory and practice, Knowl. Eng. Rev. 10(2) 115–152.

Yan Q, Shan L, Mao X, Qi Z (2003). RoMAS: a role-based modeling method for multi-agent systems, Proceedings of International Conference on Active Media Technology pp. 156-161.

Yan E, Cysneiros LM (2002). Agent-Oriented Methodologies – Towards A Challenge Exemplar, 4th Intl. Workshop on Agent-Oriented Information Systems (AOIS'02).

Zamboneli F, Jennings NR, Omicini A, Wooldridge M (2000). Agent-Oriented Software Engineering for Internet Applications, Published as chapter 13 in the book: Coordination of Internet Agents: Models, Technologies and Applications, Omicini A, Zambonelli F, Klusch M, Tolksdorf R (Eds.), Springer.

Zambonelli F, Jennings NR, Wooldridge M (2005). Multi-Agent Systems as Computational Organizations: The Gaia Methodology, In Henderson-Sellers B, Giorgini P (Eds.) Agent-oriented methodologies (Chapter 6), Hershey, PA: Idea Group.

Zhang T, Kendall EA, Jiang H (2002). An Agent-Oriented Software Engineering Methodology with Application of Information Gathering Systems for LCC, Proceedings of the Fourth International Bi-Conference Workshop on Agent-Oriented Information Systems (AOIS-2002 at CAiSE*02) pp. 1-15.

Towards auto-configuring routing protocols for wireless ad-hoc networks

M. B. Mutanga*, P. Mudali and M. O. Adigun

Department of Computer Science, University of Zululand, KwaDlangezwa, South Africa.

The importance of wireless ad-hoc networks in community and commercial connectivity cannot be underestimated because of the benefits associated with these networks. Self-organization will minimize the need for manual configuration. In essence, self-organization provides an out-of-the-box functionality such that very little technical expertise is required to setup a network. Providing unique IP addresses efficiently in ad-hoc networks is still an open research question. In general, nodes often are assumed to have addresses configured in advance, but in ad-hoc networks this is not the case and is not easily accomplished. Nodes require a unique address for packets to be delivered to the correct destination. Many protocols to address this problem have been proposed and most of them are independent from the routing protocol and hence fail to address this problem. Despite the interdependence of routing protocols and IP address auto-configuration, no much effort has been put in trying to investigate this. In this paper we argue that incorporating auto-configuration functionalities into routing protocols will address open issues in this area. We propose general solutions for use in proactive and reactive routing protocols.

Key words: Ad-hoc network, IP address, routing protocols, auto-configuration.

INTRODUCTION

The autonomous nature of wireless ad-hoc networks requires the existence of an IP address auto-configuration mechanism. However in recent years, a lot of research in ad-hoc networks has concentrated on routing protocols. The same intensity has not been applied to other important related areas, such as IP interface addressing. Routing protocols typically rely on nodes having a unique address (Cavalli and Orset, 2005). In general, nodes are often assumed to have addresses configured a priori, but in ad-hoc networks this is not the case and is not easily accomplished. Although routing protocols assume the existence of unique node addresses, the question of how to provide them remains open. A lot of IP address auto-configuration protocols have been proposed in literature. The purpose of having an address auto-configuration protocol is to manage the address space and configure nodes with addresses that are either local scope that is, IP addresses valid only within a particular ad-hoc network or global scope. Automatic configuration of nodes in wireless ad-hoc network will help in reducing administration efforts by users and network administrators (Weniger, and Zitterbart, 2004). One may argue that the problem of address auto-configuration can be solved easily by constructing a unique address from the medium access control (MAC) address. For example, IPv6 enables the construction of an address from the MAC address, which is meant to be globally unique but a major concern with this idea is the issue of location privacy (Weniger, and Zitterbart, 2004). This might also compromise on security of targeted nodes or individuals.

Automatic configuration using random numbers is therefore a viable solution to this problem but however, such a mechanism has to cope with a highly dynamic environment and uncertain network structures (Fan and Subramani, 2005). Another school of thought also argues that MAC addresses can be duplicated. The work in Weniger and Zitterbart (2004) reports that there are

*Corresponding author. E-mail: bethelmutanga@gmail.com.

instances of network adapters with unregistered or duplicate MAC addresses on the market, and also that some network adapters allow users to change the MAC address to arbitrary values. It is thus clear that automatic configuration is one of the best options to this problem.

IP address auto-configuration protocols may be classified under umbrella categories of stateless and stateful approaches. In designing these protocols, the following factors must be considered (Harish et al., 2008): (1) Network partitioning and merging, (2) Duplicate address detection (DAD), (3) Scalability, (4) Security and authentication. These factors affect the correct routing of data packets in the network. Despite this interdependence, not much effort has been put in investigating ways of integration IP address auto-configuration protocols with routing protocols. Most proposals are independent of the routing protocol hence making it difficult to detect address conflicts and network mergers. The applicability of these protocols is still debatable since most of them are tested without any other traffic on the network (routing protocol traffic, application traffic). It is not clear how these schemes affect the routing protocol traffic in terms of packet loss, throughput, delay etc. It is also not clear how routing protocol traffic will affect IP address auto-configuration as far as latency, communication overhead and address uniqueness is concerned. How these protocols interact with the routing protocol for duplicate address detection, security, detection of network merging and partitioning is not clear despite the close relationship between routing protocols and IP address auto-configuration protocols. In this paper we propose a paradigm shift. We argue that incorporating IP address automatic configuration functionalities shall solve the open issues around this area.

Routing protocol paradigms or approaches can be classified into two distinct categories namely reactive and proactive paradigms. Some schemes with characteristics of both approaches are also being developed under the umbrella term of hybrid approaches. Routing protocols periodically or otherwise, send control messages for route discovery and or maintenance. Information in such messages can be useful for IP address auto-configuration protocols, for example, nodes can detect network merging from receiving hello messages from a different network. The routing protocol can detect IP address duplicates by analysing routing information (Weniger, 2004). The proposal in (Saadi et al., 2007) has also shown that analysing routing protocol information can easily detect address conflicts without additional traffic.

In proactive routing protocols, each node maintains routing information to every other node in the network. The routing information is usually kept in a number of different tables. These tables are periodically updated and/or if the network topology changes. The routing table stores the routes (and in some cases, metrics associated with those routes) to particular network destinations. This information contains the topology of the network immediately around it.

In reactive routing protocols, routes are determined and maintained for nodes that require to send data to a particular destination. Route discovery usually occurs by flooding a route request packets through the network. When a node with a route to the destination (or the destination itself) is reached a route reply is sent back to the source node using link reversal if the route request has travelled through bi-directional links or by piggy-backing the route in a route reply packet via flooding (Mehran et al., 2004).

Characteristics of routing protocols can be explored to provide a solution to the auto-configuration problem. For example the discovery of routes in reactive routing protocols is similar to performing a duplicate address detection (DAD) procedure in stateless protocols. In this paper, we present generalized IP address auto-configuration solutions for proactive and reactive routing protocols with the intention to stimulate more research in this direction.

The rest of this paper is organised as follows: First, we discuss some research issues in IP address auto-configuration. Secondly, an overview of related work, thirdly, we outline how IP address auto-configuration functionalities can be integrated into both reactive and proactive routing protocols and finally the conclusion of the paper.

ISSUES IN IP ADDRESSING IN WIRELESS AD-HOC NETWORKS

Due to the unique characteristics of wireless ad-hoc networks, there are various issues that need to be considered when developing an IP address auto-configuration protocol. The work in Harish et al. (2008) also gives an analysis of these issues. Subsequently, we present our view and analysis of these issues:

Security

Wireless ad-hoc networks have unique characteristics thereby making it difficult to address security and authenticity issues. The work in Kumar et al (2008) gives possible attacks to the IP auto-configuration process. These attacks include Address Spoofing Attack, Address Conflict Attack, Address Exhaustion Attack, and Negative Reply Attack. Most protocols do not address security during auto-configuration at all. For example, proposals in Fazio et al. (2006), Günes and Reibel (2002), Indrasinghe et al. (2006), Kim et al. (2007) and Mutanga et al. (2008) only addressed the auto-configuration problem whilst the security issues surrounding this aspect are not addressed. The work in Cavalli and Orset (2005) and Pan et al. (2005) are some of the few proposals that consider security during automatic configuration. The proposal in Pan et al. (2005) binds each IP address with a public key, allows a node to self-authenticate itself, and thus thwarts address spoofing and other attacks associated with auto-configuration. In Cavalli and Orset (2005) a protocol that uses the buddy system technique to allocate the addresses, as well as an algorithm allowing to authenticate the participants inside the network is proposed.

Scalability

In most cases the process of IP address auto-configuration requires that nodes exchange a number of messages before a node can be allocated an IP address. These messages might either be flooded in the network or exchanged locally and they usually grow with network size leading to high overhead (Harish et al., 2008).

Most IP address auto-configuration protocols are independent of the routing protocol hence they define their own data packets to detect network merging or duplicate IP addresses. This results in increased communication and high latency overhead and might disrupt routing. Stateless approaches degrade dismally when the network grows because of the flooding mechanism that is used to detect duplicate IP addresses. Both communication overhead and latency are generally high in this approach. Some stateful approaches, such as the Prophet (Zhou et al., 2003), try to address this problem by configuring nodes using local messages only. This however compromises on the uniqueness of the address. The biggest challenge in building scalable protocols therefore is to try and reduce communication overhead without compromising on address uniqueness and latency. The range of IP addresses should also be scalable. IP addresses should not run out of availability when a large number of nodes are joining (Harish et al., 2008).

Duplicate address detection

Duplicate address detection (DAD) is usually required when either a new node joins a network or when two more independently configured networks merge. Stateless approaches use DAD when new nodes join the network. A DAD message containing the requested address is broadcast and any node using that address defends it by sending a conflict notification message. When two or more networks merge, there is need to detect and resolve duplicate IP addresses. This might require some of the nodes to relinquish their IP addresses and acquire new ones. A duplicate address detection mechanism is also required as continuous process to guard against duplicate addresses caused by erroneous allocation of duplicate addresses. This can be done by analysing routing protocol information for hints that can point to the existence of a duplicate address. Most IP address auto-configuration protocols, however, are independent of the routing protocol hence they define their own data packets to detect network merging or duplicate IP addresses. This results in high communication overhead and might disrupt routing. Incooporating IP address auto-configuration functionalities into routing protocols may be favourable in wireless ad-hoc networks since nodes are likely to be using the same routing protocol and the networks are usually administered by a single entity.

Network partitioning and merging

Network merging occurs when two or more separately configured networks come together to form one network. This can be as a result of mobility or other factors. If each partition has independently allocated or configured its own addresses, two nodes may end up sharing the same address. Therefore, after a network merger is detected, the first task is to detect address conflicts and then take corrective action, that is some nodes need to acquire new addresses. This, however, is possible if the total number of nodes from the two networks are less than the total address space. To detect network merging, some approaches make use of periodic messages that are broadcast to first hop neighbours. In MANETconf (Nesargi and Prakash, 2002), if a node receives a hello message with a different network identifier, network merging is detected. A network might also be partitioned in to two or more partitions due to various factors. Nodes need to detect this so that they can allocate the IP addresses allocated nodes in the other partition. However, when such networks merge again, duplicate IP addresses might occur. This then requires nodes to generate new partition IDs when network partition is detected.

Network merging is a common occurrence in wireless ad-hoc networks. Consider a network of 100 nodes that are scattered over a 1000 x 1000 m square area. If the nodes are randomly switched on, a lot of independent networks will be formed. To prove this point, simulations were conducted in ns2 and the results were obtained. Nodes were randomly switched-on and the auto-configuration process allowed to take place. The number of independently configured networks formed was recorded. We varied the number of participating nodes and merging was not allowed to take place during simulation so that the number of networks could be counted at the end. The experiment was run for eight times and average values were used for the analysis.

From the results obtained (Figure 1), it is interesting to note that 100 nodes on a 1400 x 1400 m area recorded as much as 20 different networks whilst 50 nodes also recorded up to 17 independent networks. From the number of independently configured networks recorded in

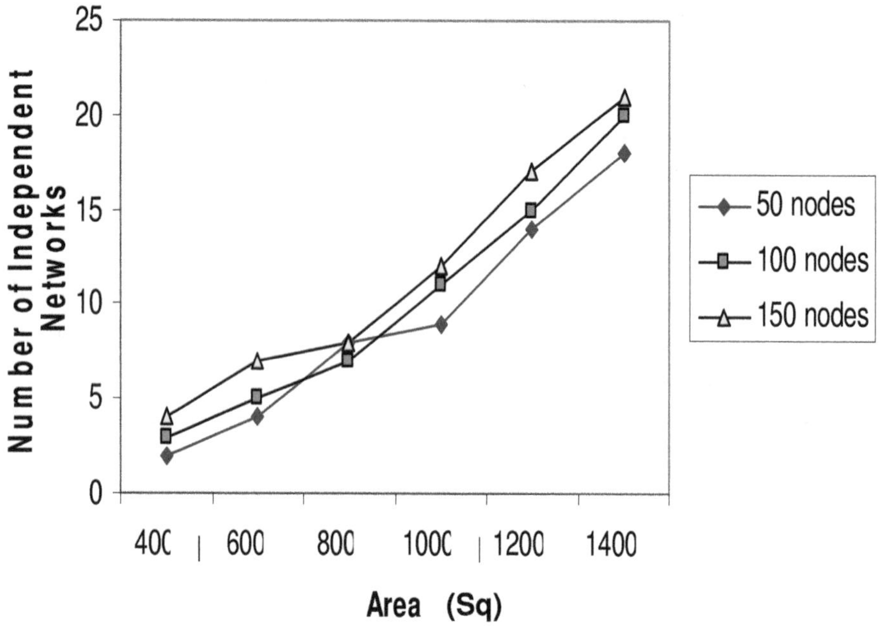

Figure 1. Number of independently configured networks.

the experiments, it is clear that factors such as the time taken for a node to detect a network merger and resolve any possible address duplications and number of packets generated by each node in order to detect and resolve a network merger are of paramount importance.

Wireless ad-hoc network scenarios usually involve relatively closed user groups (for example, community networks) or networks run by a single entity, routing protocol dependency is not an issue. This raises the possibility of incorporating IP address functionalities in the routing protocol unlike in generic networks.

CURRENT APPROACHES IN IP ADDRESS AUTO-CONFIGURATION

IP address auto-configuration protocols are generally classified into three categories namely: stateless, stateful and hybrid.

Stateless approaches

Protocols following the stateless paradigm do not maintain an address allocation table. An allocation table is a list of all IP addresses in use in a network at any given time. In this approach, nodes generate their own IP addresses and check for possible conflicts through a DAD procedure, hence most of the research classified under this approach is aimed at coming up with the most efficient DAD procedure (Mutanga et al., 2008). If a conflict is detected, the process is repeated, thus making DAD the cornerstone of the stateless paradigm.

In Strong-DAD (Perkins et al., 2001), a node randomly selects an IP address and checks whether or not it is used in a network using a DAD procedure. In fact a new node chooses two addresses: a temporary address and the actual address to use. During the IP address negotiation process described previously, new nodes use temporary IP addresses for communication. The temporary address is not verified for uniqueness. The network is flooded with an address request (AREQ) message containing the selected address. A node that uses the same address defends its address by replying with an address reply (AREP) message. If the address is currently in use, the process is started again until a free IP address is obtained. An address is assumed to be free if the timer for a DAD trial expires before receiving a conflict notification message (AREP). Due to broadcast, Strong-DAD has high communication overhead. It performs a DAD procedure every time a new node requests for an IP address. The number of failed DAD procedures increases as network size increases in size.

Due to the increase in the probability of failed DAD as the number of nodes increases, scalability is a problem in Strong-DAD. Also from the birthday paradox, address conflicts are likely to occur when each node chooses its address by random selection (Jeong et al., 2004). As the network size increase, latency and communication overhead also increase. Since the approach uses a time based DAD, address allocation latency depends on the DAD timeout and the number of DAD trials. If DAD is successful on the first attempt, address allocation latency is equal to the DAD timeout. Strong DAD does not specify how it handles the situation of more than one node requesting for the same IP address at the same time hence address uniqueness is compromised. However, the DAD proposed is likely to get a unique address if all the network nodes are reachable. Strong-DAD does not provide a way for solving the problem of two nodes using the same temporary IP address during the address negotiation process.

In AIPAC (Fazio et al., 2006), the authors proposed a stateless IP address auto-configuration protocol, AIPAC, which is based on Strong-DAD (Perkins et al., 2001). This mechanism avoids the storage of a lot of information about the network and does not produce too much traffic in the communication channels. Since Strong-DAD does not provide a way for solving the problem of two nodes using the same temporary IP address, AIPAC uses the concept of Requester and Initiator, which is defined in ManetConf. The Initiator selects an address at random among the allowed addresses, and sends in broadcast a Search_IP packet. The selected address is specified in the packet. Any node receiving this packet checks whether the address is known (whether this address belongs to it or to another node in its routing tables). If a match is detected, the node sends a Used_IP message to the Initiator. When the Initiator receives the Used_IP message, the address assignment procedure is restarted, and a new address is selected. Conversely, if no reply is received for a given time interval (Search_IP timer), the Initiator sends the Search_IP packet again, in order to face up possible errors in wireless channels. If neither replies arrive, it means that the address is not used yet. The Initiator then notifies the Requester with the NetID of the network and the IP address that it has to use.

Like Strong-DAD, this scheme has high communication overhead. It performs a DAD procedure every time a new node requests for an IP address. The number of failed DAD procedures is likely to increase as the network increases in size. This affects the overall quality of service of the network and might also increase power consumption of the nodes. This scheme does not specify how it handles the situation of more than one node requesting for the same IP address at the same time hence uniqueness in this scheme is not guaranteed. However, like Strong-DAD, the DAD proposed is likely to get a unique address if all the network nodes are reachable.

Stateful approaches

Protocols that follow the stateful paradigm assume that the addresses that are going to be assigned are not being used by any node in the network. This is achieved by guaranteeing that the nodes that participate in the allocation of IP addresses have disjoint address pools. In this case, performing a DAD is not necessary. Another way is to distribute the address allocation table to all network nodes so that they can configure new nodes since they know which IP addresses are free. This approach requires that the allocation tables be synchronized. In this case, a DAD is required to guard against a situation in which the same IP address is being requested for at the same time.

In MANETconf (Nesargi and Prakash, 2002), the authors proposed a system for the management of the IP addresses which is distributed in all the nodes of the network. A new node has to rely on a configured node (initiator), to negotiate for an address for it. Each node belonging to the network stores all the used addresses, as well as the ones that are going to be assigned to the new nodes. The initiator selects an address among the available ones, and performs a DAD procedure. This is a way for checking whether the same address is being assigned in another part of the network. If all the nodes send a positive reply for this request, the address is assigned. This process is repeated until a free IP address is obtained. All nodes in the network periodically broadcast their IP address allocation for state synchronization purposes.

If a node leaves the network gracefully, it has to release its address, by sending a bye message in broadcast. This allows the other network nodes to update their address allocation tables accordingly. For managing the merging of different networks, a single network ID is used, which is selected by the node with the lowest IP address. When nodes belonging to different networks get in contact, they detect the merging and check for possible duplicated addresses. The system has to verify also if network partitioning occurs. If some nodes do not respond to the subsequent assignment procedure of the IP address, then partitioning is detected. If such nodes also include the one that originally determined the network ID, a new one is selected by the node with the lowest IP address. Since the IP assignment operations may not take place for a long-time, and thus no partitioning can be detected, the node with the lowest IP address must periodically broadcast a message to show its presence. One cannot easily determine how often this message needs to be sent, since this depends on the dynamics of the network.

Although MANETconf is a stateful protocol it employs broadcast similar to the one used in stateless approaches. It also requires periodic state information synchronization which is bandwidth consuming. The length of the IP address assignment process in MANETConf is proportional to the network size because every node in the network takes part in the address assignment process.

In the Prophet's approach (Zhou et al., 2003), the authors proposed a novel approach that follows the stateful paradigm, but the protocol does not store an allocation table. The basic idea is to predict the allocation table using a function f(n) that is distributed among nodes. The authors argued that IP address auto configuration is the same as assignment of different numbers from an integer range, say R, to different nodes. They went on to argue that if all the addresses that have been allocated and those that are going to be allocated are known in advance, then broadcast could be avoided whilst conflict is still detectable. A way to obtain an integer sequence consisting of numbers in R, using a function f(n), was then proposed. The initial state of f(n) is called the seed. Different seeds lead to different sequences with the state of f(n) updated at the same time. The basic idea behind the approach of Prophet is as follows:

The first node, say A, chooses a random number as its IP address and uses a random state value or a default state value as the seed for its f(n).
When another node, say B, approaches A and asks for a free IP address, A uses f(n) to obtain another integer, say n2, and a state value. It then provides them to B. Node A updates its state accordingly.
Node B uses n2 generated by A as its IP address and the state value obtained from node A as the seed for its f(n).
Now nodes A and B are both able to assign IP addresses to other nodes.

Address reclamation is not necessary in prophet because the same number will reoccur in the sequence. Nevertheless, the minimal interval between two occurrences of the same number in the sequence is extremely long. The authors say when a node is assigned an old address X, the previous node with the same address X, is likely to have already left the network. As a result of this, this mechanism does not exclude the possibility of generating duplicate addresses. The mechanism employed in prophet works well with short-lived networks like the proposals in Dijkstra et al. (2006) and Saxena et al. (2005). However, prophet does not flood the network with IP request messages. The new node only communicates with its first hop neighbors and IP addresses are generated locally. This reduces both latency and communication overhead.

Hybrid approaches

Hybrid protocols combine elements of both stateful and stateless approaches. Protocols that follow this approach combine DAD with either a centrally maintained or a distributed common allocation table.

In Wise-DAD (Mutanga et al., 2008) an unconfigured node periodically broadcasts a request to join message. If there is another unconfigured node within its transmission range, a network is automatically formed. The node with the lower host identifier (HID) chooses network parameters, gives the other node an IP address and other configuration details. The HID is a randomly generated temporary IP address used by nodes before they acquire permanent IP addresses. If a configured node receives a request to join message, it assumes that an unconfigured node wants to join the network hence it will offer to act as its initiator by sending a confirmation message. The new node then selects only one of its neighbors node to act as its negotiating agent (initiator). It sends a select initiator message to the first node to respond. The initiator then generates a random IP address from the allowed addresses and checks its allocation table if there is no node in the network that have requested for or used the same IP. If the address is not known, the initiator then performs a DAD (using an address request message).

All nodes receiving an address request packet update their tables and add their IP addresses to the packet before broadcasting it. If any node is using the requested address, it defends it with an IP conflict message and this process is repeated. If no IP conflict message is received after a certain time interval, the address is assumed to be free and the initiator will send an address reply message to the new node. The address reply message will have the IP address for the new node, the network identifier (NetID) and the state information (allocation table). If a node leaves the networks gracefully, it broadcasts a goodbye message and all the nodes delete its IP address from their allocation tables. If a node leaves abruptly, immediate address reclamation is not performed. Since the node will not be sending or forwarding any data packets, other nodes will remove all passive nodes from their allocation tables. Allocation tables are not actively synchronized, they are used only as an estimate of the state information. If a node does not take part in an IP address allocation process for a long time, its IP address will be deleted when the size of the allocation table reaches a certain level because it will be assumed that the node left the network abruptly.

Compared to Strong DAD, Wise-DAD significantly reduced latency, communication overhead and address conflicts. Passively collecting state information reduces the number of DAD trials thereby both reducing latency and communication overhead. However, the number of IP address conflicts recorded was relatively high as compared to stateful approaches like prophet.

AUTO-CONFIGURING ROUTING PROTOCOLS

In order to realize the goal of integrating IP addressing functionalities into with routing protocols, there is need to design algorithms for both reactive and proactive routing protocols, it is imperative to come up with mechanisms of how routing protocols can handle: (1) Network partitioning and merging, (2) Duplicate addresses and solve them, (3) Scalability issues, (4) Security and authentication during and after configuration. These issues affect the way packets are routed in the network. For example, if two networks merge, duplicate IP addresses might occur. Most applications in the ad-hoc networks are based upon unicast communication hence routing protocols require nodes to have unique address for packets to be delivered to the correct destination (Toner and O'Mahony, 2003). Thus, the most basic operation in the

IP layer of ad-hoc networks is to successfully transmit data packets from one source to destination (Zhou, 2003). Subsequently, we present general solutions for integrating IP address auto-configuration functionalities with reactive and pro-active routing protocols.

Auto-configuration in proactive routing protocols

Here, we present an IP address auto-configuration solution for proactive routing protocols. Subsequently, a breakdown of how IP address auto-configuration can be achieved in networks running pro-active routing protocols was given.

Node admission

Nodes running pro-active routing protocols can easily adopt the stateful approach of configuring IP addresses since they store and update topology information. Proactive routing protocols, maintain an up-to-date view of the network by periodically broadcasting the link-state costs of its neighbouring nodes to all other nodes using a flooding strategy (Mehran et al., 2004). Stateful auto-configuration protocols also maintain state information that is, the list of all the nodes that are in the network at any given time. The same information can be obtained from routing tables of proactive routing protocols. It then makes sense to use the same information rather than maintaining two separate states. The concept of initiator can be adopted for the purposes of IP address negotiation.

An un-configured node periodically broadcasts a request message until it receives a reply from another node that will negotiate for an IP address for it. The initiator generates a random IP address and checks if it is in its routing table before it starts the negotiation process through a DAD procedure. If the address is in the routing table, it generates another one otherwise it will perform a DAD procedure and set a timer. If the timer expires without any node defending the requested IP address, the initiator will sends an address reply (AREP) to the new node.

On receiving an address request message other network nodes first check if the message is new or not before checking if the requested IP address has been assigned them. A message sequence number can used to determine if a message is new or not. If the address is found to be in use, an IP conflict is sent to the initiator and the process is repeated. If the message is not new, it is discarded, otherwise it will be broadcast further. Before the message is broadcast, the recipient adds its IP address to the message. As the message is passed from one node to another, a reverse path to the initiator will be contained in the packet. This allows for an IP conflict message to be sent back to the initiator.

Duplicate address detection

To detect duplicate addresses, nodes analyse routing protocol information. The proposal in Vaidya (2002) can be applied. Each node generates a random key at initialization phase, and distributes it with its IP address in all routing messages. Each node maintains keys along with IP addresses of all the other nodes in its routing table. When a node receives a routing message with an IP address that exists in its table, it checks if the keys are different. If they are different, a duplicate address is detected and steps can then be taken to inform other nodes about this duplication. The nodes with duplicated addresses will be required to acquire new ones. Using this approach, nodes can detect duplicate addresses without any additional traffic. This approach however relies on the key-address combination being unique, that is, no two nodes should have the same key and IP address at the same time. The probability of two nodes having the same key and IP address can however be minimized by increasing the range of the key.

Network merging

The concept of network IDs used in the MANETConf protocol can be adopted to handle network merging. The first node in the network generates a random network identifier to be used by all the nodes in the network. Nodes can incorporate network IDs in topology update messages. If a node receives a topology update message with a different network ID, network merging is detected. Nodes detecting the network merging can estimate the number of IP address conflicts by inspecting routing tables of both networks. Only nodes with conflicting IP addresses will then be required to relinquish their IP addresses and acquire new ones.

Auto-configuration in reactive routing protocols

Here, we present an IP address auto-configuration solution for reactive routing protocols. Subsequently, a breakdown of how IP address auto-configuration can be achieved in networks running reactive routing protocols are given.

Node admission

Nodes running reactive routing protocols can easily adopt the stateless approach with minor changes. The discovery of routes in these protocols can be likened to performing duplicate address detection (DAD) procedure in stateless protocols. Route discovery usually occurs by flooding route request packets in the network. When a node with a route to the destination (or the destination itself) is reached a route reply is sent back to the source node using link reversal if the route request has travelled through bi-directional links or by piggy-backing the route in a route reply packet via flooding (Mehran et al., 2004). A DAD message is flooded in the network just like route request messages in reactive routing protocols. We propose the introduction of a new packet similar to the route discovery packet. Minor changes can be made so that the packet can be used to check if the requested IP address is not in use. A new node contacts an already configured node to act as its initiator. To reduce the chances of DAD failing, we can introduce state information maintenance which is passively collected but not actively maintained. The best time interval for state synchronization is an area that needs to be investigated. Passively collecting state information will reduce the number of DAD trials thereby reducing latency and communication overhead. Before the initiator sends an AREQ, it first checks if the IP address is not in the allocation table.

On receiving the AREQ, nodes check if the requested address does not belong to them. If it does, an IP conflict is sent to the initiator and the process is repeated. The allocation tables need not be synchronized or periodically updated since nodes still perform DAD. The allocation tables are merely used to reduce the probability of IP address conflict during a DAD procedure. Before the message is broadcast, the recipient adds its IP address to the message. As the message is passed from one node to another, a reverse path to the initiator will be contained in the packet. When nodes receive AREQ, they also update their allocation tables using IP addresses in the reverse path list before rebroadcast the AREQ. Every node also generates a random key at start-up. The key is used for detecting duplicate addresses. Subsequently, details of how these keys can be used to detect duplicate addresses are given.

Duplicate address detection

Nodes generate keys at start-up and send them when either requesting for a route or responding to a route-request message. On route-discovery a node sends the last known key of the destination and its own key in the route discovery packet. If the destination receives a route request message with a different key, a duplicate address is detected. This also serves as a way of authenticating both the receiver and the sender before they start communicating. The receiver also checks if the sender's key is different from what it has on its table. This can conserve bandwidth since duplicate addresses are detected only when the nodes with duplicated addresses wants to receive or send data. This means that nodes with duplicate addresses can still be able to forward data on behalf of other nodes without any problems. Actually this also implies that duplicate addresses can be tolerated (and allowed to exists) as long as they do not affect the routing process. Unlike in WeakDAD (Vaidya, 2002), there is no need for keys to be carried along with routing packets but only in route discovery packets hence saving a considerable amount of bandwidth.

Network merging

To detect network merging, nodes periodically send one hop messages with their network identifiers. The network identifiers can be incorporated in the hello messages of the routing protocol. Reactive routing protocols periodically send hello messages to first hop neighbours hence no additional packets need to be defined. If a node receives a hello message with a different network ID, network merging is detected. The node that detects the network merging can then respond to the hello message notifying the other network of the possibility of the two networks merging. The two nodes can exchange their allocation tables so that they can estimate the number of address duplicates. The nodes with conflicting addresses can then notified. Another way is to make all the nodes in the network with the lower network ID to relinquish their IP addresses and starts the process of IP address requisition.

CONCLUSION AND FUTURE WORK

The advent of wireless networking has significantly reduced the costs of setting up computer networks. Wireless ad-hoc networks in particular have the potential to expand but a lot of research is still needed to realise this dream. Automatic configuration of nodes is one area that still needs investigation. The following factors are important in the design of auto-configuration protocols: Network partitioning and merging, Duplicate addressed and solve them, scalability issues and security and authentication during and after configuration. These issues affect the way packets are routed in the network.

Despite this interdependence, not much effort has been done in investigating ways of integration IP address auto-configuration protocols with routing protocols. Most proposals in literature are independent of the routing protocol hence making it difficult to detect address conflicts and network mergers. The applicability of these protocols is still debatable since most of them are tested without any other traffic on the network (routing protocol traffic, application traffic). It is not clear how these schemes affect the routing protocol traffic in terms of packet loss, throughput, delay etc. It is also not clear how routing protocol traffic affect IP address auto-configuration as far as latency, communication overhead and address uniqueness is concerned. How these protocols interact with the routing protocol for duplicate address detection, security, detection of network merging and partitioning is not clear despite the close relationship between routing protocols and IP address auto-configuration protocols. Integrating auto-configuration functionalities into routing protocols is a candidate solution to open issues to the IP address auto-configuration problem. We hope that our contributions will stimulate further research in this direction. The future focus of this work will be on implementing the proposed approaches to test the validity of our proposition.

ACKNOWLEDGMENTS

The authors appreciate the support given to the Department of Computer Science at the University of Zululand by industry partners. In addition, the authors also appreciate contributions from the Wireless Mesh Networks Group at the University of Zululand.

REFERENCES

Cavalli A, Orset J (2005). Secure hosts auto-configuration in mobile ad hoc networks. Ad Hoc Networks, 3(5): 656-667.

Dijkstra F, Van der Ham J, Cees TAM (2006). Using zero configuration technology for IP addressing in optical networks, Future Generation Comput. Syst.. 22(8): 908-914.

Fan Z, Subramani S (2005). An address autoconfiguration protocol for IPv6 hosts in a mobile adhoc Network, Comput. Commun., 28(4): 339-350.

Fazio M, Villari M, Puliafito A (2006). AIPAC: Automatic IP address configuration in mobile ad hoc networks, Comput. Commun., 29(8): 1189-1200.

Günes M, Reibel J (2002). An IP Address Configuration Algorithm for Zeroconf Mobile Multihop Ad Hoc Networks, Proceedings of the International Workshop on Broadband Wireless Ad-Hoc Networks and Services, Sophia Antipolis, France.

Harish K, Singla RK, Malhotra S (2008). Issues & Trends in AutoConfiguration of IP Address in MANET IProceed. ICCCC 2008, pp. 353-357

Indrasinghe S, Pereira R, Mokhtar H (2006). Hosts Address Auto Configuration for Mobile Ad Hoc Networks, in the proceedings of HET-NETs, West Yorkshire UK.

Jeong J, Park J, Kim H, Kim D (2004). Ad Hoc IP Address Autoconfiguration for AODV, IETF Internet-Draft.

Kim N, Ahn S, Lee Y (2007). AROD: An Address Autoconfiguration with Address Reservation and Optimistic Duplicated Address Detection for Mobile Ad Hoc Networks, Comput. Commun., 30(8): 1913-1925.

Mehran A, Tadeusz W, Eryk D (2004) A review of routing protocols for mobile ad hoc networks, Ad Hoc Networks. 2(1): 1-22

Mutanga MB, Nyandeni TC, Mudali P, Xulu SS, Adigun MO (2008). Wise-DAD Auto-Configuration for Wireless Multi-hop Networks, In the proceedings of Southern Africa Telecommunication Networks and Applications Conference.

Nesargi S, Prakash R (2002). MANETconf: configuration of hosts in a mobile ad hoc Network, in: Proceedings of the 21st Annual Joint Conference of IEEE Computer and Communication Societies, New York.

Pan W, Reeves DS, Ning P (2005) Secure Address Auto-configuration for Mobile Ad Hoc Networks, Proceedings of the Second Annual International Conference on Mobile and Ubiquitous Systems: Networking and Services.

Perkins C. Malinen T, Wakikawa R, Belding-Royer E. Sun Y (2001). IP address autoconfiguration for ad hoc networks. IETF Internet Draft.

Saadi B, Adjih C, M¨uhlethaler P, Laouiti A (2007). Duplicate Address Detection and Autoconfiguration in OLSR, J. Uni. Comput. Sci., 13(1): 4-31

Saxena N, Tsudik G, Yi JH (2005). Efficient Node Admission for Short-lived Mobile Ad Hoc Networks, Proceedings of the 13TH IEEE International Conference on Network Protocols, pp: 269 – 278.

Toner S, O'Mahony D (2003). Self-Organising Node Address Management in Ad-hoc Networks, in Springer Verlag Lecture notes in Computer Science 2775, Springer Verlag, Berlin, pp: 476-483, 2003.

Vaidya NH (2002). Weak Duplicate Address Detection in Mobile Ad Hoc Networks, Proceedings of ACM MobiHoc, Lausanne, Switzerland, pp: 206–216.

Weniger K (2004). Passive Duplicate Address Detection in Mobile Ad Hoc Networks, In IEEE Wireless Communications and Networking Conference (WCNC), New Orleans, USA.

Weniger K, Zitterbart M (2004). Address Autoconfiguration in Mobile Ad Hoc Networks: Current Approaches and Future Directions, IEEE Network Magazine Special issue on 'Ad hoc networking: data communications & topology control'.

Zhou H (2003). A Survey on Routing Protocols in MANETs. Technical Report: MSU-CSE-03-08.

Zhou H, Ni L, Mutka M (2003). Prophet address allocation for large scale manets, Ad Hoc Networks. 1(4): 423-434

6

Investigation in the deployment of a geographic information system

M. N. Lakhoua

Department of Electronics, ISSAT Mateur, Laboratory of Analysis and Command of Systems, ENIT Tunisia.
E-mail: Lakhoua@enit.rnu.tn.

After a presentation of the cereal activities in Tunisia, we present a systemic analysis of project of deployment of a geographic information system (GIS). This analysis is based on the objective oriented project planning (OOPP) method. The exploitation of the systemic analysis method enables us not only to analysis and to identify the information of the cereal activities but also to lead to an efficient management of cereal transaction. This analysis enables us to identify the information needed for the deployment of a GIS in the Office des Cereales in Tunisia.

Key words: Geographic information system, data analysis, objective oriented project planning method, specific objective, global objective.

INTRODUCTION

The geographic context, the climatic environment and the social tradition and culture of Tunisia, whose alimentary tradition is based particularly on the consumption of cereals, shows an important deficit of the national production and cereal consumption.

In Tunisia, the Office des Cereales represents the official organism of cereal commercialisation, it participate, with private co-operatives, at the harvest and the cereal storage. It possesses the monopoly in cereal importation that is intended to human consumption (Annabi, 1998). Because of the nature of activities of cereal transaction, the notion of the space is important since the movement of cereals evolve in an environment of information. Indeed, the state of the situation of the movement of the cereals in Tunisia organized currently by two systems of information: a developed classic system and using an environment of data base Oracle with tools of Visual Basic development and a new geographic information system (GIS) exploiting the notion of information layers of which the one of relative basis to the geographical localization of units of cereal storage.

In order to assure an efficient management of cereal activities, the Office des Cereales exploits a system of information that stocks currently, analysis and visualize some spatial data at a time and no spatial. This is how we studied our various applications in this environment of the GIS of the fact of its innovating aspect and of the suppleness of its communication. We exploited the structuring established by the objective oriented project planning (OOPP) method. The object of this paper is to present a systemic analysis of project of a GIS deployment based on the OOPP method (AGCD, 1991; Gu and Zhang, 1994).

PRESENTATION OF THE OOPP METHOD

In order to analyze the project of a GIS deployment, we adopt a systemic logic allowing situating the project in its intern or exterior environment. In fact, the systemic analysis belongs to a scientific tendency that analysis the elements of a complex process as a component of a set where they are in a reciprocal dependence relation. Its study field is not limited to the mechanisation of the thought: the systemic analysis is a methodology that organise the knowledge in order to optimise an action (Lakhoua, 2009).

The systemic analysis of a production system has a mission to define the general strategy of the modelling study to achieve (Landry and Banville, 2000; Lakhoua, 2008). This strategy must enable the fixation of the modelling limits, by precisely making the frontiers of the system to model and specify between the data that are really exchanged in the different component of the production system and those that the modelling study will cover.

In order to offer a model project of a GIS deployment, we adopt the OOPP method. In fact, the OOPP method (AGCD, 1991; Peffers, 2005) constitutes a tool of a global systemic modelling, enabling the analysis of a complex situation by a hierarchical decomposition until it reached an elementary level that allows for an operational planning. This method, widely used in the planning of complex projects, involves many operators and partners.

In Tunisia, OOPP method was used in development projects

financed by bilateral or multilateral co-operation mechanism (with Germany, Belgium, Canada, World bank...), in upgrading of a different structures (Training and Employment through MANFORME project, Organisation of the Tunis Mediterranean Games, 2001...) and in restructuring private and public enterprises...

The two determining steps for the OOPP analysis are (Lakhoua et al., 2006):

(a) The scheme of planning project (SPP) that consist in establishing a global diagnostic of a situation by elaborating a tree of problems using a causal logic and by transforming it to a tree of objectives ;
(b) The scheme of planning activity (SPA) that, according to a logic « Medium - Detailed » lead to an hierarchic analysis of the results to achieve.

In fact, these steps constitute a preliminary action for establishing a project that requires a global piloting and evaluation system (PES). The parameters defined as the SPA can be represented in a « Matrix of Activities » that comported: the number of the activity, the code of the activity, the designation of the activity, the responsible of the activity, the collaborators of the responsible, the objectively verifiable indicator (OVI), the verification source (VS), the necessary resources according to their categories : Infrastructure, human resources, equipment and consumables, logistic (energy, transport...), informational resources...

ANALYSIS OF THE PROJECT OF GIS DEPLOYMENT

Let's recall first of all the different phases to succeed the deployment of a GIS: Definition of needs; development of the load notebook; choice of the GIS; conception of the geographical data base and its installation; starting of the project. In order to define needs of the enterprise in GIS, we present some questions of an elaborate investigation of the office des cereales:

(a) For what domain will the GIS be used?
(b) What is the objective of the GIS?
(c) What are for results waited of the GIS?
(d) What information will be used by the GIS?
(e) What supports will be used?
(f) What circuits will information borrow?
(g)What is the procedure for the validation of information?
(h) What are files to use?
(i) What are sources of the different information?
(j) What are responsibilities at the level of the production, validation and the utilization of information?
(k) What storage of information?

The phase of development of the load notebook conditions the success of a product in part. Indeed, the quality of the product results a compromise between the demand, reliability and the final cost. In a first approach, we can distinguish the main stages in the development of a load notebook:

(i) To recover the maximum of information on the customer's needs.
(ii) To distribute these needs in four categories: functions, performances, constraints and details.
(iii) To land in a first time that the functional aspect.
(iv) To construct a hierarchical diagram of functions.
(v) To retail and to complete the diagram with the team of project.
(vi) To construct a matrix of functions while sequencing these in: indispensable, desirable or superfluous.
(vii) To establish for every function the quantitative performances, the qualitative performances and constraints.
(viii) To propose a first - project to the customer.

According to a more rigorous approach, it can be necessary, the use of methods for example the SADT method that is more suitable to the realization of a load notebook. In the case of our application, we adopted the systemic method OOPP. In order to analyze the different activities of the project of deployment of a GIS, we exploited the systemic method OOPP. The different specific objectives (SO) permitting to reach the global objective (GO) "Deployment and exploitation of a GIS" are:

(i) Visualization and localization of the geographic data;
(ii) Identification of the information of the infrastructure of the cereal storage system;
(iii) Construction of a geographical data base;
(iv) Exploitation of the GIS in the office des cereales.

The presented analysis (Figure 1) is limited to the level of the results permitting to reach the GO: "Deployment and exploitation of a GIS".

ANALYSIS AND DEPLOYMENT OF A GIS

Today, information has become at the moment a strategic weapon and its life has become very short; so, an information system of an organisation must be reliable and quick, that is, it justifies the importance of an information tool (Ayari et al., 2001; Baazaoui et al., 2000; Bernhardsen, 1993).

In fact, a GIS represents a group of information equipment, software and methodology for keyboarding, storage and data exploitation, which the majority is spatial referring, allow a simulation of a process as a grain silo, a management and a decision help (Berry, 1993; Bolstad, 2005; Caloz and Collet, 1998; Chang, 2007). A GIS allows the representation and analysis of all information with geographic character in the way that all the events are produced. As a matter of fact, it stores the world information like thematic leers that can be linked together with geography (Chesnais, 1998; Claramunt et al., 1997; CNT, 1998).

This concept, simple and powerful, shows the efficacy to solve many practical problems. The GIS exploit all the

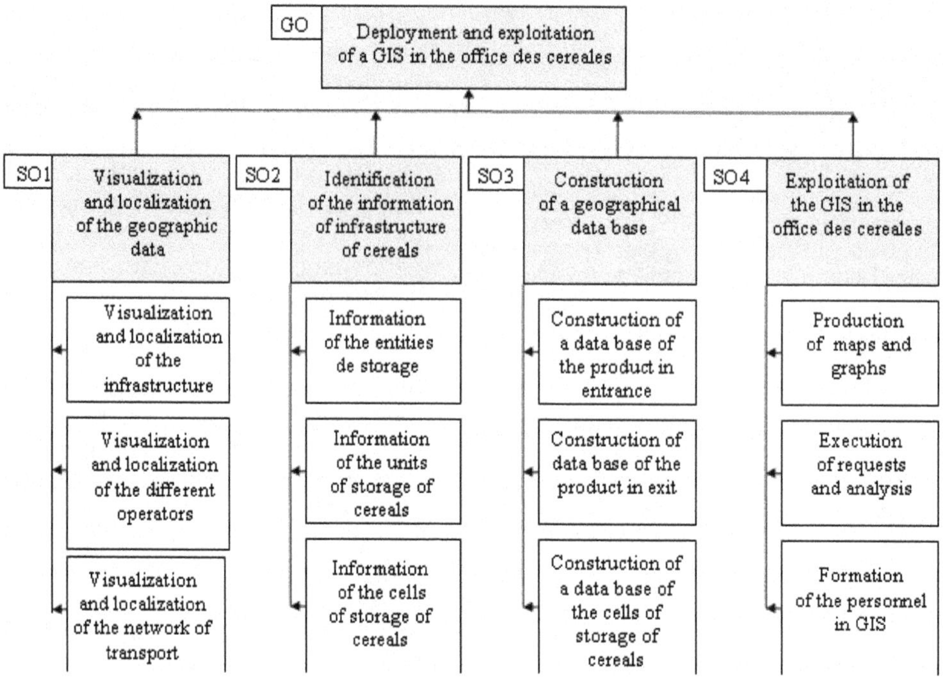

Figure 1. Analysis of a project of GIS.

Table 1. Identification of the entities of the GIS.

N°	Entity	Attribute
1	Center of storage of cereals	Code_Center Name_City Capacity_Center Type_Center Product Quantity
2	Unit of storage of cereals	Code_Unit of storage Code_Center of storage Capacity_Unit of storage Product Quantity
3	Cell of storage of cereals	Code_Cell of storage Code_Unit of storage Type_Cell of storage Capacity_Cell Product Quantity
4	Handling equipment	Code_Matériel Code_Center Number _Elevators Number_Carriers Nombre_ rockers ...

possibilities offered by data bases (request and static analysis) by a unique visualisation of them (Elangovan, 2006; Longley, 2005; Teoh, 2009; Tomlinson, 2005). We introduce the appropriate information of all the cereal storage centres. We class information by entity of storage and we indicate the identified entity (Table 1).

Figure 2 presents the different symbols used in order to represent with the GIS the infrastructure of the Office des Cereales. We exploited the MapInfo software to keyboard, manipulate and manage all cereal storage data, to do query and analysis and to display maps and graphs (Figure 3).

The list of data to keyboard on the table of received cereal produces in a grain silo: Received share produce code, origin product code, produce, origin product, quantity product, quality product, storage cell code, date of reception, and instant of reception. The list of data to keyboard on the table of expedited cereal produces of a grain silo: Expedited share produce code, product, destination code, destination produce, quantity product, quality product, storage cell code, date of expedition and instant of expedition. The execution of requests allows us to search the city capacity (Figure 4), the substructure grain silo, the cereal quality, the cereal stock, the cell stock, the length section during a cereal transfer from a centre to another.

In order to represent with the GIS the different road or railway sections used by the Office des Cereales permitting the determination of distances browsed by carriers of cereals (trucks, wagons...) with the best

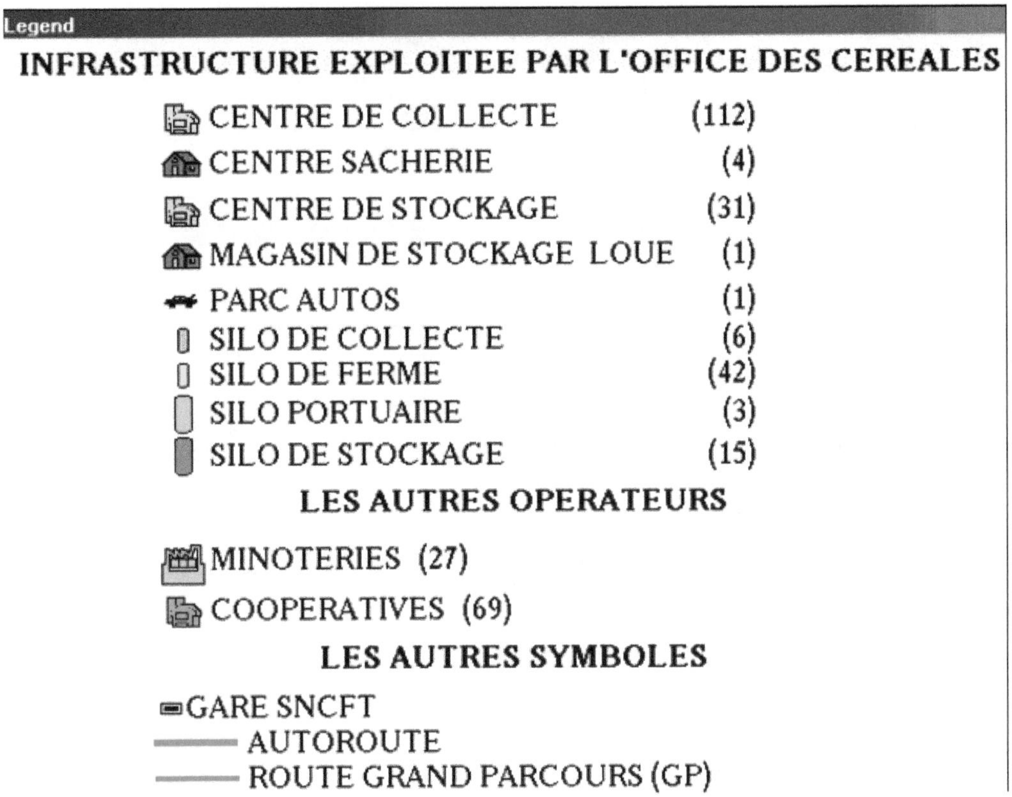

Figure 2. Different symbols with GIS.

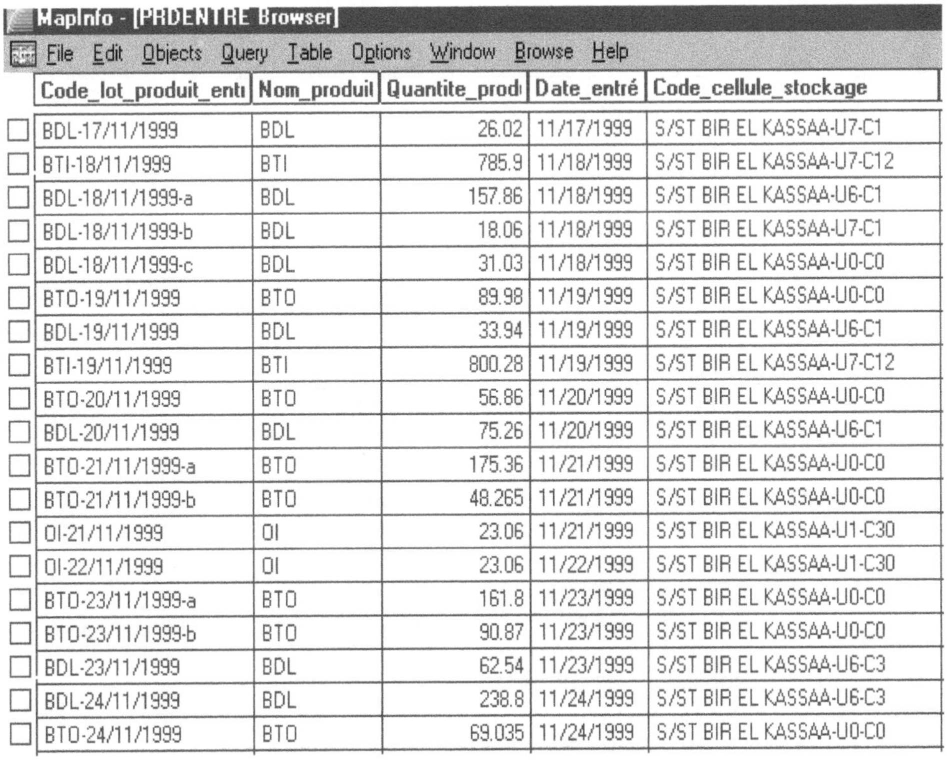

Code_lot_produit_ent	Nom_produit	Quantite_prod	Date_entré	Code_cellule_stockage
BDL-17/11/1999	BDL	26.02	11/17/1999	S/ST BIR EL KASSAA-U7-C1
BTI-18/11/1999	BTI	785.9	11/18/1999	S/ST BIR EL KASSAA-U7-C12
BDL-18/11/1999-a	BDL	157.86	11/18/1999	S/ST BIR EL KASSAA-U6-C1
BDL-18/11/1999-b	BDL	18.06	11/18/1999	S/ST BIR EL KASSAA-U7-C1
BDL-18/11/1999-c	BDL	31.03	11/18/1999	S/ST BIR EL KASSAA-U0-C0
BTO-19/11/1999	BTO	89.98	11/19/1999	S/ST BIR EL KASSAA-U0-C0
BDL-19/11/1999	BDL	33.94	11/19/1999	S/ST BIR EL KASSAA-U6-C1
BTI-19/11/1999	BTI	800.28	11/19/1999	S/ST BIR EL KASSAA-U7-C12
BTO-20/11/1999	BTO	56.86	11/20/1999	S/ST BIR EL KASSAA-U0-C0
BDL-20/11/1999	BDL	75.26	11/20/1999	S/ST BIR EL KASSAA-U6-C1
BTO-21/11/1999-a	BTO	175.36	11/21/1999	S/ST BIR EL KASSAA-U0-C0
BTO-21/11/1999-b	BTO	48.265	11/21/1999	S/ST BIR EL KASSAA-U0-C0
OI-21/11/1999	OI	23.06	11/21/1999	S/ST BIR EL KASSAA-U1-C30
OI-22/11/1999	OI	23.06	11/22/1999	S/ST BIR EL KASSAA-U1-C30
BTO-23/11/1999-a	BTO	161.8	11/23/1999	S/ST BIR EL KASSAA-U0-C0
BTO-23/11/1999-b	BTO	90.87	11/23/1999	S/ST BIR EL KASSAA-U0-C0
BDL-23/11/1999	BDL	62.54	11/23/1999	S/ST BIR EL KASSAA-U6-C3
BDL-24/11/1999	BDL	238.8	11/24/1999	S/ST BIR EL KASSAA-U6-C3
BTO-24/11/1999	BTO	69.035	11/24/1999	S/ST BIR EL KASSAA-U0-C0

Figure 3. Example of cereal transfer.

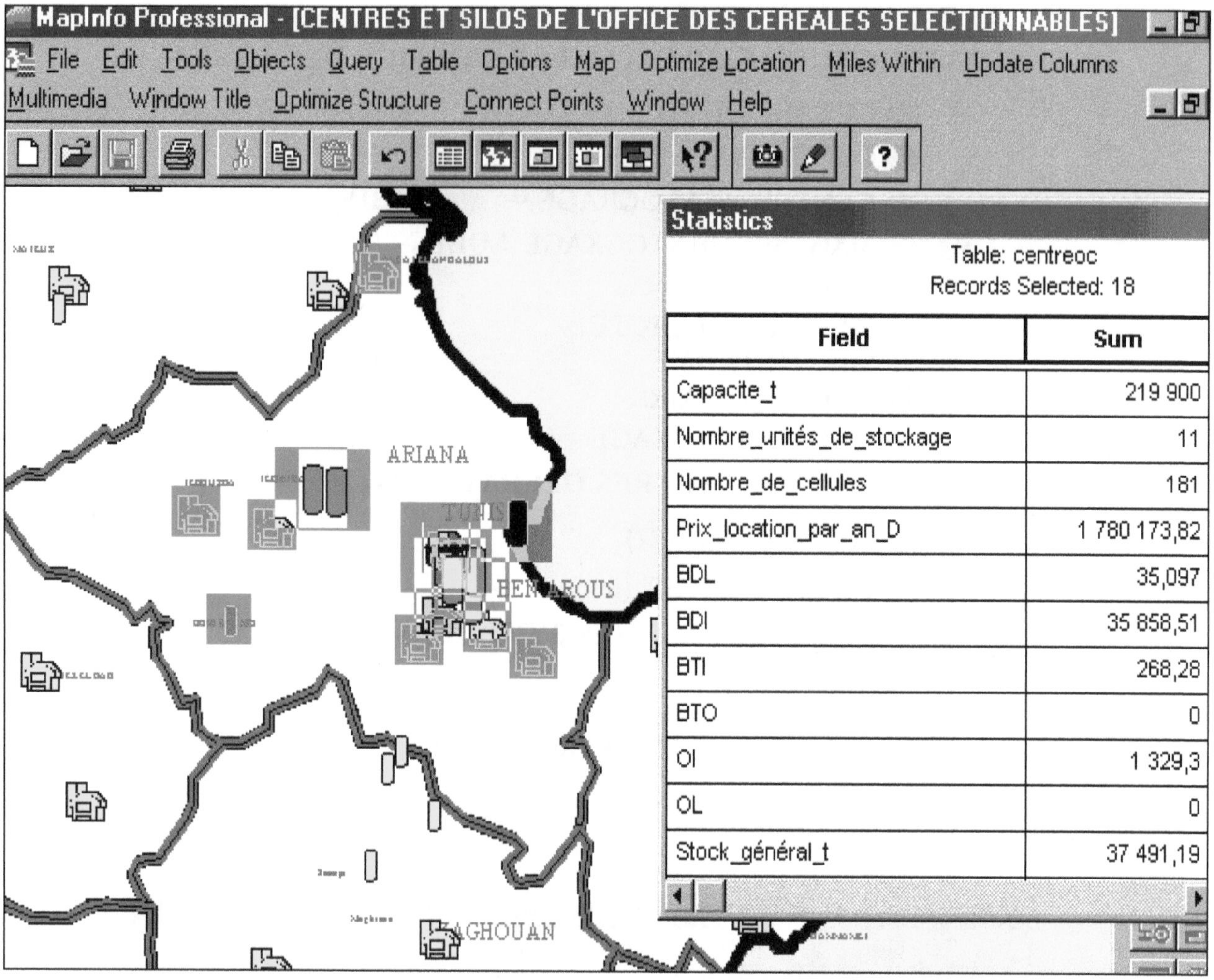

Figure 4. Evolution of the stock of cereals. Yellow key represent, not selected grain silos, while red key indicates selected grain silos in Ariana.

precision, it is necessary to exploit the well stocked data by satellites (Figure 3).

CONCLUSION

A GIS differs from other computerized information systems in two major respects. First, the information in this type of system is geographically referenced. Secondly, a GIS has considerable capabilities for data analysis and scientific modelling, in addition to the usual data input, storage, retrieval and output functions.

In this paper, we presented an investigation in the deployment of a GIS in the Office des Cereales in Tunisia. A systemic analysis based on the OOPP method of the project was presented. This application of GIS offer many tools to create interactive queries, analyze spatial information, edit data, maps, and present the results of all these operations.

REFERENCES

AGCD (1991). Manuel pour l'application de la «Planification des Interventions Par Objectifs (PIPO)», 2ème Edition, Bruxelles.

Annabi M (1998). Plan Directeur de Stockage des Céréales. Atelier PIPO, Sidi Thabet. Tunisie.

Ayari H, Mansouri T, Zante P (2001). Réalisation d'une base de données géographique et mise en place d'un SIG sur les bassins versants de lacs et barrages collinaires de la dorsale et du CapBon. Tunisie.

Bâazaoui H, Faïz S, Ghézala H (2000). Introduction au Data Mining Spatial. JSFT'2000. Tunisie.

Bernhardsen T (1993). Geographic information systems, Arendal, Viak IT.

Berry JK (1993). Beyond mapping: concepts, algorithms and issues in GIS. Fort Collins. GIS World.

Bolstad P (2005). GIS Fundamentals: A first text on Geographic Information Systems, Second Edition. White Bear Lake, MN: Eider Press, p. 543

Caloz R, Collet C (1998). Système d'Information Géographique, Manuel SIRS.

Chang K (2007). Introduction to Geographic Information System, 4th Edition. McGraw Hill.

Chesnais M (1998). Un SIG pour la gestion des déplacements urbains à Sfax. Tunisie.
Claramunt C, Coulondre S, Libourel T (1997). Autour des méthodes orientées objet pour la conception des SIG. Revue de géomatique, (7)3-4: 233-257.
CNT (1998). Projet National Mobilisateur : Sécurité alimentaire, Rapport final. Tunisie.
Elangovan K (2006). GIS: Fundamentals, Applications and Implementations", New India Publishing Agency, New Delhi" 208.
Gu P, Zhang Y. (1994). OOPPS: an object-oriented process planning system, Comput. Ind. Eng., 26(4): 709-731.
Lakhoua MN (2008). Analyse systémique d'un environnement de production en vue d'implanter un système d'information, Thèse de doctorat. ENIT. Tunisie.
Lakhoua MN (2009). Analysis and Modelling of Industrials Systems in order to develop an Information System. RCIS IEEE, Fes, Morocco.
Lakhoua MN, Ben JT, Annabi M (2006). State of the art of Strategic Planning. ICTTA'06, IEEE, Damascus, Syria, OCT (2002). Pour une stratégie de développement du transport ferroviaire des céréales, Séminaire sur le transport ferroviaire des céréales. Tunisie.
Landry M, Banville C (2000). Caractéristiques et balises d'évaluation de la recherche systémique, RTSG, 2 :1.
Longley PA, Goodchild MFI, Maguire DJ, Rhind DW (2005). Geo. Info. Syst. Sci. Chichester: Wiley. 2nd edition.
Teoh Chee H (2009). An Integrated GIS Database Server for Malaysian Mapping, Cadastral and Location-Based Systems (LBS). World Congress on Computer Science and Information Engineering. Vol.4: 162-167.
Peffers K (2005). Planning for IS applications: a practical, information theoretical method and case study in mobile financial services, Info. Manage., 42(I3)483-501.
Tomlinson RF (2005). Thinking about GIS: Geographic Information System Planning for Managers. ESRI Press. Congress Comput. Sci. Inf. Eng., (4)162 – 167.

Hidden markov model based Arabic morphological analyzer

A. F. Alajmi*, E. M. Saad and M. H. Awadalla

Communication and Electronics Department, Faculty of Engineering, Helwan University, Egypt.

Natural language processing tasks includes summarization, machine translation, question understanding, part of speech tagging, etc. In order to achieve those tasks, a proper language representation must be defined. Roots and stems are considered as representations for some of those systems. A word needs to be processed to extract its root or stem. This paper presents a new technique that extracts word weights, by stripping of prefixes and suffixes from a given word. This technique is based on Hidden Markov Model (HMM). A path from a start state to the end state represents a word, each state constitute letters of a word. States are prefixes, weights, and suffixes. The best selected path should have the highest likelihood of a word. The approach results in a promising 95% performance.

Key words: Natural language processing, morphology, hidden markov model, stem.

INTRODUCTION

The Arabic word is characterized by a well defined letters organization. Words are originated from sections of 3 letters called tri-root, or 4 letters called quad-root, which is the basic block of a word. Furthermore, different forms of words with possibly different meanings are generated from those roots based on well established morphological rules, which are called weights. Thus, by detecting those weights, a word can be reversed into its original root. Over 300 weights represent all forms of an Arabic word, but adding prefixes and suffixes complicate the detection of a word root.

Features are the basis of a text processing system, and in our case, those features are words in a given text. The word by itself does not provide a good representation of a text due to its inflation. Therefore, segmentation of a surface word - word which appears in a text- is a must in order to assure a more efficient text processing system. Thus, further processing of a word is needed to produce better features. One way is to use a stem, which is a result of stripping prefixes, suffixes, and infixes from a word and thus provides better representation. Stem, sometimes referred to as the root, has a drawback of grouping words with possibly different meaning under one root that will affect the accuracy of the outcome of such a system. Another way of presenting a word is the words' weight, which is extracted by stripping prefixes and affixes. The process will minimize the number of features and, preserve the meaning of the word.

In this paper, a new statistical approach is presented based on Hidden Markov Model to extract words' weights and roots. This approach identifies three segments of a given surface word - word in a text. A word is represented by different states. States in the model are divided into three segments. The first segment represents prefixes, the second segment represents the weights that the word belongs to, and the third segment represents the suffixes which a word might be attached to. Word may or may not have a prefix or a suffix. A set of states (path) represents a word, where each letter of the input word is represented by a single state. Furthermore, the extraction of Arabic word weights may lead to word type (noun, verb) detection. Weights may represent nouns, verbs, or both. It will be shown that our approach will detect over 90% of word type, and 95% for weight extraction.

As far as we know, there were no works done on the

*Corresponding author. E-mail: om_mo3ath@yahoo.com, alajmi@ieee.org, alajmi@acm.org.

extraction of a word weight. Most of the research focuses on the root, and stem detection. Deferent techniques were used to extract roots, or stems. Most are rule based, and few are statistical based. The presented technique is considered as a morphological analyzer, which will serve as a weight extractor, a root and stem extractor, a word type identifier. It can also be used to convert a word into its singular state by weights conversion rules (for example, مسلمات to مسلمة).

The next section presents some of the previous works about other morphological systems developed. Following this, we describe the Hidden Markov Model for weight extraction. Finally, we present the results of our system and conclude with a list of future improvements identified as a result of the evaluation.

PREVIOUS WORK

Various morphological systems were developed in literatures. Almost all the system focused on extracting roots or stems. Morphological systems are categorized as statistical driven methods (Al-Sahmsi and Guessoum, 2006; Mohamed et al., 2009; Ahmed and Nürnberger, 2007; Sinane et al., 2008), machine translation driven methods (Chen and Gey, 2002) and rule based methods (El-Hajar et al., 2010; Larkey et al., 2002, 2005; Buckwalter, 2002; Al-Ameed et al., 2005; Khoja and Garside,1999; Darwish, 2002).

A Hidden Markov Model Based part of speech approach was introduced in the works of Al-Sahmsi and Guessoum (2006). It uses HMM to resolve Arabic text POS (Part of Speech) tagging ambiguity through the use of a statistical language model developed from Arabic corpus. The paper presents the characteristics of the Arabic language and the POS tag set that has been selected. It then introduces the methodology followed to develop the HMM for Arabic. For the POS-tagging problem, observation sequence is a sequence of words. The transition probabilities are obtained from the trigram model and the emission probabilities are obtained from the lexical trigram model. The states of the HMM model are the POS tags. A training corpus of Arabic news articles has first been stemmed using the Buckwalter's stemmer, and then, tagged manually with proposed tag set. Then, a trigram language model was built for the tagged training corpus. The trigram language model computes lexical probabilities. Then, the POS tag sequences was obtained from the training corpus and created a trigram Arabic language model based on the POS tag corpus. Next, lexical and contextual probabilities were used to determine the HMM model's parameters as follows: contextual probabilities were transition probabilities and lexical probabilities were the emission probabilities. Once matrices A and B were computed, search needs to be performed to find the POS tag sequence that maximizes the product of the lexical and contextual probabilities. The proposed HMM POS tagger achieved a performance of 97%.

El Hajar et al. (2010) combine morphological analysis with Hidden Markov Model (HMM) and rely on the Arabic sentence structure to produce Arabic Part-Of-Speech Tagging. The morphological analysis is used to reduce the size of the tags lexicon by segmenting Arabic words in their prefixes, stems, and suffixes due to the fact that Arabic is a derivational language. HMM is used to represent the Arabic sentence structure in a hierarchical manner. Each tag in this system is used to represent a possible state of HMM and the transitions between tags (states) are governed by the syntax of the sentence. A corpus is manually tagged and then used for training and testing this system. Experiments conducted on the data set have given a recognition rate of 96%.

Arabic stemming algorithms can be classified, according to the desired level of analysis (El-Hajar et al., 2010), as either stem-based or root-based algorithms. Stem-based algorithms, remove prefixes and suffixes from Arabic words, while root-based algorithms reduce stems to roots. Light stemming refers to the process of stripping off a small set of prefixes and/or suffixes without trying to deal with infixes.

One light stemmer is Larkey et al. (2002), who used a predefined list of prefixes and suffixes to produce a prefix/stem/suffix form. The maximum number of prefixes it can remove is 3, and the maximum number of letters in a suffix is 2. Thus, it fails to remove prefixes that have more than three letters long and suffixes that have more than two letters long. Larkey et al. (2005) revisited the light stemmers and developed another one called light10 that exploits the possibility of having more prefixes and suffixes in the list.

Another light stemmer introduced in Buckwalter (2002), returns all valid segmentations based on the fact that an Arabic prefix length can go from zero to four letters, and the stem can consist of one or more letters, and the suffix can consist of zero to six letters. It returns stems rather than roots. It is based on a set of lexicons of Arabic stems, prefixes, and suffixes, with truth tables indicating their legal combinations. The three dictionaries list possible prefixes, Arabic stems, and possible suffixes. The three compatibility tables indicate compatible prefix/ stem category pairs, compatible prefix/suffix category pairs, and compatible stem/suffix category pairs.

Al-Ameed et al. (2005) is based on the elimination of the Arabic character "و" if it is the beginning of the word, of specific list of prefixes and the suffixes. This stemmer is not dictionary driven, so it cannot apply a criterion that an affix can be removed only if what remains is an existing Arabic word. The stemmers work blindly on words even if they are not found in a word list. It attempts to remove strings which would be found reliably as affixes far more often than they would be found as the beginning or end of an Arabic stem without affixes. The light stemmers do not remove any string that would be considered Arabic prefixes by itself.

Khoja and Garside (1999) presented a simple morphological analyzer, where layers of prefixes and suffixes are removed, then a list of patterns and roots are checked to determine whether the remainder could be a known root with a known pattern applied. If so, it returns the root. Otherwise, it returns the original word, unmodified. This system also removes terms that are found on a list of 168 Arabic stop words.

Taghva et al. (2005) introduced a stemmer without a root dictionary. It uses a similar approach to extract roots as Khoja's approach, but without using a root dictionary or lexicon, and performs as well as a light stemmer. This method is based on the elimination of several sets of affixes, and on the application of several patterns. This method does not use any dictionary to extract the Arabic root. To implement this algorithm, they have defined several sets of the affixes, D diacritic. P3 P2 P1 prefix of three, two, and one letter. And S3 S2 S1, suffix of three, two, one letter, and several sets of pattern models of four, five and six letters. Furthermore, a three, four, five letters roots Models were defined.

Chen and Gey (2002) developed two Arabic stemmers and an Arabic stop list at TREC 2001. The two researchers created a machine translation (MT) based stemmer and a light stemmer. The stemmer based on translation was relied on the idea of translating the Arabic word to the English, after removing English stop words, then, extract the base word in English, then translate this word in Arabic to the root for example: أطفالنا (our children), remove "our" is a word, أطفالنا is apparent that in relation to "child". So أطفالنا is related to طفل. The light stemmer (Chen and Gey, 2002) was called Berkeley which shares many of prefixes and suffixes that should be removed with the light stemmers developed by Larkey et al. (2002) and the one developed by Darwish (2002). They identified other sets of prefixes and suffixes. They start by counting the words that begin with a given prefix, and the number of words ending with the given suffixes. At the end, the prefixes that must be removed are identified: 19 three-letters, 14 two-letters, and 3 one letter, and the suffixes: 18 two-letters, 4 one letter. To remove the prefixes and suffixes in the predefined sets, each algorithm proposes their own rules.

A statistical method which belongs to the "N-gram" class was developed by Ahmed and Nürnberger (2007) and Sinane et al. (2008). An n-gram is a subsequence of n letters from a given word to predict the next letter in such a sequence. It is based on the concept of words similarity or dissimilarity. Two words are considered similar if they have several common substrings of N letters. Two words are considered dissimilar if they do not have common different substrings of N characters. N-gram was implemented with bi-gram N=2 and tri-gram N=3. Similarity or dissimilarity statistical coefficients are calculated between the processing word and a list of roots are extracted from a dictionary to extract the root of a word. The roots that have the highest for similar or lowest for dissimilar coefficient are named as probable roots.

THE PROPOSED APPROACH

Hidden Markov Model is one of the most important machine learning models in speech and language processing (Jurafsky and Martin, 2000). HMM is a probabilistic sequence classifier, given a sequence of units (in our case letters) and its job is to compute the probability distribution over possible labels and choose the best label sequence.

The Hidden Markov Model is a finite set of states, and a set of transitions between states that are taken based on the input observations. Each of which is associated with a probability distribution (Lawrence, 1989). Weights are augmented; where each transition is associated with a probability of how likely state a transit to state b. Transitions among the states are governed by a set of probabilities called transition probabilities. In a particular state, an outcome or observation can be generated, according to the associated probability distribution. It is only the outcome, not the state visible to an external observer and therefore, states are ``hidden" to the outside; hence the name Hidden Markov Model (Lawrence, 1989).

A Markov chain is a special case of a weighted auto-maton in which the input sequence uniquely determines which states, sequence will go through. In our case the sequence represents a word.

Weight extraction

Hidden Markov Model is used to extract Arabic word weights. HMM is represented by a set of states and a set of transitions from one state to another. A given word is tested through the model by using states as the letters of the word, and the transition from start state 0 to end state will represent the full word. The model will output the path which yields the highest probability. There are two probability matrices, the state transition probability matrix, and the emission probability matrix. State transition matrix will provide the probability of going from state i to state j. Furthermore, the emission probability matrix will provide the probability of emitting an observation in a given state i, observations are the alphabets of the Arabic language plus a special character called "Shadda" "شدة", a total of 31 observation is considered.

Elements of the proposed Hidden Markov Model are:

A set of N states $S = s_1 s_2 \ldots s_N$ representing the number of states of the model, each state represent one letter of a word, and a path from state s_i to s_j represent a word. N = 172 states.

A transition probability matrix A. $A = a_{11} a_{12} \ldots a_{nn}$, where a_{ij} represents the probability of moving from state i to state j, $A = \{a_{ij}\}$. That is going from one letter to the next in a given word.

A sequence of K observation $O = o_1 o_2 \ldots o_k$ each drawn from the vocabulary $V = v_1, v_2, \ldots v_V$, V represents Arabic letters plus some special letters. The number of observation symbols in the alphabet, M =31.

A sequence of emission probabilities $E = e_i(o_k)$, each sequence expresses the probability of an observation o_k being generated from a state i.

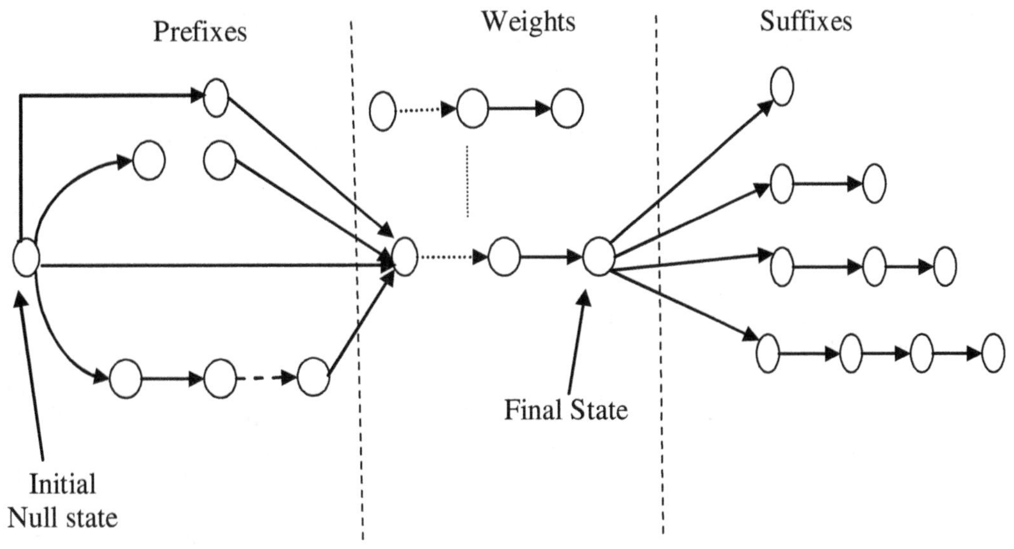

Figure 1. Proposed model.

Table 1. Example of words decoding

Word	Prefix	Weight	suffix	length	Weight
Fsayakfekahma	Will be	Enough	For them	10	FAL
Muslim	-	Muslim	they	6	mFAL
Yalaabn	ya	play	they	5	FAL
Aljamee	the	all	-	6	FAeL

A special (start) state and a final (end) state S_0, S_F which are not associated with observations. The proposed model has one null initial state and multiple end states. End state can be the last state of any valid weight states, or a suffix state.

For example, a word "مسلمون" (Muslims) has six letters, adding a null state, it should start with state 0 and goes up to six states depending on A (transition probability), and E (emission probability). There could be multiple correct paths for the word, but the only one with the highest probability will be accepted as a valid solution. In the case of our example, a path of states, 0, 8, 15, 16, 17, 170, 171, state 0, as a starting null state, state 8 will represent the letter "" and it is considered as a part of the prefix states group, and it only prefixes a noun, so the word will be identified as a noun. State 15 up to 17 represent the weight "F3L" (فعل=سلم) and it is also the root of the word. States 170, and 171 (ون) are the suffixes of the word, and it is special for plurals. Other words are found in the same way (Figure 1).

First, we define the number of states S in the system. A total of 172 states were identified as prefixes, weights, or suffixes. Prefixes are represented by 15 states. States are logically divided into three groups that identify the set of prefixes state group, the set of weights states group, and the set of suffixes states group. Weights are represented by 82 states, and suffixes are represented by 75 states. We start with one initial null state, and multiple end states. An end state is the last state of any valid end state of a weight, or a suffix state. Observations are 28 Arabic letters added to it shadah (شدّة), Alef maqsora (ى) and Taa (ة), and we distinguish between Alef and Hamza (أ and ا). A total of 31 observations is embedded. Figure 1 shows the proposed model design.

A word may or may not have a prefix. Prefixes are of length up to 7, for example the word (وبالاستخدام). The word has a prefix of length 7. A word without prefixes or suffixes could be of size 3 - 4 - 5 - 6 - 7 with infixes. A word may or may not have a suffix. Suffixes could be of length up to 4. For example, the word (فعاليّات) has a suffix of length four letters.

For example, a word (اجتمعنا) will have one prefix, and two suffixes, leaving 4 letters to represent the pattern (افتعل), which is a verb in the past tense (as shown in Table 1). Hidden Markov Model is characterized by three problems, the evaluation problem, the decoding problem, and the learning problem. Evaluation is also referred to as computing the likelihood, given an HMM $\lambda = (A, E)$ and a sequence of letters $O = o_1, o_2, \ldots, o_k$, find the pro-bability that the word letter are generated by the model, $p\{O \mid \lambda\}$. Forward algorithm (Jurafsky and Martin, 2000) is used to compute such likelihood.

Furthermore, decoding will discover the best hidden state sequence (S) in the model that produces the word. Given a word is represented by letters $O = o_1, o_2, \ldots, o_k$ and HMM $\lambda = (A, E)$. The discovery of the hidden sequence depends upon the way most likely state sequence is defined. It can be interpreted as a search in a graph whose nodes are formed by the states of the HMM in each of the time instant $k, 1 \le k \le K$. Viterbi algorithm (Jurafsky and Martin, 2000) solves this problem where the whole state sequence with the maximum likelihood is found.

In addition to evaluation and decoding, the learning problem is needed to extract model parameters from a training set. Learning is defined as, given a model λ and a sequence of letters (a word) $O = o_1, o_2, \ldots, o_k$, how should we adjust the model parameters in order to maximize $p\{O \mid \lambda\}$, that is to learn the HMM parameters A, and E.

The input to the learning algorithm would be unlabeled sequence of observations O (letters) and a vocabulary of potential hidden states S which simply means the word and the correct path of states it should have. Standard algorithms for HMM training are Forward-backward, and Baum Welch algorithm. The Algorithm will train both the transition probabilities, A, and the Emission Probability, E, of the HMM. Generally, the learning problem is how to adjust the HMM parameters, so that the given set of observations (words) is represented by the model in the best way for the weight-root extraction system. The Forward-Backward Algorithm was used to train our system.

Word type detecting

The proposed system can extract the word type (Verb-Noun) depending on different criteria. The detection of a word type (N, V) may depend on any of the following: Prefixes; suffixes; weights; word preceding the word in question (particles).

Some prefixes are attached only to nouns (for example, ال), others may only precede verbs (for example, ي). The same concept follows the suffixes attached to nouns only (for example, ات), and other attached to verbs only (for example, نَ). If word type was not detected by prefixes and suffixes then we check for the extracted word's and suffixes then we check for the extracted word's weight. Weights are either belonging to nouns, or verbs, or common between them. For example, the word (احتبس) has the weight (افتعل) which is a verb; whereas, the word (مركب) has the weight (مفعل) which is a noun. An example of common weight is (فاعل). Words preceding the word in question may detect a word type. For example, words like (في) only precede nouns and words such as (لم) only comes before verbs. Those preceding words are considered as stop words in a text processing system. Over 90% of word types can be detected by the given method. Weights might also help in part-of-speech tagging.

Bi-gram word model

Hidden Markov Model will provide the most probable path for the given sequence of letters that represents a word. The relation between two consecutive letters is not preserved by the model. Therefore, a bi-gram model was constructed from the training words to preserve the letter to letter succession. This is done because of a problem detected upon testing the decoding phase of the HMM. A word which begins and ends with letters that has a high possibility of being a prefix or a suffix can be interpreted wrongly by the system. For example, the word (نشرت) begins with a letter (ن) which can be a prefix and ends with the letter (ت) which can be a suffix. The correct path is to consider the last letter as a suffix, but the system may consider wrongly the first letter as a prefix. To prevent this, Two, 28 × 28 matrices were constructed with Arabic alphabetic as the rows and the columns of the matrix. The value is considered as the probability of going from letter A to letter B in the beginning of the word for the first matrix, and the probability of going from letter A to letter B at the end of the word for the second matrix. It was found that, having the sequence (نش) as the first two letters of a word is more probable (14%) than having the sequence (رت) as the last two letters of the word (2%).

EXPERIMENT AND RESULTS

About 15 million words were used to train the model. Those words constitute all possible different forms that a word could have. Words were generated by the aid of Arabic dictionary (Ar-Rhazi, 1989; Al-Asmar, 2009). Based on word root, and possible weights for those roots, different forms of a word were generated. The generated words were attached to different prefixes and suffixes following Arabic morphological rules. The following are the procedure to produce the Hidden Markov Model parameters: Collect words' roots and patterns for those roots from Arabic dictionaries; generate different forms of a word using morphological rules; add suffixes and prefixes to resulting words; use the final result to train the model using forward-Backward algorithm.

The result is two matrices, one for state transition probability, and the other for observation emission probability. State transition matrix will provide the probability of going from state si to state sj. Emission probability matrix will provide the probability of emitting a letter E in state si. These matrices are used as inputs for the Viterbi algorithm to decode a given word. The algorithm was altered to give all possible paths, and not only the one with the highest probability. In order to extract the correct path, further rules have to be applied, which are: End states must not be before the last state of any valid weight (pattern); prefix and suffix matching table must be applied. For example prefix "ي" does not match suffix "ت"; check the Bi-Gram generated matrices probability if the first and the last letters of the word are probable prefix and suffix.

The words were decoded using Veterbi Algorithm. Those words (training set) were extracted from different documents. The following are the processing procedure of a text in order to extract weights and roots: Tokenizing words and eliminating all punctuation; Hamza must all be normalized to one shape "أ"; altered veterbi algorithm is used to decode the words, and find all possible paths; apply the weights correctness rules, and prefix-suffix matching table; select the path with highest probability; states which belongs to the weights' states are identified, thus, extract the root. Table 2 shows an example of the text decoding.

Testing of 50, randomly selected documents from the internet, shows an average count of 400 words after tokenization. The results were compared manually against Arabic dictionary to compare between the correct and the outcome of the system. The presented approach achieved a promising accuracy of 95%. It was found that 2% of error is due to spelling mistake.

CONCLUSION

Arabic is a highly inflected language. The wide range of word forms and the large variety of prefixes and suffixes complicate the extraction of precise features for a text

Table 2. Test result.

Input string	State transition	P of emission	P of state transition	Expected
She Eats	0-3-37-38-39-40-41	0.000616	0.006813	Ttfaal
They Feel	0-5-7-8-9-102-103-	0.0001037160	0.0029909289	Yafalon
Increase	0-2-25-26-27-28	0.000001	0.011867	Eftaal

processing system. Therefore, a preprocessing technique is needed to unify similar words into a single feature before further processing of the text. Root is aimed at finding the base letters which represent a word in a dictionary and, stemming simply refers to stripping prefixes and suffixes from a word. Also, the root may represent a group of words that may have different meaning such as the word (مجتمع=community) and the word (جامع=Mosque) that belongs to the same root (جمع), but has different meaning.

Arabic words are structured in well known patterns called weights thus "weights" are selected in this paper as a feature of an Arabic text. Weights are closer to stems, except some of the prefixes that belong to the weight which will not be removed. The presented approach is based on Hidden Markov Model. Each state in a model is considered as a letter of a word, a word is represented by consecutive states, from start to end. Two questions to be answered are; what is the likelihood of a path for a word, and what is the probability of emitting the letter of a word in a given state of the path. The model was trained with a collection of words extracted from Arabic dictionaries and, it was ensured that words constitute a verity of prefixes, suffixes, and weights. Different rules have to be applied before selecting the path with highest probability. States are distinguished as prefixes or the weight or suffixes from the selected path. Testing the system with different documents which belongs to different categories, a 95 % correctness was accomplished by this paper. The weights of document's words were manually checked against Arabic dictionary to compare with the extracted result.

In the future, we aim at studying the reduction of the extracted weights by grouping weights with similar meaning and different states (single, plural, past, present) into unified ones. Furthermore, the selected features will be tested in text processing task (for example, clustering) against the root features for a comparison.

REFERENCES

Ahmed F, Nürnberger A (2007). N-grams Conflation Approach for Arabic, ACM SIGIR Conference, Amsterdam.

Al-Ameed H, Al-Ketbi S, Al-Kaabi K, Al-Shebli K, Al-Shamsi N, Al-Nuaimi N, Al-Muhairi S (2005) Arabic Light Stemmer: A new Enhanced Approach. The Second International Conference on Innovations in Information Technology (IIT'05).

Al-Asmar R (2009). The Detailed Lexicon in Morphology. Scientific book publisher. (Arabic Book)

Al-Sahmsi F, Guessoum A (2006). A hidden Markov Model – Based POS Tagger for Arabic. 8es Journees internationals d'Analyse statistique des Donnees Textuelles.

Ar-Rhazi MB (1989). Mukhtar Us-Sihah, Librairie du Liban. (Arabic Book)

Buckwalter T (2002). Buckwalter Arabic Morphological Analyzer. the Linguistic Data Consortium, University of Pennsylvania.

Chen A, Gey F (2002). Building an Arabic stemmer for information retrieval.

Darwish K (2002), Building a shallow Arabic Morphological Analyzer in one day, Proceedings of the ACL-02 workshop on Computational approaches to semitic languages, pp.1-8, July 11, Philadelphia, Pennsylvania

El-Hajar A, Hajar M, Zreik K (2010). A System for Evaluation of Arabic Root Extraction Methods. fifth international Conference on Internet and Web Applications and Services.

Jurafsky D, Martin JH (2000). Speech and Language Processing An Introduction to Natural Language Processing Computational Linguistics and Speech Recognition, Volume: 21, Prentice Hall.

Khoja S, Garside R (1999). Stemming Arabic Text. Technical report, Lancaster University, Lancaster, U.K.

Larkey L, Ballesteros L, Connell M (2005). Light Stemming for Arabic IR Arabic Computational Morphology: Knowledge-based and Empirical Methods, A.Soudi, A. van en Bosch, and Neumann, G., Editors. Kluwer/Springer's serieson Text, Speech, and Language Technology.

Larkey LS, Ballesteros L, Connel ME (2002). Improving Stemming for Arabic Information Retrieval: Light Stemming and Co-occurrence Analysis. Proc. of the 25th annual international ACM SIGIR conference on Research and development in information retrieval, pp. 275 – 282.

Lawrence RR (1989). A tutorial on Hidden Markov Models and selected applications in speech recognition, Proceed. IEEE, 77: 2.

Mohamed El-Hadj, Al-Sughayeir IA, Al-Ansari AM (2009). Arabic Part of Speech Tagging Using the Sentence Structure. 2nd international Conference on Arabic Language Resources & Tools. Cairo.

Sinane M, Rammal M, Zreik K (2008). Arabic documents classification using N-gram, Conference ICHSL6, Toulouse.

Taghva K, Elkoury R, Coombs J (2005). Arabic Stemming without a root dictionary.

8

A study of indoor positioning by using trigonometric and weight centroid localization techniques

Hakan Koyuncu* and Shuang Hua Yang

Computer Science Department, Loughborough University, Loughborough, United Kingdom.

An indoor positioning system was developed to provide a fast and easy determination of unknown position coordinates. Wireless sensor nodes (WSN) are employed in a test area. Trigonometry techniques were employed to determine the position of the unknown objects by employing numerical analysis techniques on received signal link quality indicator (LQI) values. The distances between the unknown object position and the WSNs are calculated by using curve fitting techniques on received LQI values. Weight centroid localization (WCL) algorithm was introduced on the results of the trigonometry techniques to improve the position accuracy. An application program (AP) was developed to control and display all the results.

Key words: Wireless sensor nodes (WSN), weight centroid localization (WCL), transmitter, receiver, received signal strengths (RSS), received signal strength indicator (RSSI), link quality indicator (LQI), application program (AP).

INTRODUCTION

Wireless sensor nodes (WSN) technology is widely used to realize the positions of objects in different environments. It is employed for variety of indoor position detection (Lionel, 2004). There are many types of position identification systems using optical (Want et al., 1992, 1997), ultrasonic (Ward et al., 1997; Harter et al., 1999) and RF wireless technologies (Bahl and Padmanabhan, 2000; Hightower et al., 2000; http://www.aimglobal.org/technologies/rfid/; Konrad et al., 2005). Each has their own strengths as well as limitations.

WSN technology has several advantages such as having no contact and none line-of-sight nature. All transmitters can be read in extreme environmental conditions (http://www.aimglobal.org/technologies/, 2005; koyuncu and Yang, 2010).

To define the exact coordinates of the unknown sensor node, there is a need to measure the distances between the unknown node and the known transmitter nodes. These measurements require to measure the time of interval (TOA) or to measure the time difference of arrival (TDOA). Due to the difficulties of time measurements resulting from synchronization of WSNs and complicated electronics, these mea-surement techniques are not frequently employed. Received signal strengths (RSS) values are used to realize the unknown positions.

RSS values are represented in the form of LQI values by the Zigbee devices. In the study, WSNs are strategically placed in indoors and identified as transmitter nodes. An unknown sensor node which is also a WSN was identified as an unknown receiver mobile node. The receiver mobile node receives the transmitted signal packets in the form of LQI values from transmitter nodes, sends them to an attached PC. The topology is illustrated in Figure 1.

The wireless sensor node localization can be defined as finding the location of an unknown mobile node with respect to distances between the transmitter nodes and the unknown node. In this study, A well known weight centroid localization (WCL) method was employed. Unknown positions are calculated by dividing the test area into triangles and using numerical analysis technique to determine the locations of the unknown objects with respect to known WSNs.

RSSI and LQI

Received signal strength indicator (RSSI) is a parameter to identify the incoming radio signal. The transmitter

*Corresponding author. E-mail: h.koyuncu@lboro.ac.uk.

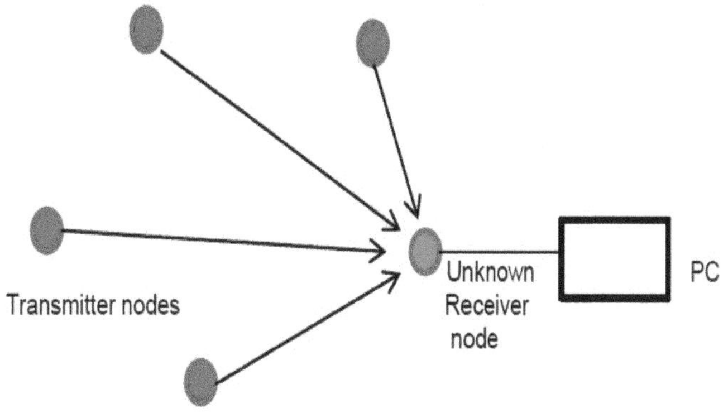

Figure 1. Topology of wireless sensor nodes.

power (P_T) at the transmitter node directly affects the received power (P_R) at the receiver device. The free space transmission equation (Rappaport, 1996), is given in Equation 1.

$$P_R = P_T . G_T . G_R . \left(\frac{\lambda}{4\pi d} \right)^2 \quad (1)$$

Where, P_T = transmit power. P_R = received power. G_T = gain of transmitter. G_R = gain of receiver. π = wave length. d = distance between transmitter and receiver. As it is seen in Equation 1, the received power decreases with the inverse square of the distance. In WSNs, the received signal strength is converted to RSSI. It is defined as the ratio of the received power to a reference power (P_{REF}) where P_{REF} = 1mW. Hence, RSSI can be expressed as:

$$RSSI = 10.\log \frac{P_R}{P_{REF}} \quad (2)$$

It can be concluded from here that RSSI value is also inversely proportional with d values. In practice propagating radio signal is effected and interfered by many environmental factors. Hence, in many applications, RSSI has a high variance and the localization of unknown node becomes very imprecise.

Another method of distance determination is carried out by LQI of transmission. According to IEEE 802.15.4 standards, LQI is identified as the strength of the received signal. It is proportional to RSSI and has a value between 0 to 255 (Ergen, 2004). Hence, RSSI can be directly mapped to LQI (Zigbeready, 2007). The transmitter nodes transmit the signal packets continuously. The receiver mobile node logs the LQI of the incoming signal packets and sends them to PC.

The position of the transmitter node varied between 0 and 40 m with respect to receiver mobile node. The recordings of LQI values received by the receiver mobile node are carried out in obstacle free outdoor space. The recording process is carried out with each transmitter. It was observed that their LQI versus distance plotting's were close to each other. An average plot of 4 transmitters is carried out and presented in Figure 2.

LQI of incoming radio signals decreases with increasing distance "d" between transmitter and the receiver in free space. Hence, LQI measurements versus distance curve also display a close correlation between LQI and the distance d (Ralf, 2007).

The free space model for recordings of LQI values versus d distances is used to calibrate the indoor values of d with respect to LQI for short distances. The test area in the study had no obstacles and it was approximated to a free space model for short distances. The reflections from the outside walls were considered negligible. A curve fitting technique (MATLAB v.9) is employed and a 5th polynomial curve is best fitted with 95% confidence boundaries on the recorded LQI values as seen in Figure 3. The curve fitted equation for the received LQI data between 0 and 40 m is generated by MATLAB and is shown in Equation 3.

$$LQI(d) = P_1.x^5 + P_2.x^4 + P_3.x^3 + P_4.x^2 + P_5.x^1 + P_6 \quad (3)$$

Where P_1 = -6.939exp (-005), P_2 = 0.007404 , P_3 = -0.2938, P_4 = 5.369 , P_5 = -46.14 , P_6 = 228.3.

A numerical analysis technique which is identified as bisectioning algorithm (http://en.wikipedia.org/wiki/Bisection_method), is used first time to determine the distance between the unknown node and each transmitter once its corresponding LQI value is known.

It is also called root finding method which repeatedly bisects the interval between the transmitter and the receiver and then selects a sub interval in which a root must lie for further processing. When an unknown LQI value is received from a transmitter and recorded in computer, its corresponding d value will be calculated by applying bisectioning algorithm with Equation 3.

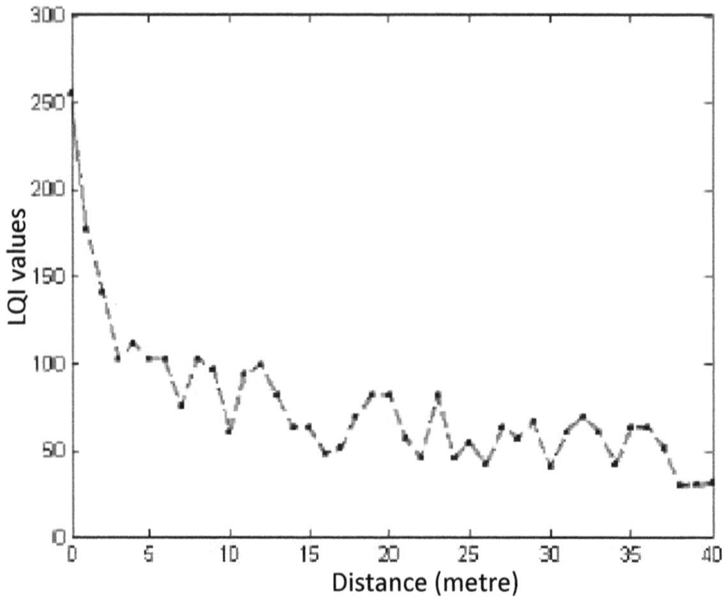

Figure 2. LQI values versus distance in m.

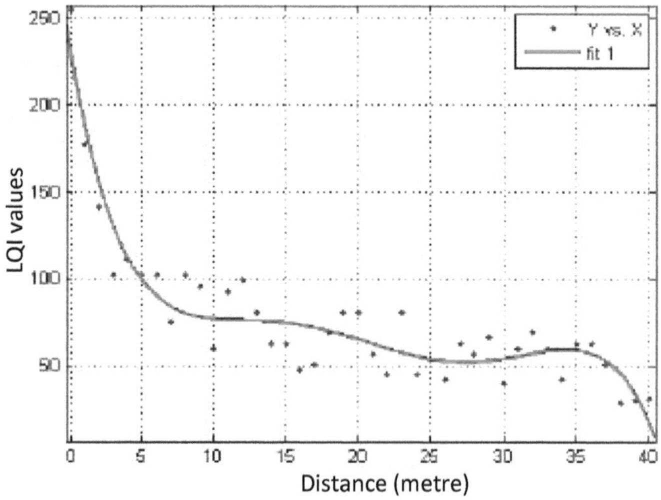

Figure 3. Curve fitted LQI values.

Trigonometric techniques will be employed with these d values to determine the positions of the unknown nodes. WCL technique will also be employed at a later stage to refine the previously calculated positions of the unknown nodes.

TRIGONOMETRY

Recordings of LQI values are carried out by the unknown mobile node in the test area. The corresponding d distance for each LQI is also calculated by using numerical methods. The block diagram of the rectangular test area is shown in Figure 4. The unknown mobile node P has four d values (d_A, d_B, d_C, d_D) at every location. Each of them corresponds to the distance between a transmitter and itself.

The unknown node P(x, y) could be in anywhere in the test area. The trigonometric equations corresponding to x and y coordinates of point P in $B_1B_2B_3B_4$ test area can be given by:

$$x^2 + y^2 = d_A^2 \tag{4}$$

$$y^2 + (5 - x)^2 = d_B^2 \tag{5}$$

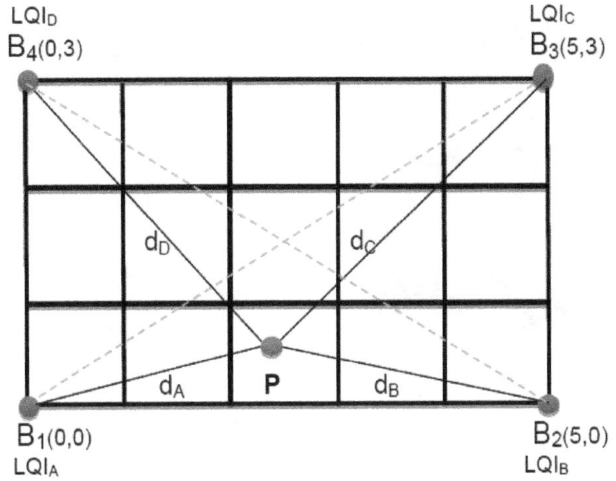

Figure 4. 5 × 3 m test area with B_i transmit- ters and P unknown mobile node.

$$(5-x)^2+(3-y)^2=d_C^2 \quad (6)$$

$$x^2+(3-y)^2=d_D^2 \quad (7)$$

Where B_1B_2 is the x axis and B_1B_4 is the y axis with B_1 is the (0, 0) coordinate center.

The test area is divided into sub sections in the shape of triangles and the coordinates of the unknown node are calculated with respect to these triangles. There are 4 triangles in test area which are $B_1B_2B_4$, $B_1B_2B_3$, $B_1B_4B_3$ and $B_4B_3B_2$. The unknown node could be in any one of these triangles. For example if P(x,y) is inside or outside the $B_1B_2B_4$ triangle, the x,y coordinates can be calculated as:

$$P_1(x,y)=\left(\frac{d_a^2-d_b^2+25}{10},\frac{d_a^2-d_d^2+9}{6}\right) \quad (8)$$

Similarly $P_2(x, y)$ for $B_1B_2B_3$ triangle is:

$$P_2(x,y)=\left(\frac{d_a^2-d_b^2+25}{10},\frac{d_b^2-d_c^2+9}{6}\right) \quad (9)$$

$P_3(x,y)$ for $B_1B_4B_3$ triangle is:

$$P_3(x,y)=\left(\frac{d_b^2-d_c^2+25}{10},\frac{d_a^2-d_d^2+9}{6}\right) \quad (10)$$

$P_4(x, y)$ for $B_4B_3B_2$ triangle is:

$$P_4(x,y)=\left(\frac{d_d^2-d_c^2+25}{10},\frac{d_b^2-d_c^2+9}{6}\right) \quad (11)$$

By using these equations, unknown coordinates of the unknown node P(x, y) can be calculated by substituting (d_a, d_b, d_c, d_d) values in Equations 8 to 11 with respect to 4 triangles in the rectangular test area.

WCL

WCL introduces weights to improve the localization (Jan, 2007). Weight function is expressed by w_{ij} and the estimated position of the unknown node is defined by:

$$P_i(x,y)=\frac{\sum_{j=1}^{n}(w_{ij}.B_j(x,y))}{\sum_{j=1}^{n}w_{ij}} \quad (12)$$

Weight function w_{ij}, depends on the distance of the unknown receiver node to transmitter node. Shorter distances have more weight than longer distances. Therefore, w_{ij} and d_{ij} are inversely proportional and this relationship is expressed as:

$$w_{ij}=\left(\frac{1}{d_{ij}}\right)^k \quad (13)$$

d_{ij} is the distance between transmitter B_j and unknown receiver node P_i. k is the degree. The distance is raised to high powers of k in order to get longer distances to have lower weights. But if a very high degree k is used, estimated position moves to the closest transmitters and the position error e increases. Hence there is an optimal k value exists for minimum error e. This k value is determined as 1 in the literature.

Figure 5. Transmitter (Left), Receiver (Right).

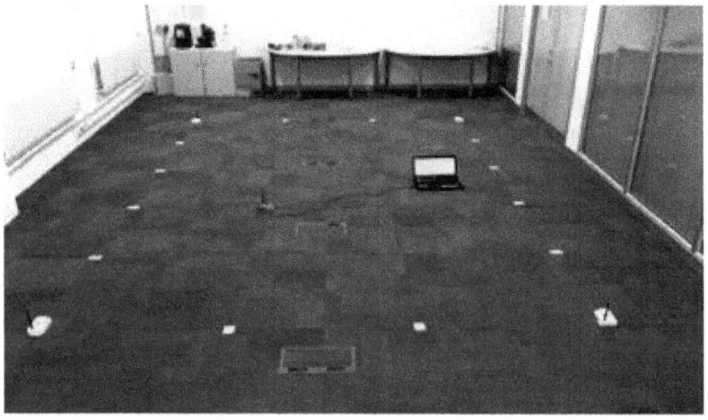

Figure 6. Test bed area.

The position error e is represented by the distance between the actual position, (x_r, y_r) and the estimated position, (x_e, y_e) of the unknown node. It is expressed as:

$$e = \sqrt{(x_e - x_r)^2 + (y_e - y_r)^2} \quad (14)$$

Positions of several unknown nodes will be determined and their error margins with respect to their actual positions will be calculated with Equation 14.

IMPLEMENTATION

JENNIC JN5139 wireless sensor nodes were deployed in the experiments (http://www.jennic.com/jennic_support/application). The Zigbee Home Sensor demo program was used to program JN5139 active devices to work as fixed transmitter nodes and mobile receiver node, respectively (http://www.jennic.com/files/support_documentation). The active transmitter/receiver pair used in this study is shown in Figure 5.

JN5139 receiver is interfaced to a PC through a USB port. ZigBee protocol which is based on the IEEE 802.15.4 protocol in the 2.4 GHz band is used during the data communication between the fixed and mobile nodes.

The test bed is on a single empty floor inside a building as seen Figure 6. A rectangular grid of 5 x 3 m is defined over the two-dimensional floor plane and all the unknown node positions are limited to grid points. Any position in the rectangular test area is implemented by P(x, y) coordinates. WSN trans-mitters are placed in the 4 corners of this test area.

The unknown mobile receiver node is positioned at any point in the test area interfaced to a computer. For the grid area of 5 x 3 m, there are 24 grid points. Receiver node is placed at each grid point and 4 LQI readings at each grid point are recorded by the receiver.

A total of 24 x 4 = 96 LQI entries are recorded in the data base. Each entry in the database includes a mapping of the grid coordinate (x, y) and d distances (d_A, d_B, d_C, d_D) of each grid point to 4 transmitters. Received LQI values exhibit a strong correlation with the receiver aerial orientation as well as its location. The LQI measurements at one location vary depending on the orientation. In the analytical model, the variations due to aerial orientation have been averaged out when the LQI is recorded for 4 compass directions by the receiver.

The outdoor free space recordings of LQI values at short ranges of less than 5 meters were approximately same with the obstacle free indoor test area recordings. Hence the radio wave reflections from the walls around the test area were considered negligible.

A visual C# based application program (AP), has been developed to control entire data manipulation and calculation process. As a result of communication between the mobile receiver and 4 transmitter nodes at every grid point, 4 LQI values and the grid coordinates are transferred to PC. Additionally, the distances (d_A, d_B, d_C, d_D), between each grid point and 4 transmitter nodes are also calculated. All the relevant data in the PC is further put in the form of a database by using Microsoft access.

CALCULATIONS

Trigonometry method

During measurements, AP measures four LQI values at an unknown location in the grid. These LQI values are recorded and the corresponding d values, (d_A, d_B, d_C, d_D) are calculated by using numerical methods on the fitted curve in Figure 3.

Once 4 d values are identified for each unknown location they are used to calculate the unknown coordinates P(x, y) of the unknown location by using previous four triangles defined as $P_1(x, y)$, $P_2(x, y)$, $P_3(x, y)$ and $P_4(x,y)$. These coordinates together with corresponding LQI and d values are tabulated in Table 1. In conclusion, unknown location (x, y) coordinates are calculated for each triangle and there are 4 calculated P(x, y) values for each unknown location.

Table 1. P(x,y) unknown coordinates for each triangle test area.

Unknown (x,y) position coordinates	LQI values of mobile node at unknown positions				d values calculated with bisectioning algorithm for each LQI values				P_1, P_2, P_3, P_4 points calculated with trigonometric methods							
	LQI_A	LQI_B	LQI_C	LQI_D	d_A	d_B	d_C	d_D	$P_1(x,y)$		$P_2(x,y)$		$P_3(x,y)$		$P_4(x,y)$	
1, 1	110	120	125	150	3.43	2.96	2.96	2.03	2.80	2.78	2.80	1.50	2.03	2.78	2.03	1.50
1, 2	105	100	95	180	3.43	3.43	3.43	1.17	2.50	3.24	2.50	1.50	1.45	3.24	1.45	1.50
2, 1	95	145	95	137	3.43	2.34	3.43	2.65	3.13	2.29	3.13	0.44	2.02	2.29	2.02	0.44
3, 0	95	145	93	145	3.43	2.34	3.43	2.34	3.13	2.55	3.13	0.44	1.86	2.55	1.86	0.44
3, 2	97	151	108	132	3.43	2.03	3.43	2.65	3.26	2.29	3.26	0.21	2.02	2.29	2.02	0.21
4, 1	92	129	121	111	3.43	2.65	2.96	3.43	2.97	1.50	2.97	1.20	2.80	1.50	2.80	1.20

Table 2. Distances between P and respective triangle corners for each unknown location.

Unknown locations	Calculated P(x, y) points and their distances to respective triangle corners			
	P_1(2.8, 2.7)	P_2(2.8, 1.5)	P_3(2.0, 2.7)	P_4(2.0, 1.5)
(1, 1)	dA=3.94	dA=3.17	dA=3.44	dC=3.32
	dB=3.54	dB=2.66	dC=2.97	dB=3.32
	dD=2.8	dC=2.66	dD=2.04	dD=2.52
	P_1(2.5, 3.2)	P_2(2.5, 1.5)	P_3(1.4, 3.2)	P_4(1.4, 1.5)
(1, 2)	dA=4.09	dA=2.91	dA=3.55	dC=3.84
	dB=4.09	dB=2.91	dC=3.55	dB=3.84
	dD=2.51	dC=2.91	dD=1.47	dD=2.09
	P_1(3.13, 2.29)	P_2(3.13, 0.44)	P_3(2.02, 2.29)	P_4(2.02, 0.44)
(2, 1)	dA=3.88	dA=3.16	dA=3.05	dC=3.92
	dB=2.95	dB=1.92	dC=3.05	dB=3.00
	dD=3.21	dC=3.16	dD=2.14	dD=3.25
	P_1(3.13, 2.55)	P_2(3.13, 0.44)	P_3(1.86, 2.55)	P_4(1.86, 0.44)
(3, 0)	dA=4.04	dA=3.16	dA=3.16	dC=4.04
	dB=3.16	dB=1.92	dC=3.16	dB=3.16
	dD=3.16	dC=3.16	dD=1.92	dD=3.16
	P_1(3.26, 2.29)	P_2(3.26, 0.21)	P_3(2.02, 2.29)	P_4(2.02, 0.21)
(3, 2)	dA=3.99	dA=3.27	dA=3.05	dC=4.07
	dB=2.87	dB=1.74	dC=3.05	dB=2.98
	dD=3.34	dC=3.27	dD=2.14	dD=3.44
	P_1(2.97, 1.5)	P_2(2.97,1.20)	P_3(2.8,1.5)	P_4(2.8,1.2)
(4, 1)	dA=3.33	dA=3.21	dA=3.17	dC=2.83
	dB=2.51	dB=2.35	dC=2.66	dB=2.50
	dD=3.33	dC=2.70	dD=3.17	dD=3.32

WCL method

Weighted centroid localization will be introduced with the unknown P(x, y) points to improve their position accuracies. The distances between the P(x, y) and the corners of the corresponding triangle are calculated and used as weights in final recalculation of P(x, y) values. These distance values are tabulated in Table 2.

Recalculated P(x, y) values by using WCL are identified as Q(x, y). Calculation of $Q_1(x, y)$ is shown in Equation 14

Table 3. Calculated unknown position coordinates with error margins.

Unknown locations	$Q_1(x,y)$	$Q_2(x,y)$	$Q_3(x,y)$	$Q_4(x,y)$	Ave= $(Q_1+Q_2+Q_3+Q_4)/4$	Error (m)
(1,1)	1.5, 1.1	3.5, 1.0	1.5, 2.2	3.0, 2.0	2.4, 1.6	1.5
(1,2)	1.3, 1.3	3.3, 1.0	1.1, 2.3	2.6, 2.2	2.1, 1.7	1.3
(2,1)	1.8, 1.0	3.6, 0.8	1.4, 2.1	3.2, 1.8	2.5, 1.4	0.6
(3,0)	1.7, 1.0	3.6, 0.8	1.3, 2.1	3.2, 1.9	2.5, 1.5	1.5
(3,2)	1.9, 0.9	3.7, 0.7	1.4, 2.1	3.3, 1.8	2.6, 1.4	0.7
(4,1)	1.9, 0.9	3.5, 1.0	1.8, 2.0	3.5, 1.8	2.7, 1.4	1.3
Total average error $=(e_1+........e_6)/6$ =						1.1

as an example.

$$Q_1(x,y)=\frac{\frac{1}{d_A}(0,0)+\frac{1}{d_B}(5,0)+\frac{1}{d_D}(0,3)}{(\frac{1}{d_A}+\frac{1}{d_B}+\frac{1}{d_D})} \quad (14)$$

For each unknown location, 4 Q(x, y) values are obtained by using WCL techniques. The average of them represented the final position coordinates of the unknown location (Table 3).

Error calculations from all unknown positions revealed an average error distance of 1.1 m with the optimum weight function of w = 1/d. The average error distance calculations are later compared with the results in the literature.

CONCLUSIONS

In this study, determination of unknown positions by using trigonometric methods is investigated. Test area is divided into sub areas in triangle shapes and unknown position coordinates are calculated with respect to each triangle. Hence, each unknown (x, y) position coordinates had 4 calculated P(x, y) coordinates.

Numerical analysis techniques are introduced first time and the distance between transmitting and receiving WSNs are calculated with respect to LQI values. Received LQI values of WSN nodes are calibrated in free space with respect to distance between transmitter and receiver nodes and the calibration curve was used to calibrate the indoor LQI values for short ranges.

Free space calibration model for short ranges is used first time in obstacle free indoors. The modeling showed similar error distance results with the literature and justified its usage. WCL technique is employed to improve the calculated position accuracy. Distances between the calculated P(x, y) coordinates and the corners of respective triangles are used as weights. These weights are introduced with WCL techniques in each triangle and new unknown position coordinates Q(x, y) are calculated.

The average accuracy between the unknown position and the calculated position is found as 1.1 m. This was similar to the error values of calculated in the literature. For example in reference (Bal et al., 2010), average accuracy error was 1 to 2 m at indoors. In references (ni et al., 2004; Sugano et al., 2006), the average errors were 1 and 1.5 to 2 m, respectively.

Our application of numerical analysis technique to determine the d distances from LQIs introduced a new look into the randomness of the LQIs. An empirical formula is introduced to calculate d values from received LQI values. The error distance calculations revealed that the weight function w_i = 1/d produced the minimum error distances between the actual and the calculated coordinates. There were a few coordinates which did not follow this trend. This was due to the variance of LQI values in time. Finally, Trigonometric method together with WCL method produced a hybrid method of position calculation. This hybrid method generated an error margin of 1.1 m similar to literature. Hence, it can be an acceptable new technique for position detection in indoors.

REFERENCES

Bahl P, Padmanabhan VN (March 2000). RADAR: An in-building RF-based user location and tracking system,in: Proceedings of IEEE INFOCOM 2000, Tel-Aviv, Israel (March 2000), http://www.research.Microsoft.com/padmanab/papers/infocom2000.pdf.

Bal M, Xue H, Shen W, Ghenniwa H (2010). A 3D indoor location tracking and visualization system based on WSNs, IEEE, 978-1-4244-6587, pp. 1584-1590

Ergen SC (2004). "Zigbee/IEEE 802.15.4 Summary" http://pages.cs.wisc.edu/~suman/courses/838/papers/zigbee.pdf

Harter A, Hopper A, Steggles P, Ward A, Webster P (August 1999). The anatomy of a context aware application, In proceedings of the 5th annual ACM/IEEE International conference on Mobile Computing and Networking, pp. 59-68.

Hightower J, Wantand R, Borriello G (February 2000). SpotON: An indoor 3D location sensing technology based on RF signal strength, UW CSE00-02-02, February 2000, http://www.cs.washington.edu/homes/jeffro/pubs/hightower2000indoor/hightower2000indoor.pdf RadioFrequencyIdentification (RFID) homepage, http://www.aimglobal.org/technologies/rfid/ http://en.wikipedia.org/wiki/Bisection_method http://www.aimglobal.org/technologies/rfid/text-Awareness (LoCA 2005) at Pervasive 2005, May 2005 http://www.jennic.com/files/support_documentation/ JN-AN-1052-

ZigBee-Home-documentation/ Sensor-Demo-1v3.pdf http://www.jennic.com/jennic_support/application notes/jn-an 1052_home_sensor_demonstration_using_zigbee.

Jan BR (2007). Frank Gola- towski "weighted centroid localization in zigbee-based sensor networks", CELISCA centerfor life science automation, 2007.

Konrad L, Welsh M (2005). "MoteTrack: A Robust, Decentralized Approach to RF-Based Location Tracking," Proceedings of the International Workshop on Locationand Con13-RadioFrequencyldentification (RFID) homepage.

Koyuncu H, Yang SH (2010). " A survey of indoor positioning and object locating systems", IJCSNS, 10(5): 121-128

Lionel M, Yunhao NI (2004). LiuYiuChoLauand Abhishek P. Patil ; LANDMARC: IndoorLocation Sensing Using Active RFID Wireless Networks, 10: 701-710.

Ni LM, liu Y, Lau YC, Patil A (2004). Landmarc,indoor location sensing using active RFID, wireless Networks 10, Kluwer academic Publishers, pp. 701-710

Ralf G (2007). "Localization in zigbee-based wireless sensor networks" Technical report University of Rostock, Institute MD.

Rappaport TS (1996). Wireless Communication: principles and practice, Prentice hall Inc, New Jersey.

Sugano M, Kawazone T, Ohta Y, Murata M (2006). Indoor localization system using RSSI measurement of WSN based on zigbee Standard, ın proceedings wireless and optical communi- cations, IASTED/ACTA press, pp. 1-6

Texas instruments" Zigbeready RF transceiver" http://focus.ti.com/lit/ds/swrs041b/swrs041b.pdf, 2007.

Want R, Hopper A, Falcao V, Gibbons J (January 1992). The active Badge location system,ACM Transactions on Information systems, 40(1): 91-102.

Want R, Schilit B, Adams N, Gold R, Gold- berg D, Petersen K, Ellis J, Weiser M (1997). TheParctabUbiquitous Computing Experiment", BookChapter: "Mobile Computing", Kluwer Publishing, Edited by Tomas z Imielinski, Chapter 2: 45-101, ISBN 0-7923-9697-9.

Ward A, Jones A, Hopper A (1997). A neq location technique for the active office , In IEEE personal Communication Magazine, 4(5): 42-47.

A least square approach to analyze usage data for effective web personalization

S. S. Patil

Rajarambapu Institute of Technology Rajaramnagar/CSE, Sangli, India. E-mail: patil.sachin.s@gmail.com.

Web server logs have abundant information about the nature of users accessing it. The analysis of the user's current interest based on the navigational behavior may help the organizations to guide the users in their browsing activity and obtain relevant information in a shorter span of time (Sumathi and Padmaja, 2010). Web usage mining is used to discover interesting user navigation patterns and can be applied to many real-world problems, such as improving Web sites/pages, making additional topic or product recommendations, user/customer behavior studies, etc (Ratanakumar, 2010). Web usage mining, in conjunction with standard approaches to personalization helps to address some of the shortcomings of these techniques, including reliance on subjective lack of scalability, poor performance, user ratings and sparse data (Mobasher et al., 2002; Eirinaki and Vazirgiannis, 2003; Khalil et al., 2008; Forsati et al., 2009; Mobasher et al., 2001). But, it is not sufficient to discover patterns from usage data for performing the personalization tasks. It is necessary to derive a good quality of aggregate usage profiles which indeed will help to devise efficient recommendation for web personalization (Cooley et al., 1997; Srivatsava et al., 2000; Agarwal and Srikant, 1994). Also, the unsupervised and competitive learning algorithms has help to efficiently cluster user based access patterns by mining web logs (Hartigan and Wong, 1979; Ng et al., 2007; Memon and Dagli, 2003). This paper presents and experimentally evaluates a technique for finely tuning user clusters based on similar web access patterns on their usage profiles by approximating through least square approach. Each cluster is having users with similar browsing patterns. These clusters are useful in web personalization so that it communicates better with its users. Experimental results indicate that using the generated aggregate usage profiles with approximating clusters through least square approach effectively personalize at early stages of user visits to a site without deeper knowledge about them.

Key words: Aggregate usage profile, least square approach, web personalization, recommender systems, expectation maximization.

INTRODUCTION

Tremendous growth of unstructured information available on internet and e-commerce sites makes it very difficult to access relevant information quickly and efficiently. Web data research has encountered a lot of challenges such as scalability, multimedia and temporal issues etc. Web user drowns to huge information facing the problem of overloaded information.

Web personalization is the process based on users past behavior for providing users with relevant content including massive information of web pages link, relevant data, products etc. Traditionally, collaborative filtering technique was employed to do this task. It generally produces recommendations on objects yet not rated by user, by matching the ratings of current user for objects with those of similar users. To increase the user click rate and service quality of Internet on a specific website, Web developer or designer needs to know what the user really wants to do and its interest to customize web pages to the user by learning its navigational pattern. Various approaches are defined to unreal the applicative techniques to get higher and corrective recommendations for user surf.

OVERVIEW OF RELATED WORK

Various approaches have been devised for recommender

systems (Mobasher et al., 2002; Eirinaki and Vazirgiannis, 2003; Khalil et al., 2008; Forsati et al., 2009). The explicit feedback from the user or rating on items help to match interest with online clustering of users with "similar interest" to provide recommendations. But practically, it leads toward limitations of scalability and performance (Mobasher et al., 2001) due to the lack of sufficient user information. Other approaches relating usage mining are implied to discover patterns or usage profiles from implicit feedback such as page visits of users.

The offline pattern discovery using numerous data mining techniques are used to provide dynamic recommendations based on the user's short term interest. "Web Personalizer" a usage based Web Personalization system using Web mining techniques to provide dynamic recommendations was proposed by Mobasher et al. (2001). According to Mehrdad et al. (2009), a novel approach using LCS algorithm improves the quality of the recommendations system for predictions by classifying user navigation patterns. K-means clustering followed by classification for recommender systems (AlMurtadha et al., 2010) is used to predict the future navigations and has improved the accuracy of predictions. Recent developments for online personalization through usage mining have been proposed. In Mobasher et al. (2002), experimental evaluation of two different techniques such as PACT and ARHP based on the clustering of user transactions/pageviews, respectively for the discovery of usage profiles was proposed.

According to Şule and Ozsu (2003), Poisson parameters to determine the recommendation scores helped to focus on the discovery of user's interest in a session using clustering approach. They are used to recommend pages to the user. This novel approach in Şule and Ozsu (2003) involving integrated clustering, association rules and Markov models improved web page prediction accuracy. Various clustering algorithms had helped to group the user sessions as like K-means, Fuzzy C-means and subtractive clustering (Chiu, 1994; Bezdek, 1973; Ratanakumar, 2010; Memon and Dagli, 2003). The clusters formed as a result of applying these algorithms are aggregated to form web profiles. The recommendation engine uses these profiles, to generate pages for recommendation. In Vasumathi and Govardhan (2005) and Spiliopoulou (2000), formal concept analysis approach is used to discover user access patterns represented as association rules from web logs which can then be used for personalization and recommendation.

However, the existing system does not satisfy users particularly in large web sites in terms of the quality of recommendations. This paper proposes to classify user navigation patterns through web usage mining system and effectively provide online recommendation. The tested results on ritindia.edu dataset indicate to improve the quality of the system for recommendations.

METHODOLOGY

Personalization using usage mining consists of four basic stages. The process embeds of:

1. Data Preprocessing
2. Pattern discovery
3. Pattern recognition
4. Recommendation process

Classifying and matching an online user based on his browsing interests for recommendations of unvisited pages has been employed in this paper using usage mining to determine the interest of "similar" users. The recommendation (Mobasher et al., 2000) consists of offline component and online component. The offline component involves data preprocessing, pattern discovery and pattern analysis. The outcome of the offline component is the derivation of aggregate usage profiles using web usage mining techniques. The online component is responsible for matching the current user's profile to the aggregate usage profiles to generate the necessary recommendations.

Data preprocessing

Preprocessing is the primary task of personalization involving cleansing of data, session and user identification, page view and transaction identification (Mobasher et al., 2000; Sumathi et al., 2010; Suresh and Padmajavalli, 2006). Let there be set of pages P = $\{p_1, p_2, p_3, p_4, \ldots, p_n\}$ and set of n sessions, S = $\{s_1, s_2, s_3, \ldots, s_n\}$ where each $s_i \in S$ is a subset of P. A file consisting of session profile of user requests for pages is maintained.

In Sumathi and Padmaja (2010), for a particular session, a session-pageview matrix is maintained consisting of a sequence of page requests in that session. A row representing a session and every column represents a frequency of occurrence of pageview visit in a session. Then the weight of the pageview is determined by evaluating the importance of a page in terms of the ratio of the frequency of visits to the page with respect to the overall page visits in a session and is represented by a weighted session-pageview matrix. Each session s_i is modeled as a vector over the n-dimensional space of pageviews.

Pattern discovery

The primary task of pattern discovery is to find out the hidden patterns using various mining techniques such as clustering, association rule, classification etc., which helps to uncover the user behavior with respect to the site. It is an offline task which helps to determine sessions with similar navigational patterns/interest from the user session file. Clustering technique is employed to determine the session clusters using model-based expectation maximization as in Sumathi and Padmaja (2010). The profile interest is learnt by determining an aggregate usage profile using the formula:

$$wt(pg, up_c) = 1/nc \sum_{s \in c} w^s_{pg} \quad (1)$$

Wherein w^s_{pg} represents the weight of the page in session $s \in c$ and nc represents the number of sessions in cluster c. Table 1 shows the aggregate usage profiles for 6 clusters under 13 distinct categories of pageviews URLs (explained in experimental evaluation).

Pattern recognition

The individual profile effectiveness is measured using weighted average visit percentage. It is to represent the significance of user's

Table 1. Aggregate usage profiles.

Page view	C					
	C0	C1	C2	C3	C4	C5
Aboutkes	0.013	0.000	0.006	0.689	0.003	0.066
Aboutrit	0.002	0.006	0.589	0.456	0.082	0.000
Courses	0.023	0.000	0.043	0.004	0.823	0.078
Departments	0.000	0.009	0.003	0.001	0.023	0.889
Facilities	0.003	0.432	0.028	0.033	0.000	0.083
Faculty	0.007	0.003	0.789	0.073	0.032	0.071
Admission	0.946	0.001	0.016	0.000	0.646	0.946
Placement	0.004	0.843	0.000	0.023	0.014	0.000
Lifeatrit	0.000	0.009	0.022	0.012	0.765	0.004
Contact	0.005	0.017	0.013	0.000	0.001	0.923
Mission-vision	0.478	0.047	0.003	0.004	0.008	0.003
Achievements	0.001	0.011	0.034	0.003	0.013	0.801
Academics-at-rit	0.002	0.708	0.049	0.028	0.022	0.000

interest in the cluster. If the aggregate usage profiles consist of m clusters and k pages, then the significance in the cluster can be determined as follows:

$$\max_{i=0}^{m} (wt(pg_j, up_i)), 1 \le j \le 13 = M_{I(j)} \quad (2)$$

Where I (j) is the index of the maximum value in each page and $M_{I(j)}$ represents the maximum value. Also the weight of page is considered as per pageview j. This maximization function is used to recommend pages to users belonging to a profile/cluster.

Recommendation process

The recommendation engine is the online component of a usage-based personalization system. The goal of personalization based on anonymous Web usage data is to compute a recommendation set for the current (active) user session, consisting of the objects (links, ads, text, products, etc.) that most closely match the current user profile. Recommendation set can represent a long/short term view of user's navigational history based on the capability to track users across visits.

The test data of user sessions are taken as sequence of pages in time order. An active window size is fixed and those many pages are taken from the user session as active session. Then the similarity between the active session and all the cluster profiles is calculated using a vector similarity measure and the most similar profile selected for recommendations (Sumathi and Padmaja, 2010; Mobasher et al., 2002; Mobasher et al., 1999). If an active session is represented as s_i and cluster as c_k, then their similarity can be measured as follows:

$$sim(s_j, c_k) = \frac{\sum_{i-1}^{n} w_{i,j} * w_{i,k}}{\sqrt{\sum_{i-1}^{n} w_{i,j}^2 * \sqrt{\sum_{i-1}^{n} w_{i,k}^2}}} \quad (3)$$

Where $w_{i,j}$, represents weight of page i in active session j and $w_{i,k}$, represents weight of page i in cluster k. The method of *least squares* assumes that the best-fit similarity of a given type is the matching score that has the minimal sum of the deviations squared (*least square error*) from a given set of data. Suppose that the data points are sim (s_1,c_1), sim (s_2,c_2),...., sim (s_j,c_k) where s_j is the independent variable and c_k is the dependent variable. The fitting score (s_j) has the deviation (error) d from each data point, that is, $d_1 = c_1 - (s_1)$, $d_2 = c_2 - (s_2)$... $d_n = c_n - (s_n)$. According to the method of *least squares*, the best matching score has the property that:

$$\Pi = d_1^2 + d_2^2 + \ldots + d_n^2 = \sum_{i-1}^{n} d_i^2 = \sum_{i-1}^{n} [c_i - f(s_i)]^2 = \text{a min.} \quad (4)$$

$$sim'(sj,ck) = sim(sj,ck) - \Pi \quad (5)$$

This *least square error* approach helps to fine tune the scores such as to approximate user clusters based on similar web access patterns on their usage profiles. Then a recommendation score for each page view p in the selected cluster/profile is calculated. If C is the most similar cluster/profile to the active session S, then a recommendation score for each page view p in C is as:

$$\text{Rec}(S, p) = \sqrt{\text{weight}(p, C) * \text{sim}'(s_j, c_k)} \quad (6)$$

Profiles having a similarity greater than a threshold value μ_c are selected as matching clusters in the decreasing order of their scores. The weight of pageview p in C is computed twice that is, directly and indirectly but to compensate the impact, square root in the above function is taken and results are normalized to value between 0 and 1. If the pageview p is in the current active session, then its recommendation value is set to zero. These matching clusters can be used for recommending pages instantaneously which have not been visited by the user. Figure 1 shows the overall process of web personalization using web usage data.

Experimental evaluation

This section provides a detailed experimental evaluation of the profile generation techniques. The privately available data set at the University of Shivaji, containing web log files of ritindia.edu web site have been used for this research. It includes the page visits of users who visited the "ritindia.edu" web site in period of June 2006 to April 2011. The initial log file produced a total of 16,233 transactions and the total number of URLs representing pageviews was 27. By using support filtering for long transactions, pageviews appearing in less than 0.5% or more than 85% of transactions were eliminated. Also, short transactions with at least 5 references were eliminated. The visits are recorded at the level of URL category and in time order, which includes visits to major 13 distinct categories of pageviews URLs. Each sequence in the dataset corresponds to a user's request for a page. The 13 categories are shown in Table 2.

A clustering model is estimated using approximately 15,000 samples within the dataset. They are further classified into training and testing sets. Dataset is split into 70% training and 30% testing sets such that the model is designed using training set and then evaluated using test samples for performance. Applying the clustering algorithm for Expectation Minimization with 12 iterations

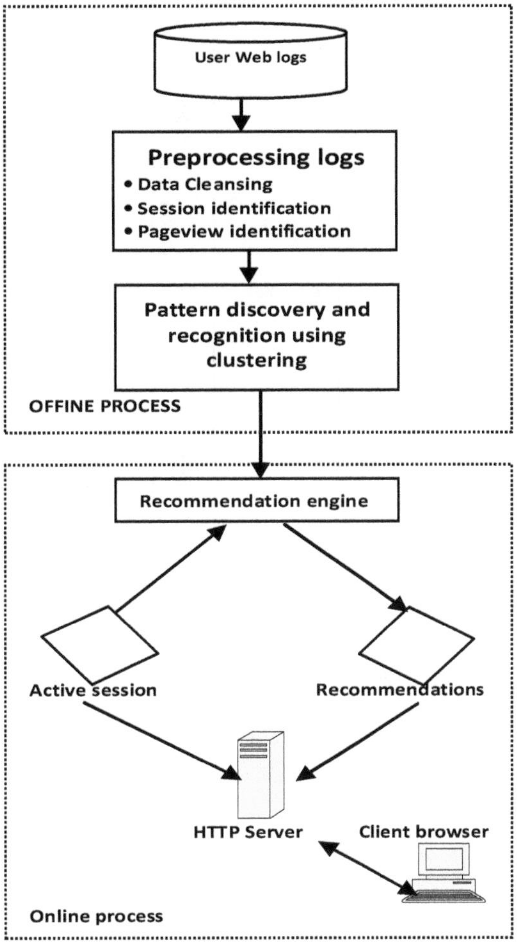

Figure 1. The overall process of personalization.

Table 2. Thirteen distinct categories of page views URLs.

Id	Category
1	aboutkes
2	aboutrit
3	courses
4	departments
5	facilities
6	faculty
7	admission
8	placement
9	lifeatrit
10	contact
11	mission-vision
12	achievements
13	academics-at- rit

results in 6 major clusters. Each cluster represents several sessions of navigational patterns representing "similar" interest in the web pages or the usage profile and the aggregate usage profile is determined using Equation 1. During the online phase, the pages visited in a session are stored in a user session file and after each page visit, the relative frequency of pageviews in the active session is determined. An active session with sliding window size 'n' (in our experiment, the size is 5 as it represents the average number of page visits in the dataset) consists of the current page visit and the most recent n-1 pages visited. The window slides, as the user

Table 3. Page visits in the sliding window.

Session	Order of visit	Window	Active session (page visited)				
1	1	1	1	0	0	0	0
1	2	2	1	8	0	0	0
2	1	1	1	0	0	0	0
2	2	2	1	8	0	0	0
2	3	3	1	8	13	0	0
3	1	1	1	0	0	0	0
3	2	2	1	13	0	0	0
3	3	3	1	13	1	0	0
3	4	4	1	13	1	13	0
3	5	5	1	13	1	13	1
3	6	6	13	1	13	1	7
3	7	7	1	13	1	7	1

Table 4. Frequency of page visited/weighted page view

Session	Order of visit	Aboutkes	Aboutrit	Courses	Department	Facilities	Faculty	Admission	Placement	Lifeatrit	Contact	Mission-vision	Achievement	Academis-at-rit
1	1	1	0	0	0	0	0	0	0	0	0	0	0	0
1	2	1	0	0	0	0	0	0	1	0	0	0	0	0
2	1	1	0	0	0	0	0	0	0	0	0	0	0	0
2	2	1	0	0	0	0	0	0	1	0	0	0	0	0
2	3	1	0	0	0	0	0	0	1	0	0	0	0	1
3	1	1	0	0	0	0	0	0	0	0	0	0	0	0
3	2	1	0	0	0	0	0	0	0	0	0	0	0	1
3	3	2	0	0	0	0	0	0	0	0	0	0	0	1
3	4	2	0	0	0	0	0	0	0	0	0	0	0	2
3	5	3	0	0	0	0	0	0	0	0	0	0	0	2
3	6	2	0	0	0	0	0	1	0	0	0	0	0	2
3	7	3	0	0	0	0	0	1	0	0	0	0	0	1

browses through various pages. Now, using the cosine similarity measure, the active session is matched with the aggregate usage profiles and matching cluster(s) having value greater than the threshold and are used for recommending pages exceeding threshold that have not been visited by the user. For example, consider the following 3 sessions consisting of page visits:

1 8
1 8 13
1 13 1 13 1 7 1

The sliding window consists of the pages 1 13 1 13 1 in the fifth page visit. Tables 3 and 4 represent the page visits and frequency of visited pages in the sliding window.

Table 5. Matching clusters.

Session	Order of visit/ window	Page visited	C0	C1	C2	C3	C4	C5
1	1	1	0.000	0.000	0.245	0.000	0.169	0.000
1	2	8	0.000	0.000	0.000	0.076	0.243	0.000
2	1	1	0.023	0.000	0.334	0.000	0.043	0.000
2	2	8	0.000	0.000	0.332	0.031	0.223	0.013
2	3	13	0.025	0.192	0.000	0.000	0.332	0.000
3	1	1	0.000	0.023	0.034	0.333	0.000	0.000
3	2	13	0.020	0.000	0.000	0.014	0.223	0.336
3	3	1	0.000	0.012	0.000	0.443	0.000	0.020
3	4	13	0.013	0.000	0.043	0.258	0.014	0.256
3	5	1	0.000	0.012	0.033	0.000	0.000	0.276
3	6	7	0.000	0.013	0.344	0.000	0.017	0.000
3	7	1	0.012	0.000	0.000	0.344	0.000	0.032

Table 6. Recommendation set for session 1, session 2 and session 3.

Session	Order of visit/ window	Active session window (pages)	Matching cluster(s)	Recommendation pages
1	1	1	2,4	2,3,6,7,9
1	2	1->8	2,3,4	2,3,6,7,9
2	1	1	2,4	2,3,6,7,9
2	2	1->8	2,3,4	2,3,6,7,9
2	3	1->8->13	1,2,3,4	2,3,6,7,9,11
3	1	1	2,4	2,3,6,7,9
3	2	1->13	2,4,5	2,3,4,6,7,9, 10,12
3	3	1->13->1	2,3,4,5	2,3,4,6,7,9, 10,12
3	4	1->13->1->13	2,3,4,5	2,3,4,6,7,9, 10,12
3	5	1->13->1->13->1	2,3,4,5	2,3,4,6,7,9, 10,12
3	6	13->1->13->1->7	2,3,4,5	2,3,4,6,9,10,12
3	7	1->13->1->7->1	2,3,4,5	2,3,4,6,9,10,12

It states the weight of the pageview by evaluating the importance of a page in terms of the ratio of the frequency of visits to the page with respect to the overall page visits in the active session.

Clusters greater than the threshold value, are chosen to be matching clusters as shown in Table5. This table depicts the comparative study of aggregate usage profiles and the maximization function to show recommendations. It has been found that when the user visits page 1 (window size 1), the appropriate clusters, exceeding the threshold value are cluster 2 and 4. It is seen that pages 2, 3, 6, 7, 9 can be recommended from cluster 2 and 4. Similarly, when the user visits page 8 subsequent to page visit 1(window size 2), the appropriate matching clusters are cluster 2, cluster 3 and cluster 4. As the window size increases to the fixed size limit (n = 5), correspondingly, the matching clusters for the visited page(s) in the active session and the recommendations are dynamic in nature. Table 6 shows the recommended set of pages for all 3 demo sessions.

As compared to experimental study in Sumathi and Padmaja (2010), the recommendation of pages for demo sessions is calculated on Equation 3 for measuring similarities of sessions. Then the pages are recommended in the session as per Equation 6 for simple similarities of clusters which provides a less precision for recommending the matching scores of clusters. As compared to same, the least square approach analysis in our study helps to find deviations and to refine further the recommendations as per Equation 6 with similarity measures. In Sumathi and Padmaja (2010), if the previous 3 demo samples are measured, then the recommendation set varies a lot recommending less pages under given threshold.

CONCLUSION AND FUTURE WORK

The ability to collect detailed usage data at the level of individual mouse click provides Web-based companies with a tremendous opportunity for personalizing the Web experience of clients. The practicality of employing Web usage mining techniques for personalization is directly related to the discovery of effective aggregate profiles that can successfully capture relevant user navigational patterns and can be used as part of usage-based recommender system to provide real-time personalization.

In this work, the primary objective was to classify and match an online user based on his browsing interests.

Identification of the current interests of the user based on the short-term navigational patterns instead of explicit user information has proved to be one of the potential sources for recommendation of pages. In particular context of anonymous usage data, these work under least square approximation show promise in creating effective personalization solutions that can help retain and convert unidentified visitors based on their activities in the early stages of their visits. Future work involves with various types of transactions derived from user sessions, such as to isolate specific types of "content" pages in the recommendation process. Also, the plan is to incorporate client-side agents and use of optimization techniques to assess the quality of recommendations.

REFERENCES

Agarwal R, Srikant R (1994). Fast Algorithms for Mining Association Rules in Large Database. Procd. Conf. on Very Large Data Bases, USA., 1: 12-15.

AlMurtadha Y, Sulaiman M, Mustapha N, Udzir N (2010). Mining Web Navigation Profiles for Recommendation System. Inform. Technol. J., 9: 790-796.

Bezdek J (1973). Fuzzy Mathematics in Pattern Classification, Cornell Univ. PhD Thesis.

Chiu S (1994). Fuzzy Model Identification Based on Cluster Estimation. J. Intelligent Fuzzy Syst., 2(3): 268-278

Cooley R, Mobasher B, Srivatsava J (1997). Web Mining: Information and Pattern Discovery on the World Wide Web. IEEE., 9: 558-567.

Eirinaki M, Vazirgiannis M (2003). Web mining for Web personalization.ACM, 3(1): 1-27

Forsati R, Meybodi M, Ghari N (2009). Web Page Personalization based on Weighted Association Rules. Internet Conf. Electron. Comp.Tech., 1: 130-135.

Hartigan T, Wong A (1979). A K-Means Clustering Algorithm. Appl. Statistics, 28: 100-108.

Khalil F, Jiuyong L,Hua W (2008). Integrating Recommendation Models for Improved Web Page Prediction Accuracy. Australa. Conf. Comp. Sci., 74: 91-100.

Mehrdad J, Norwati M, Ali M, Nasir B (2009). A Recommender System for Online Personalization in the WUM Applications. Procd. World Congress Engr. Comp. Sci., 9(2).

Memon K, Dagli C (2003). Web Personalization using Neuro-Fuzzy Clustering. IEEE., 1: 525-529.

Mobasher B, Cooley R, Srivatsava J (1999). Creating Adaptive Web Sites Through Usage-Based Clustering of URLs. Proc. KDEX '99. Workshop on Knowledge and Data Engineering Exchange.

Mobasher B, Cooley R, Srivatsava J (2000). Automatic Personalization Based on Web Usage Mining. ACM., 43:142-151.

Mobasher B, Dai H, Luoand T, Nakagawa (2001). Improving the effectiveness of collaborative filtering on anonymous Web usage data. IJCAI, Seattle.

Mobasher B, Honghua D, Tao L, Nakagawa M (2002). Discovery and Evaluation of Aggregate Usage Profiles for Web Personalization. ACM., 6: 61-82.

Ng K, Junjie M, Huang J, Zengyou Y (2007). On the Impact of Dissimilarities Measure in K-modes Clustering Algo. IEEE., 29(3).

Ratanakumar J (2010). An Implementation of Web Personalization Using Mining Techniques. J. Theoretical Appl. I. T., 5(1): 67-73.

Spiliopoulou M (2000). Web usage mining for Web Site Evaluation. ACM., 43(8): 127-134.

Srivatsava J, Cooley R, Deshpande M, Tan P (2000). Web Usage Mining: Discovery and Applications of Usage Patterns from Web Data. ACM., 1: 12-23.

Şule G, Ozsu M (2003). A User Interest Model for Web Page Navigation. DMAK, Seoul, 1: 46-57.

Sumathi C, Padmaja R, Valli, Santhanam T (2010). J. Comp. Sci., 1: 785-793.

Sumathi CP, Padmaja Valli R (2010).Automatic Recommendation of Web Pages in Web Usage Mining. Internet J. Comp. Sci. Engr., 2(9).

Suresh R, Padmajavalli R (2006). Overview of Data Preprocessing in Data and Web Usage Mining. IEEE., 1: 193-198.

Vasumathi D, Govardhan A (2005). Efficient Web Usage Mining Based On Formal Concept Analysis. IFIP., 163(2): 99-108.

10

A shift-add algorithm for computing Bezier curves

GU Feng

ZheJiang Technical Institute of Economics, Hangzhou, China. E-mail:coolfun630@hotmail.com

A shift-add algorithm based on coordinate rotation digital computer algorithm for computing Bezier curves was presented in this paper. This algorithm can be implemented in basic computing system (which deals only with shift, add and logical operations) which exists in many areas. Convergence of the algorithm was proved. Error estimation was analyzed. A numerical experiment was carried out to validate algorithm's effectiveness and efficiency.

Key words: Bezier curve, shift-add algorithm, basic computing system, CORDIC, approximation.

INTRODUCTION

Bezier curves are very popular in CAD/CAM and other curve fitting systems. Bezier spline of degree *n* (order *n*+1) can be obtained by deCasteljau algorithm as an interpolation between (*n*+1) control points P_0, P_1, ... , P_n . The general expression for Bezier curve $P(t)$ of degree *n* (order *n*+1) is

$$B_0^0(t) = 1,$$

$$B_i^k(t) = (1-t)B_i^{k-1}(t) + tB_{i-1}^{k-1}(t), \text{ (}k\text{=1, 2, , }n.\ i\text{=0, 1, …, }k.)$$

$$P(t) = \sum_{i=0}^{n} B_i^n(t)P_i$$

where $B_i^k(t)$ (*k*=0,1,2,…,*n*. *i*=0,1,…,*k*) are Bernstein polynomials, P_i (*i*=0,1,…,*n*) are control points (Aumann, 1997; Catherine and Sonya, 2003; Farin 1997).

Different methods for constructing Bezier curves were developed (Catherine and Sonya, 2003; Han et al., 2008; Popiel and Noakes, 2006). Existing algorithms for constructing Bezier curves usually run in advanced computing systems. In this paper we discuss how to computing Bezier curves in a basic computing system. A basic computing system deals only with shift, add and logical operations. Basic computing systems exist in many application systems such as industrial control systems, military application systems, medical application systems, etc. Single chip microcomputers and Field Programmable Gate Arrays (FPGA) are good examples. Coordinate rotation digital computer (CORDIC) algorithms are well known shift-add algorithms for computing a wide range of elementary functions including trigonometric, hyperbolic, linear and logarithmic functions (Volder, 1959; Muller, 2006; Neil, 1998). CORDIC algorithms have been generalized (Feng, 2006; Xiaobo et al., 1991). Their convergences and error estimations have been analyzed (Feng, 2006). With the development of hardware technique, these fast-united shift-add algorithms can be implemented in hardware system (even multipliers need not be used) (Ray, 1998). These algorithms can also be coded with assembly language.

In this paper a shift-add algorithm based on CORDIC algorithm for computing Bezier curves is presented.

Variables that are made used of include:

A, $(a_{ij})_{n\times n}$: matrixes.

$B_i^k(t)$ (*k*=0,1,2,…,*n*. *i*=0,1,…,*k*): Bernstein polynomials of degree *k*.

BSx , BSy ,*bst*: coordinates of a point on a Bezier curve.

$b_j^i(t)$: real values of Bernstein polynomials of degree *i*.

$bs(t)$: real value of a Bezier curve.

$F_N(x,\delta)$: *x*'s measurement expansion with $\{\delta_i\}_0^\infty$.

I: identity matrix.

i,j,k,n,m,N: integer variables.

P_i (*i*=0,1,…,*n*): control points.

P_i^x , P_i^y , P_i^u (*i*=0,1,…,*n*): coordinates of a control point P_i.

$R(\delta)$: the measurement radius of a normal series

$\{\delta_i\}_0^\infty$.

$sg(x)$: the sign function.

s, s_i (i=0,1,...): sign of a number.

t,u,v,w, w_1 ,x,y,z, x_i , y_i , z_i (i=0,1,...): real variables.

ε , ε_i (i=0,1,...): the upper bound of error.

$\{\delta_i\}_0^\infty$: a normal series.

DESCRIPTION OF THE ALGORITHM

A sign function and a positive number series (Feng, 2006) are defined as follows;

$$sg(x)=\begin{cases}1 & x\geq 0\\ -1 & x<0\end{cases}$$

$$\{\delta_i\}_0^\infty = \{2^{-i}\}_0^\infty$$

Let $\{P_i=(P_i^x,P_i^y)\}_0^n$ be control points. $B_i^k(t)$ (k=0,1,2,...,n. i=0,1,...,k. $t\in[0,1]$) denote Bernstein polynomials,. ε is the upper bound of error. The shift-add algorithm for computing Bezier curves consists of one main program and three subprograms.

Subprogram 1: UV(u,v,ε).

1° if u=0 or v=0 then result:=0. Stop.
2° s:=1.
if u<0 then
begin
s:=-s;
u:=-u.
end;
if v<0 then
begin
s:=-s;
v:=-v.
end;
3° m:=0;
while $u>1$ do
begin

$u:=\frac{u}{2}$;

m:= m+1.
end;
4° N:=2;

$\varepsilon:=2^{-m}\times\varepsilon$;

while $\delta_{N-2}>\varepsilon$ do N:=N+1;

5° i:=1; $x_1:=u$, $y_1:=v$, $z_1:=0$.

6° while i<N do
begin

$s_i:=sg(x_i)$;

$x_{i+1}:=x_i+s_i\times\delta_i$;

$z_{i+1}:=z_i+s_i\times\delta_i\times y_1$;

i:=i+1;
end;

7° $z_N:=s\times 2^m\times z_N$.

result: = z_N . Stop.

Subprogram2: Bernstein (n,t,ε).

1° $B_0^0:=1$;
for i:=1 to n
begin

$B_{-1}^i:=0$;

$B_{i+1}^i:=0$;

end;

2° $\varepsilon_1:=\varepsilon\times 2^{-1}$;

while $UV(\varepsilon_1,n,\varepsilon\times 2^{-1})>\varepsilon$ do $\varepsilon_1:=\varepsilon_1\times 2^{-1}$;

3° for i:=1 to n
for j:=0 to i

$B_j^i(t):=$ UV($1-t,B_j^{i-1}(t),\varepsilon_1$)+UV($t,B_{j-1}^{i-1}(t),\varepsilon_1$);

4° Output $B_j^n(t), j=0,...,n.$ Stop.

Subprogram3: BS($n,t,P_{i=0...n}^u,\varepsilon$).

1° w:=0;
for i:=0 to n

$w:=w+sg(P_i^u)\times P_i^u$;

w:=w+1;

$w_1:=UV(w,n+1,\varepsilon\times 2^{-1})$;

$\varepsilon_1:=\varepsilon$;

while $UV(\varepsilon_1,w,\varepsilon\times 2^{-1})>\varepsilon$ do $\varepsilon_1:=\varepsilon_1\times 2^{-1}$;

$\varepsilon_2:=\varepsilon$;

while $UV(\varepsilon_2,w_1,\varepsilon\times 2^{-1})>\varepsilon$ do $\varepsilon_2:=\varepsilon_2\times 2^{-1}$;

2° Bernstein (n,t,ε_1);

bst:=0;
3° for i:=0 to n

$bst:=bst+UV(P_i^u,B_i^n(t),\varepsilon_2)$;

4° Output *bst.* Stop.

Main program: Bezier Curve $(n,t,P_{i=0...n},\varepsilon)$

1° BSx =BS($n,t,P^x_{i=0...n},\varepsilon$).

2° BSy =BS($n,t,P^y_{i=0...n},\varepsilon$).

3° Output BSx , BSy . Stop.

Remarks,

1. Only operations shifting (i.e. $2^{-i}\times t$) and adding were concerned in the algorithm.
2. The determination of iteration number N in Subprogram 1 is based on Theorem 1.
3. In Subprogram 2, $\varepsilon_1 \le \frac{\varepsilon}{2n}$.
4. In Subprogram 3, $\varepsilon_1 \le \frac{\varepsilon}{\sum_{i=0}^{n}|P_i^u|+1}$,

$$\varepsilon_2 \le \frac{\varepsilon}{(n+1)\left(\sum_{i=0}^{n}|P_i^u|+1\right)}.$$

5. Experience showed that Subprogram 1 usually runs not more than 28 steps, so it is a fast algorithm.

CONVERGENCE AND ERROR ESTIMATION OF THE ALGORITHM

$\{\delta_i\}_0^\infty = \{2^{-i}\}_0^\infty$ is a normal series, with measurement radius $R(\delta)=\sum_{i=0}^{\infty}\delta_i = 2$ (Feng, 2006).

Let $A=\begin{pmatrix}0 & 0\\ 1 & 0\end{pmatrix}$. There are $A^i=\begin{pmatrix}0 & 0\\ 0 & 0\end{pmatrix}(i=2,3,......)$,

and $e^{Ax}=\sum_{i=0}^{\infty}\frac{(Ax)^i}{i!}=I+Ax=\begin{pmatrix}1 & 0\\ x & 1\end{pmatrix}$.

Let $x\approx F_N(x,\delta)=\sum_{i=0}^{N}sg(x_i)\delta_i$ be *x*'s measurement expansion with $\{\delta_i\}_0^\infty$ $R(\delta)=\sum_{i=0}^{\infty}\delta_i=2$ (Feng, 2006).

There is,

$$\begin{pmatrix}1 & 0\\ x & 1\end{pmatrix}=e^{Ax}\approx e^{A\sum_{i=0}^{N}sg(x_i)\delta_i}=\prod_{i=0}^{N}e^{Asg(x_i)\delta_i}=\prod_{i=0}^{N}\begin{pmatrix}1 & 0\\ sg(x_i)\delta_i & 1\end{pmatrix},$$

$$\begin{pmatrix}y\\ xy\end{pmatrix}=\begin{pmatrix}1 & 0\\ x & 1\end{pmatrix}\begin{pmatrix}y\\ 0\end{pmatrix}\approx\prod_{i=0}^{N}\begin{pmatrix}1 & 0\\ sg(x_i)\cdot\delta_i & 1\end{pmatrix}\begin{pmatrix}y\\ 0\end{pmatrix}.$$

It is equivalent to the following iterative process,

$$\begin{cases}x_0=0,\ \ z_0=0\\ s_i=sg(x-x_i)\\ x_{i+1}=x_i+s_i*2^{-i}\\ z_{i+1}=z_i-s_i*2^{-i}*y\quad i=1,2,\cdots\cdots\end{cases}\qquad(1)$$

When *n* is big enough, there are $x_{n+1}\approx x$, $z_{n+1}\approx xy$.

5° and 6° of Subprogram1 UV(u,v,ε) in the description of algorithm is based on iterative process (1).

Theorem1: Let $\{\delta_i\}_0^{+\infty}=\{2^{-i}\}_0^{+\infty}$. If $x\in[-R(\delta),R(\delta)]=[-2,2]$ then,

(a) $\{x_i\}$ defined by iterative process (1) converges to *x* and there is
$|x-x_N|\le\delta_{N-1}$.

(b) $\{z_i\}$ defined by iterative process (1) converges to xy and there is an error estimation,
$|z_N-xy|\le|y|(1+|x|)(1+\delta_N)\delta_N$.

(c) $\{z_i\}$ in Subprogram1 UV(u,v,ε) converges to xy. Its calculation error is not more than ε.

Proof: (a) From iterative process (1) it is easy to know that $x_N-x_{N+k}=\sum_{j=N}^{N+k-1}s_j\delta_j$.

From Lemma 1 in (Feng, 2006). there is

$$|x_N-x_{N+k}|=\sum_{j=N}^{N+k-1}\delta_j\le\sum_{j=N}^{\infty}\delta_j\le\delta_{N-1}$$

$\therefore\{x_i\}$ is a Cauchy series. From construct of algorithm there must be $x_i\to x\,(i\to\infty)$.

Let $k\to\infty$ there is $|x-x_N|\le\delta_{N-1}$.

(b) Let *x*'s measurement expansion with $\{\delta_i\}_0^\infty$ be $x=\sum_{i=0}^{\infty}s_i\delta_i$ [4], and $\left\|(a_{ij})_{n\times n}\right\|_\infty=\max_{1\le i\le n}\sum_{j=1}^{n}|a_{ij}|$.

For $A=\begin{pmatrix}0 & 0\\ 1 & 0\end{pmatrix}$, $\|A\|_\infty = 1$.

$$\left\|e^{Ax}\right\|_\infty = \left\|\begin{pmatrix}1 & 0\\ x & 1\end{pmatrix}\right\|_\infty = 1+|x|.$$

Because N>0, from Lemma 1 in [4] there is

$$|z_N - xy| \le \left\| e^{Ax}\begin{pmatrix}y\\0\end{pmatrix} - e^{A\sum_{i=0}^{N} s_i\delta_i}\begin{pmatrix}y\\0\end{pmatrix}\right\|_\infty$$

$$\le \left\| e^{Ax} - e^{A\sum_{i=0}^{+N} s_i\delta_i}\right\|_\infty \left\|\begin{pmatrix}y\\0\end{pmatrix}\right\|_\infty = \left\|\begin{pmatrix}y\\0\end{pmatrix}\right\|_\infty \left\|e^{Ax}\right\|_\infty \left\| I - e^{-A\sum_{i=N+1}^{+\infty} s_i\delta_i}\right\|_\infty$$

$$= \left\|\begin{pmatrix}y\\0\end{pmatrix}\right\|_\infty \left\|e^{Ax}\right\|_\infty \left\| I - \left(I + \sum_{k=1}^{+\infty} \frac{\left(-A\sum_{i=N+1}^{+\infty} s_i\delta_i\right)^k}{k!}\right)\right\|_\infty$$

$$= \left\|\begin{pmatrix}y\\0\end{pmatrix}\right\|_\infty \left\|e^{Ax}\right\|_\infty \left\| A\cdot \sum_{i=N+1}^{+\infty} s_i\delta_i \cdot \sum_{k=0}^{+\infty} \frac{1}{k+1} \frac{\left(-A\sum_{i=N+1}^{+\infty} s_i\delta_i\right)^k}{k!}\right\|_\infty$$

$$\le \left\|\begin{pmatrix}y\\0\end{pmatrix}\right\|_\infty \left\|e^{Ax}\right\|_\infty \|A\|_\infty \left|\sum_{i=N+1}^{+\infty} s_i\delta_i\right| \left\| e^{\left|A\sum_{i=N+1}^{+\infty} s_i\delta_i\right|}\right\|_\infty$$

$$= \left\|\begin{pmatrix}y\\0\end{pmatrix}\right\|_\infty \left\|e^{Ax}\right\|_\infty \|A\|_\infty \sum_{i=N+1}^{+\infty} \delta_i \cdot \left\| e^{\left|\sum_{i=N+1}^{+\infty} s_i\delta_i\right| A}\right\|_\infty$$

$$= |y|(1+|x|)\cdot \sum_{i=N+1}^{+\infty}\delta_i \cdot \left(1 + \left|\sum_{i=N+1}^{+\infty} s_i\delta_i\right|\right)$$

$$\le |y|(1+|x|)\cdot(1+\delta_N)\cdot\delta_N$$

$$< |y|(1+|x|)\cdot\delta_{N-1}.$$

(c) If *u*=0 or *v*=0 procedure just simply output result *uv*=0.

When $uv \ne 0$, *u* and *v* were pre-processed as $uv = s\times 2^m \times u_1 v_1$ in 2° and 3° of Subprogram1 UV (u, v, ε). Here is 1 or -1. u_1 and v_1 were limited in (0,1]. From (b), for result z'_N of 6° there is

$$|z'_N - u_1v_1| < |u_1|(1+|v_1|)\cdot\delta_{N-1} \le 2\delta_{N-1} < \delta_{N-2}$$

In 4° of the procedure, iterative number N was set to ensure $\delta_{N-2} \le 2^{-m}\times\varepsilon$. So for last result $z_N = s\times 2^m \times z'_N$ there is

$$|z_N - uv| < 2^m \times \delta_{N-2} \le \varepsilon.$$

Proven.

Theorem 2: $B_j^n(t)\,(j=0,\dots,n)$ in Subprogram2 Bernstein (n, t, ε) are calculated values of Bernstein polynomials. The upper bound of calculation error is ε.

Proof: We use inductive reasoning to prove result. For *n*=1,

$$B_{-1}^0(t)=0, B_0^0(t)=1, B_1^0(t)=0.$$

$$B_{-1}^1(t)=0,$$

$$B_0^1(t) = UV(1-t, B_0^0(t), \varepsilon_1) + UV(t, B_{-1}^0(t), \varepsilon_1),$$

$$B_1^1(t) = UV(1-t, B_1^0(t), \varepsilon_1) + UV(t, B_0^0(t), \varepsilon_1),$$

$$B_2^1(t)=0.$$

From procedure we know $\varepsilon_1 \le \frac{\varepsilon}{2n}$. So calculation errors of $B_0^1(t)$ and $B_1^1(t)$ are not more than $2\times\varepsilon_1 \le \frac{\varepsilon}{n}$. Inductive assuming calculation errors of $B_j^{i-1}(t)$ (*j*=0,…,*i*-1) are not more than $\frac{(i-1)\varepsilon}{n}$. Let real values of Bernstein polynomials be $b_j^i(t)$, real calculation error of $UV(1-t, B_j^{i-1}(t), \varepsilon_1)$ be ε_j. There is,

$$\left|B_j^i(t) - b_j^i(t)\right| =$$

$$\left|UV\left(1-t, B_j^{i-1}(t), \varepsilon_1\right) + UV\left(t, B_{j-1}^{i-1}(t), \varepsilon_1\right) - (1-t)b_j^{i-1}(t) - tb_{j-1}^{i-1}(t)\right|$$

$$= \left|(1-t)B_j^{i-1}(t) + \varepsilon_j + tB_{j-1}^{i-1}(t) + \varepsilon_{j-1} - (1-t)b_j^{i-1}(t) - tb_{j-1}^{i-1}\right|$$

$$\le (1-t)\left|B_j^{i-1}(t) - b_j^{i-1}(t)\right| + t\left|B_{j-1}^{i-1}(t) - b_{j-1}^{i-1}\right| + 2\times\frac{\varepsilon}{2n}$$

$$\le (1-t)\frac{(i-1)\varepsilon}{n} + t\frac{(i-1)\varepsilon}{n} + \frac{\varepsilon}{n}$$

$$= \frac{i\varepsilon}{n} \quad j=0,1,\dots,i.$$

That means the upper bound of calculation errors of $B_j^n(t)$ (j=0,1, … ,n) is ε. Result proved.

Theorem 3: The upper bound of calculation error of

Table 1. Calculated values of the cubic Bezier curve.

t	Bernstein polynomials of degree 3				The cubic Bezier curve	
	$B_0^3(t)$	$B_1^3(t)$	$B_2^3(t)$	$B_3^3(t)$	*X(t)*	*Y(t)*
0.0	1.0000000075	0	0	0	0.300000003	0.300000005
0.1	0.7290000054	0.2429999958	0.0269999989	0.0009999999	0.332900002	0.375600005
0.2	0.5120000014	0.3839999993	0.0959999994	0.0079999999	0.371200002	0.424800001
0.3	0.3429999989	0.4410000002	0.1890000007	0.0270000002	0.414300002	0.451200003
0.4	0.2159999976	0.4319999992	0.2880000021	0.0640000011	0.461600002	0.458400001
0.5	0.1250000279	0.3750000084	0.3750000084	0.1250000028	0.512500013	0.450000021
0.6	0.0640000011	0.2880000021	0.4319999992	0.2159999976	0.566400000	0.429600001
0.7	0.0270000002	0.1890000007	0.4410000002	0.3429999989	0.622700002	0.400800003
0.8	0.0079999999	0.0959999994	0.3839999993	0.5120000014	0.680800003	0.367200000
0.9	0.0009999999	0.0269999989	0.2429999958	0.7290000054	0.740100005	0.332400003
1.0	0	0	0	1.0000000075	0.800000007	0.300000005

bst in Subprogram3 BS ($t, P^u_{i=0\dots n}, \varepsilon$) is ε.

Proof: Let real values of Bernstein polynomials be $b_j^i(t)$, real value of Bezier spline be $bs(t)=\sum_{i=0}^{n} P_i^u b_i^n(t)$, real calculation error of $UV(P_i^u, B_i^n(t), \varepsilon_2)$ be ε_i, $0<\varepsilon_i\le\varepsilon_2$. Because $\varepsilon_1 \le \dfrac{\varepsilon}{\sum_{i=0}^{n}|P_i^u|+1}$ and $\varepsilon_2 \le \dfrac{\varepsilon}{(n+1)\left(\sum_{i=0}^{n}|P_i^u|+1\right)}$, we have,

$$|bst-bs(t)| = \left|\sum_{i=0}^{n} UV(P_i^u, B_i^n(t), \varepsilon_2) - \sum_{i=0}^{n} P_i^u b_i^n(t)\right|$$

$$= \left|\sum_{i=0}^{n}\left(P_i^u B_i^n(t)+\varepsilon_i\right) - \sum_{i=0}^{n} P_i^u b_i^n(t)\right|$$

$$= \left|\sum_{i=0}^{n} P_i^u B_i^n(t) + \sum_{i=0}^{n}\varepsilon_i - \sum_{i=0}^{n} P_i^u b_i^n(t)\right|$$

$$\le \left|\sum_{i=0}^{n} P_i^u B_i^n(t) - \sum_{i=0}^{n} P_i^u b_i^n(t)\right| + (n+1)\varepsilon_2$$

$$\le \sum_{i=0}^{n}|P_i^u|\left|B_i^n(t)-b_i^n(t)\right| + (n+1)\frac{\varepsilon}{(n+1)\left(\sum_{i=0}^{n}|P_i^u|+1\right)}$$

$$\le \left(\sum_{i=0}^{n}|P_i^u|\right)\varepsilon_1 + \frac{\varepsilon}{\sum_{i=0}^{n}|P_i^u|+1}$$

$$\le \left(\sum_{i=0}^{n}|P_i^u|\right)\frac{\varepsilon}{\sum_{i=0}^{n}|P_i^u|+1} + \frac{\varepsilon}{\sum_{i=0}^{n}|P_i^u|+1} = \varepsilon$$

Result proved.

Theorem 4: The upper bound of calculation error of Bezier curves with this algorithm is $\sqrt{2}\varepsilon$.

Proof: Let $BSx(t)=\sum_{i=0}^{n} P_i^x b_i^n(t)$ and $BSy(t)=\sum_{i=0}^{n} P_i^y b_i^n(t)$ denote *x* value and *y* value of Bezier curve. From Theorem 3, both values' calculation error are not more than ε, then the overall error is not more than of $\sqrt{\varepsilon^2+\varepsilon^2}=\sqrt{2}\varepsilon$. Proven.

NUMERICAL EXPERIMENT

Experiment 1: Given 4 control points (0.3, 0.3), (0.4, 0.6), (0.6, 0.4), (0.8, 0.3) and the upper bound of error $\varepsilon=5\times10^{-7}$. Using algorithm presented in this paper to compute a cubic Bezier curve. Results are shown below. Iteration of Subprogram1 UV(u, v, ε) is not more than 28 steps.

Real velues of Bernstein polynomials and the cubic Bezier curve are shown in . Tables 1, 2 and Figure 1,

Experiment 2: For another set of control points, (0, 0.8), (0.3, 0.4),(0.6, 0.2), (0.9, 0.6), and the upper bound of

Table 2. Real values of the cubic Bezier curve.

t	Bernstein polynomials of degree 3				The cubic Bezier curve	
	$B_0^3(t)$	$B_1^3(t)$	$B_2^3(t)$	$B_3^3(t)$	*X(t)*	*Y(t)*
0.0	1	0	0	0	0.3	0.3
0.1	0.729	0.243	0.027	0.001	0.3329	0.3756
0.2	0.512	0.384	0.096	0.008	0.3712	0.4248
0.3	0.343	0.441	0.189	0.027	0.4143	0.4512
0.4	0.216	0.432	0.288	0.064	0.4616	0.4584
0.5	0.125	0.375	0.375	0.125	0.5125	0.45
0.6	0.064	0.288	0.432	0.216	0.5664	0.4296
0.7	0.027	0.189	0.441	0.343	0.6227	0.4008
0.8	0.008	0.096	0.384	0.512	0.6808	0.3672
0.9	0.001	0.027	0.243	0.729	0.7401	0.3324
1.0	0	0	0	1	0.8	0.3

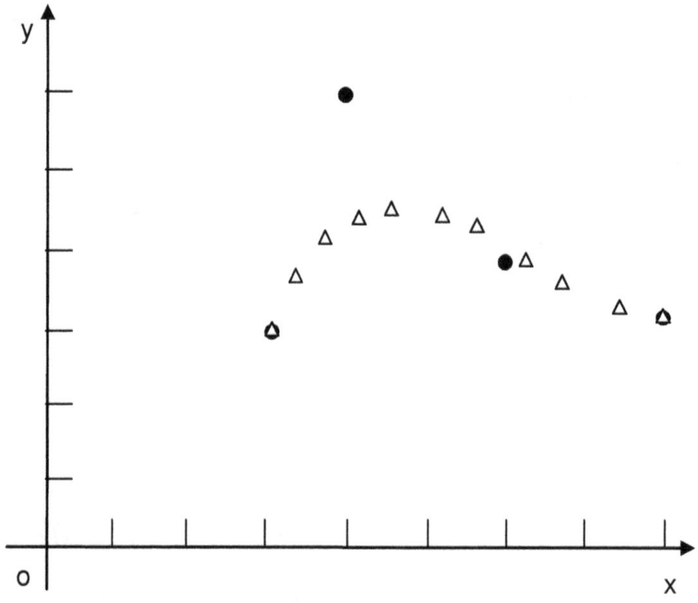

Figure 1. Data points of the cubic Bezier curve.

error $\varepsilon = 5\times10^{-7}$, computing results of a cubic Bezier curve are shown in Table 3 and Figure 2.

Results for Bernstein polynomials of degree 3 are the same as those in experiment 1. Iteration of Subprogram1 UV(u, v, ε) is not more than 27 steps.

Experiment 3: For control points (0, 0.8), (0.5, 0.3), (0.9, 0.6) and the upper bound of error $\varepsilon = 5\times10^{-7}$, generate a quadratic Bezier curve. Calculated values and real values of both Bernstein polynomials and the Bezier curve are shown in Table 4 and Figure 3. Iteration of Subprogram1 UV (u, v, ε) is not more than 25 steps. Real velues of Bernstein polynomials of degree 2 and the quadratic Bezier curve are shown in Table 5 and Figure 3, all calculation errors are under control.

Conclusion

Above are some discussions for a shift-add algorithm based on CORDIC algorithm for computing Bezier curves. This algorithm can be implemented in basic computing system which exists in many areas.

Theoretical analysis showed the convergence of the algorithm. Error estimations were provided. A numerical experiment was carried out to validate the algorithm's effectiveness and efficiency. We can say this is a fast,

Table 3. Calculated values and real values of the cubic Bezier curve.

t	Calculted values		Real values	
	X(t)	Y(t)	X(t)	Y(t)
0.0	0	0.800000015	0	0.8
0.1	0.090000034	0.686400012	0.09	0.6864
0.2	0.179999988	0.587799971	0.18	0.5872
0.3	0.269999984	0.504799997	0.27	0.5048
0.4	0.359999997	0.441600026	0.36	0.4416
0.5	0.450000046	0.400000053	0.45	0.4
0.6	0.540000019	0.382400008	0.54	0.3824
0.7	0.630000006	0.391199973	0.63	0.3912
0.8	0.719999982	0.428799986	0.72	0.4288
0.9	0.810000010	0.497600000	0.81	0.4976
1.0	0.900000011	0.600000007	0.9	0.6

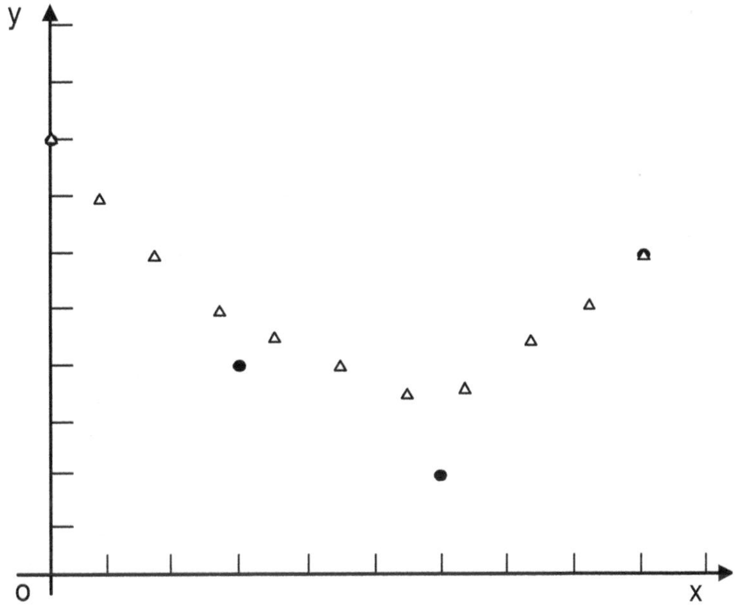

Figure 2. Data points of the cubic Bezier curve.

Table 4. Calculated values of the quadratic Bezier curve.

t	Bernstein Polynomials of degree 2			The quadratic Bezier curve	
	$B_0^2(t)$	$B_1^2(t)$	$B_2^2(t)$	*X(t)*	*Y(t)*
0.0	1.000000030	0	0	0	0.8000000060
0.1	0.809999984	0.180000040	0.010000005	0.0990001645	0.7080000041
0.2	0.639999995	0.319999983	0.039999995	0.1959999453	0.6319999767
0.3	0.490000025	0.420000018	0.090000007	0.2910000278	0.5720000536
0.4	0.369999993	0.480000002	0.160000005	0.3840000637	0.5280000117
0.5	0.250000030	0.500000060	0.250000030	0.4750000805	0.5000000894
0.6	0.160000005	0.480000002	0.359999993	0.5640000482	0.4880000045
0.7	0.090000007	0.420000018	0.490000025	0.6510000743	0.4920000095
0.8	0.039999995	0.319999983	0.639999995	0.7359999453	0.5119999767
0.9	0.010000005	0.180000040	0.809999984	0.8190001329	0.5480000255
1.0	0	0	1.000000030	0.9000000328	0.6000000119

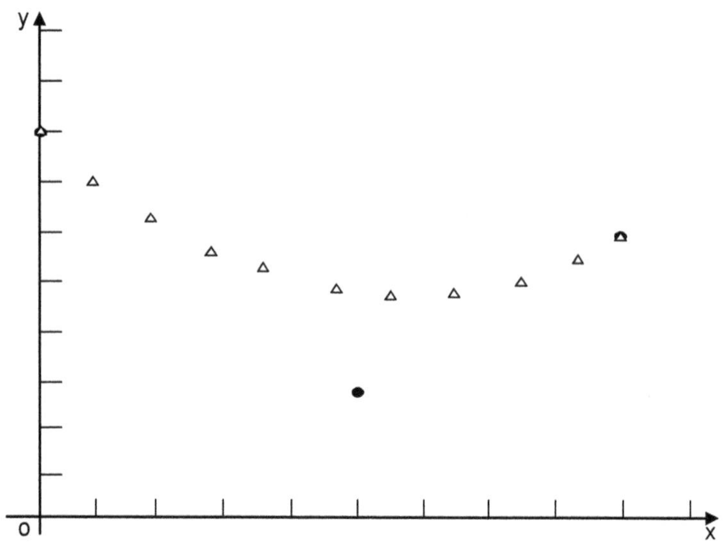

Figure 3. Data points of the quadratic Bezier curve.

Table 4. Calculated values of the quadratic Bezier curve.

t	Bernstein Polynomials of degree 2			The quadratic Bezier curve	
	$B_0^2(t)$	$B_1^2(t)$	$B_2^2(t)$	*X(t)*	*Y(t)*
0.0	1.000000030	0	0	0	0.8000000060
0.1	0.809999984	0.180000040	0.010000005	0.0990001645	0.7080000041
0.2	0.639999995	0.319999983	0.039999995	0.1959999453	0.6319999767
0.3	0.490000025	0.420000018	0.090000007	0.2910000278	0.5720000536
0.4	0.369999993	0.480000002	0.160000005	0.3840000637	0.5280000117
0.5	0.250000030	0.500000060	0.250000030	0.4750000805	0.5000000894
0.6	0.160000005	0.480000002	0.359999993	0.5640000482	0.4880000045
0.7	0.090000007	0.420000018	0.490000025	0.6510000743	0.4920000095
0.8	0.039999995	0.319999983	0.639999995	0.7359999453	0.5119999767
0.9	0.010000005	0.180000040	0.809999984	0.8190001329	0.5480000255
1.0	0	0	1.000000030	0.9000000328	0.6000000119

Table 5. Real values of the quadratic Bezier curve.

t	Bernstein Polynomials of degree 2			The quadratic Bezier curve	
	$B_0^2(t)$	$B_1^2(t)$	$B_2^2(t)$	*X(t)*	*Y(t)*
0.0	1	0	0	0	0.8
0.1	0.81	0.18	0.01	0.099	0.708
0.2	0.64	0.32	0.04	0.196	0.632
0.3	0.49	0.42	0.09	0.291	0.572
0.4	0.36	0.48	0.16	0.384	0.528
0.5	0.25	0.5	0.25	0.475	0.5
0.6	0.16	0.48	0.36	0.564	0.488
0.7	0.09	0.42	0.49	0.651	0.492
0.8	0.04	0.32	0.64	0.736	0.512
0.9	0.01	0.18	0.81	0.819	0.548
1.0	0	0	1	0.9	0.6

effective and efficient algorithm and could be of many applications.

REFERENCES

Aumann G (1997). Corner cutting curves and a new characterization of Bezier and B-spline curves. Computer Aided Geometric Design, 14(5):449-474.

Catherine C, Sonya S (2003). Circular Bernstein--Bézier spline approximation with knot removal. J. Comput. Appl. Math., 155(1):177-185.

Farin G (1997). Curves and Surfaces for Computer-aided Geometric Design: A Practical Guide, 4th Ed. Academic Press, San Diego.

Feng G (2006). Convergence and Error Estimation of Coordinate Rotating Algorithm and Its Expansion. Chn. J. Num. Math. Applications. 28(2):1-9.

Han X, Ma Y, Huang X (2008). A novel generalization of Bezier curve and surface. J. Comput. Appl. Math., 217(1):180-193.

Muller JM (2006). Elementary Functions, Algorithms and Implementation. Birkhauser Boston. 1st edition, 1997. 2nd edition, pp.133-156.

Neil Eklund (1998). CORDIC: Elementary Function Computation Using Recursive Sequences. International Conference on Technology in Collegiate Mathematics (ICTCM). p. 11.

Popiel T, Noakes L (2006). C-2 spherical Bezier splines. Computer Aided Geometric Design., 23(3):261-275.

Ray Andraka (1998). A Survey of CORDIC Algorithms for FPGA Based Computers. In Proceedings of the 1998 ACM/SIGDA Sixth International Symposium on Field Programmable Gate Arrays(FPGA) pp.191-200

Volder JE (1959). The CORDIC Computing Technique. IRE Transactions on Electronic Comput., 8(9):330-334.

Xiaobo H, Ronald H, Steven B (1991). Expanding the Range of Convergence of the CORDIC Algorithm. IEEE Transactions on Comput., 40(1):13-21.

Blind signal separation based on generalized laplace distribution

M.EL-Sayed Waheed, Osama Abdo Mohamed and M.E. Abd El-Aziz*

Department of Mathematics, Faculty of science, Zagzig University, Egypt.

Blind Signal Separation is the task of separating signals when only their mixtures are observed. Recently, Independent Component Analysis has become a favorite method of researchers for attacking this problem. We propose a new score function based on Generalized Laplace Distribution for the problem of blind signal separation for supergaussian and subgaussian. To estimate the parameters of such score function we used Nelder-Mead algorithm for optimizing the maximum likelihood function of Generalized Laplace Distribution. To blindly extract the independent source signals, we resort to FastICA approach. Simulation results show that the proposed approach is capable of separating mixture of signals.

Key words: Independent component analysis (ICA), generalized laplace distribution (GLD), maximum likelihood (ML), Nelder-Mead (NM).

INTRODUCTION

A blind source separation (BSS) algorithm aims to recover sources from a number of observed mixtures. The problem that it is solving can be formulated statistically as follows: given M-dimensional random variable vector $\mathbf{x}(t)=[x_1(t),..,x_M(t)]^T$ that arises from linear combination of the mutually independent components of N-dimensional unknown random variable $\mathbf{s}(t)=[s_1(t),..,s_N(t)]^T$ represented mathematically as

$$\mathbf{x}(t)=\mathbf{A}\mathbf{s}(t) \quad \mathbf{t}=1,2,..,M, \qquad (1)$$

Where $\mathbf{x}\in\mathbf{R}^M$, $\mathbf{s}\in\mathbf{R}^N$ and A is an M x N mixing matrix. Here, R denotes the field of real numbers. The class of algorithms that handle such a problem is also called independent component analysis (ICA). When the number of the mixtures is equal to that of the sources (that is, M=N), the objective can be refined to find an N x N invertible square matrix W such that

$$\mathbf{u}(t)=\mathbf{W}\mathbf{x}(t) \quad \mathbf{t}=1,2,..,N, \qquad (2)$$

Where the components of estimated source $\mathbf{u}(t)=[u_1(t),...,u_N(t)]^T$ are mutually independent as much as possible. This must be done as accurately as possible with the assumption that no more than one source has a Gaussian distribution. Current algorithms can meet this objective within a permutation and scaling of the original sources. In general, the majority of BSS approaches perform ICA, by essentially optimizing the negative log-likelihood (objective) function with respect to the unmixing matrix W such that

$$L(\mathbf{u},\mathbf{W})=\sum E[\log p_{u_i}(u_i)]-\log|\det(\mathbf{W})| \qquad (3)$$

Where E [.] represents the expectation operator and $p_{u_i}(u_i)$ is the model for the marginal probability density function (pdf) of u_i, for all $i=1,2,...,n$. Normally, matrix W is regarded as the parameter of interest and the pdfs of the sources are considered to be nuisance parameters. In effect, when correctly hypothesizing upon the distribution of the sources, the maximum likelihood (ML) principle leads to estimating functions, which in fact are the score functions of the sources (Cardoso, 1998).

*Corresponding author. E-mail: abd_el_aziz_m@yahoo.com.

$$\varphi_i(u_i) = -\frac{d}{du_i}\log p_{u_i}(u_i) \quad (4)$$

In principle, the separation criterion in (3) can be optimized by any suitable ICA algorithm where contrasts are utilized (Cardoso, 1998). A popular choice of such a contrast-based algorithm is the so-called fast (cubicly) converging Newton-type (fixed-point) algorithm, normally referred to as FastICA (Hyvarinen and Oja, 1997), and based on:

$$\mathbf{W}_{k+1} = \mathbf{W}_k + \mathbf{D}(\mathrm{E}[\varphi(\mathbf{u})\mathbf{u}^T] - diag(E[\varphi_i(u_i)u_i]))\mathbf{W}_k$$
(5)

Where, as defined in Karvanen and Koivunen (2002)

$$\mathbf{D} = \mathrm{diag}(1/(\mathrm{E}[\varphi_i(u_i)u_i] - \mathrm{E}[\varphi_i'(u_i)])) \quad (6)$$

With $\varphi(t) = [\varphi_1(u_1), \varphi_2(u_2), \ldots, \varphi_n(u_n)]^T$ being valid for all $i = 1, 2, \ldots, n$. In the ICA framework, accurately estimating the statistical model of the sources at hand is still an open and challenging problem (Cardoso, 1998). Practical BSS scenarios employ difficult source distributions and even situations where many sources with very different pdfs are mixed together. Since these densities are often unknown, unrealistic assumptions about the score functions employed that can seriously compromise the performance and convergence properties of the algorithms in question can be made. This calls for a FastICA method that introduces source adaptively through a well-matched parametric (adaptive) score function (Kokkinakis and Nandi, 2006).

GENERALIZED LAPLACE DISTRIBUTION (GLD)

Subbotin (1923) proposed a generalization of the Laplace distribution with pdf:

$$f_i(x|\mu_i,\sigma_{p_i},p_i) = \frac{1}{2p_i^{1/p_i}\sigma_{p_i}\Gamma(1+1/p_i)}\exp\left(-\frac{|x-\mu_i|^{p_i}}{p_i\sigma_{p_i}^{p_i}}\right) \quad (7)$$

Where $-\infty < \mathbf{x} < \infty$, μ_i is the location parameter, σ_{p_i} is the scale parameter, $p_i > 0$ is the shape parameter and $\Gamma(\alpha)$ is the Gamma function, defined by

$$\Gamma(\alpha) = \int_0^\infty t^{\alpha-1}e^{-t}dt$$

The incomplete gamma function defined by

$$\gamma(\alpha, x) = \int_0^x z^{\alpha-1}e^{-z}dz$$

The complementary incomplete gamma function defined by

$$\Gamma(\alpha, x) = \int_x^\infty z^{\alpha-1}e^{-z}dz$$

The generalized Laplace is sometimes referred to as the exponential power function distribution. This distribution is widely used in Bayesian inference (Box and Tiao, 1962; Tiao and Lund, 1970). Estimation issues related to Equation (7) are discussed in [Agr 'o, 1995; Zeckhauser and Thompson, 1970). Using the definition of the incomplete gamma functions, one can write the cdf corresponding to (7) as

$$F_i(u) = \left(1/(2\Gamma(1/p_i))\right)\begin{cases}\Gamma\left(\frac{1}{p_i}\right)+\gamma\left(\frac{1}{p_i},\frac{(\mu_i-u)^{p_i}}{p_i\sigma_{p_i}^{p_i}}\right) & u>\mu_i\\ \Gamma\left(\frac{1}{p_i},\frac{(\mu_i-u)^{p_i}}{p_i\sigma_{p_i}^{p_i}}\right) & u\le\mu_i\end{cases}$$
(8)

Example for GLD

Consider random numbers generated form GLD with parameters $p = [2, 4, 3]$, $\mu = [= -2, 0, 4,]$ and $\sigma = [0.5, 0.1, 0.9]$ in which its probability density function (pdf) (g, h, f) respectively as shown in Figure 1. In this example we see that the GLD contain (Laplace and Gaussian as special case).

THE OBJECTIVE FUNCTION

Based on Equation (4) we can obtain family of parametric or score functions by twice differentiable GLD of Equation (7). By substituting Equation (7) into (4) for the source estimates u_i, it quickly becomes obvious that our proposed objective function

$$\varphi_i(u_i|\mu_i,\sigma_{p_i},p_i) = sign(u_i-\mu_i)\frac{|u_i-\mu|^{p_i-1}}{\sigma_{p_i}^{p_i}} \quad (9)$$

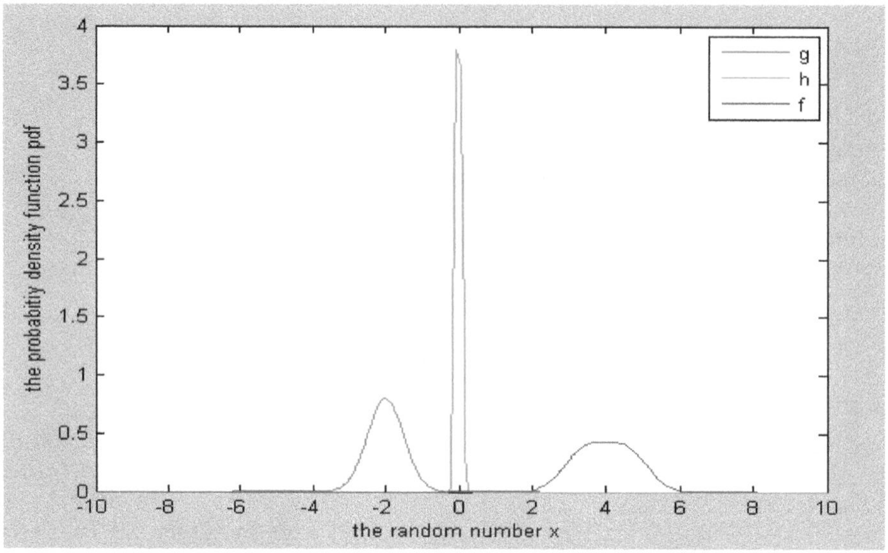

Figure 1. Probability density function for GLD with different parameters.

This objective function can be used to modeling large amount of signals such as speech and types of challenging heavy- and light-tailed distributions. We can obtain special case of Equation (9) at $\mu_i = 0$, $p_i = 1$ and $\sigma_i = 1$

$$\varphi_i(u_i) = sign\ (u_i) \tag{10}$$

In which this special case is the standard threshold activation function which is suitable for speech signals or (Laplacian pdf).

ESTIMATION OF THE GLD PARAMETERS

To refine those further, we can resort to ML. For a sequence of mutually independent Data $\mathbf{u} = [u_1, u_2, ..., u_N]$ of sample size N with density as defined in Equation (7) $g_i(u_i \mid \mu, \sigma_p, p)$ the ML estimates are uniquely defined by their log-likelihood function as

$$L(u \mid \mu, \sigma_p, p) = -\log \prod_{i=1}^{N} g(u_i \mid \mu, \sigma_p, p)$$

$$= -\sum_{i=1}^{N} \log(g(u_i \mid \mu, \sigma_p, p)) \tag{11}$$

Usually, ML parameter estimates are obtained by first differentiating the log-likelihood function in Equation (11) with respect to the GLD parameters and then by equating those derivatives to zero (Shin et al., 2005).

Estimation of the location and scale parameters

By deriving the log-likelihood function with respect to μ and σ_p and by equalizing the obtained expressions to zero, we have the following equations:

$$\frac{\partial L}{\partial \mu} = -\sum_{i=1}^{N} | u_i - \mu |^{p-1} sign(u_i - \mu) = 0 \tag{12}$$

$$\frac{\partial L}{\partial \sigma} = -N + \frac{1}{\sigma_p^p} \sum_{i=1}^{N} | u_i - \mu |^p = 0 \tag{13}$$

The Equation (12) does not have, in general, an explicit solution and is solved by means of numerical methods, while from Equation (13) we get the maximum likelihood estimator of σ as follow:

$$\hat{\sigma}_p = \left(\frac{\sum_{i=1}^{N} | u_i - \mu |^p}{N} \right)^{1/p} \tag{15}$$

Estimation of the shape parameter p

The methods presented in literature are based on the likelihood function and on indices of kurtosis.

Estimation of p by means of the maximum likelihood method

If we want to determine the maximum likelihood estimator of the shape parameter p, the equation that we obtain by deriving the log-likelihood function (11) is:

$$\frac{\partial L}{\partial p} = -\frac{N}{p^2}[\log(p)+\Psi(1+1/p)-1]+\frac{1}{p^2\sigma_p^2}\sum_{i=1}^{N}|u_i-\mu|^p - \frac{1}{p\sigma_p^p}[\log(\sigma_p)\sum_{i=1}^{N}|u_i-\mu|^p-\sum_{i=1}^{N}|u_i-\mu|^p \log|u_i-\mu \tag{14}$$

Where $\Psi(.)$ is the digamma function, which is the first derivative of the logarithm of the gamma function. The equation (14) can be solved by using numerical methods. Moreover, Agr`o (1995) uses this method showing that it does not work well for small samples, even though it provides good results for samples of size greater than 50 - 100.

Estimation of p by means of indices of kurtosis

These estimation procedures take into account the relationship between the shape parameter p and the kurtosis. The usually used indices of kurtosis are:

$$\beta_2 = \frac{\mu_4}{\mu_2^2} = \frac{\Gamma(1/p)\Gamma(5/p)}{[\Gamma(3/p)]^2} \tag{15}$$

$$VI = \frac{\sqrt{\mu_2}}{\mu_1} = \frac{\sqrt{\Gamma(1/p)\Gamma(3/p)}}{\Gamma(2/p)} \tag{16}$$

$$I = \frac{1}{VI} \tag{17}$$

$$\beta_p = \frac{\mu_{2p}}{\mu_p^2} = p+1 \tag{18}$$

Where

$$\mu_r = \sigma_p^p \, p^{r/p} \frac{\Gamma[(r+1)/p]}{\Gamma(1/p)} \tag{19}$$

Is the absolute moment of grade r. The index β_p, called generalized index of kurtosis, the estimators of the indices of kurtosis above described are given by:

$$\hat{\beta}_2 = \frac{n\sum_{i=1}^{n}(u_i-M)^4}{[\sum_{i=1}^{n}(u_i-M)^2]^2} \tag{20}$$

$$V\hat{I} = \frac{\sqrt{n\sum_{i=1}^{n}(u_i-M)^2}}{\sum_{i=1}^{n}|u_i-M|} \tag{21}$$

$$\hat{I} = \frac{1}{V\hat{I}} \tag{22}$$

$$\hat{\beta}_p = \frac{n\sum_{i=1}^{n}|u_i-M|^{2\hat{p}}}{(\sum_{i=1}^{n}|u_i-M|^{\hat{p}})^2} = \hat{p}+1 \tag{23}$$

Where M is the arithmetic mean.

Alternative method used to maximize the ML equation in (11) to ensure the estimated parameters, this done by resorting to the Nelder-Mead (NM) method direct search method. The appeal of the NM optimization technique lies in the fact that it can minimize the negative of the log-likelihood objective function given in Equation (11), essentially without relying on any derivative information. Despite the danger of unreliable performance (especially in high dimensions), numerical experiments have shown that the NM method can converge to an acceptably accurate solution with substantially fewer function evaluations. Good numerical performance and a significant improvement in computational complexity for our estimation method. Therefore, optimizations with the NM technique produce a good estimation for three parameters in GLD.

SIMULATIONS

Here, simulation results are shown to verify the performance of the proposed algorithm using Generalized Laplace Distribution as objective (cost) function in which we used NM to estimate the parameters before using FastICA.

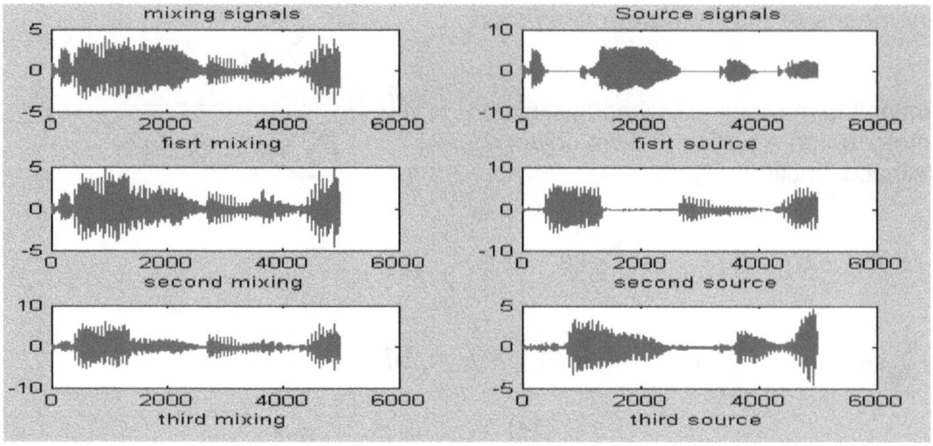

Figure 2. The mixing signals in left and original signals in right.

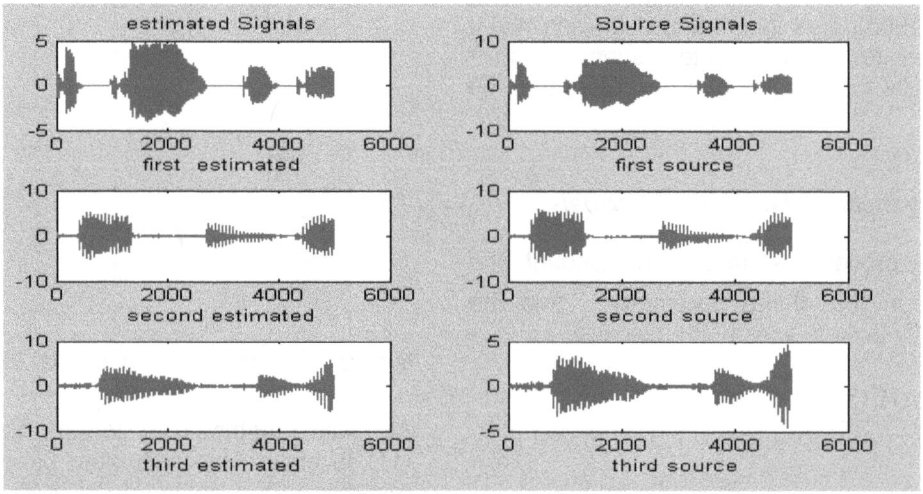

Figure 3. The estimated signals in left with scales, permutation and original signals in right.

Example 1

Consider three speech signals as sources, mixing matrix A and demixing matrix W are given as follow

$$\mathbf{A} = \begin{pmatrix} .56 & .79 & .37 \\ .75 & .65 & .56 \\ .17 & .32 & .48 \end{pmatrix} \text{ And } \mathbf{W} = \begin{pmatrix} .0109 & .0340 & .260 \\ .0024 & .0467 & .0415 \\ .0339 & .0192 & .0017 \end{pmatrix}$$

By using the equation $\mathbf{x} = \mathbf{A}\mathbf{s}$ we obtain mixed signals as shown in Figure (2) where mixing signals in left and original signals in right. We recover the source by using FastICA and we show the estimated signals in left with scales, permutation and original signals in right in Figure (3).

Example 2

Consider a three sources in which they are random number from GLD but with parameters $p=[2,1,6]$, $\mu=[=-2,0,4,]$ and $\sigma=[0.5,0.1,0.9]$

$$\mathbf{s}_1 = \mathrm{GLDrnd}(\mu(1\ ), \sigma(1), p(1), n)\ ,$$
$$\mathbf{s}_2 = \mathrm{GLDrnd}(\mu(2\ ), \sigma(2), p(2), n)\ ,$$
$$\mathbf{s}_3 = \mathrm{GLDrnd}(\mu(3\ ), \sigma(3), p(3), n)\ ,$$

At n=600

$$\mathbf{A} = \begin{pmatrix} .50 & .6 & .37 \\ .35 & .65 & .60 \\ .25 & .92 & .5 \end{pmatrix} \text{ And } \mathbf{W} = \begin{pmatrix} 2.55 & -1.40 & .-0.84 \\ 2.03 & -9.91 & 9.80 \\ -.4333 & 0.84 & -0.312 \end{pmatrix}$$

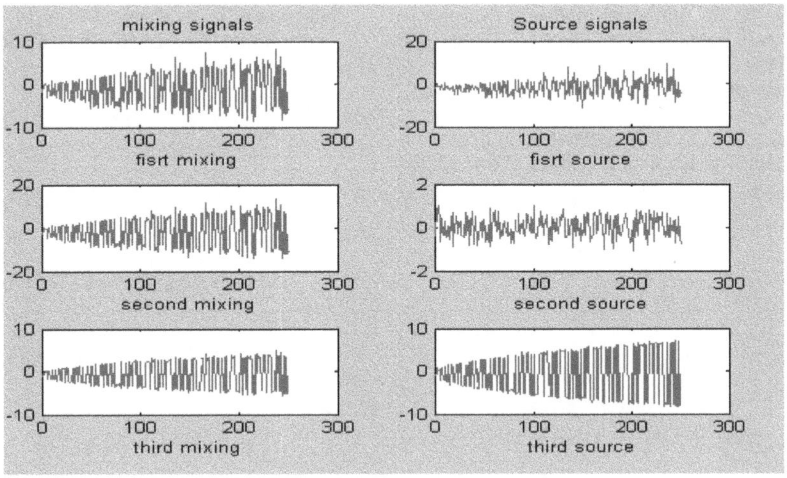

Figure 4. The mixing signals in left and original signals in right.

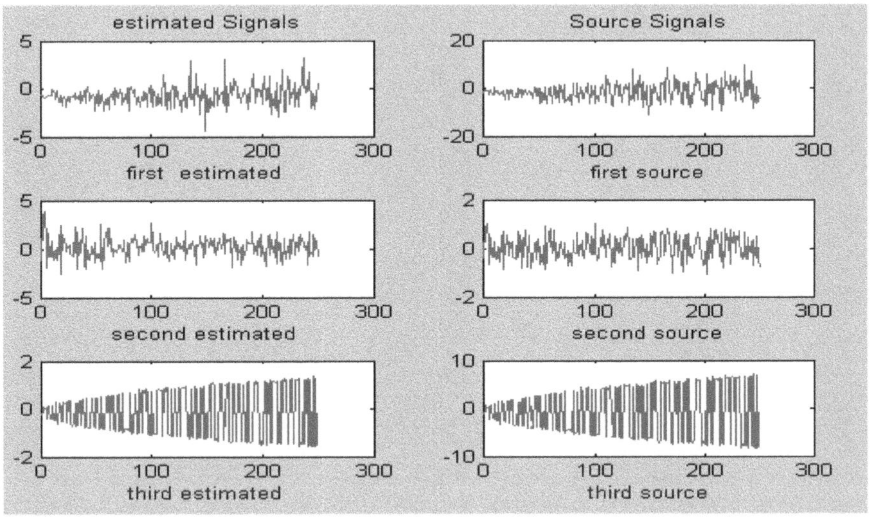

Figure 5. The estimated signals in left with scales, permutation and original signals in right.

Based on the equation of mixed X = AS we obtain mixed signals as shown in Figure (4) where mixing signals in left and source signals in right. We obtain the source signals by using FastICA and we show the estimated signals in left and original signals in right in Figure (5).

Conclusions

This paper introduces a new family of score functions based on Generalized Laplace Distribution for BSS in which this family contain Laplace and Gaussian distributions as special cases. To estimate the parameters of these functions, we have chosen to maximize the ML equation with the NM optimization method as alternative method to derive the ML equation. To blindly extract the source signals we resort to FastICA. Simulation results show that the proposed approach is capable of separating mixtures of signals.

REFERENCES

Agr 'o G (1995). Maximum likelihood estimation for the exponential power function parameters. Comm. Stat. Simul. Comput., 24(2): 523-536.

Box GEP, Tiao GC (1962). A further look at robustness via Bayess theorem. Biometrika, 49: 419-432.

Cardoso JF (1998). Blind signal separation: Statistical principles. Proc. IEEE, 86(10): 2009-2025.

Hyvarinen A, Oja E (1997). A fast fixed-point algorithm for independent component analysis. Computation, 9(7): 1483-1492.

Karvanen J, Koivunen V (2002). Blind separation methods based on Pearson system and its extensions. Signal Process., 82(4): 663-673.

Kokkinakis K, Nandi AK (2006). Flexible score functions for blind separation of speech signals based on generalized gamma probability density functions. Proc. IEEE Int. Conf. Acoustics Speech Signal Process. Toulouse, France, May 1419, 1: 1217-1220.

Shin JW, Chang JH, Kim NS (2005). Statistical modeling of speech signals based on generalized gamma distribution. IEEE Signal Process. Lett., 12(3): 258-261.

Subbotin MT (1923). On the law of frequency of errors. Mat. Sb., 31: 296-300.

Tiao GC, Lund DR (1970). The use of OLUMV estimators in inference robustness studies of the location parameters of a class of symmetric distributions. J. Am. Stat. Assoc., 65: 371-386.

Zeckhauser R, Thompson M (1970). Linear regression with non-normal error terms. Rev. Econ. Stat., 52: 280-286.

12

Fast matrix multiplication techniques based on the Adleman-Lipton model

Aran Nayebi

727 Moreno Avenue, Palo Alto, California, United States of America 94303-3618. E-mail: aran.nayebi@gmail.com.

On distributed memory electronic computers, the implementation and association of fast parallel matrix multiplication algorithms has yielded astounding results and insights. In this discourse, we use the tools of molecular biology to demonstrate the theoretical encoding of Strassen's fast matrix multiplication algorithm with DNA based on an *n*-moduli set in the residue number system, thereby demonstrating the viability of computational mathematics with DNA. As a result, a general scalable implementation of this model in the DNA computing paradigm is presented and can be generalized to the application of all fast matrix multiplication algorithms on a DNA computer. We also discuss the practical capabilities and issues of this scalable implementation. Fast methods of matrix computations with DNA are important because they also allow for the efficient implementation of other algorithms (that is inversion, computing determinants, and graph theory) with DNA.

Key words: DNA computing, residue number system, logic and arithmetic operations, Strassen algorithm.

INTRODUCTION

The multiplication of matrices is a fundamental operation applicable to a diverse range of algorithms from computing determinants, inverting matrices, and solving linear systems to graph theory. Indeed, Bunch and Hopcroft (1974) successfully proved that, given an algorithm for multiplying two $n \times n$ matrices in $O(n^{\alpha})$ operations where $2 < \alpha \leq 3$, then the triangular factorization of a permutation of any $n \times n$ nonsingular matrix, as well as its inverse can be found in $O(n^{\alpha})$ operations. The standard method of square matrix multiplication requires $2n^3$ operations. Let ω be the smallest number such that $O(n^{\omega+\varepsilon})$ multiplications suffice for all $\varepsilon > 0$. Strassen (1969) presented a divide-and-conquer algorithm, using noncommutative multiplication to compute the product of two matrices (of order $m2^k$) by $m^3 7^k$ multiplications and $(5 + m)m^2 7^k - 6m^2 2^{2k}$ additions. Thus, by recursive application of Strassen's algorithm, the product of two matrices can be computed by at most $(4.7)n^{\log_2 7}$ operations. Following Strassen's work, Coppersmith and Winograd (1990) were able to improve the exponent to 2.38.

Their approaches and those of subsequent researchers rely on the same framework. For some k, they devised a method to multiply matrices of order k with $m \lll k^3$ multiplications and recursively apply this technique to show that $\omega < \log_k m$ (Robinson 2005). Only until recently, it was long supposed that, ω could take on the value of 2 without much evidence. Using a group-theoretic construction, Cohn et al. (2005) rederived the Coppersmith-Winograd algorithm to describe several families of wreath product groups that yield nontrivial upper bounds on ω, the best asymptotic result being 2.41. They also presented two conjectures in which either one would imply an exponent of 2.

Unfortunately, although these improvements to Strassen's algorithm are theoretically optimal, they lack pragmatic value. In practice, only the

Strassen algorithm is fully implemented and utilized as such:

$$X = \begin{pmatrix} X_{00} & X_{01} \\ X_{10} & X_{11} \end{pmatrix}, \quad Y = \begin{pmatrix} Y_{00} & Y_{01} \\ Y_{10} & Y_{11} \end{pmatrix}, \quad Q = \begin{pmatrix} Q_{00} & Q_{01} \\ Q_{10} & Q_{11} \end{pmatrix},$$

For even integers m, n, and k, let $X \in R^{m \times k}$ and $Y \in R^{k \times n}$ be matrices with product $Q \in R^{m \times n}$, and set

where $X_{ij} \in R^{m/2 \times k/2}$, $Y_{ij} \in R^{k/2 \times n/2}$, and $Q_{ij} \in R^{m/2 \times n/2}$. Then perform the following to compute $Q = XY$,

M_0: $= (X_{00} + X_{11})(Y_{00} + Y_{11})$,
M_1: $= (X_{10} + X_{11})Y_{00}$,
M_2: $= X_{00}(Y_{01} - Y_{11})$,
M_3: $= X_{11}(-Y_{00} + Y_{10})$,
M_4: $= (X_{00} + X_{01})Y_{11}$,
M_5: $= (-X_{00} + X_{10})(Y_{00} + Y_{01})$,
M_6: $= (X_{01} - X_{11})(Y_{10} + Y_{11})$,
$Q_{00} = M_0 + M_3 - M_4 + M_6$,
$Q_{01} = M_1 + M_3$,
$Q_{10} = M_2 + M_4$,
$Q_{11} = M_0 + M_2 - M_1 + M_5$.

Even if the dimension of the matrices is not even or if the matrices are not square, it is easy to pad the matrices with zeros and perform the aforementioned algorithm. Typically, computations such as this one are performed using electronic components on a silicon substrate. In fact, it is a commonly held notion that 'most' computers should follow this model. In the last decade however, a newer and more revolutionary form of computing has come about, known as DNA computing. DNA's key advantage is that it can make computers much smaller than before, while at the same time maintaining the capacity to store prodigious amounts of data. Since Adleman's (1994) pioneering paper, DNA computing has become a rapidly evolving field with its primary focus on developing DNA algorithms for NP-complete problems. However, unlike quantum computing in recent years, the viability of computational mathematics on a DNA computer has not yet been fully demonstrated, for the whole field of DNA-based computing has merged to controlling and mediating information processing for nanostructures and molecular movements. In fact, only recently have the primitive operations in mathematics (that is addition, subtraction, multiplication, and division) been implemented Thus, the general problem dealt with in this paper is to explore the feasibility of computational mathematics with DNA.

Fujiwara et al. (2004) proved a DNA representation of binary integers using single strands and presented procedures for primitive mathematical operations through simple manipulations in DNA. It is important to note that, the work of Fujiwara et al. (2004) and those of subsequent researchers have relied upon a fixed-base number system. The fixed-base number system is a bottleneck for many algorithms, as it restricts the speed at which arithmetic operations can be performed and increases the complexity of the algorithm. Parallel arithmetic operations are simply not feasible in the fixed-base number system because of the effect of a carry propagation. Recently, Zheng et al. (2009) have presented an improved DNA representation of an integer based on the residue number system (RNS) and give algorithms of arithmetic operations in $Z_M = \{0, 1, \cdots, M - 1\}$ where Z_M is the ring of integers with respect to modulo M. Their results exploit the massive parallelism in DNA mainly because of the carry-free property of all arithmetic operations (except division, of course) in RNS.

In this paper, we present a parallelization method for performing Strassen's fast matrix multiplication methods on a DNA computer. Although DNA-based methods for the multiplication of boolean (Oliver, 1997) and real-numbered matrices (Zhang and Wang, 2009) have been proven, these approaches run in the traditional $O(n^3)$ time, by using digraphs and are not divide-and-conquer like Strassen's algorithm (and hence are not particularly efficient when used with DNA). Divide-and-conquer algorithms particularly benefit from the parallelism of the DNA computing paradigm because distinct sub-processes can be executed on different processors. The critical problem addressed in this paper is to provide a DNA implementation of Strassen's algorithm, while keeping in mind that in recent years, it has been shown that the biomolecular operations suggested by the Adleman-Lipton model are not very reliable in practice. More specifically, the objectives we aim to accomplish in this research paper are the following:

1. To provide a revised version of the Adleman-Lipton model that better handles recursive ligation and overcomes the confounding of results with the complexity of tube content.
2. To establish a systematic approach of representing and adding and subtracting matrices using DNA in the RNS system.
3. Next, based on this representation system, we describe an implementation of the Cannon algorithm with DNA at the bottom level.
4. And lastly, we present a method to store the

different sub-matrices in different strands, and we prove a mathematical relation between the resultant matrix and the sub-matrices at recursion level *r*.

Our approach uses the Cannon algorithm at the bottom level (within a tube containing a memory strand) and the Strassen algorithm at the top level (between memory strands). We show that the Strassen-Cannon algorithm decreases in complexity as the recursion level *r* increases (Nguyen et al., 2005). If the Cannon algorithm is replaced by other parallel matrix multiplication algorithms at the bottom level (such as the Fox algorithm), our result still holds. The difficulty that arises is that, in order to use the Strassen algorithm at the top level, we must determine the sub-matrices after the recursive execution of the Strassen formula *r* times and then find the resultant matrix. On a sequential machine, this problem is trivial; however, on a parallel machine this situation becomes much more arduous. Nguyen et al. (2005) present a method for electronic computers to determine all the nodes at the unspecified level r in the execution tree of the Strassen algorithm, thereby allowing for the direct calculation of the resultant matrix from the sub-matrices calculated by parallel matrix multiplication algorithms at the bottom level.

Thus, we show that this result can theoretically be obtained using DNA, and combined with a storage map of sub-matrices to DNA strands and with the usage of the Cannon algorithm at the bottom level, we have a general scalable implementation of the Strassen algorithm on Adleman's DNA computer. The reason why we concentrate on the Strassen algorithm is that it offers superior performance over the traditional algorithm for practical matrix sizes less than 1020 (Nguyen et al., 2005). However, our methods are also applicable to 'all' fast matrix multiplication algorithms on a DNA computer, as these algorithms are always in recursive form (Pan, 1984). In addition, our results can be used to implement other algorithms, such as inversion and computing determinants on a DNA computer, since matrix multiplication is almost ubiquitous in application.

PRELIMINARY THEORY

The residue number system

Here, we introduce the residue number system because it will be used later on as a basis for the representation system of matrices using DNA, and exploits the mass parallelism of DNA. The residue number system is defined by a set of pairwise, coprime moduli $P = \{q_{n-1}, \cdots, q_0\}$. An integer in RNS is represented as a vector of residues with respect to the moduli set *P*. As a consequence of the Chinese remainder theorem, for any integer $x \in [0, M-1]$ where $M = \prod_{i=0}^{i=n-1} q_i$, each RNS representation is unique. As stated by Zheng et al. (2009), the vector $(x_{n-1}, \cdots, x_0)$ denotes the residue representation of *x*.

It has been previously mentioned that, one of the important characteristic of RNS is that, all arithmetic operations except for division are carry-free. Thus, for any two integers $x \rightarrow (x_{n-1}, \cdots, x_0) \in Z_M$ and $y \rightarrow (y_{n-1}, \cdots, y_0) \in Z_M$ we obtain the following from Paun et al. (1998):

$$|x \circ y|_M \rightarrow \left(|x_{n-1} \circ y_{n-1}|_{q_{n-1}}, \cdots, |x_0 \circ y_0|_{q_0}\right),$$

in which $\circ$ is any operation of addition, subtraction, or multiplication.

The Adleman-Lipton model

Here, we present a theoretical and practical basis for our algorithms. By the Adleman-Lipton model, we define a test tube *T* as a multi-set of (oriented) DNA sequences over the nucleotide alphabet {*A*, *G*, *C*, *T*}. The following operations can be performed as follows:

1. Merge (T_1, T_2): Merge the contents in tube T_1 and tube T_2, and store the results in tube T_1;
2. Copy (T_1, T_2): Make a copy of the contents in tube T_1 and store the result in tube T_2;
3. Detect (*T*): For a given tube *T*, this operation returns "True" if tube *T* contains at least one DNA strand, else it returns "False";
4. Separation (T_1, *X*, T_2): From all the DNA strands in tube T_1, take out only those containing the sequences of *X* over the alphabet {*A*, *G*, *C*, *T*} and place them in tube T_2;
5. Selection (T_1, *l*, T_2): Remove all strands of length *l* from tube T_1 into tube T_2; $\begin{bmatrix}\sigma_0\sigma_1\\ \overline{\sigma_0\sigma_1}\end{bmatrix}$,
6. Cleavage (*T*, $\sigma_0\sigma_1$): Given a tube *T* and a sequence $\sigma_0\sigma_1$, for every strand containing then the cleavage operation can be performed as such:

$$\begin{bmatrix}\alpha_0\sigma_0\sigma_1\beta_0\\ \alpha_1\overline{\sigma_0\sigma_1}\beta_1\end{bmatrix} \xrightarrow{Cleavage(T,\sigma_0\sigma_1)} \begin{bmatrix}\alpha_0\sigma_0\\ \alpha_1\overline{\sigma_0}\end{bmatrix}, \quad \begin{bmatrix}\sigma_1\beta_0\\ \overline{\sigma_1}\beta_1\end{bmatrix},$$

where the overhead bar denotes the complementary strand.

7. Annealing (T): Produce all feasible double strands in tube *T* and store the results in tube *T*

(the assumption here is that ligation is executed after annealing);
8. Denaturation (T): disassociate every double strand in tube *T* into two single strands and store the results in tube *T*;
9. *Empty* (*T*): Empty tube *T*.

According to Paun et al. (1998), the complexity of each of the aforementioned operations is $O(1)$.

Revised Adleman-Lipton model through ligation by selection

In practice, the recursive properties of our implementation of the Strassen-Canon algorithm require a massive ligation step that is not feasible. The reason is that, in practice, the biomolecular operations suggested by the Adleman-Lipton model are not completely reliable. This ligation step cannot produce longer molecules as required by our implementation, and certainly not more than 10 to 15 ligations in a row. Not to mention that both the complexity of the tube content and the efficiency of the enzyme would obscure the results. As a result of these considerations, the operations *Separation* (T_1, X, T_2) and *Annealing* (T) function with questionable success when applied to a complex test tube, especially when recursion is used.

Therefore, in order for matrix multiplication under the Adleman-Lipton model to be completely reliable in practice and the aforementioned problems circumvented, these streptavidin based operations must be improved upon. That way, the parallelization offered by DNA can be utilized as an important mathematical tool with performance capabilities comparable to the electronics. One way we propose to overcome this potential setback of ligation is to use a modified ligation procedure that can handle longer molecules in place of the original, termed "ligation by selection" presented by Kodumal and Santi (2004). Ligation by selection (LBS) is a method to ligate multiple adjacent DNA fragments that does not require intermediate fragment isolation and is amenable to parallel processing, therefore reducing the obfuscation of the results by the complexity of tube content. Essentially in LBS, fragments that are adjacent to each other are cloned into plasmid markers that have a common antibiotic marker, a linking restriction site for joining the fragments, a linking restriction site on the vector, and each vector has a unique site to be used for restriction-purification and a unique antibiotic marker. The method is applied to efficiently stitch multiple synthetic DNA fragments of 500 to 800 bp together to produce segments of up to 6000 bp (Kodumal and Santi, 2004). For a cogent and complete explanation of ligation by selection we refer the reader to Kodumal and Santi (2004).

To utilize LBS recursively, the alteration of resistance markers and restriction-purification sites of acceptor and donor vectors that occur in each LBS cycle must be accounted for, in order to minimize the number of cycles required in parallel processing. As opposed to conventional ligation, the advantages that LBS has are (Kodumal and Santi, 2004):

1. The avoidance of the need to isolate, purify, and ligate individual fragments,
2. The evasion of the need for specialized MCS linkers,
3. And most importantly, the ease with which parallel processing of operations may be applied.

Hence, in order for the Adleman-Lipton model to be more reliable in the recursive operations our implementation of Strassen's algorithm requires, we replace the ligation procedure of the Adleman-Lipton model with LBS.

DNA MATRIX OPERATIONS IN RNS

DNA Representation of a matrix in RNS

We extend the DNA representation of integers in RNS presented in Zheng et al. (2009) to representing an entire matrix *Y* in RNS by way of single DNA strands.

$$Y = \begin{pmatrix} y_{11} & y_{12} & \cdots & y_{1t} \\ y_{21} & y_{22} & \cdots & y_{2t} \\ \vdots & \vdots & \ddots & \vdots \\ y_{t1} & y_{t2} & \cdots & y_{tt} \end{pmatrix}$$

The key here is the RNS representation of each element y_{qr} in the hypothetical matrix *Y* with $1 \le q \le t$ and $1 \le r \le t$ by way of DNA strands. We first utilize the improved DNA representation of *n* binary numbers with *m* binary bits as described in Zheng et al. (2009) for the alphabet $\sum$:

$\sum = \{A_i, B_j, C_0, C_1, E_0, E_1, D_0, D_1, 1, 0, \#|0 \le i \le M - 1, 0 \le j \le m\}$.

Here, A_i indicates the address of *M* integers in RNS; B_j denotes the binary bit position; C_0, C_1, E_0, E_1, D_0, and D_1 are used in the *Cleavage* operation; # is used in the *Separation* operation; and 0 and 1 are binary numbers. Thus, in the residue digit position, the value of the bit y_{qr} with a bit address of i and a bit position of j can be represented by a single DNA strand $(S_{i,j})y_{qr}$ $(S_{i,j})_{qr} = (D_1B_jE_0E_1A_iC_0C_1V\,D_0)y_{qr}$, for $V\in\{0, 1\}$. Hence, the matrix Y can be represented as such:

$$Y = \begin{pmatrix} (D_1B_jE_0E_1A_iC_0C_1VD_0)_{y_{11}} & (D_1B_jE_0E_1A_iC_0C_1VD_0)_{y_{12}} & \cdots & (D_1B_jE_0E_1A_iC_0C_1VD_0)_{y_{1t}} \\ (D_1B_jE_0E_1A_iC_0C_1VD_0)_{y_{21}} & (D_1B_jE_0E_1A_iC_0C_1VD_0)_{y_{22}} & \cdots & (D_1B_jE_0E_1A_iC_0C_1VD_0)_{y_{2t}} \\ \vdots & \vdots & \ddots & \vdots \\ (D_1B_jE_0E_1A_iC_0C_1VD_0)_{y_{t1}} & (D_1B_jE_0E_1A_iC_0C_1VD_0)_{y_{t2}} & \cdots & (D_1B_jE_0E_1A_iC_0C_1VD_0)_{y_{tt}} \end{pmatrix} \quad (2)$$

Where each strand-element is not necessarily distinct. The reader must keep in mind that M integers in RNS defined by the n-moduli set P can be represented by $2M(m + 1)$ different memory strands, whereas in the binary system, the representation of M integers requires $2M(1 + \sum_{i=0}^{i=n-1} m_i)$ different memory strands.

Residue number arithmetic with matrices

From (1), it is apparent that the operation $\circ$ is carry-free, thereby allowing for the employment of parallel procedures in all residue digits. In Zheng et al. (2009) two properties are given for the modular operation involving two integers $x \rightarrow (x_{n-1}, \cdots, x_0)$ and $y \rightarrow (y_{n-1}, \cdots, y_0)$ in RNS defined by the set $P = \{2^{m_{n-1}}, 2^{m_{n-2}} - 1, \cdots, 2^{m_0} - 1\}$.

Next, the procedures *RNSAdd* and *RNSDiff* add and subtract two integers in RNS defined by the moduli set P, respectively. The pseudocode for *RNSAdd* and *RNSDiff* is given in Zheng et al. (2009), and we refer the reader to that source (note that the pseudocode of Zheng et al. (2009) for both algorithms utilizes the operations of the Adleman-Lipton model extensively).

Lemma 1: *For* $\forall j,\ m_{n-1} \in \mathbb{N}$, *if* $j < m_{n-1}$ *then* $|2^j|_{2^{m_{n-1}}} = 2^j$ *else* $|2^j|_{2^{m_{n-1}}} = 0$.

Lemma 2: *For* $l = 0, \cdots, n-2$, *let* $x_l + y_l = z_l$ *where* $z_l = (z_{l(m_l)}, \cdots, z_{l0})$. *If* $z_l > 2^{m_l} - 1$, $|z_l|_{2^{m_l}-1} = 1 + \sum_{j=0}^{m_l-1} z_{lj}2^j$.

Instead, we provide some background on the two procedures. The inputs are $2n$ tubes T_l^X and T_l^Y (for $l = 0, \cdots, n-1$) containing the memory strands representing the elements x_{qr} and y_{qr} of $t \times t$ matrices X and Y, respectively. Once, either operation is complete, it returns n tubes T_l^{Rsum} and T_l^{Rdiff} containing the result of residue addition or subtraction, respectively. We also use the following n temporary tubes for *RNSAdd*, namely, T_{temp}, T_{sum}, and T_{sum}. Similarly for *RNSDiff*, the n temporary tubes, T_{temp}, T'_{diff}, and T'_{diff} are used. Thus, based on Lemma 1 and 2, we introduce the following two algorithms for matrix addition and subtraction in RNS which will be used when dealing with the block matrices in Strassen's algorithm. For the sake of example, we are adding (and subtracting) the hypothetical $t \times t$ matrices X and Y. Essentially, the *RNSMatrixAdd* and *RNSMatrixDiff* algorithms employ *RNSAdd* and *RNSDiff* in a nested FOR loop.

Matrix addition

The procedure *RNSMatrixAdd* is defined as:

Algorithm 1: RNSMATRIXADD(T_X, T_Y)

```
for q ← 0 to t
  do
  {for r ← 0 to t
     do
     {RNSAdd(T_{n-1}^{x_qr}, ..., T_0^{x_qr}, T_{n-1}^{y_qr}, ..., T_0^{y_qr});
```

Matrix subtraction

The procedure *RNSMatrixDiff* is defined as:

Algorithm 2: RNSMATRIXDIFF(T_X, T_Y)

```
for q ← 0 to t
  do
  {for r ← 0 to t
     do
     {RNSDiff(T_{n-1}^{x_qr}, ..., T_0^{x_qr}, T_{n-1}^{y_qr}, ..., T_0^{y_qr});
```

STRASSEN'S ALGORITHM REVISITED

Bottom-level matrix multiplication

Although, a vast repository of traditional matrix multiplication algorithms can be used between processors (or in our case, test tubes containing memory strands; however for the sake of brevity, we shall just use the term "memory strand" or "strand"), we will employ the Cannon algorithm (Cannon, 1969) since it can be used on matrices of any dimension. We will only discuss square strand arrangements and square matrices for simplicity's sake. Assume that we have p^2 memory strands, organized in a logical sequence in a $p \times p$ mesh. For $i \geq 0$ and $j \leq p - 1$, the strand in the ith row and j^{th} column has coordinates (i, j).

The matrices X, Y, and their matrix product Q are of size $t \times t$, and again as a simplifying assumption, let t be a multiple of p. All matrices will be partitioned into $p \times p$ blocks of $s \times s$ sub-matrices where $s = t/p$. As described by Nguyen et al. (2005), the mesh can be perceived as an amalgamation of rings of memory strands in both the horizontal and vertical directions (opposite sides of the mesh are linked with a torus interconnection). A successful DNA implementation of Cannon's algorithm requires communication between the strands of each ring in the mesh where the blocks of matrix X are passed 'in parallel' to the left along the horizontal rings and the blocks of the matrix Y are passed to the top along the vertical rings. Let X_{ij}, Y_{ij}, and Q_{ij} denote the blocks of X, Y, and Q stored in the strand with coordinates (i, j). The Cannon algorithm on a DNA computer can be described as such:

Algorithm 3: $\text{CANNON}(T_{X_{ij}}, T_{Y_{ij}})$

for i^{th} column $\leftarrow 0$ **to** i
  do
$\{\text{LeftShift}(T_{X_{ij}})$
for j^{th} column $\leftarrow 0$ **to** j
  do
$\{\text{UpShift}(T_{Y_{ij}})$
$\forall$ strands (i, j)
  do
$\{\text{ValueAssignment}(T_{X_{ij}Y_{ij}}, T_{Q_{ij}})$

  do $(p-1)$ times

$$\begin{cases} \text{LeftShift}(T_{X_{ij}}) \\ \text{UpShift}(T_{Y_{ij}}) \\ \text{ValueAssignment}\left(T_{\text{RNSMatrixAdd}(T_{Q_{ij}}, T_{X_{ij}Y_{ij}})}, T_{Q_{ij}}\right) \end{cases}$$

Note that the procedure *UpShift* can be derived from Zheng et al. (2009) *LeftShift*. Now we examine the run-time of the Cannon algorithm. The run time can be componentized into the communication time and the computation time, and the total communication time is

(1) $2p\alpha + (2B\beta t^2)/p$,

and the computation time is

(2) $(2t^3 t_{comp})/p^2$,

Where, t_{comp} is the execution time for one arithmetic operation, α is the latency, β is the sequence-transfer rate, the total latency is $2p\alpha$, and the total sequence-transfer time is $2p\beta B(m/p)^2$ with B as the number of sequences to store one entry of the matrices. According to Nguyen et al. (2005), the running time is

(3) $T(t) = (2t^3 t_{comp})/p^2 + 2p\alpha + (2B\beta t^2)/p$.

Matrix storage pattern

The primary difficulty is to be able to store the different sub-matrices of the Strassen algorithm in different strands, and these sub-matrices must be copied or moved to appropriate strands if tasks are spawned. Hence, we present here a storage map of sub-matrices to strands based on the result of Luo and Drake (1995) for electronic computers. Essentially, if we allow each strand to have a portion of each sub-matrix at each recursion level, then we can make it possible for all strands to act as *one* strand. As a result, the addition and subtraction of the block matrices performed in the Strassen algorithm at all recursion levels can be performed in parallel without any inter-strand communication (Nguyen et al., 2005). Each strand performs its local sub-matrix additions and subtractions in RNS (via our *RNSMatrixAdd* and *RNSMatrixDiff* algorithms). At the final recursion level, the block matrix multiplications are calculated using our DNA implementation of the Cannon algorithm.

For instance, if we suppose that the recursion level in the Strassen-algorithm is r, and let $n = t/p$, $t_0 = t/2$, and $n_0 = t_0/p$ for $n, t_0, n_0 \in$ N, then the run-time of the Strassen-Canon algorithm is:

$T(t) = 18T_{add}(t/2) + 7T(t/2)$,

where $T_{add}(t/2)$ is the run-time to add or subtract block matrices of order $t/2$. Additionally, according to (9) of Nguyen et al. (2005),
$T_t = (2(7/8)^r t^3 t_{comp})/p^2 + (5(7/4)^r t_{comp})/p^2 + (7/4)^r 2p\alpha$.
Since the asymptotically significant term

$(2(7/8)^r t^3 t_{comp})/p^2$ decreases as the recursion level r increases, then for t significantly large, the Strassen-Cannon algorithm should be faster than the Cannon algorithm. Even if the Cannon algorithm is replaced at the bottom level by other parallel matrix multiplication algorithms, the same result holds.

Recursion removal

As has been previously discussed, in order to use the Strassen algorithm between strands (at the top level), we must determine the sub-matrices after r times recursive execution and then to determine the resultant matrix from these sub-matrices. Nguyen et al. (2005) recently presented a method on electronic computers, to ascertain all of the nodes in the execution tree of the Strassen algorithm at the unspecified recursion level r and to determine the relation between the sub-matrices and the resultant matrix at level r. We extend it to the DNA computing paradigm. At each step, the algorithm will execute a multiplication between 2 factors, namely the linear combinations of the elements of the matrices X and Y, respectively. Since we can consider that each factor is the sum of all elements from each matrix, with coefficient of 0, -1, or 1 (Nguyen et al., 2005), then we can represent these coefficients with the RNS representation of numbers with DNA strands described as such:

$(\{D_1B_1E_0E_1A_0C_0C_10D_0,\ D_1B_0E_0E_1A_0C_0C_10D_0\},$
$\{D_1B_1E_0E_1A_0C_0C_10D_0,\ D_1B_0E_0E_1A_0C_0C_10D_0\},$
$\{D_1B_1E_0E_1A_0C_0C_10D_0,\ D_1B_0E_0E_1A_0C_0C_10D_0\}),$
$(\{D_1B_1E_0E_1A_{-1}C_0C_11D_0,\ D_1B_0E_0E_1A_{-1}C_0C_11D_0\},$
$\{D_1B_1E_0E_1A_{-1}C_0C_11D_0,\ D_1B_0E_0E_1A_{-1}C_0C_11D_0\},$
$\{D_1B_1E_0E_1A_{-1}C_0C_11D_0,\ D_1B_0E_0E_1A_{-1}C_0C_11D_0\}),$
or
$(\{D_1B_1E_0E_1A_1C_0C_10D_0,\ D_1B_0E_0E_1A_1C_0C_11D_0\},$
$\{D_1B_1E_0E_1A_1C_0C_10D_0,\ D_1B_0E_0E_1A_1C_0C_11D_0\},$
$\{D_1B_1E_0E_1A_1C_0C_10D_0,\ D_1B_0E_0E_1A_1C_0C_11D_0\}),$

respectively. For the sake of brevity, we shall denote the latter three equations as $(0)_{RNS}$, $(-1)_{RNS}$, and $(1)_{RNS}$, respectively. This coefficient is obtained for each element in each recursive call and is dependent upon both the index of the call and the location of an element in the division of the matrix by 4 sub-matrices (Nguyen et al., 2005). If we view the Strassen-Cannon algorithm's execution as an execution tree (Nguyen et al., 2005), then each scalar multiplication is correlated on a leaf of the execution tree and the path from the root to the leaf represents the recursive calls leading to the corresponding multiplication. Furthermore, at the leaf, the coefficient of each element (either $(0)_{RNS}$, $(-1)_{RNS}$, or $(1)_{RNS}$) can be determined by the combination of all computations in the path from the root. The reason is that since all of the computations are linear, they can be combined in the leaf (which we will denote by t_l). Utilizing the nomenclature of Nguyen et al. (2005), Strassen's formula can be depicted as such:

For $l = 0 \cdots 6$,

$$t_l = \sum_{i,j=0,1} x_{ij} SX(l,i,j) \times \sum_{i,j=0,1} y_{ij} SY(l,i,j),$$

And

$$q_{ij} = \sum_{l=0}^{6} t_l SQ(l,i,j),$$

in which

$SX =$

l\ij	00	01	10	11
0	$(1)_{RNS}$	$(0)_{RNS}$	$(0)_{RNS}$	$(0)_{RNS}$
1	$(0)_{RNS}$	$(1)_{RNS}$	$(0)_{RNS}$	$(0)_{RNS}$
2	$(0)_{RNS}$	$(0)_{RNS}$	$(1)_{RNS}$	$(1)_{RNS}$
3	$(-1)_{RNS}$	$(0)_{RNS}$	$(1)_{RNS}$	$(1)_{RNS}$
4	$(1)_{RNS}$	$(0)_{RNS}$	$(-1)_{RNS}$	$(0)_{RNS}$
5	$(0)_{RNS}$	$(0)_{RNS}$	$(1)_{RNS}$	$(1)_{RNS}$
6	$(0)_{RNS}$	$(0)_{RNS}$	$(0)_{RNS}$	$(1)_{RNS}$

$SY =$

l\ij	00	01	10	11
0	$(1)_{RNS}$	$(0)_{RNS}$	$(0)_{RNS}$	$(0)_{RNS}$
1	$(0)_{RNS}$	$(0)_{RNS}$	$(1)_{RNS}$	$(0)_{RNS}$
2	$(-1)_{RNS}$	$(1)_{RNS}$	$(0)_{RNS}$	$(0)_{RNS}$
3	$(1)_{RNS}$	$(-1)_{RNS}$	$(0)_{RNS}$	$(1)_{RNS}$
4	$(0)_{RNS}$	$(-1)_{RNS}$	$(0)_{RNS}$	$(1)_{RNS}$
5	$(0)_{RNS}$	$(1)_{RNS}$	$(0)_{RNS}$	$(1)_{RNS}$
6	$(-1)_{RNS}$	$(1)_{RNS}$	$(1)_{RNS}$	$(-1)_{RNS}$

$SQ =$

l\ij	00	01	10	11
0	$(1)_{RNS}$	$(1)_{RNS}$	$(1)_{RNS}$	$(1)_{RNS}$
1	$(1)_{RNS}$	$(0)_{RNS}$	$(0)_{RNS}$	$(0)_{RNS}$
2	$(0)_{RNS}$	$(1)_{RNS}$	$(0)_{RNS}$	$(0)_{RNS}$
3	$(0)_{RNS}$	$(1)_{RNS}$	$(1)_{RNS}$	$(1)_{RNS}$
4	$(0)_{RNS}$	$(0)_{RNS}$	$(0)_{RNS}$	$(1)_{RNS}$
5	$(0)_{RNS}$	$(1)_{RNS}$	$(0)_{RNS}$	$(0)_{RNS}$
6	$(0)_{RNS}$	$(0)_{RNS}$	$(0)_{RNS}$	$(1)_{RNS}$

At recursion level r, t_l can be represented as such:

For $l = 0 \cdots 7^k - 1$,

$$t_l = \sum_{i,j=n-1} x_{ij} SX_k(l,i,j) \times \sum_{i,j=0,n-1} y_{ij} SY_k(l,i,j),$$

And

$$q_{ij} = \sum_{l=0}^{7^k-1} t_l SQ_k(l, i, j).$$

It is easy to see that $SX = SX_1$, $SY = SY_1$, $SQ = SQ_1$; however, the difficulty that arises is to determine the values of the matrices SX_k, SY_k, and SQ_k in order to have a general algorithm. The following relations were proved in Nguyen et al. (2006), and we shall prove that these results hold with DNA:

$$SX_k(l, i, j) = \prod_{r=1}^{k} SX(l_r, i_r, j_r),$$

$$SY_k(l, i, j) = \prod_{r=1}^{k} SY(l_r, i_r, j_r),$$

$$SQ_k(l, i, j) = \prod_{r=1}^{k} SQ(l_r, i_r, j_r).$$

First, we shall extend the definition of the tensor product for arrays of arbitrary dimensions (Nguyen et al., 2006) by representing the tensor product in RNS by way of single DNA strands.

Proposition

Let A and B be arrays of the same dimension l and of size $m_1 \times m_2 \times \cdots \times m_l$ and $n_1 \times n_2 \times \cdots \times n_l$, respectively. The elements of A and B are represented using RNA by way of DNA strands as presented in detail previously in this paper. The tensor product can thus be described as an array of the same dimension and of size $m_1n_1 \times m_2n_2 \times \cdots \times m_ln_l$ in which each element of A is replaced with the product of the element and B. This product can be computed with the algorithm RNSMult which is recognized by a serial of operations of the RNSAdd algorithm detailed in Zheng et al. (2009). $P = A \otimes B$ where $P[i_1, i_2, \cdots, i_l] = A[k_1, k_2, \cdots, k_l]B[h_1, h_2, \cdots, h_l]$. $1 \leq \forall j \leq l$, $i_j = k_jn_j + h_j$ (k_jn_j and h_j will be added with RNSAdd).

If we let $P = \otimes_{i=1}^{i=n} A_i = (\cdots(A_1 \otimes A_2) \otimes A_3) \cdots \otimes A_n)$ where A_i is an array of dimension l and of size $m_{i1} \times m_{i2} \times \cdots \times m_{il}$, the following theorem allows us to directly compute the elements of *P. All* products and sums of elements can be computed with *RNSMult* and *RNSAdd*, respectively.

Theorem 1. If we let $j_k = \sum_{s=1}^{n} \left(h_{sk} \prod_{r=s+1}^{n} m_{rk}\right)$, then $P[j_1, j_2, \cdots, j_l] = \prod_{i=1}^{n} A_i[h_{i1}, h_{i2}, \cdots, h_{il}]$.

Proof: We give a proof by induction. For $n = 1$ and $n = 2$, the statement is true. Assume it is true with n, then we shall prove it is true with $n+1$.

$$P_{n+1}[v_1, v_2, \cdots, v_l] = \prod_{i=1}^{n+1} A_i[h_{i1}, h_{i2}, \cdots$$

where

$$v_k = \sum_{s=1}^{n+1}\left(h_{sk} \prod_{r=s+1}^{n+1} m_{rk}\right),$$

for $1 \leq \forall k \leq l$. Hence, $P_{n+1} = P_n \otimes A_{n+1}$.

Furthermore, by definition,

$$P_{n+1}[j_1, j_2, \cdots, j_l] = P_n[p_1, p_2, \cdots, p_l]A_{n+1}[h_{(n+1)}, h_{2(n+1)}, \cdots, h_{l(n+1)}] = \prod_{i=1}^{n+1} A_i[h_{i1}, h_{i2}, \cdots, h_{il}],$$

Where

$$j_k = \sum_{s=1}^{n}\left(h_{sk} \prod_{r=s+1}^{n+1} m_{rk}\right) + h_{k(n+1)} = \sum_{s=1}^{n+1}\left(h_{sk} \prod_{r=s+1}^{n+1} m_{rk}\right)$$

Theorem 2. $SX_k = \otimes_{i=1}^{i=k} SX$, $SY_k = \otimes_{i=1}^{i=k} SY$, and $SQ_k = \otimes_{i=1}^{i=k} SQ$.

Proof. We give a proof by induction. For $k = 1$, the statement is true. Assume it is true with k, then we shall prove that it is true with $k + 1$. Thus, at level $k + 1$ of the execution tree, for $0 \leq l \leq 7^{k+1} - 1$

$$T_l = \left(\sum_{i \geq 0, j \leq 2^{k+1}-1} X_{k+1,ij} SX_{k+1}(l, i, j)\right) \times \left(\sum_{i \geq 0, j \leq 2^{k+1}-1} Y_{k+1,ij} SY_{k+1}(l, i, j)\right).$$

It follows that at level $k + 2$, for $0 \leq l \leq 7^{k+1} - 1$ and $0 \leq l \leq 6$,

$$T_l[l'] = \sum_{i' \geq 0, j' \leq 1}\left(\sum_{i \geq 0, j \leq 2^{k+1}-1} X_{k+1,ij}[i', j'] SX_{k+1}(l, i, j) SX(l', i', j')\right.$$

$$\sum_{i' \geq 0, j' \leq 1}\left(\sum_{i \geq 0, j \leq 2^{k+1}-1} Y_{k+1,ij}[i', j'] SY_{k+1}(l, i, j) SY(l', i', j\right.$$

where $X_{k+1,ij}[i', j']$ and $Y_{k+1,ij}[i', j']$ are $2^{k+2} \times 2^{k+2}$

matrices obtained by partitioning the matrices $X_{k+1,ij}$ and $Y_{k+1,ij}$ into 4 sub-matrices (we use i' and j' to denote the sub-matrix's quarter). We represent l, l' in base 7 RNS, and i, j, i', j' in base 2 RNS. Since $X_{k+1,ij}[i', j'] = X_{k+2,ij}[\overline{ii'}_2, \overline{jj'}_2]$, then for $0 \leq \overline{ll'}_{(7)} \leq 7^{k+1} - 1$,

Moreover, for $0 \leq \overline{ll}_{(7)} \leq 7^{k+1} - 1$,

$$M[\overline{ll'}_{(7)}] = \left(\sum_{\overline{ii'}_{(2)} \geq 0, \overline{jj'}_{(2)} \leq 2^{k+1}-1} X_{k+2}[\overline{ii'}_{(2)}, \overline{jj'}_{(2)}] SX_{k+1}(l,i,j) SX(l',i',j') \right) \times \left(\sum_{\overline{ii'}_{(2)} \geq 0, \overline{jj'}_{(2)} \leq 2^{k+1}-1} Y_{k+2}[\overline{ii'}_{(2)}, \overline{jj'}_{(2)}] SY_{k+1}(l,i,j) SY(l',i'j') \right).$$

$$M[\overline{ll'}_{(7)}] = \left(\sum_{\overline{ii'}_{(2)} \geq 0, \overline{jj'}_{(2)} \leq 2^{k+1}-1} X_{k+2}[\overline{ii'}_{(2)}, \overline{jj'}_{(2)}] SX_{k+2}\left(\overline{ll'}_{(7)}, \overline{ii'}_{(2)}, \overline{jj'}_{(2)}\right) \right) \times \left(\sum_{\overline{ii'}_{(2)} \geq 0, \overline{jj'}_{(2)} \leq 2^{k+1}-1} Y_{k+2}[\overline{ii'}_{(2)}, \overline{jj'}_{(2)}] SY_{k+2}\left(\overline{ll'}_{(7)}, \overline{ii'}_{(2)}, \overline{jj'}_{(2)}\right) \right).$$

We also have

$SX_{k+2}(\overline{ll'}_7, \overline{ii'}_2, \overline{jj'}_2) = SX_{k+1}(l,i,j)SX(l',i',j')$,

and

$SY_{k+2}(\overline{ll'}_7, \overline{ii'}_2, \overline{jj'}_2) = SY_{k+1}(l,i,j)SY(l',i',j')$.

Thus,

$SX_{k+2} = SX_{k+1} \otimes SX = \otimes_{i=1}^{i=k+2} SX$,
$SY_{k+2} = SY_{k+1} \otimes SY = \otimes_{i=1}^{i=k+2} SY$,

and

$SQ_{k+2} = SQ_{k+1} \otimes SQ = \otimes_{i=1}^{i=k+2} SQ$.
We can form the following sub-matrices:

$$T_l = \sum_{i,j=0,2^r-1} X_{ij} \left(\prod_{u=1}^{r} SX(l_u, i_u, j_u) \right) \times \sum_{\substack{i,j=0,2^r-1 \\ l=0\cdots 7^r-1}} Y_{ij} \left(\prod_{u=1}^{r} SX(l_u, i_u, j_u) \right).$$

As a result of our storage map of sub-matrices to strands presented earlier in this paper, the following sub-matrices can be 'locally' determined within each strand, and their product T_l can be computed by our DNA implementation of the Cannon algorithm:

$$\left(\sum_{\substack{i=0,2^r-1 \\ j=0,2^r-1}} X_{ij} \left(\prod_{u=1}^{r} SX(l_u, i_u, j_u) \right) \right)$$

And

$$\left(\sum_{\substack{i=0,2^r-1 \\ j=0,2^r-1}} Y_{ij} \left(\prod_{u=1}^{r} SY(l_u, i_u, j_u) \right) \right)$$

All of the sub-matrices are added with the *RNSMatrixAdd* algorithm presented earlier in this paper. Lastly, it is important to note that we have derived a method to directly compute the sub-matrix elements of the resultant matrix via the application of matrix additions (using the *RNSMatrixAdd* algorithm) instead of backtracking manually down the recursive execution tree to compute:

$$Q_{ij} = \sum_{l=0}^{7^r-1} T_l SQ_r(l,i,j) = \sum_{l=0}^{7^r-1} T_l \left(\prod_{u=1}^{r} SQ(l_u, i_u, j_u) \right).$$

CONCLUSION

Our general scalable implementation can be used for all of the matrix multiplication algorithms that use fast matrix multiplication algorithms at the top level (between strands) on a DNA computer. Moreover, since the computational complexity of these algorithms decreases when the recursion level *r* increases, we can now find optimal algorithms for all particular cases. Of course, as mentioned previously in this paper, the current science of DNA computing does not guarantee a perfect implementation of the Strassen algorithm as described herein; for now, these results should be regarded as primarily theoretical in nature.

REFERENCES

Adleman L (1994). Molecular Computation of Solutions to Combinatorial Problems. Science, 266: 1021-1024.

Bunch R Hopcroft J (1974). Triangular Factorization and Inversion by Fast Matrix Multiplication. Math. Compt., 28: 231-236.

Cannon L (1969). A cellular computer to implement the kalman filter algorithms. Ph.D. Thesis, pp. 1-228.

Cohn H, Kleinberg R, Szegedy B, Umans C (2005). Group-Theoretic Algorithms for Matrix Multiplication.Proc. of the

Coppersmith D, Winograd S (1990). Matrix multiplication 46th Annual Symp. on Found. of Compt. Sci., 379-388.

Fujiwara A, Matsumoto K, Chen W (2004). Procedures for logic and arithmetic operations with DNAmolecules. Int. J. Found. Comput. Sci., 15: 461-474.

Kodumal S, Santi D (2004). DNA ligation by selection. BioTechniques, 37: 34-40.

Luo Q, Drake J (1995). A scalable parallel strassen's matrix multiplication algorithm for distributed memory computers. Proc. of the ACM symp. Appl. Comp., pp. 221-226.

Nguyen D, Lavallée I, Bui M (2005). A General Scalable Implementation of Fast Matrix Multiplication.Algorithms on Distributed Memory Computers. Proc. Sixth Inter. Conference Soft. Engin., pp. 116-122.

Nguyen D, Lavallée I, Bui M (2006). A New Direction to Parallelize Winograd's Algorithm on Distributed Memory Computers. Proc. of the Third Inter. Conference on High Perf. Scientific Compt., pp. 445-457.

Oliver J (1997). Matrix Multiplication with DNA. J. Mol. Evol., 45: 161-167.

Pan V (1984). How can we speed up matrix multiplication?. SIAM Rev., 26: 393-416.

Paun G, Rozenberg G, Salomaa A (1998). DNA computing. Springer-Verlag.

Robinson S (2005). Toward an Optimal Algorithm for Matrix Multiplication. SIAM News, 38: 1-3.

Strassen V (1969). Gaussian elimination is not optimal. Number. Math., 13: 354-356.

Zhang G, Wang S (2009). Matrix Multiplication Based on DNA Computing. ICNC, 5: 167-170.

Zheng X, Xu J, Li W (2009). Parallel DNA arithmetic operation based on n-moduli set. Appl. Math. Compt., 212: 177-184.

Managing distribution of national examinations using geospatial technologies: A case study of Pumwani and Central divisions

David Ndegwa Kuria[1]*, Moses Murimi Ngigi[2], Josephine Wanjiru Wanjiku[1] and Rachel Kavutha Kasumuni[2]

[1]Department of Geomatic Engineering and Geospatial Information Science, Kimathi University College of Technology, P. O. Box 657 – 10100, Nyeri, Kenya.
[2]Department of Geomatic Engineering and Geospatial Information Systems, Jomo Kenyatta University of Agriculture and Technology, P. O. Box 62000 – 00200, Nairobi, Kenya.

Most of the spatially referenced data held by the Kenya national examination council (KNEC) are in analogue hard copy format. This necessitates large storage facilities for storing the paper maps, which have low retrieval speeds. Additionally, wear and tear are occasioned during retrieval and handling, and sometimes some of the data is lost. In this form data sharing is difficult and reproduction usually involves high costs per unit. The purpose of this paper is to implement a geographic information system (GIS) which will lower cost per unit, by allowing higher retrieval speeds, smaller storage facilities requirements, while facilitating data sharing. This GIS will perform all the tasks of the current manual system and in addition, provide functionality to aid in the efficient management of the Kenya national examination council data. To accomplish this, existing hardcopy data was digitized and cleaned. New data was collected, processed, analyzed and stored in the form of a geodatabase. This geodatabase stores both the spatially related data and the attribute data. This geodatabase can be used to answer many questions, but for this work, we emphasize the aspect of efficiency in exam distribution. To determine the most efficient routes to follow in the distribution of examinations during the examination period, a geometric network was prepared which was then used to determine the best routes. In this research, a prototype GIS has been developed. Visualization and comparison can be easily performed using the digital maps produced from the implemented system. The GIS database created can be used for purposes of querying and can be revised whenever new information is available. Shortest distances analysis and efficient distribution route determination were performed using spatial analysis and network analysis tools. From the distribution analysis, the service area analysis is demonstrated as giving a more realistic spatial extent of coverage compared to the buffering approach. From these analyses, the services area analysis and buffering approach showed areas of 980.96 and 223.15 Ha being beyond zone 5.

Key words: Geographic information systems, network analysis, route location.

INTRODUCTION

The Kenya national examinations council (KNEC) was established in 1980 under the KNEC Act of Parliament (CAP, 225A) of the Laws of Kenya (GoK, 1980). It was established to take over the functions previously undertaken by the defunct East African Examinations Council and the Ministry of Education to conduct school, post school and other examinations.

A narrow view of geographic information system (GIS) is that it is a computer system for the input, manipulation, storage and output of digital spatial data (Konecny, 2003). It is the integrated computer hardware and software that captures, stores, analyzes, and displays geographically referenced information (Tomlinson, 2007). It can also be defined as an organized collection of

*Corresponding author. E-mail: dn.kuria@gmail.com.

computer hardware and software, with supporting data and personnel, that captures, stores, manipulates, analyses, and displays all forms of geographically referenced information (Clarke and Langley, 1996; Birkin et al., 1996). There are as many views of GIS as uses and users with some viewing it as a way to automate the production of maps, while others see it as a complex system capable of solving geographic problems and supporting spatial decisions, with the power of GIS being an engine for analyzing data and revealing new insights. Still, others view it as a tool for maintaining complex inventories that adds spatial perspectives to existing information systems, allowing spatially distributed resources to be tracked and managed (Longley et al., 2005).

GIS has many uses in education such as being used as a teaching aid (Johansson, 2003; Zwartjes, 2010), to help with facilities management, vehicle routing, district boundary mapping, safety and preparedness, amongst a host of others (ESRI, 2010). There is a specific focus on education planning and the uses to which geographical information can be put in this context, with particular reference to the situation in Kenya. Some uses of GIS within the education sector are determination of spatial distribution of schools and the analysis of spatially referenced data (Mulaku and Nyadimo, 2011).

The traditional role of educational planners, that of planning school location, has been supplanted in recent years by additional tasks such as school improvement agenda (strategies to improve quality of school curricula) and examination target setting (Mulaku and Nyadimo, 2011). The latter target extends to KNEC, as the monitoring of performance is important, as it is not just schools which have to set targets for improved performance. There are many activities that must be carried out and monitored, largely through the use of data collected. Every time provisions are reviewed there are major changes in terms of financial cost and upheavals in schooling, which can affect the education of the youth (Langley, 1997). It is a complex situation which most of the time must be monitored, and changes implemented in as non-disruptive a manner as possible. In order to assist in this monitoring and analysis, role planners can utilize geographic information. All educational data have a spatial element and it is thus possible to visualize the enormous potential GIS holds for generating and analyzing huge datasets of geographic information, by schools, by local authorities and over time, nationally. The main uses of a GIS are, as in most other fields, the easy visualization of data and performance of sophisticated spatial analyses. KNEC has been using hardcopy maps for planning distribution and identification of various infrastructures necessary to successfully distribute and man the examinations. The hardcopy maps not needed are filed and stored and those required retrieved manually. These traditional methods of acquiring, storing and analyzing spatially referenced data have been proven to be costly and inflexible. There are several of reasons for adopting a GIS for the KNEC: Currently, the council does not have its data in digital form that can allow them to view the location of schools. At this time they only possess paper maps of the schools, which in some cases are already outdated. A geodatabase would allow the council to locate any school easily. Furthermore, visualization of the schools can be done in a more efficient fashion using data in digital form in comparison to using paper maps. Some of the issues that organizations dealing with spatially referenced data must contend with include:

1. Spatial information is poorly maintained or is often outdated: This takes the form of outdated maps. Attendant long delays in processing map revisions or inaccurate data records and summaries leads to user mistrust of the quality of the information.
2. Spatial data is not recorded or stored in a standardized way: The coordinate systems differ and map scales vary, making it difficult to use multiple data sets together.
3. The spatial data may not be defined in a consistent manner: In some cases, different organizations may require that similar data be organized using different classification systems to suit their peculiar needs.
4. Data is not shared: This arises from fear of misuse or because potential users may not know of the existence or whereabouts of the data. As a result different users keep their own copy of the original data leading to duplication of data. This results in the existence of different versions, which are not updated simultaneously.
5. Data retrieval and manipulation capabilities are inadequate: The retrieval of information such as routine reports may be too slow and the ability to perform complex or special purpose analyses of spatial information may be limited or non-existent.
6. New demands made by the organization: Such demands cannot be met using the prevailing information system in the organization. The organization's mandate may be changed or a new legal requirement may take effect that cannot be satisfied without the capabilities of GIS, or at least computerization of existing records.

The vision of KNEC is to be an efficient testing and evaluation center for quality education, while its mission is to objectively test and evaluate the curriculum to enhance and safeguard globally accepted certification standards (KNEC, 2008). The core functions of KNEC are as follows: (a) Development of school and post-school examinations, (b) registration of candidates for various examinations, (c) administration and processing of examinations, (d) certification of candidates' results, (e) researching into examinations and school curricula and, (f) evaluation, assessment and equation of certificates from other examining bodies.

The examinations developed and administered by KNEC are as follows: (i) Kenya certificate of primary

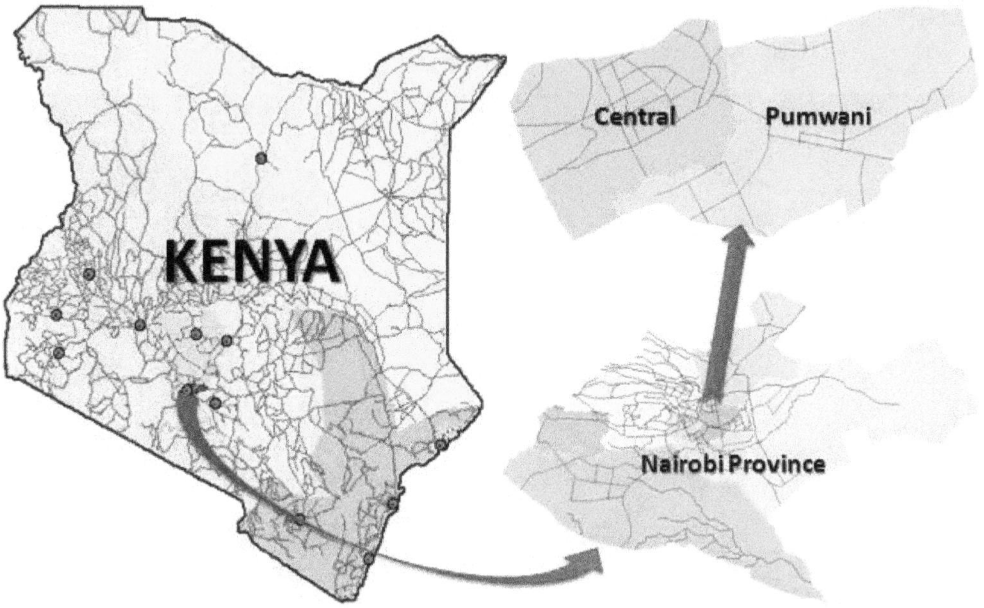

Figure 1. The study area adopted in the pilot phase.

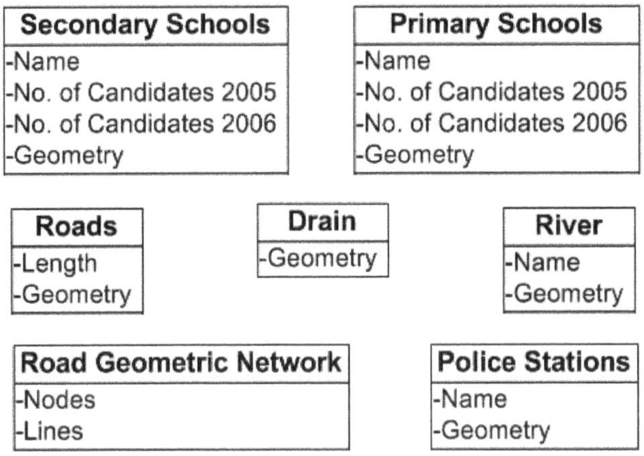

Figure 2. Feature classes and associated key attributes.

education (KCPE), (ii) Kenya certificate of secondary education (KCSE), (iii) Primary teachers examination (PTE) for both pre-service and in-service trainees, (iv) Teacher certificate in adult education (TCAE), (v) Post school examinations in business and technical subjects and, (vi) English proficiency examinations for law graduates seeking to join Kenya School of Law.

A GIS implementation will help improve maintenance of the maps as they are in digital form compared to the traditional analogue format. The objective of this research is to develop a GIS to assist the KNEC in managing examination related issues. Some of the features of this GIS will be improved efficiency in distribution of examinations, ability to evaluate schools well served by the existing distribution centers and determining routes to follow when distributing from a center to far flung schools. These features are in addition to the visualization capabilities of a GIS which can be used to generate maps showing the spatial distribution of schools.

MATERIALS AND METHODS

Study area

The study area is located in Nairobi province and lies between 36°48′39.532″ E to 36°53′1.021″ E and 1°14′59.266″ S to 1°17′51.45″ S with an approximate area of 24.535 km². It covers the two division of Central division and Pumwani division. It has about 30 primary schools and 17 secondary schools. Figure 1 shows the geographic location of the study area. In this area, there are two police stations that are usually used as the central distribution points for examination purposes. These are the Central Police Station and Kamukunji Police Station. The spatial data used in this research was provided by the Geomatic Engineering and Geospatial Information Systems (analog topographic maps). Attribute information on registration and enrollment in schools was provided by the KNEC.

To achieve the objectives of this research, the activities were divided into two main components: Data capture and network analysis. Data capture entailed conversion of existing analog data into digital form. The data collected was collated with attribute data from.

KNEC to come with data representation portrayed in Figure 2. Six main feature classes were identified of which the key were Primary Schools, Secondary Schools, Police Stations and Roads. These data were stored in a geodatabase, after which a geometric network was constructed. This network comprises of links and nodes with the links representing possible path segments that can be followed, and the nodes representing possible turning points. Common network operations include computational processes to find the shortest, least-cost, or most-efficient path (path finding), to analyze network connectivity (tracing), and to assign portions of a

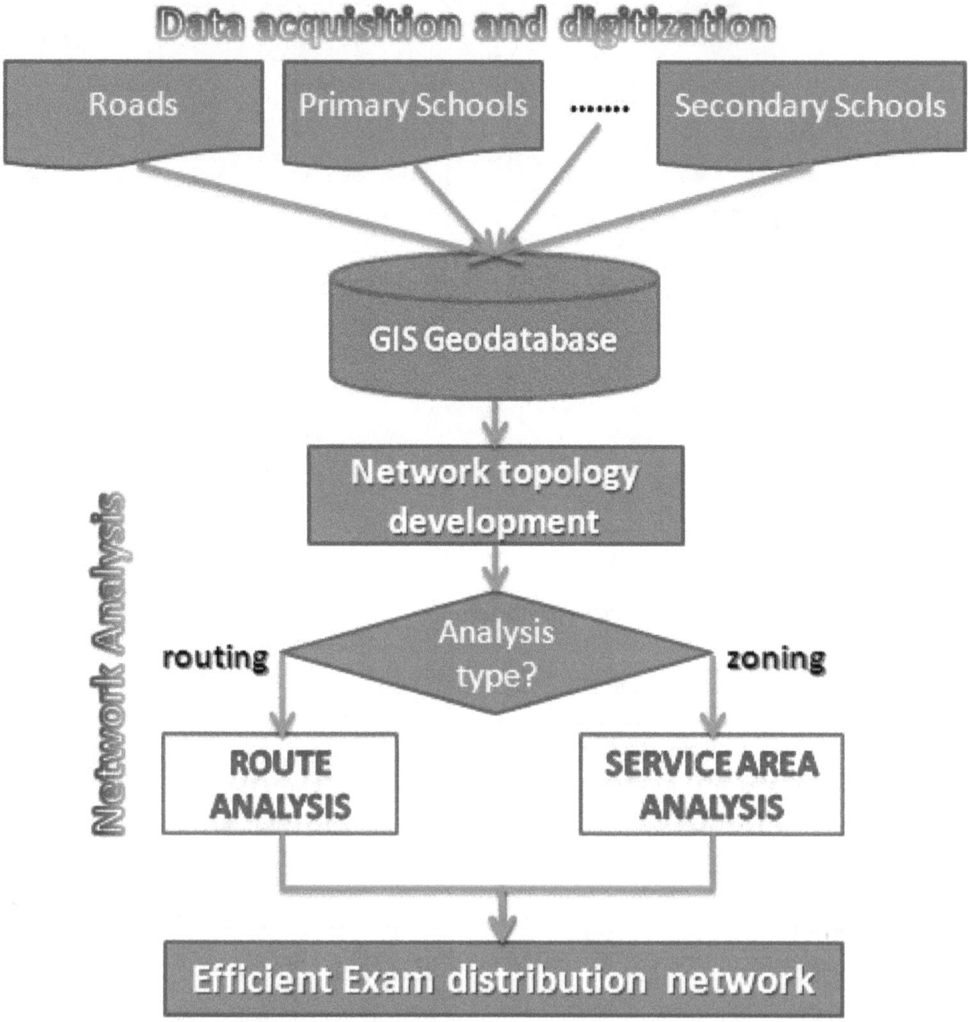

Figure 3. Methodology workflow adopted in this research.

network to a location based on some given criteria (allocation) (Jiang and Claramunt, 2004). The geometric network generated was used in "Service area analysis" and "Route analysis".

A network service area is a region that encompasses all accessible streets (that is, streets that are within specified impedance). For instance, a one-hour service area for a point on a network includes all the streets that can be reached within one hour or minutes from that point. Service areas also help evaluate accessibility. Concentric service areas show how accessibility varies with impedance (ESRI, 2010a). The notion of impedance is borrowed from electronics and refers to the resistance to traffic flow encountered when traversing the network.

Using route analysis, one can find the best way to get from one location to another or to visit several locations. The locations can be specified interactively by placing points on the screen, entering an address, or using points in an existing feature class or feature layer. In this way, in the event of needing to visit more than two points, the best route can be determined for the order of locations as specified by the user.

Depending on the type of analysis desired, a route can be selected (shortest in terms of length) between the distribution center and examination centers, or a service area can be produced showing how well the existing distribution centers are able to serve the examination centers. This scheme's workflow is represented by Figure 3.

RESULTS AND DISCUSSION

The geodatabase and geometric network developed in the research were used to answer a variety of queries spanning simple to complex queries. This geodatabase is then useful for many purposes, such as preparing charts and reports, visualization of special purpose maps, posing queries to the system and generating the efficient distribution map. For example, the geodatabase can be used to assess the trend in registration of candidates across years for both primary and secondary school students. Figure 4 shows the variation of students' registration between 2005 and 2006 for the Kenya Certificate of Primary Education. Figure 5 shows the registration of students for the Kenya Certificate of Secondary Education for the same two years. These two

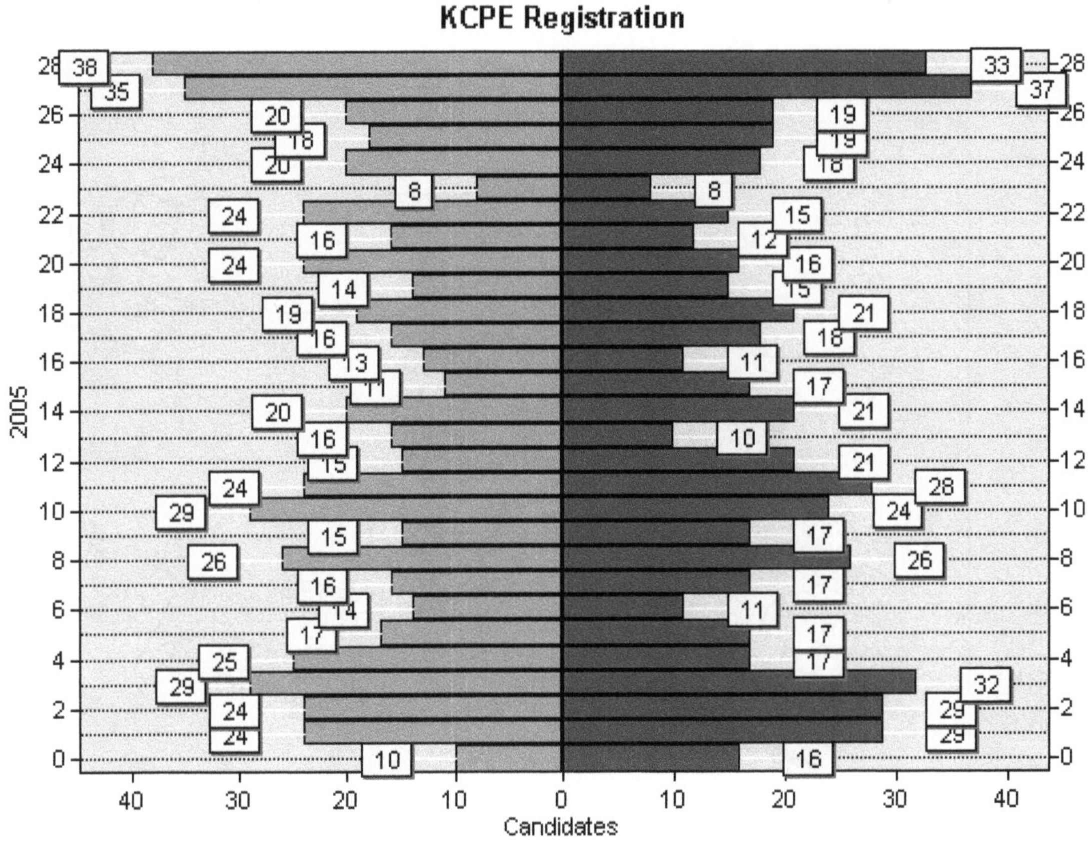

Figure 4. Graphing capabilities - KCPE registration for 2005 and 2006 compared.

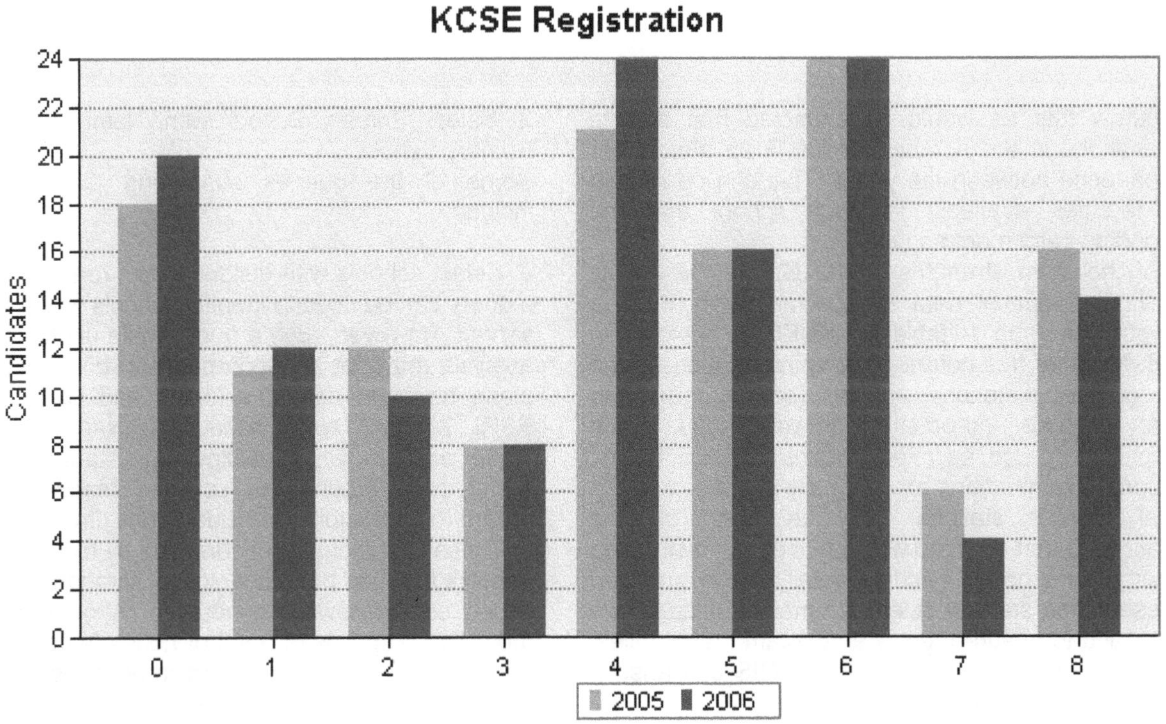

Figure 5. Graphing capabilities - KCSE registration.

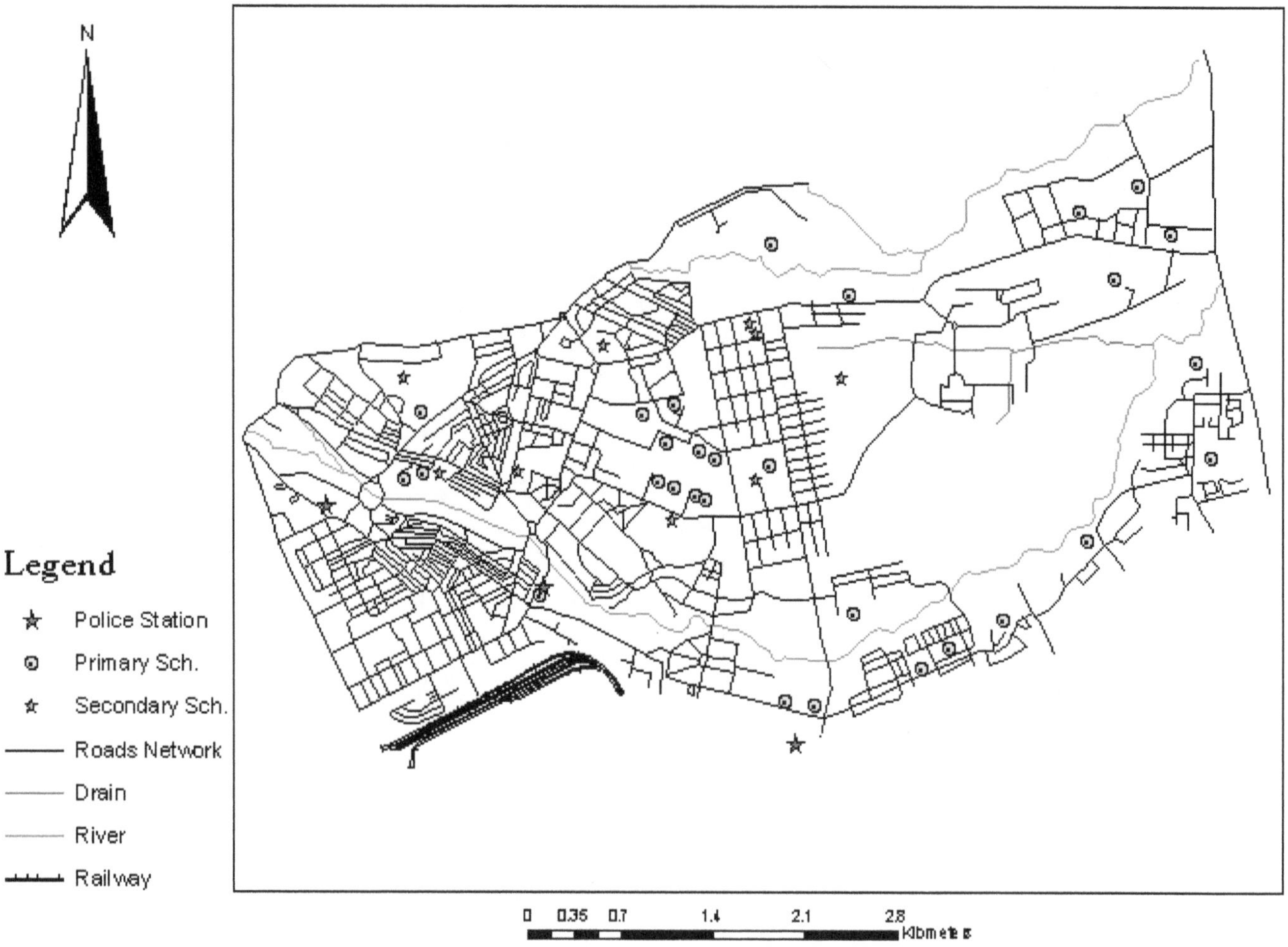

Figure 6. KNEC special purpose map.

figures show that as would be expected that despite slight variations in the numbers, there is an almost 1:1 correspondence between the years. This can be related to the facilities available in each school and the corresponding catchment population.

One of the main strengths of the GIS is the quality visualization of spatial data as special maps. Such a special purpose map suitable for KNEC is depicted in Figure 6. Maps of this nature contain information on the location of Police stations, schools (both primary and secondary), roads (geometric network) and some basemap layers such as rivers, drains and rail tracks. The national examinations are normally dispersed to the divisional police stations on the eve of the examinationsso that the following day they get distributed to the targeted schools. Security detail is also provided from these police stations to ensure maintenance of law and order and to ensure there are no exam irregularities.

Some of the simple queries that this GIS can answer include selection queries such as:

1. Select schools with 'No. of candidates 2005' > 100

2. Select 'Primary School' with 'Name' = 'Guru Nanak Primary School'

Some of the queries supporting planning purposes include:

a. Select schools with distance from roads > 1 km: Such a query can be used to identify schools which are not well served. However, such a query while useful for proximity analysis may not be appropriate in distribution analysis along transport networks (Jiang and Claramunt, 2004; ESRI, 2010a). This is because it uses the idea behind 'buffer analysis' which utilizes equidistant generation of a buffer zone around the selected feature without due regard to accessibility considerations (impedances).

b. These limitations are addressed by the road geometric network that has been developed, through which network based analyses were conducted. A geometric network topology comprises of a set of nodes (stops), link(routes) and barriers (hindrances). An impedance value can be calculated for each of the links to describe the resistance to flow along that particular link. It is possible to incorporate many factors in the calculation of impedances

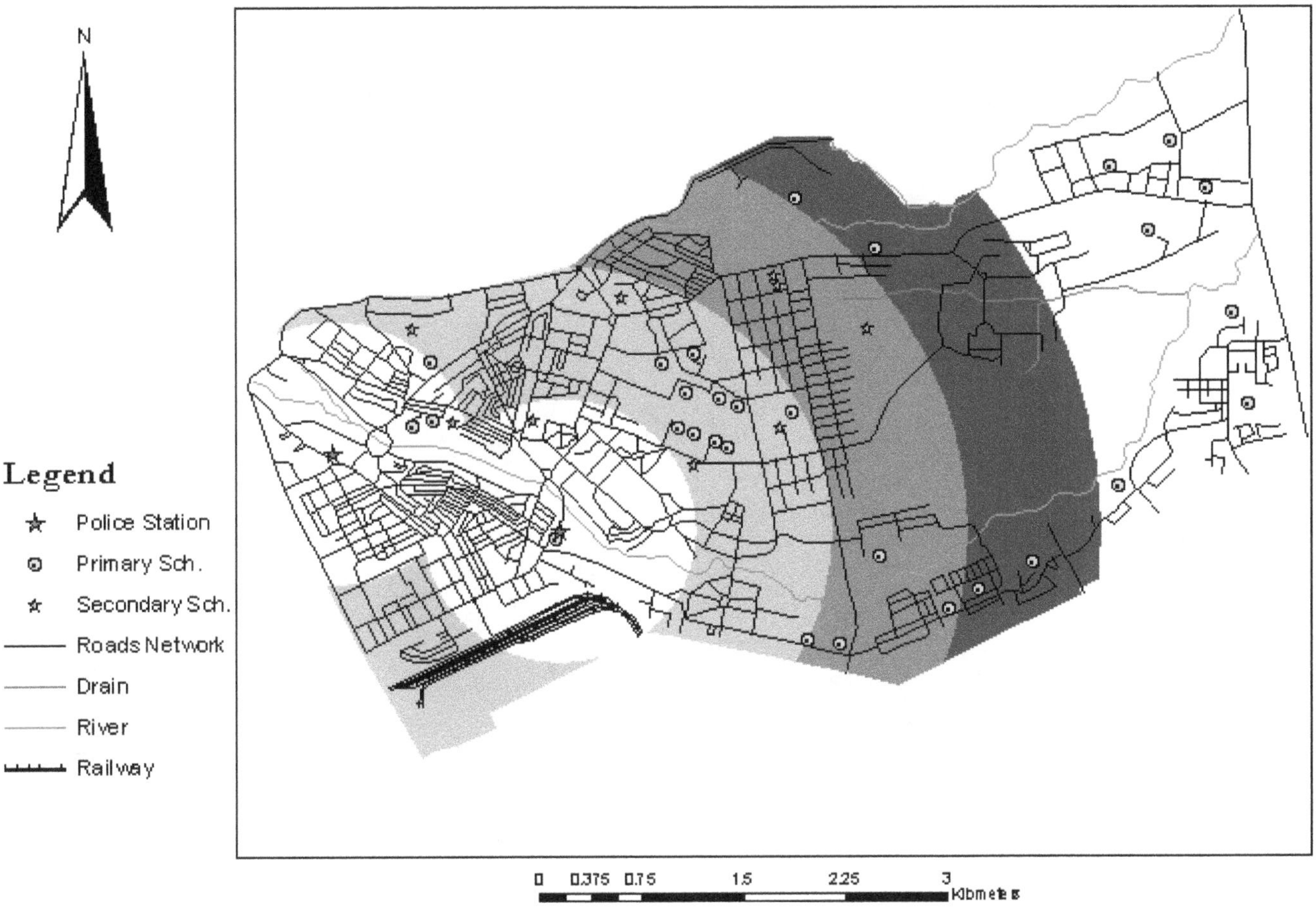

Figure 7. Buffer zoning to show how well the distribution centers serve the exam centers.

to motions such as wind speed and direction, slope of the link, road class hierarchy (can lower class road join a road of a higher class directly?), road surface condition (describing friction) etc. In this research to begin with, it is assumed that all the links have the same impedance and uses simple link length to perform the network analysis. Using this assumption, the network developed can answer the query.

C. Which is the shortest and fastest route from a point A to a point B?

In this research, the shortest route will also be flagged out as the fastest route too. However, by considering the factors outlined in the foregoing, it is clear that the shortest route to some point may not necessarily be the fastest route (most economical route).

Two types of network analyses were undertaken in this research: route analysis and service area analysis. Route analysis chooses the most appropriate route based on the criteria given (impedances) in the links and nodes, bearing in mind any barrier (physical or otherwise) that may have been placed at some sections of the network (e.g. if there are road works on some sections of a road in the network, such a road will not be available and alternate routes will be determined). Service area analysis determines how well facilities in a network are served or are serving the area (ESRI, 2010a). Buffering may accomplish more or less the same objective, but it has the shortcoming that it does not consider accessibility aspects. To clarify this fact, the two approaches are compared in Figures 7 and 8. In both cases, the zoning interval is 1 km. it can be seen that at 5 km there are still some schools that are not well served. These are in the far flung parts of the Pumwani division. These two approaches show that the current distribution of the police stations is not optimal for distribution of exams. Several approaches can be used to address this: (i) Create a police station in the Pumwani division appropriately located in the better networked portion of region to the extreme right of the division or (ii) other police stations in the neighboring divisions could be used to ameliorate this deficiency if they are used in the network analysis.

In the buffering approach the geometric network is not considered as having a significant impact on the zones, it is totally ignored. To offset this limitation, service area analysis incorporates the geometric network in the zoning. Zones are designated along possible routes originating from the distribution centers. Figure 8 shows

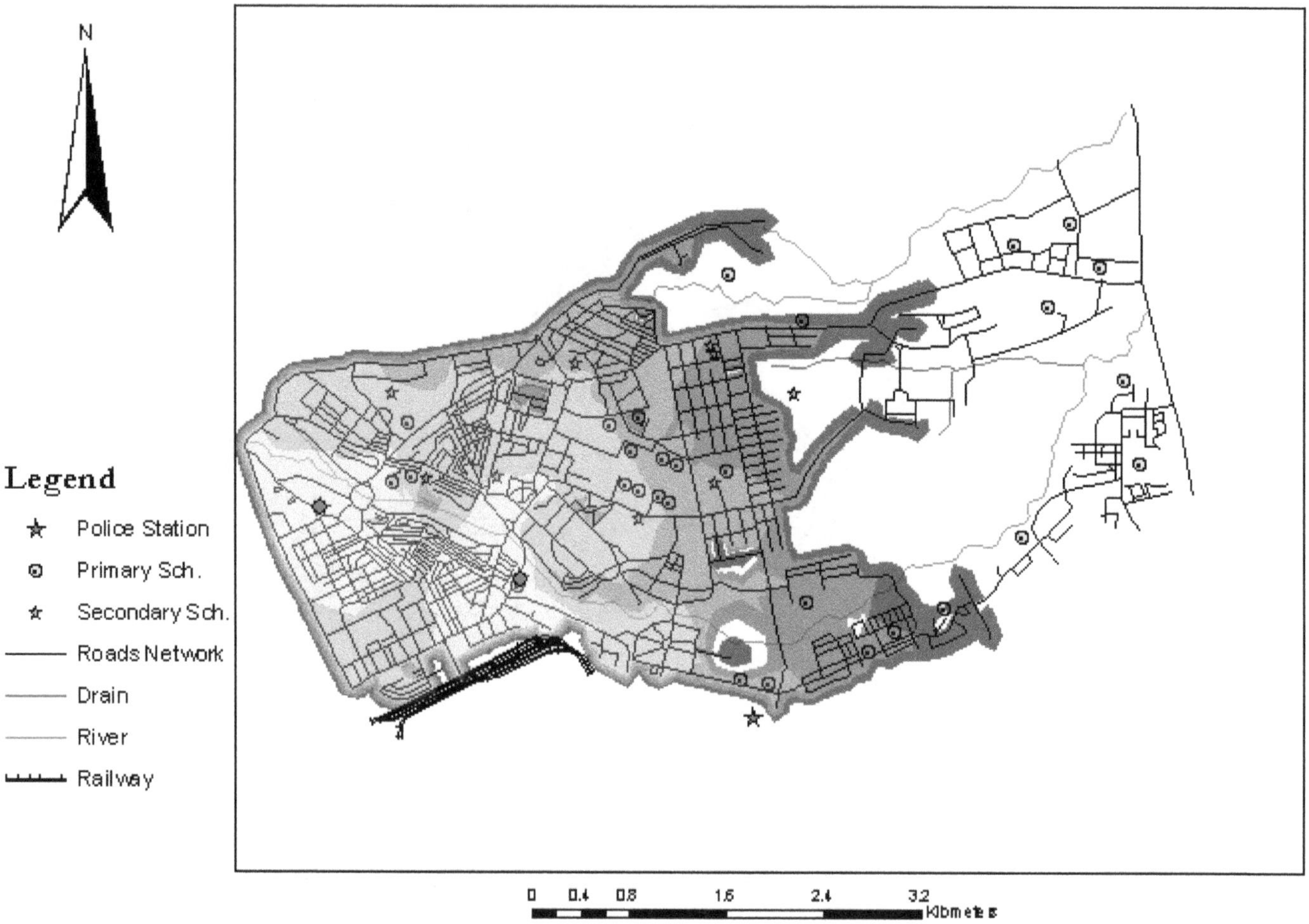

Figure 8. Service area analysis showing the effectiveness of the existing distribution network.

Table 1. Area comparison for service area viz. buffering approaches.

Zone (Km)	Service area (Ha)	Buffering (Ha)	Difference (Ha)
1	254.52	535.74	281.21
2	460.31	552.89	92.58
3	328.96	436.66	107.70
4	287.19	385.81	98.62
5	141.58	319.28	177.70
Total	1,472.56	2,230.37	757.81

the service area zoning. It is clear that there are areas that are not well served in the intermediate zones, especially where there is an inadequate road network but would have been flagged as adequately served from the buffer analysis only.

Comparing Figures 7 and 8, it can be seen that it is important to consider the distribution network's impact. There are some schools that are found within the buffer zones but are missing out in the service area zones since they can not be accessed using the existing road network.

Table 1 shows the quantitative comparison of the two approaches. Overall, it is clear that the service area analysis all round returns smaller area as it gives regard to the nature of the road network. The combined area of the divisions considered was evaluated as 2,453.52 Ha meaning that the service area analysis flags 980.96 Ha as completely beyond zone 5 while 223.15 Ha is what is beyond zone 5 from the buffering approach.

Another form of analysis possible with a geometric network which was executed in this research is route analysis. Route analysis allows one to determine alternative routes depending on the conditions that the user specifies. Creating a route can mean finding the

Figure 9. Route analysis without barriers.

quickest, shortest, or most scenic route, depending on the impedances chosen. If the impedance is time, then the best route is the quickest route. Hence, the best route can be defined as the route that has the lowest impedance, or least cost, where the impedance is chosen by the user. Any cost attribute can be used as the impedance when determining the best route (ESRI, 2008).

In this research, two scenarios are considered: (i) Network without any barriers in which case the shortest distance is computed (this research assumes uniform impedance in which case the shortest route is also the best route) throughout the network (Figure 9) and (ii) network in which barriers (e.g. roads underconstructions/ renovation and accident occurrences) are placed on some of the paths (Figure 10) to simulate situations where some routes maybe temporarily unusable.

In both scenarios the two distribution centers are the origins and four prospective destinations. Figure 9 shows the routes to the destinations following the shortest paths corresponding to scenario 1. In the second scenario, three barriers are introduced along the shortest paths picked in scenario 1. Figure 10 show the new alternative shortest paths through the same points.

Conclusion

A prototype GIS has been developed, capable of answering simple attribute and spatial queries and visualization of spatial data. This GIS has at its core a geodatabase that will be useful in efficient and effective planning for better management and decision making by KNEC. It addresses the challenge of fast data access, retrieval, manipulation and storage that the agency has grappled with in managing the schools information. A geometric network using roads data has been developed that can be used to perform efficient routing between distribution centers and various examination centers. This network has been demonstrated as being capable of showing examination centers that are not well served by the existing distribution network. It has also been shown

Figure 10. Route analysis circumventing three (3) barriers.

that with respect to determining a distribution network, it is better to use service area analysis rather than buffer analysis.

Several improvements are recommended, but which can follow after the prototype has been implemented. First, it is recommended that the geodatabase developed in this research can be connected to other KNEC and education sector related databases (e.g. teacher-student ratios, teaching resource facilities etc). This will improve the utility of the overall system as such information can be linked to the spatial data to unravel unique relationships hidden in the data.

Secondly, it is recommended that information about impedance factors (contributors) be collected and incorporated to improve the value of the results obtained from the system. From the findings of the research, it is proposed that a new distribution center should be designated or established in Pumwani division to ease the distribution strain. This center will serve the far flung schools in the division. It is further recommended that the prototype should be extended to cover the whole of Nairobi province and ultimately nationally.

ACKNOWLEDGEMENTS

The authors wish to appreciate facilitation during data acquisition and execution of the research quest by the Jomo Kenyatta University of Agriculture and Technology. The three anonymous reviewers who reviewed the manuscript gave critical insights and their remarks have greatly helped improve the manuscript and their contribution is appreciated.

REFERENCES

Birkin M, Clarke GP, Clarke M and Wilson AG (1996). Intelligent GIS, Geoinformation. Cambridge.

Clarke GP, Langley R (1996). The potential of GIS and spatial modelling for planning in the new education market. Environment and Planning C, Government and Policy, 14: 301-323.

ESRI (2008). Network Analysis. ArcGIS desktop help. ESRI Press, California.

ESRI (2010). *GIS for Schools.* Retrieved october 12, 2011, from GIS for Education: http://www.esri.com/industries/k-12/index.html.
ESRI (2010a). Types of network analysis layers. ESRI Press, California.
Government of Kenya (1980). Kenya National Examination Council Act, CAP 255A. Laws of Kenya. Government Printers, Nairobi.
Jiang B and Claramunt C (2004). Topological analysis of urban street networks. Environment and Planning B: Planning and Design, 31: 151-162.
Johansson T (2003). GIS in Teacher Education – Facilitating GIS. Retrieved October 13, 2011, from Scan GIS: http://www.scangis.org/scangis2003/papers/20.pdf.
Kenya National Examination Council (2008). Mission and vision. Retrieved September 14 2010, from KNEC: http://www.examscouncil.or.ke/mission.php.
Konecny G (2003). Geoinformation: Remote sensing, photogrammetry and Geographic Information Systems. Taylor and Francis, London.
Langley R (1997). The use and development of GIS and spatial interaction models for planning in education. PhD thesis. University of Leeds, Leeds.
Longley PA, Goodchilde MF, Maguire D J and Rhind DW (2005). Geographic Information Systems and Science. John Wiley and Sons Ltd, Chichester.
Mulaku GC and Nyadimo E (2011). GIS in Education Planning: The Kenyan School Mapping Project. Surv. Rev., 43(323): 567-578.
Tomlinson R (2007). Thinking about GIS: Geographic Information System Planning for Managers (Third ed.). ESRI Presss, California.
Zwartjes L (2010). iGuess: Introducing GIS Use in Education in Several Subjects. Retrieved Oct. 12, 2011, from iGuess Project: http://www.iguess.eu/uploads/docs/geotech03.pdf.

14

Cross layer based miss detection ratio under variable rate for intrusion detection in WLAN

Ravneet Kaur

Department of Computer science and Engineering, Beant College of Engineering and Technology, Gurdaspur Punjab, India. E-mail: reet.kahlon@gmail.com.

The emphasis for the use of wireless LAN in industry is on robustness, reliability and security. Almost any given single secruity mechanism (such as MAC filtering) alone may be easily overcome by attackers. However, proper configuration and implemetation of the maximum possible security mechanism must be used to form a multiple security layers, to provide the best possible wireless protection. The present paper deals with cross layer based miss detection ratio under variable rate for intrusion detection in WLAN. In cross layer based intrusions detection, the decision is based on the combine on weight value of two or more layer. So the decision is not based on single layer, it will reduce false positive rate. Two different layers, physical and MAC have been used in the present study and the results have been compared with existing technique.

Key words: Reciever signal strength (RSS), time taken for RTS-CTS handshake (TT), radio frequency (RF).

INTRODUCTION

Owing to developments made in the wireless technology in the recent years, wireless LAN is rapidly winning acceptance as an alternate solution for many applications in industrial environments. The high degree of flexibility it provides within the plant can lead to cost reduction during both installation and operation. Features such as fast roaming times, coverage, worldwide acceptance and proven security concepts have further increased the attractiveness of wireless solution in business and industry. A wireless network is not as secure as compare the wired network because the data is transferred on air so any intruder can use hacking techniques to access that data. Indeed it is difficult to protect the data and provide the user a secure information system for lifetime. An intrusion detection system aim to detect the different attacks against network and system. An intrusion detection system should be capable for detecting the misuse of the network whether it will be by the authenticated user or by an attacker. They detect attempts and active misuse either by legitimate users of the information systems or by external (Mukherjee et al., 1994). The aim of intruder is to gain the access of the privileges. Generally, this show that intruder want information which is protected.

INTRUSION DETECTION SYSTEM

Inevitably, the best intrusion prevention system will fail. A system's second line of defense is intrusion detection, and this has been the focus of much research in recent years (Dasgupta, 2002; Debar et al., 1999; Denning, 1987; Thamilarasu et al., 2005; Jeyanthi, 2005; Lim et al., 2003)

Types of intrusion detection systems

There are two types of intrusion detection system: First, network based intrusion detection system (NIDS) which resides on network. Second, host based intrusion detection system (HIDS) which resides on host that is computer system (Rakesh, 2010; Madhavi, 2008; Shafiullah, 2010; Zhang and Lee, 2000)

Network based intrusion detection system (NIDS)

Network based intrusion detection system resides on network. It exists as software process on hardware system. It change the network interface card (NIC) into promiscuous mode, that is, the card passes all traffic on the network to the NIDS software. The software includes the rules which are used to analyze the traffic. It analyzes the incoming packets against these rules to determine the signature of the attacker. Whether this traffic signature is of any attacker or not, if it is of interest then events are generated (Mukherjee et al., 1994; Dasgupta, 2002; Debar et al., 1999).

The data source to NIDS is raw packets. It utilizes a network adapter which is running in promiscuous mode to monitor and analyze the network. There are four common techniques to identify attack.

(a) Frequency or threshold crossing.
(b) Correlation of lesser events.
(c) Statistical anomaly detection.
(d) Pattern, expression or byte code matching.

NIDS is not limited to read all the incoming packets only. But also learn the valuable information on outgoing traffic. With this feature the attacker form inside the monitored network are identified.

Host based intrusion detection system (HIDS)

Host based IDS are embedded on host computer. It exists as a software process on a system. So it examines the log entries in system for specific information. It identifies the new entries and compares them to pre configured rules. It also works on rule based, if the entry match to the rule, then it will generate alarm that this is not a legal user.

Anomaly based detection

Anomaly detection attempts to model the normal behavior. Any occurring event which violates this model behavior is reflecting to be suspicious. It aim is to detect the patterns that do not conform normal behavior. The pattern that does not conformed as normal are called anomalies (Wang et al., 2009; Bal, 2009).

Misuse based detection

The equations are an exception to the prescribed specifications of this template. You will need to determine whether or not your equation should be typed using either the times new roman or the symbol font (please no other font). To create multileveled equations, it may be necessary to treat the equation as a graphic and insert it into the text after your paper is styled.

CROSS LAYER BASED TECHNIQUE

Cross layer based technique is used to make decision that whether there is an attacker or not by combining the result of two or more layer in TCP protocol (Wang et al., 2009; Bal, 2009).

Monitoring received signal strength (RSS)

A measure of energy which is observed by the physical layer at the antenna of the receiver is called received signal strength (RSS). In IEEE 802.11 networks, while performing MAC clear channel measurement and in roaming operations, the RSS indication value is used. The radio frequency (RF) signal strength can be measured through absolute (decibel mill watts - dBm), or relative (RSSI) manner.

Exact RSS value from sender to receiver is not easy to assume as mention previously. To assume exact value of RSS the attacker has to be present on the same location which is not possible. The radio equipment used by the receiver have to be same for identify exact value of RSS. Moreover there should be same level of reflection, refraction, and interface. Even if the sender is fixed, RSS value seems to vary a little and it is proved that it is almost not possible to guess. This restricts the attacker from using the radio equipment to spoof the RSS clearly by the receiver.

A dynamic profile is build of the computer node which are communicating depend upon the RSS value from a server. Any sudden or unusual changes can be marked as doubtful activity which indicates the possible session of hijacking attack. Any sudden changes in the RSS dynamic profile can be marked as doubtful activity with a higher confidence level because BSs are generally immobile. On the other hand, if the MS is mobile, then its respective RSS values will vary quickly which can be observed by the server. Therefore, the uncertainty of the wireless medium can be used in the favor of intrusion detection, where the attacker is unable to know what RSS values to spoof. Therefore, it is effective for the session hijacking attacks and it does not need any additional bandwidth consumption. For example, based on the observed RSS values at the server it can develop a dynamic RSS profile for both MS2 and BS when a valid MS2 has an active session with a BS (Figure 1). If an attacker MS1 hijacks MS2 through isolating from the network and spoofing its MAC address then the server will pick up the abrupt changes in the RSS profile of MS2's MAC and gives an alert signal. Since they depend on the MS1's actual location, radio equipment and surrounding environment the RSS values for the MS2's MAC address will change.

In another situation, if the attacker MS1 spoofs the base station BS then it will also get detected as the dynamic RSS profile for the BS undergoes sudden

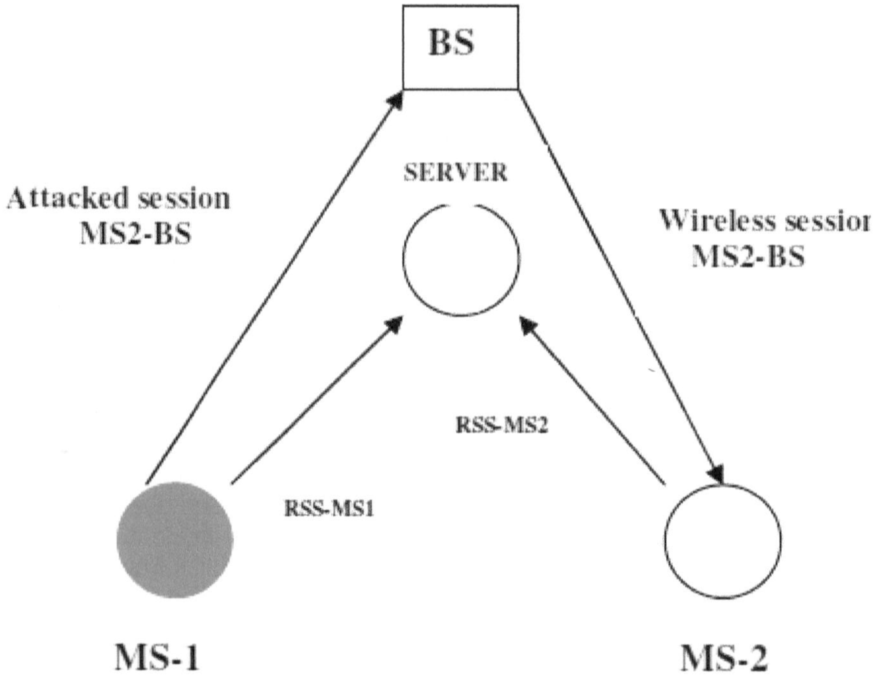

Figure 1. Received signal strength (RSS).

variations. Therefore, this mechanism gives detection for both session hijacking and man-in-the-middle attacks which is targeted at either MSs or BSs.

Monitoring time taken For RTS-CTS handshake

Virtual carrier sensing is created using RTS-CTS which makes the transmission of data frames possible without collision. The successful delivery of the CTS frame from the receiver shows that the receiver is received the senders RTS frame successfully and ready for receiving the data. The time taken to complete the RTS-CTS handshake between itself and receiver that is, TT can be examined by the sender. This is the total time taken for the RTS frame to travel from the sender to receiver and also for the CTS frame to send an acknowledgement. RTS-CTS handshake is free from collisions with any network node.

The TT values for a fixed transmission rate are not affected because the size of RTS and CTS frames are fixed and makes the TT betoneen two nodes as an unspoofable parameter. So this cannot be easily guessed by an attacker when tracking the waves. Since it is calculated by the sender of the RTS-CTS handshake, it is also protected from snooping. Since it is a measurement related to the entity measuring, the attacker should be exactly at the same location as the sender. Also, the attacker should use the same radio equipment with the same attenuation and antenna gain. In order to predict the values of TT betoneen the sender and receiver as measured by the sender, the attacker should receive the radio waves after the same number of reflections and refractions. It can also be calculated without any particular computation.

From the intrusion detection point of view, a mechanism which is used to detect the session hijacking attacks uses the quick and sudden changes in the TT betoneen the two nodes. Server can measure the time elapsed betoneen when it detects RTS frame from the sender to receiver and when it detects a return CTS from the receiver back to the sender that is, TT. For understanding, this time can be represented as:

$$TT = TT_M - TT_{s-r} - TT_{m-s} \tag{1}$$

Where, TT_{s-r} is time taken for a RTS frame to cover the distance betoneen the sender and the server, TT_{m-s} - time taken for a RTS frame to cover the distance betoneen the server and the receiver, TT_M - time taken for a $RTS - CTS$ handshake to complete betoneen a sender and receiver as observed by the server. But the server does not know these actual values.

Monitoring observed TT values at the server provides a reliable passive detection mechanism for session hijacking attacks since TT is an unspoofable parameter related to its measuring entity. Also, this cannot be guessed because its exact value depends on;

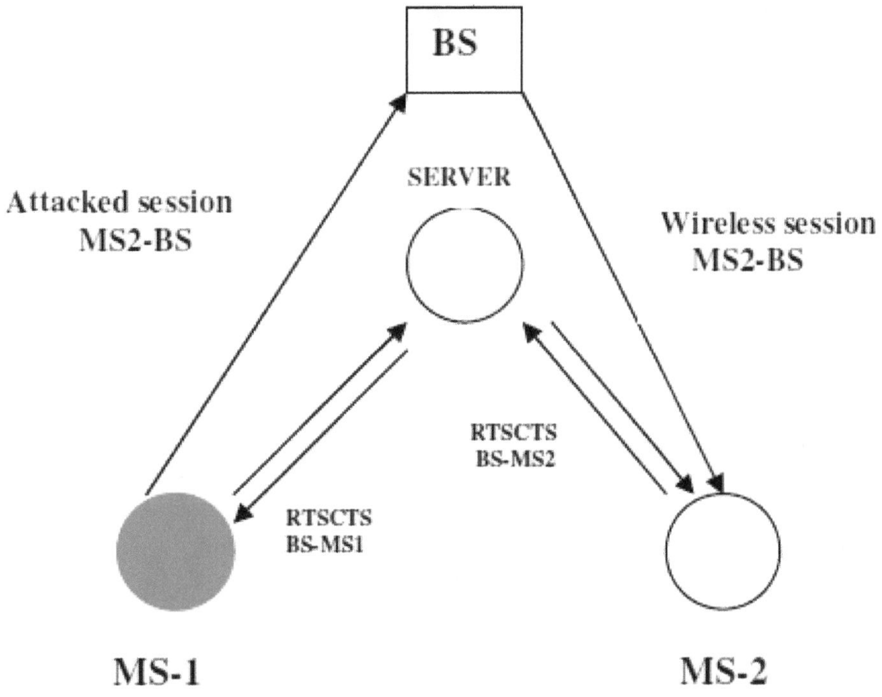

Figure 2. Round trip time (RTT).

1. The position of the receiver and the server
2. The distance betoneen the server and receiver
3. The environment around the receiver and the server.

This is a property which cannot be measured or spoofed by an attacker when tracking the network traffic or using a specialized radio equipment. It has been proposed (Bal, 2009) that changes in TT betoneen two communicating nodes can be observed by a passive server and the sudden variations are marked as suspicious. This helps to detect the attacker who tries to take over a receiver's session by isolating it off the network and spoofing its MAC address. On the other hand, the $RTS-CTS$ handshake which originates from the receiver is used to detect the session hijacking attacks which aims the sender.

For example, the server can develop a dynamic RSS profile which gets constantly updated per session and it calculates the TT for every $RTS-CTS$ handshake from both MS2 and BS when a valid MS2 has an active session with a BS (Figure 2). If an attacker MS1 hijacks MS2 through spoofing its MAC address then the server will observe abrupt changes in the TT for MS2 and gives an alert signal. Also, to detect the man-in-the-middle attacks against BS, TT values from $RTS-CTS$ handshakes betoneen MS2 and BS which originates from MS2 can be registered by the server in the MS2's profile. The Server executes the following algorithm, to detect the attackers.

Detection algorithm

Step 1: Server measures RSS
Step 2: Server measures TT
Step 3: Server calculates the on eight W as.,

$$W = w1.\delta_{RSS} + w2.\delta_{TT} \quad (2)$$

Where δ_{RSS} = Variation of RSS and δ_{TT} = Variation of TT. $w1$ and $w2$ are two constants, which can be fine tuned.
Step 4: If $W > Dthr$, (where $Dthr$ is the detection threshold) Then MS is an attacker.

This technique has been successfully applied for intrusion detection in mobile adhoc network (Bal, 2009). The present study aims to determine the application of the technique proposed by Bal (2009) for WLAN system in order to study the effect of range on the performance asonell as compared to existing techniques.

EXPERIMENTAL ASPECT IN PRESENT STUDY

The following hardware/software platforms have been used to conduct the proposed study:

1. Hardware platform: INTEL CORE i5 n series processor.

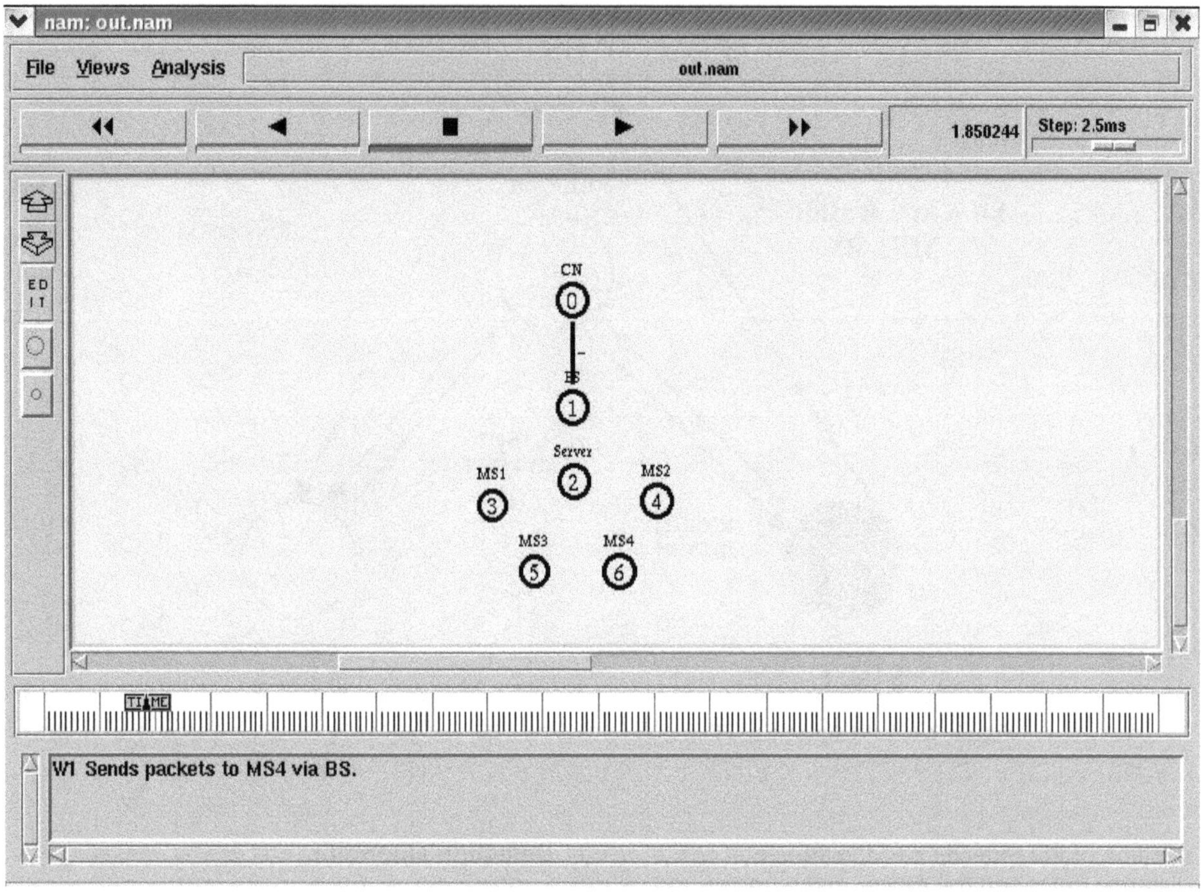

Figure 3. Simulation scenario.

2. Software platform: LINUX OS and Ns 2 simulator.

The number of wireless network devices will soon surpass the number of wired devices, and the amount of research in the area of wireless networking is increasing at a similar rate (Madhavi, 2008). Wireless research often involves a test bed implementation and/or a simulation study. Network simulators allow researchers to analyze the behavior of these wireless devices at every level. As a result, these simulations are capable of producing very large amounts of data. The simulation community has made available many types of scripts (e.g., tracegraph to parse and analyze this output data, but visualization of the data is needed to further aid understanding of the output. A good visualization package is important, because the human visual system is unrivaled in pattern recognition and offers the ability to process large amounts of data quickly and clearly (Debar et al., 1999). Visualization adds to the understanding gained via statistical analysis. As one show in this paper, certain erroneous network behaviors could go undetected without visualizations.

The Network simulator 2 (NS-2) is a popular and powerful simulation environment, and the number of NS-2 users has increased greatly in recent years. Although, it was originally designed for wired networks, NS-2 has been extended to work with wireless networks, including wireless LANs, mobile ad hoc networks, and sensor networks.

RESULTS AND DISCUSSION

In order to test the protocol, the NS2 simulator is used. The experimental consist of 1 wired node, 1 base station and 4 master stations with one server. One compares our proposed cross-layer based intrusion detection technique with the radio frequency fingerprinting (RFF) technique. Figure 3 shows the snapshot of experimental setup for the present study.

Effect of varying rate on miss detection ratio

In the first experiment, the attack traffic rate is varied as 50,100,150,200 and 250 kb. Figure 4 shows the misdetection ratio of our cross-layer technique and RFF. From the figure, one can see that the misdetection ratio is

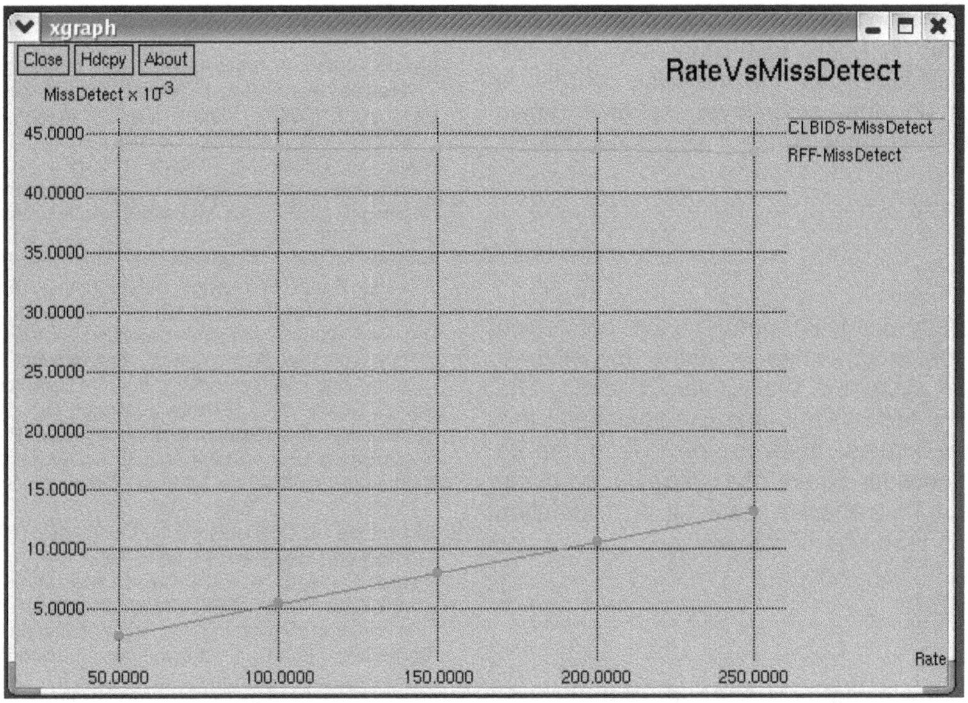

Figure 4. Rate Vs miss detection ratio.

significantly less in the cross-layer scheme when compared with RFF scheme, since it accurately detects the intrusion.

The purposed technique is based on cross layer, where two layers have been used that is, physical layer and MAC layer. On physical layer, one computes the RSS value, which is evaluated by the receiver at destination node. RSS value is computed by the omnidirectional antenna at receiver node. Second on MAC layer RTS/CTS handshake time is computed. RTS/CTS is used to avoid collision on network. The combine result value is submitted to the server, which becomes the threshold value Dthr and when a new session is made the server will compare the current RSS and RTS/CTS time taken with the previous value Dth. If that value is less than previous value then it is an attacker. RSS value depends upon the type of antenna being used as well as the reflection, refraction and interference. If an attacker want to pretend as the authenticated user by accessing its MAC address, but using this technique the attacker is unable to identify the RSS value because he may not be using same antenna and even there is not same reflection, refraction and interference. So he is unable to know the exact value.

RTS/CTS fame makes the transmission of packets without collision. RTS/CTS time taken is computed by the sender. A successful delivery of CTS frame from receiver to sender shows that RTS frame is delivered to the receiver. RTS/CTS frame has a fixed transmission rate. This makes TT parameter unspoofable, so the attacker is unable to detect TT parameter. As describe in previous cases, it is difficult for an attacker to access the session, because only with MAC address he cannot access the session, the server is computing RSS and RTS/CTS time taken (which is not exactly as the authenticated user). This shows that this technique will reduce the chance of intrusion. Moreover, due to combine result of two layers the false positive rate is also reduced.

Conclusion

In the scenario, there are 1 wired node, 1 base station and 4 master stations (1 as server). The transmission range is set from 100 to 400 m. The antenna used here is omnidirectional, with two way propagation. There are two domains with one cluster in each, 1 node in first cluster and 6 in the second cluster. When the simulation starts the RSS value and RTS/CTS handshake time is captured. The threshold value is taken by the packet size plus the channel idle time. Then the procedure to check the attacker is started where one gets the delta RSS, TT values by subtracting it from current values form the previous values. Both of these values are evaluated by multiplying two of the eight parameters of W1 and W2. Then the combine result of these is checked against the Dth (threshold value). If it is less than the Dth value then that person is an attacker.

Purposed technique is compared with the figure printing technique and the simulation result shows that the cross layer based intrusion detection system (CLBIDS) technique is better technique than the RFF technique. It is concluded that the misdetection ratio is significantly less in the cross-layer scheme when compared with RFF scheme, since it accurately detects the intrusion.

Future work

The effect of other dominant performance enhancing parameters will be incorporated in future for efficient intrusion detection system in the wireless domain. The future scope of this technique is one can implement this technique in many wireless hardware devices. It can be implemented in network where the decision is made whether to accept that attacker data for a destination node by computing RSS and TT values.

Impact of study

Wireless mesh networking has been a cost-effective technology that provides wide-coverage broadband wireless network services. They benefit both service providers with low cost in network deployment, and end users with ubiquitous access to the Internet from anywhere at any time. However, as wireless mesh network (WMN) proliferate security and privacy issues associated with this communication paradigm have become more and more evident and thus need to be addressed. The present study will be useful to provide a good foundation to implement real time detection.

ACKNOWLEDGEMENTS

The author is thankful to Dr. Jatinder Singh Bal (Dean and Professor, Computer Science and Engineering Desh Bhagat Enggineering College, Moga) for critical discussion as well as constant help during the present study. The constant encouragement provided by Dr. H S Johal as well as Mr. Dalwinder Singh and Deepak Prashar, Lovely Professional University Jalandhar is also acknowledged.

REFERENCES

Bal JS (2009). A cross layer based intrusion detection technique for wireless network. Int. J. Comput. Sci. Inf. Secur., p. 5.

Dasgupta D (2002). Cougaar Based Intrusion Detection System (Cids). Cs Technical Report No. Cs- 02- 001.

Debar H, Dacier M, Onespi A (1999). Towards A Taxonomy of Intrusion-Detection Systems. Computer Networks, pp. 805-822.

Denning D (1987). An Intrusion-Detection Model. IEEE Trans. Softw. Eng., 13(2): 222-232.

Jeyanthi H (2005). Enhancing Intrusion Detection in Wireless Networks Using Radio Frequency Fingerprinting. IEEE Trans. Dependable Secure Computi., pp. 18-22.

Lee WY (2000). Intrusion Detection in Wireless Ad-Hoc Networks. Proc. of the Sixth Annual International Conference on Mobile Computing And Networking, Boston: Massachussetts, pp. 26-31.

Lim Y, Schmoyer T, Levine J, Oonen HL (2003). Wireless Intrusion Detection and Response. Proc of IEEE Workshop On Information Assurance United States Military Academy, pp. 22-26.

Madhavi S (2008). An Intrusion Detection System In Mobile Adhoc Networks. Int. J. Secur. Appl., 2(3): 11-17.

Mukherjee B, Heberlein LT, Levitt KN (1994). Network Intrusion Dtetction. Ieee Network, pp. 8-10.

Rakesh S (2010). A Novel Cross Layer Intrusion Detection System in MANET. Proc. IEEE International Conference on Advanced Information Networking and Applications, pp. 38-48.

Shafiullah K (2010). Framework for Intrusion Detection in IEEE 802.11 Wireless Mesh Networks. Int. Arab J. Inf. Technol., 7(4): 50-55.

Thamilarasu G, Balasubramanian A, Mishra S, Sridhar R (2005). A Cross-Layer Based Intrusion Detection Approach For Wireless Ad Hoc Networks. Proc. IEEE International Conference on Mobile Adhoc and Sensor Systems Conference, p. 861.

Wang X, Wong JS, Stanley F, Basu S (2009). Cross-layer Based Anomaly Detection in Wireless Mesh Networks. Ninth Annual International Symposium on Applications and the Internet.

15

A review on advances in iris recognition methods

Fuad .M. Alkoot

HITN-PAAET P. O. Box 4575, Alsalmia, 22046, Kuwait. E-mail: f_alkoot@yahoo.com. Tel: +965 66012265.

Iris recognition is one of the most accurate identity verification systems. Since its initial introduction by J. Daughman, many methods have been proposed to enhance the performance. We present an overview of the latest research on iris recognition by categorizing the research in four groups outlined as localization, segmentation, coding and recognition. We present the latest developments explaining advances to solve problems existing at each of iris recognition stages.

Key words: Biometrics, identity verification, iris recognition, pattern recognition, iris segmentation, iris localization and iris code.

INTRODUCTION

Iris background

Identity verification and identification is becoming increasingly popular. Initially fingerprint, voice and face have been the main biometrics used to distinguish individuals. However, advances in the field have expanded the options to include other biometrics such as iris, retina, ear, vein, gait, smell and more. Among the large set of options, it has been shown that the iris (Daugman, 2004) is the most accurate biometric. We aim at presenting the latest advances that resolve common problems associated with iris recognition.

The iris is the elastic, pigmented, connective tissue that controls the pupil. The iris is formed in early life in a process called morphogenesis where it begins to form during the third month of gestation (Kronfeld, 1962). The structures creating its striking patterns are developed in the eight month (Wolff, 1948), although pigment accretion may continue into the first postnatal years. Once fully formed, the texture is stable throughout life while the pattern becomes permanent after puberty. The iris of the eye has a unique pattern, from eye to eye and person to person. Each iris is a meshwork of melanocyte and fibroblast cells (Johnston, 1992). The colour depends on the density of the cells and the concentration of pigment. Contrary to blue eyes, brown eyes have high cell densities and large amounts of pigmentation. The layers of the iris have both ectodermal and mesodermal origin, consisting of (from back to front): a darkly pigmented epithelium; pupillary dilator and sphincter muscles; a vascularized stroma (connective tissue of interlacing ligaments containing melanocytes); and an anterior layer with a genetically determined (Imesh et al., 1997) density of melanin pigment granules. The combined effect is a visible pattern displaying distinctive features such as arching ligaments, crypts, ridges, and a zigzag collarette (Figure 1).

The richness, uniqueness, and immutability of iris texture, as well as its external visibility, make the iris suitable for automated and highly reliable personal identification. This means that the probability of finding two people with identical iris patterns is almost zero (Daugman and Downing, 2001b). Although the iris stretches and contracts to adjust the size of the pupil in response to light, its detailed texture remains largely unaltered apart from stretching and shrinking. Such distortions in the texture can readily be reversed mathematically in analyzing an iris image, to extract and encode an iris signature that remains the same over a wide range of papillary dilations. These unique features of the iris present it as the best biometric identification method. Besides its use as a biometric identification feature, iris code has also been used as a secret key. Ziauddin and Dailey (2010) generate a biometric secret key based on an iris code. They manipulate the key information using error correcting codes that increase reliability and robustness of the system. The resulting system has a higher security rate compared to cryptography based keys.

There are few papers surveying the latest work on iris recognition. Daugman (2007) attempts to survey the advances in iris recognition in a detailed mathematical

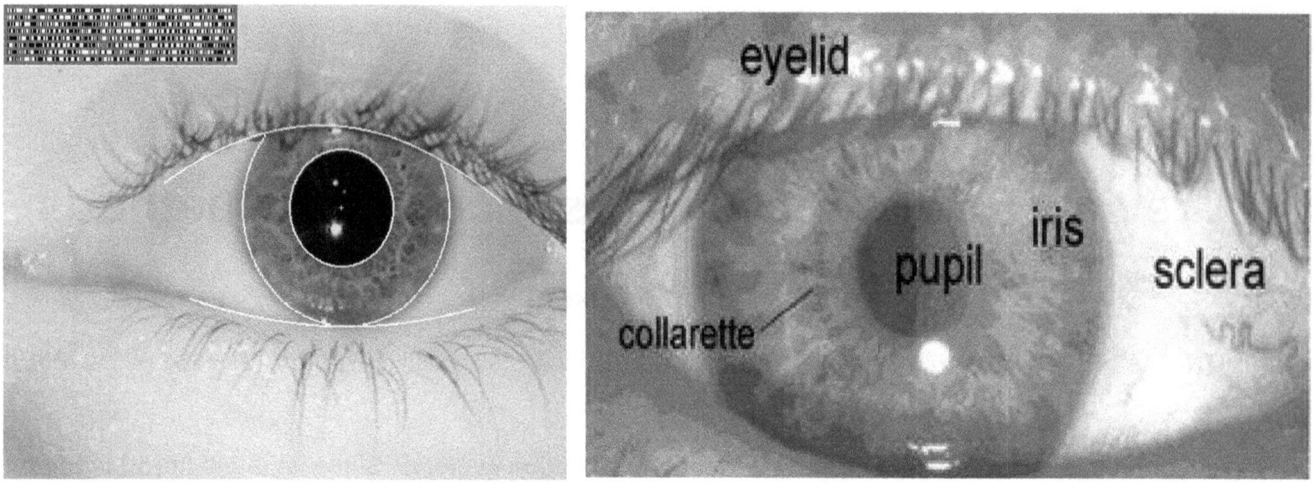

Figure 1. A sample of an iris of a human.

analysis of how some problems were solved. He discusses methods for detecting and modeling the iris inner and outer boundaries with active contours, leading to more flexible embedded coordinate systems, Fourier-based methods for solving problems in iris trigonometry, statistical inference methods for detecting and excluding eyelashes and exploring of score normalizations. Ng et al. (2008) present a survey on different iris recognition methods with an emphasis on methods that improve speed and accuracy. They also discuss benchmark databases. Popescu-Bodorin and Balas (2010) presents an overview of major algorithms where they present a tabular comparison of methods used at each of the three stages by 16 prominent papers. They show that good alternatives to Daugmans method exist. Popescu-Bodorin and Balas (2010) presents three artificial intelligence challenges in iris recognition systems: to build an exploratory supervised intelligent agent for iris recognition; to build at least a rudimentary control unit enabling an exploratory agent to act independently based on its own decisions; and describe radial iris movement through approximate equations formulated in the framework of discrete image topology. New recognition results based on the first publicly available set of processing tools for University of Bath Iris Image Database (UBIID) are also presented.

In this paper, we present the latest developments explaining advances to solve problems associated with image acquisition such as non-frontal face images and off angle iris. Problems at the segmentation stage such as iris boundary detection problems, ghosts caused by visible light, degraded system performance due to noisy iris images, and many problems due to inaccuracies at earlier stages. We also discuss advances that lead to improvement in iris system performance, improvement in iris coding methods, and improvement in recognition methods. We also present a review on a comparative study of different iris methods to find the effect of different parameters on the recognition rate, and to find an answer to the question of which approach is most suitable for extracting iris features.

Subsequently, in primary iris recognition systems present the initial work of J. Daugman and the proposed modifications. The other parts of the work present the latest research on iris categorised according to the four stages of the iris recognition system localization, segmentation, coding and recognition, followed by performance enhancement and the paper is then to concluded.

Primary iris recognition systems

Daugman (1993) presented a prototype system for iris recognition and reported that it has excellent performance on a diverse database of many images. Daugman (1994) also proposed a system for automatic identification of persons based on iris analysis. First, the system acquires through a video-camera a digitized image of an eye of the human to be identified. Then, it isolates the iris if it is present within the image and defines a circular pupillary boundary between the iris and pupil portions of the image, and it defines another circular boundary between the iris and sclera portions of the image, using arcs that are not necessarily concentric with the pupillary boundary. Then the system establishes a polar coordinate system on the isolated iris image, the origin of the coordinate system being the centre of the circular pupillary boundary. It then defines a plurality of annular analysis bands within the iris image, these analysis bands excluding certain pre-selected portions of the iris image likely to be occluded by the eyelids, eyelashes, or specular reflection from an illuminator. The portion of the iris image lying within these annular analysis bands is analyzed and encoded employing a special signal processing means comprising a multiscale, self-similar set of quadrature bandpass filters in polar coordinates, to generate an iris code of fixed length and having a universal format for all irises. The resulting code is stored as a reference code. Because of the universal format and length of all such iris codes, comparisons among different iris codes are efficient and simple. Specifically, a comparison between any two iris codes is achieved by computing the elementary logical XOR (exclusive-OR) between all their corresponding bits, and then computing the norm of the resulting binary vector. The result is a Hamming distance between the two iris code vectors. The universal format of iris codes also lends itself to rapid parallel search across large data bases of stored reference iris codes in order to determine the identity of an individual.

To perform an identification using the reference code, the system generates from an identification subject an identification code. Then, the system compares the identification code with the reference code, to ascertain the Hamming distance between the codes. This distance is then converted into a calculated likelihood that the two codes originated from the same iris, and hence from the same person, by computing the probability that the observed matching fraction of bits in the two codes could match by chance if the two codes were independent. A preselected criterion applied to this measured Hamming distance generates a "yes" or "no" decision and the confidence level for the decision is provided by the calculated probability. Daugman (2003b) outlines the steps of an iris recognition process as follows: Assessing the image focus, scribing specular reflections, localising the eye and the iris, fitting the pupillary boundary, detecting and fitting both eyelids, removing eyelashes and contact lens artifacts, demodulation and iris code creation, and XOR comparison of any two iris codes.

Wildes et al. (1994) described a prototype system for personal verification based on automated iris recognition. These recent prototype systems considered a number of implementation issues from the practical point of view. Both the systems of Daugman (2003b) and Wildes et al. (1994) concentrated on ensuring that repeated image captures produced irises in the same location within the image, had the same resolution, and were glare-free under fixed illumination. These requirements were essential for the accurate extraction of iris features in order for processing to be successful. The prototype of Wildes et al. (1994) relied on image registration, which is very computationally demanding. Daugman's system filters transformed images with oriented, quadrature pair, bandpass filters and coarsely quantizes the resulting representation for byte-wise matching. Both systems in Daugman (1993) and Wildes et al. (1994) have been much more extensively tested on databases of hundreds of images and have been shown to produce remarkable results.

Further, Daugman and Downing (2001b) and Daugman (2003b) presented a study where they have assessed the randomness and singularity of iris patterns, and their phenotypic distinctiveness as biometric identifiers, based on video images acquired in public trials of pattern recognition methods proposed in Daugman (1993). They have found that the probability of two different irises agreeing by chance in more than 70% of their phase sequence is about one in 7 billion. The detailed phase information was extracted from each isolated iris pattern using complex-valued two-dimensional Gabor wavelets. Also, they have compared images of genetically identical irises, from the left and right eyes of 324 persons, and from monozygotic twins. They have found that their relative phase sequence variation generated the same statistical distribution as did unrelated eyes.

A complete active system that uses the Daugman approach described in the foregoing is presented by Hanna et al. (1996), where for image acquisition a machine vision technique was used. The user stands in front of the system an image of his iris is acquired, and the identity is verified or refuted. The system consisted of a stereo pair of wide field-of-view (WFOV) cameras, a narrow field-of-view (NFOV) camera, a pan-tilt mirror allowing the NFOV to be moved relative to the WFOV, a real time vision computer, and a front end computer. The system actively finds the position of the user's eye and acquires a high resolution image to be passed to Daugman's system.

Looking at the iris recognition process from imaging to matching we can categorize the operation in 4 independent stages, as follows. An iris recognition system operates by initially localizing or detecting the iris in the image. Then segmentation techniques are applied to extract the iris from the image, this stage involves also masking to remove eyelids and eyelashes. Next Daugman's techniques are applied to convert the iris image to a unique iris code. After storage of the iris code, recognition and identification by reading the iris can be performed. Many approaches for iris identification have been proposed to improve speed and performance. To further enhance the performance some have combined results of several recognition approaches while others have used confidence measures. Attempts have been made to perform recognition at difficult conditions and to measure iris quality to increase the robustness of the identification technique.

IRIS LOCALISATION AND DETECTION

At the first stage of the iris recognition system, the iris must be detected and localized. Many researchers have studied iris recognition techniques in unconstrained environments, where the probability of acquiring non-ideal iris images is very high due to off-angles, noise, blurring and occlusion. Inaccuracies at this early stage detrimentally affect the performance at the next stages. Some methods underperform when frontal images have an angle. Perez et al. (2010) proposed a method based on particle swarm optimization (PSO) to generate templates for frontal face localization in real time. Additionally, the PSO templates in iris localization outperformed other methods.

He et al. (2010) use Adaboost for iris detection, where they adopt Haar-like features for object representation. The topological properties of the Haar-like features enhancement are used to enhance robustness of Adaboost learning.

After detection iris outer and inner boundaries must be drawn. The outer boundary may be occluded by eyelids; therefore, many methods have been presented for localizing the eyelids.

Kranauskas and Masiulis (2009) present a study on eyelid localization considering image focus for iris recognition, while Jang et al. (2008) proposes a detection algorithm that can be used to detect eyelid regions.

Min and Park (2009) propose an automatic eyelid and eyelash detection method based on the parabolic Hough model and Otsu's thresholding method. They apply the parabolic Hough transform to the normalized iris image, rather than to the original image to reduce the dimension of the parameter space and limit the parameter search range, decreasing computational load. For automatically separating the eyelash region Otsu's method is applied to the proposed feature that is obtained by combining the intensity and local standard deviation values.

SEGMENTATION

After finding an iris in the image, its boundary must be marked including the upper and lower eyelid boundaries. Next the eyelashes and reflections must be detected and removed. In less constrained environments iris recognition becomes difficult due to significant variation of eye position and size. Existence of eyebrows, eyelashes, glasses and contact lenses, and hair, together with illumination changes all make the segmentation task more difficult. Many have proposed different segmentation methods to tackle the recognition tasks. An iris segmentation method for non-ideal iris images is proposed in Jeong et al. (2010), where Adaboost is used to compensate for detection error caused by the edge detection operations. They also use colour segmentation to remove ghosts caused by visible light.

Another problem is noisy iris images which degrade the system performance. Tan et al. (2010) present an iris segmentation algorithm that achieves an optimum performance for noisy iris recognition tasks. Their method consists of different stages; initially a clustering scheme is proposed and the iris region is extracted from the non iris regions such as eyelashes, eyebrow, glass frame, hair, etc then the boundary is localized followed by a 1-D filter to tackle eyelashes and shape irregularity. Finally eyelashes and shadow occlusions are detected via a learned prediction model based on intensity statistics between different iris regions.

Labati and Scotti (2010) propose another segmentation method for noisy iris recognition that initially locates the centres of the pupil and the iris in the input image. Then two image strips containing the iris boundaries are extracted and linearized. The last step locates the iris boundary points in the strips and it performs a regularization operation by achieving the exclusion of the outliers and the interpolation of missing points. Authors in Li et al. (2010) also present a segmentation based method to detect iris in noisy images. First, the eye position and size are determined; second, in the eye region the limbic and then the pupillary boundaries are localized; third, the upper and lower eyelids are located; and finally the specular highlight is removed.

In an attempt to improve the performance of an iris recognition system, Sankowski et al. (2010) presented a segmentation approach that yielded the second in the NICE-I competition (Noisy Iris Challenge Evaluation – Part I), in which iris segmentation algorithms were evaluated and compared. The proposed stages were as follows: reflections localization, reflections filling in, iris boundaries localization and eyelids boundaries localization. These stages were a combination of methods proposed by the authors and methods proposed by others and improved by the authors.

Proença and Alexandre (2010) present an analysis of the relationship between the segmentation inaccuracy and the increase in the error rate of the iris recognition method. They recommend the development of methods that detect inaccurate segmentations.

IRIS CODING

Following the segmentation of the iris image, it is coded and stored at the registration stage or compared to a stored one at the identification or recognition stage. As outlined in Iris localisation and detection, Daugman was the first to present a prototype system for iris recognition (Daugman, 1993). At the coding stage his proposed system establishes a polar coordinate system on the isolated iris image, the origin of the coordinate system being the centre of the circular pupillary boundary. It then defines a plurality of annular analysis bands within the iris image. The portion of the iris image lying within these annular analysis bands is analyzed and encoded employing a special signal processing means comprising a multi-scale, self-similar set of quadrature bandpass filters in polar coordinates, to generate an iris code of fixed length and having a universal format for all irises.

Boles and Boashash (1998) proposed a new algorithm for extracting unique features from images of the iris of the human eye and representing these features using the wavelet transform (WT) zero crossings (Mallat, 1991). A

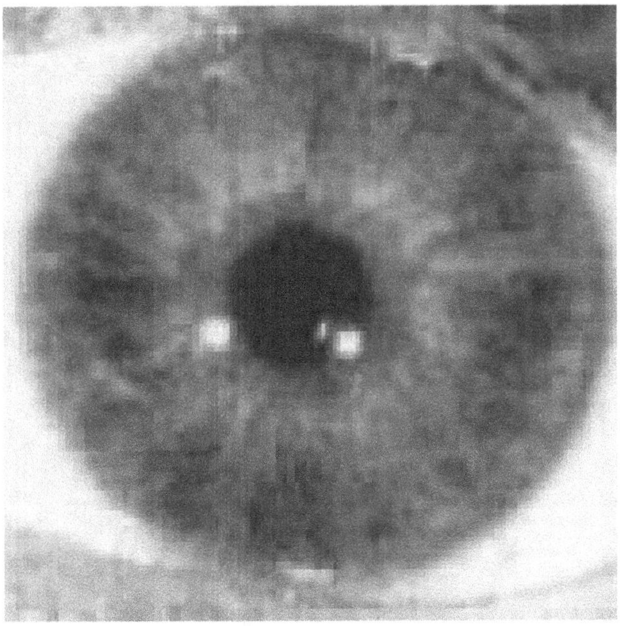

Figure 2. Sample iris image.

wavelet function that is the first derivative of a cubic spline is used to construct the representation. They have only dealt with samples of the grey-level profiles and used these to construct a representation in order to study the characteristics of the irises. Input images are pre-processed to extract the portion containing the iris. Then they proceeded to extract a set of one dimensional (1-D) signals and obtained the zero-crossing representations of these signals. The main idea of the proposed technique is to represent the features of the iris by fine-to-coarse approximations at different resolution levels based on the WT zero-crossing representation. To build the representation, a set of sampled data is collected, followed by constructing the zero-crossing representation based on its dyadic WT. Their process of information extraction starts by locating the pupil of the eye, which can be done using any edge detection technique. Knowing that it has a circular shape, the edges defining it are connected to form a closed contour. The centroid of the detected pupil is chosen as the reference point for extracting the features of the iris. The grey level values on the contours of virtual concentric circles, which are centred at the centroid of the pupil, are recorded and stored in circular buffers. In other words, the dimensions of the irises in the images are scaled to have the same constant diameter regardless of the original size in the images. Furthermore, the extracted information from any of the virtual circles has to be normalized to have the same number of data points. Then a zero-crossing representation is generated from the normalized iris signature.

The dyadic wavelet transform decomposes a signal into a set of signals at different resolution levels. The information at the finer resolution levels is strongly affected by noise. In order to reduce this effect on the zero-crossing representation, only a few low-resolution levels, excluding the coarsest level, were used. Their algorithm is a model-based one in which the original signatures of the different irises to be recognized were represented by their zero-crossing representations. These representations are then stored in the database of the system and are referred to as models. The main task is to match an iris in an image, which is referred to as an unknown, with one of the models whose representations are stored in the database.

The advantage of the method presented in Boles and Boashash (1998) is processing 1-D iris signatures rather than the 2-D images as used in both Daugman (1993) and Wildes et al. (1994). However, their technique has been tested on a small number of real images (with and without noise). Figure 2 shows a sample image and the corresponding extracted data set and its wavelet transform are shown in Figure 3. Figure 4 illustrates the zero-crossing representation of the iris of Figure 2.

Lim et al. (2001) decomposed an iris image into four levels using 2-D Haar wavelet transform and quantized the fourth-level high-frequency information to form an 87-bit code. A modified competitive learning neural network (LVQ) was adopted for classification. Park et al. (2003) used a directional filter bank to decompose an iris image into eight directional subband outputs and extracted the normalized directional energy as features. Bae et al. (2003) projected the iris signals onto a bank of basis vectors derived by independent component analysis and quantized the resulting projection coefficients as features. The global texture features of the iris were extracted by means of well-known Gabor filters at different scales and orientations (Ma et al., 2002a). Based on the experimental results and analysis obtained in Ma et al. (2002a), Ma et al. (2002b) constructed a bank of spatial filters, whose kernels are suitable for iris recognition, to represent the local texture features of the iris and achieved much better results. From the methods described above, it can be concluded that there are four main approaches to iris representation: phase-based methods (Daugman, 2001a, 2003a), zero-crossing representation (Daugman and Downing, 1995; Sanchez-Avila and Sanchez-Reillo, 2002), texture analysis (Lim et al., 2001; Sanchez-Avila and Sanchez-Reillo, 2002; Wildes et al., 1996; Zhu et al., 2000) and intensity variation analysis (Ma et al., 2003).

IRIS RECOGNITION AND IDENTIFICATION

At the registration stage, following iris coding, the identity of each subject can be stored along with the iris code. Next, at the recognition stage, iris codes of queries are compared against the stored iris codes to verify or identify the query. Recognition error rate may increase if the performance at any of the previous stages is degraded. Attempts have been made to improve the

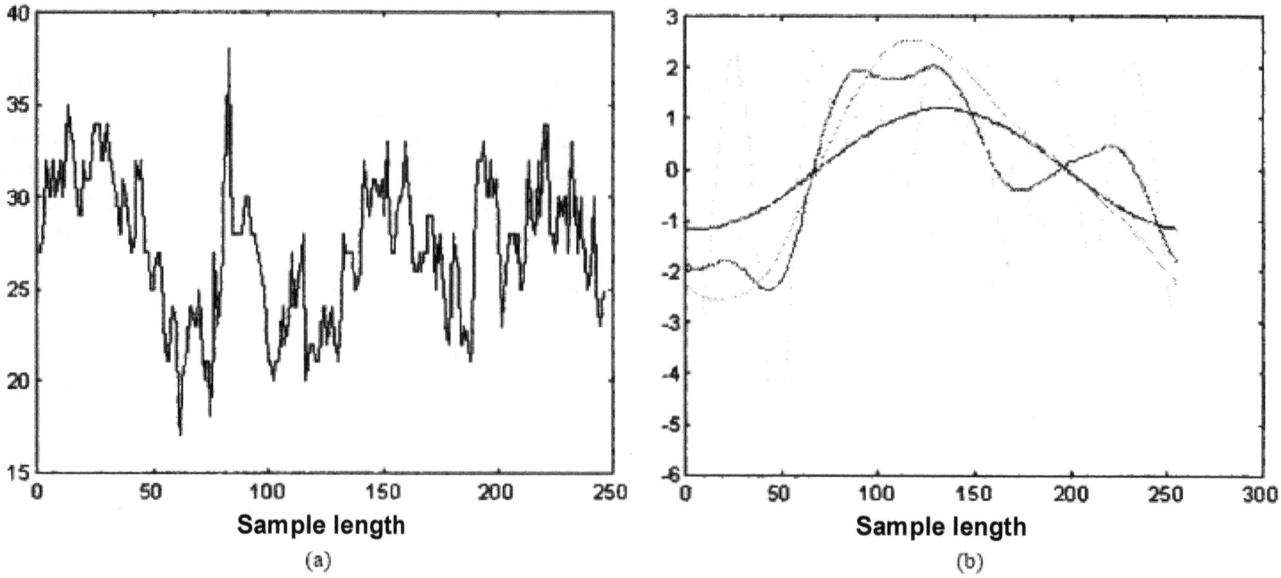

Figure 3. (a) Sample iris signature from the image of Figure 1. (b) Lowest four resolution levels of the wavelet transform.

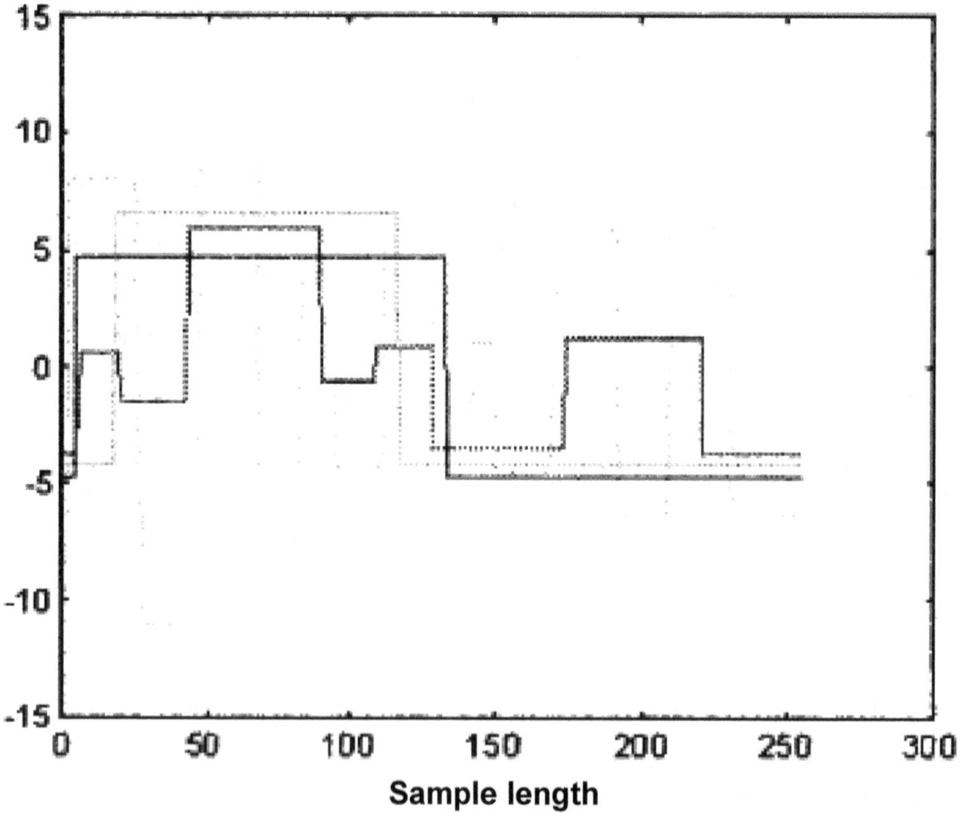

Figure 4. Zero-crossing representation of the iris of Figure 3.

recognition error rate by compensating for these degradations.

For example to deal with off-angle iris, which occurs at the first stage, Abhyankar and Schuckers (2010) propose a bi-orthogonal wavelet network using several neural networks for each angle. Their system recognizes

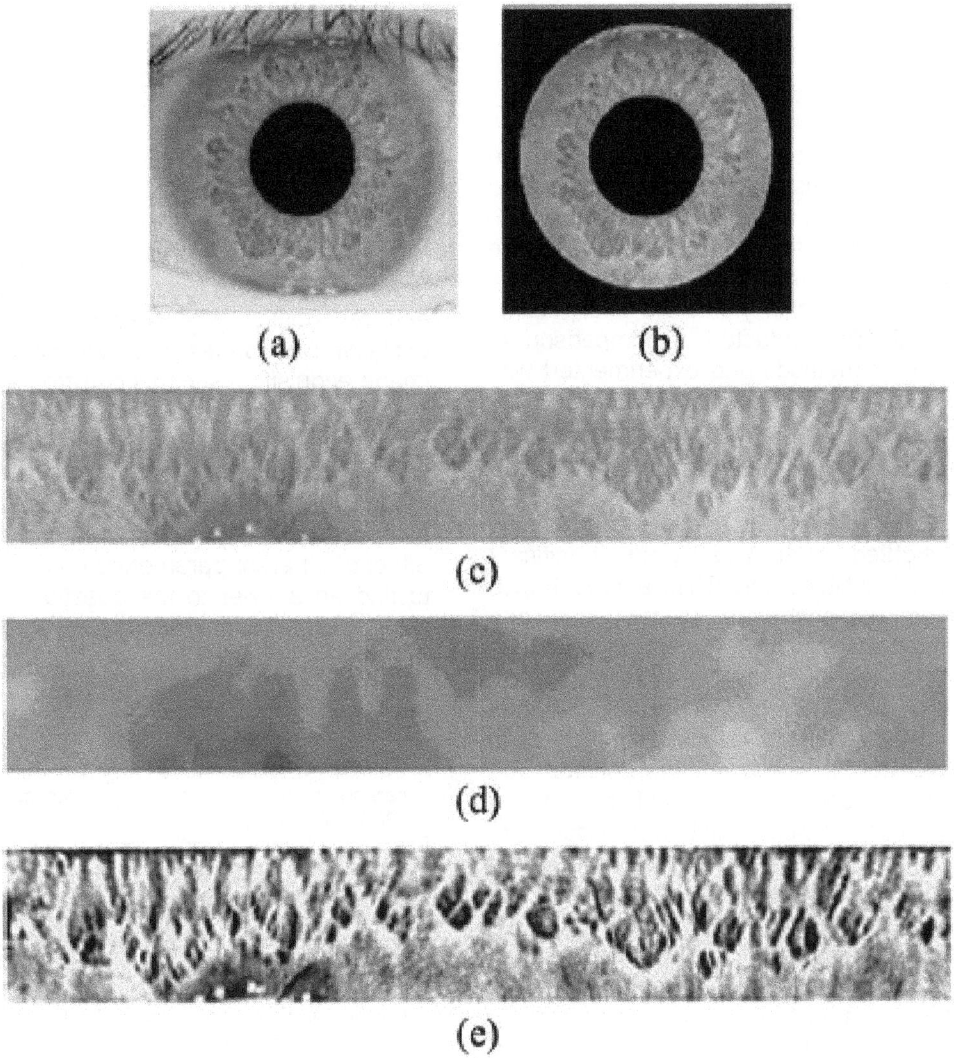

Figure 5. Iris image preprocessing: (a) original image; (b) localized image; (c) normalized image; (d) estimated local average intensity; and (e) enhanced image.

recognizes all classes efficiently up to an angular deformation of less than 45°.

Huang et al. (2002) proposed an iris recognition method which constructs a basis function for the training set using independent component analysis (ICA), represents iris pattern with ICA coefficients, determines the centre of each class by competitive learning mechanism and finally recognizes the pattern based on Euclidian distances. They have shown that their system can work well for lured iris image, variable illumination, and interference of eyelids and eyelashes.

It is possible to repeat the first stage if problems that detrimentally affect the recognition rate are detected at a later stage. Jang et al. (2008) propose a new focus assessment method for iris recognition systems, which combines the wavelet transform method and the Support Vector Machine (SVM). The proposed wavelet-based method, detects omni-directional high-frequency which is the characteristic of iris patterns and estimates focus values by using the ratio of high and low – frequency sub-band averages. The SVM reduces the error rate of the wavelet-based method by finding the optimum threshold.

Kumar et al. (2003) utilized correlation filters to measure the consistency of iris images from the same eye. The correlation filter of each class was designed using the two-dimensional (2-D) Fourier transforms of training images. If the correlation output exhibited a sharp peak, the input image was determined to be from an authorized subject, otherwise an imposter.

A feature correlation evaluation approach is proposed by Du et.al. (2010) to determine iris image quality(Figure 5). This is needed especially for determining the quality of compressed images where artificial patterns are introduced. Their proposed approach can discriminate artificial iris patterns from natural iris patterns in uncompressed images. It can also measure iris image quality of non-compressed and compressed images.

PERFORMANCE ENHANCEMENT

To find which approach is most suitable and to find the advantage of each of the existing recognition systems a comparative analysis must be conducted. Furthermore, to improve the recognition rate of the best available approach, the results of several of the existing systems can be combined. To find which yields the best results, Kumar and Passi (2010) conducted a comparison of different iris recognition methods and experimented with combining the decisions of these approaches. They compare the performance of four different approaches for iris recognition: DCT, FFT, Haar wavelet and Log-Gabor filter. The experimental results suggest that the combination of Log-Gabor and Haar wavelet matching scores using weighted sum rule yield significant improvement over either filter alone. Their approach also uses minimum computational time as they use one training image, in contrast to other methods that use several.

Another analysis to find the effect of different parameters on the recognition rate is conducted in Hollingsworth et al. (2009), where authors consider the effect of dilation on the recognition rate and find a relation between the difference between dilation measures of enrolment and recognition and the recognition rate. They recommend recording the dilation measure for every iris code to be used as a confidence measure.

To answer the question of which approach is most suitable for extracting iris features, Ma et al. (2004) carried out an extensive quantitative comparison among some existing methods and provided detailed discussions on the overall experimental results. They have discussed that the iris consists of many irregular small blocks, such as freckles, coronas, stripes, furrows, crypts, and so on. Furthermore, the distribution of these blocks in the iris is also random. Such randomly distributed and irregular blocks constitute the most distinguishing characteristics of the iris. As such, local sharp variations denote the most important properties of a signal. In their framework, they recorded the position of local sharp variation points as features instead of locating and recognizing those small blocks. The characteristics of the iris can be considered as a sort of transient signals. Local sharp variations are generally used to characterize the important structures of transient signals. Ma et al. (2004) constructed a set of 1-D intensity signals which are capable of retaining most sharp variations in the original iris image. The position of local sharp variation points is recorded as features. A special class of 1-D wavelets has been adopted in their work to represent the resulting 1-D intensity signals: the dyadic wavelets that satisfy such requirements as well as incur lower computational cost. For matching purpose, they have proposed a two-step approach: (1) the original feature vector is expanded into a binary feature vector (called feature transform), (2) the similarity between a pair of expanded feature vectors is calculated using the XOR operation.

CONCLUSION

We have presented an overview of the latest research on iris recognition by categorizing the research in four groups outlined as localization, segmentation, iris coding and recognition. We present the latest developments explaining advances to solve problems associated with image acquisition such as non-frontal face images and off angle iris. We also discuss advances that lead to improvement in iris recognition system performance, improvement in iris coding methods, and improvement in recognition methods. We also present a review on a comparative study of different iris methods to find the effect of different parameters on the recognition rate, and to find an answer to the question of which approach is most suitable for iris recognition.

REFERENCES

Abhyankar A, Schuckers S (2010). A novel biorthogonal wavelet network system for off-angle iris recognition. Pattern recognition. 43(3): 987-1007.

Bae K, Noh S, Kim J (2003). Iris feature extraction using independent component analysis. In Proc. 4th Int. Conf. Audio- and Video-Based Biometric Person Authentication. pp. 838-844.

Boles WW, Boashash B (1998). A Human Identification Technique Using Images of the Iris and Wavelet Transform. IEEE Transaction on Signal Processing, 46(4).

Daugman J (1993). High confidence visual recognition of persons by test of statistical independence. IEEE Trans. Pattern Anal. Machine Intell., 15: 1148-1161.

Daugman J (1994). United States Patent Number: 5291560.

Daugman J, Downing C (1995). Demodulation, predictive coding, and spatial vision. J. Opt. Soc. Am. A 12: 641-660.

Daugman J (2001a). Statistical richness of visual phase information: update on recognizing persons by iris patterns. Int. J. Comput. Vis. 45(1): 25-38.

Daugman J, Downing C (2001b). Epigenetic randomness, complexity and singularity of human iris patterns, Proc. R. Soc. Lond. B 268: 1737-1740.

Daugman J (2003a). Demodulation by complex-valued wavelets for stochastic pattern recognition. Int. J. Wavelets, Multi-Res. and Info. Processing. 1(1): 1-17.

Daugman J (2003b). The importance of being random: statistical principles of iris recognition. Pattern Recognition, 36: 279-291.

Daugman J (2004). How iris recognition works, IEEE trans. On sys. for video tech. 14(1).

Daugman J (2007). New methods in iris recognition", IEEE Trans. On Sys., Man, and Cybernetics-part B. 37(5).

Du Y, Belcher C, Zhou Z, Ives R (2010). Feature correlation evaluation approach for iris feature quality measure. Signal processing, 90(4):1176-1187.

Hanna K, Mandelbaum R, Mishra D, Paragano V, Wixson L (1996). A System for Non-intrusive Human Iris Acquisition and Identification. IAPR Workshop on Machine Vision Applications. pp.12-14.

He Z, Tan T, Sun Z (2010). Topology modeling for Adaboost-cascade based object detection", Pattern recognition letters, 31(9).

Hollingsworth K, Bowyer KW, Flynn PJ (2009). Pupil dilation degrades iris biometric performance. Computer vision and image understanding, 113(1).

Huang Y, Luo S, Chen E (2002). An Efficient Iris Recognition System. Proc. 1st Int'l. Conf. Machine Learning and Cybernetics, China.
Imesh PD, Wallow I, Albert DM (1997). The color of the human eye: a review of morphologic correlates and of some conditions that affect iridial pigmentation, Surv. Ophthalmol., 41(2): 117-123.
Jang J, Park KR, Kim J, Lee Y (2008). New focus assessment method for iris recognition systems. Pattern recognition letters. 29(13).
Jang YK, Kang BJ, Park KR (2008). A study on eyelid localization considering image focus for iris recognition. Pattern recognition letters, 29(11).
Jeong DS, Hwang JW, Kang BJ, Park KR, Won CS, Park DK, Kim J (2010). A new iris segmentation method for non-ideal iris images. Image and vision computing, 28(2): 254-260.
Johnston R (1992). Can iris patterns be used to identify people? Los Alamos National Laboratory, Chemical and Laser Sciences Division Annual Report LA-12331-PR, pp. 81-86.
Kranauskas BJ, Masiulis R (2009). Iris recognition by local extremum points of multiscale Taylor expansion. Pattern recognition. 42(9).
Kronfeld PC (1962) Gross anatomy and embryology of the eye, In: *The eye*, vol. 1 (ed. H. Davson), London: Academic Press.
Kumar A, Passi A (2010). Comparison and combination of iris matchers for reliable personal authentication. Pattern recognition, 43(3): 1016-1026.
Kumar B, Xie C, Thornton J (2003). Iris verification using correlation filters. In Proc. 4th Int. Conf. Audio- and Video-Based Biometric Person Authentication, pp. 697-705.
Labati RD, Scotti F (2010). Noisy iris segmentation with boundary regularization and reflections removal. Image and vision computing, 28(2): 270-277.
Li P, Liu X, Xiao L, Song Q (2010). Robust and accurate iris segmentation in very noisy iris images. Image and vision computing. 28(2).
Lim S, Lee K, Byeon O, Kim T (2001). Efficient iris recognition through improvement of feature vector and classifier. ETRI J. 23(2): 1-70.
Ma L, Wang Y, Tan T (2002a). Iris recognition based on multichannel Gabor filtering," in Proc. 5th Asian Conf. Computer Vision. I: 279-283.
Ma L, Wang Y, Tan T (2002b). Iris recognition using circular symmetric filters," in Proc. 16th Int. Conf. Pattern Recognition. II: 414-417.
Ma L (2003). Personal identification based on iris recognition. Ph.D dissertation, Inst. Automation, Chinese Academy of Sciences, Beijing, China.
Ma L, Tan T, Wang Y, Zhang D (2004). Efficient Iris Recognition by Characterizing Key Local Variations. IEEE Transactions on image processing, 13(6).
Mallat SG (1991). Zero-crossings of a wavelet transform. IEEE Trans. Inform. Theory, 37(14): 1019-1033.
Min TH, Park RH (2009). Eyelid and eyelash detection method in the normalized iris image using the parabolic Hough model and Otsu's thresholding method. Pattern recognition letters. 30(12).
Ng RYF, Tay YH, Mok KM (2008). A review of iris recognition algorithms. International Symposium on Information Technology, Malaysia.
Park C, Lee J, Smith M, Park K (2003). Iris-based personal authentication using a normalized directional energy feature. In Proc. 4th Int. Conf. Audio- and Video-Based Biometric Person Authentication. pp. 224-232.
Perez CA, Aravena CM, Vallejos JI, Estevez PA, Held CM (2010). Face and iris localization using templates designed by particle swarm optimization, Pattern recognition letters, 31(9): 857-868.
Popescu-Bodorin N, Balas VE (2010). AI challenges in iris recognition. Processing tools for Bath iris image database. In Proceedings of the 11th WSEAS international conference on Automation and information.
Proença H, Alexandre LA (2010). Iris recognition: Analysis of the error rates regarding the accuracy of the segmentation stage. Image and vision computing, 28(1): 202-206.
Sanchez-Avila C, Sanchez-Reillo R (2002). Iris-based biometric recognition using dyadic wavelet transform. IEEE Aerosp. Electron. Sys. Mag., 17: 3-6.
Sankowski W, Grabowski K, Napieralska M, Zubert M, Napieralski A (2010). Reliable algorithm for iris segmentation in eye image. Image and vision computing, 28(2).
Sheela SV, Vijaya PA (2010). Iris Recognition Methods - Survey. International Journal of Computer Applications 3(5): 19-25.
Tan T, He Z, Sun Z (2010). Efficient and robust segmentation of noisy iris images for non-cooperative iris recognition. Image and vision computing, 28(2).
Wildes R (1994). A system for automated iris recognition," in Proc. 2nd IEEE Workshop Applicat. Comput. Vision, pp. 121-128.
Wildes R, Asmuth J, Green G, Hsu S, Kolczynski R, Matey J, McBride S (1996). A machine-vision system for iris recognition," Mach. Vis. Applic., 9:1-8.
Wolff E (1948). The anatomy of the eye and orbit, London: H. K. Lewis.
Zhu Y, Tan T, Wang Y (2000). Biometric personal identification based on iris patterns. In Proc. Int. Conf. Pattern Recognition. II: 805-808.
Ziauddin S, Dailey MN (2010). Robust iris verification for key management", Pattern Recognition letters, 31(9).

Modelling and simulation of electrical machines on the basis of experimental frequency response characteristics

Abdesslem Lamari

High Institute of Applied Sciences and Technology (ISSAT), Department of Electronics, Route de Tabarka 7030, Mateur, Tunisia. E-mail: atriua@hotmail.com.

The mathematical models of the Asynchronous Electrical machines developed on the basis of the experimental frequency-response characteristics are proposed in this paper. The latter ones are recommended for investigating the transient processes occurring at short-circuits and connections of the electrical machines to the bus bars of electrical system taking into account of their rotor speed changes.

Key words: Asynchronous machines, frequency-response, networks connections short-circuit.

INTRODUCTION

Methods of frequency-response characteristics have received wide acceptance in the scientific-research and engineering practical activity for investigating and evaluating the transient conditions of the AC machines in electrical systems (Khemliche et al., 2004; Shiqin et al., 2008; Canay, 1994). These methods make possible to carry out the direct application of the experimental initial data in the form of frequency-response characteristics of the separate electrical system elements or of the system as a whole. Such approach, in some special cases when the system internal structure is indeterminate, has much potential for yielding the more precise calculations of the transient processes.

The calculation technique for determining the transients by the use of the frequency-response characteristics of synchronous machine stator admittance in the direct, $Y_d(js)$, and quadrature, $Y_q(js)$, axes or the circle diagram of an induction motor was proposed in (Khemliche et al., 2004; Shiqin et al., 2008; Liuchen, 1996; Guha and Kar, 2006). The graphic-analytical methods for determining the armature current and electromagnetic torque of the synchronous machine were developed in the cited monograph too. The methods being considered allow carrying out more accurate calculations of the transient processes taking into account the following characteristic features:

- Electromagnetic asymmetry of the rotor;
- Representation of the turbogenerator solid rotor by means of the equivalent circuits corresponding to the high order transfer function of the damper system;
- Current displacement in the windings of electrical machines;
- Saturation phenomenon in the main and leakage paths of the magnetic fluxes of the AC machines;
- External impedance inserted in the armature winding of the AC machine.

Methods of frequency-response characteristics did not get wide dissemination in due course though. In fact, the great amount of information on the frequency-response characteristics of the synchronous machines and induction motors compiled by now and availability of the developed method designed for synthesizing the equivalent circuits adequately reflecting the initial frequency-response characteristics of the AC electrical machines open up fresh opportunities for improving and further development of the frequency-response methods for investigating the transients in electrical machines.

The objective of this paper is to develop the mathematical models of the asynchronous machines based on the experimental frequency-response characteristics for investigating the transients at short-circuits and connections of the AC machines in electrical system taking into consideration the occurring speed changes of the AC machine rotor.

BASIC RELATIONS

The mathematical relations realizing the graphic-analytical approach (Khemliche et al., 2004; Shiqin et al., 2008; Liuchen, 1996) to determine the components of the stator phase current and electromagnetic torque at short-circuits or connections of the synchronous machines rotating at the synchronous speed to the electrical system are obtained in (Burakov and Arkkio, 2007; Lam and Yee, 1998; Arjona and MacDonald, 1999; Houdouin and Gilles, 2004). When the machine with the rotor asymmetry operates at the short-circuit with the speed changes relative to the synchronous speed or it is connected to the network at the given slip, determining the components of the generalized stator current vector is carried out in the following way:

We find the average value of the steady-state current $I_{s0_{av}}$ for the s at the first instant of the transient process:

$$I_{s0_{av}} = Y_{av}(js)_{s0} \tag{1}$$

Where

$$Y_{av}(js) = \frac{Y_d(js)+Y_q(js)}{2}$$

We determine the pulsating component of the steady-state current

$$\Delta I_{s0} = (R_e[\Delta Y(js)_{s0}] - j.\mathrm{Im}[\Delta Y(js)_{s0}]).e^{-j2\delta_0} \tag{2}$$

Where

$$\Delta Y(js) = \frac{Y_d(js)+Y_q(js)}{2}, \qquad \delta_0 = \text{angle between}$$

The q-axis of the rotor and the voltage vector at the infinite bus of an electrical system; We find the changes in the steady-state current with time, taking into account the difference in the rotor parameters on axes of its electrical and magnetic symmetry,

$$I_{S0}(t) = (I_{S0_{av}} + \Delta I_{S0}e^{-j2st}).e^{j.\omega.t} \tag{3}$$

We determine the aperiodic current component

$$I_{S1_{av}} = Y_{av}(js)_{-(1-s)} \tag{4}$$

And the periodic current of the frequency close to the doubled one

$$\Delta I_{S1} = (\mathrm{Re}[\Delta Y(js)_{-(1-s)}]j.\mathrm{Im}[\Delta Y(js)_{-(1-s)}])e^{-j.2.\delta_0} \tag{5}$$

Aperiodic current and the current component caused by the rotor asymmetry are changed in accordance with the following expression

$$I_{S1}(t) = -[I_{S1_{av}}.e^{j.\omega_n.\omega t} - \Delta I_{S1}.e^{-j2(1-S-\omega_n)\omega t}]e^{-t/\tau_a} \tag{6}$$

The natural angular frequency of the aperiodec current vector, ω_n and the time constant of its decaying, τ_a, are defined for the average complex admittance $Y_{av}(js)$ at the slip $s = -(1-s)$ by equations

$$\omega_n = \mathrm{Im}[Y_{av}(js)_{s=-(1-s)}].R_{S0} \tag{7}$$

$$\tau_a = \frac{1}{\omega_n = \mathrm{Im}[Y_{av}(js)_{s=-(1-s)}].R_{S0}.\omega} \tag{8}$$

The initial value of the periodic component of the transient current, I_{S2} is determined by recognizing that

$$I_{S0}(t)_{t=0} + I_{S1}(t)_{t=0} + I_{S2}(t)_{t=0} = 0$$

Generally, the initial value of the current vector $I_{S2}(t)_{t=0}$ does not coincide with the d-axis of a rotor (including the connections of the synchronous machine occurring at the angle $(\delta_0 = 0)$ resulting in aperiodic current components in both axes of the rotor symmetry.

Implementation of the method proposed is associated with representing the initial frequency-response characteristics in the form of equivalent circuits in the d- and q-axis of a synchronous machine. The latter ones, e.g., the equivalent circuit in d-axis shown in Figure 1 may be used for determining the changes in the periodic current components with time (Ronkowski, 2008).

The mentioned equivalent circuits allow obtaining the initial values $(I_{S2_{dk}}, I_{S2_{ql}})$ and the time constants (τ_{dk}, τ_{ql}) of the exponential components of the periodic armature current $I_{S2}(t)$ so in the d-and q-axis we have;

$$\tau_{dk} = \frac{x_{kD}}{\omega.r_{kD}}, I_{S2_{dk}} = \frac{1}{x_{kD}}, k = 1,2,\dots, N;$$
$$\tau_{ql} = \frac{x_{lQ}}{\omega.r_{lQ}}, I_{S2_{ql}} = \frac{1}{x_{lQ}}, l = 1,2,\dots, M \tag{9}$$

From the above, it might be assumed that the time-dependence of the periodic current follows the law;

$$I_{S2}(t) = \left(\sum_{k=1}^{N} I_{S2_{dk}}.e^{-t/\tau_{dk}}\right).e^{j.(1-S)\omega.t}.e^{j\delta_0}$$
$$+\left(\sum_{l=1}^{M} I_{S2_{ql}}.e^{-t/\tau_{ql}}\right).e^{j.(1-S)\omega.t}.e^{j\delta_0} \tag{10}$$

Where N, M= quantity of the elementary equivalent

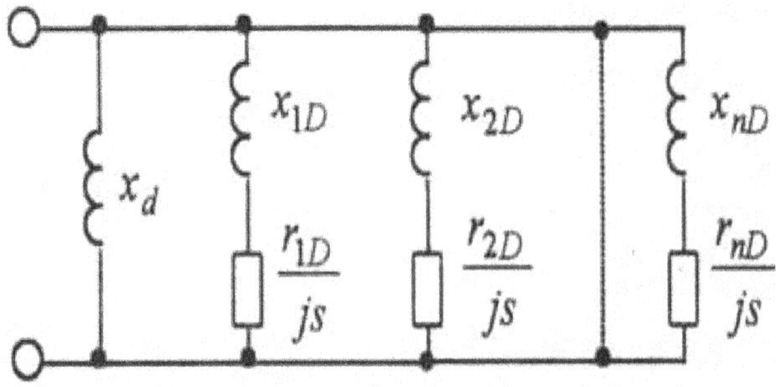

Figure 1. Equivalent circuit of the synchronous machine rotor.

rcuits of the rotor in d- and q-axis, respectively.

In the general case the initial I_{S2} current components in the d- and q-axis should be converted in proportion to the projection of the I_{S2} current vector on the direct, I_{S2d}, and quadrature I_{S2q} rotor axes, e.g.,

$$\begin{aligned} I_{S2d} &= \text{mod}[I_{S2}(t)_{t=0}].\cos(\varphi - \delta_0), \\ I_{S2q} &= \text{mod}[I_{S2}(t)_{t=0}].\sin(\varphi - \delta_0) \end{aligned} \qquad (11)$$

Where φ = argument of the $I_{S2}(t)_{t=0}$ current vector (the angle between the current vector and the real axis of the complex plain).
Then;

$$\begin{aligned} I_{S2_{dk}} &= \frac{1}{x_{kD}} . \frac{I_{S2d}}{\sum \frac{1}{x_{kD}}}, \\ I_{S2_{ql}} &= \frac{1}{x_{lQ}} . \frac{I_{S2q}}{\sum \frac{1}{x_{lQ}}} \end{aligned} \qquad (12)$$

The total generalized vector of the transient armature current comprises the vector sum of separate components:

$$I_S(t) = U.[I_{S0}(t) + I_{S1}(t) + I_{S2}(t)] \qquad (13)$$

Where V= voltage across the terminals of an armature winding at the short-circuit condition or connection of a synchronous machine to the network.

The instantaneous values of the phase currents are determined as a projection of the generalized current vector on the motionless time axes of the appropriate phases:

$$\begin{aligned} i_A(t) &= \text{mod}[I_S(t)].\cos(\alpha(t) + \gamma_0), \\ i_B(t) &= \text{mod}[I_S(t)].\cos(\alpha(t) + \gamma_0 - \frac{2}{3}\pi), \\ i_C(t) &= \text{mod}[I_S(t)].\cos(\alpha(t) + \gamma_0 + \frac{2}{3}\pi) \end{aligned} \qquad (14)$$

Where $\alpha(t)$ =time-dependent argument of the total generalized vector of the armature current.

It is evident that the dynamic properties of an induction machine can be described in full measure by means of a single frequency-response characteristic $Y(js)$. In this case, the expressions obtained above will not contain the additional current components ΔI_{S0} and ΔI_{S1} they are no needs in decomposition of the I_{S2} current on the d- and q-axis components either (Kirtley, 1994).

In accordance with the general approach the electromagnetic torque is determined using the current and flux linkage complexes, regardless of the rotor symmetry of the AC machine, by the expression:

$$T = \text{Re}[j\psi_s.\overset{*}{I}_s] = R_e[j(\psi_{S0} + \psi_{S1})(\overset{*}{I}_{S0} + \overset{*}{I}_{S1} + \overset{*}{I}_{S2})] \qquad (15)$$

The magnetic linkages in (15) can be presented more detail as follows:

$$\psi_S = \psi_{S0} - \psi_{S1} = e^{j\omega t} - e^{j\omega_n t} e^{-t/\tau_a} \qquad (16)$$

As may be seen from the Equations (15) and (16), the electromagnetic torque can be presented as the sum of the vector products of the currents by flux linkage components. For example, the product of the vector I_{S0} by the vector ψ_{S0} produces the steady-state torque being numerically equal to the vertical projection of the current vector at the rated voltage across the terminals of the stator winding.

The influence of the separate current and torque components on the features of the transient process having been analyzed, it is possible to simplify the mathematical model of an electrical machine with the given accuracy.

At researching the electromechanical transients connected with the speed variations of AC machine rotor one should consider the simultaneous solution of the equations deduced above and the supplementary equation of the rotor relative motion. The latter one can be written in the following form:

$$M\frac{ds}{dt} = T - T_{mech} \qquad (17)$$

Where T_{mech} =shaft torque developed by the prime mover; M =inertia constant.

PARAMETERS OF THE ALGORITHM

If the influence of the rotor acceleration is not taken into account the following problem algorithm considering the rotor speed changes can be suggested:

The transient process is divided into small uniform intervals of time;
The speed increment over the given interval is determined by solving the Equation (17) as follows:

$$\Delta s = \frac{T - T_{mech}}{M}\Delta t;$$

The sustained component of the I_{S0} current is calculated at the constant speed obtained for the given time interval. The amplitude of the I_{S1} current component decaying with the time constant τ_a is calculated at the initial value of the rotor speed (at the beginning of the first interval).

The natural angular frequency, ω_n , and the time constant, τ_a, of the aperiodic currant component are re-counted using Equation (7),(8) in relation to the slip changes of a rotor.

The amplitude of the I_{S2} current component caused by the transient currents in the rotor circuits is determined at the rotor slip corresponding to the first instant of the process.

It should be pointed out that the angular speed of the I_{S2} current being taken into account in (Lam and Yee, 1998) varies with the slip changes. The rotor slip dependence of the natural angular frequency and the time constant of decaying the magnetic flux ψ_{S1} are taken into account by equation (Lei and Namuduri, 2009).

ESTIMATION OF MODEL VALIDITY

The efficiency of application of the frequency-response characteristics for calculating the transient process can be demonstrated with the following examples:

1. Short-circuit at the terminals of the stator winding and connection to the network without excitation of the model turbo generator of the MT-3type:

$$(S_n = 30KVA, V_n = 414V, I_n = 41.8A,$$
$$x_d = 1.453; x_q = 1.394; R_{S0} = 0.00624 p.u.)$$

In the case being considered the influence of the sign and initial slip value at connecting the generator to the network as well as the influence of the rotor speed changes at the transient conditions were analyzed.

2. Connection to the network of the unexcited turbo generator of the ТГВ-200 type:

$$S_n = 235MVA, V_n = 15.75KV, I_n = 8635A,$$
$$x_d = 1.9; x_q = 1.89; R_{S0} = 0.0012 p.u.$$

When calculating the electromechanical transients the errors being brought about by simplifying the complicated equivalent circuits, reflecting the electromagnetic of the solid rotor, were considered.

3. Starting of the induction motor of the ДАЗО-1914-10/12A type:

$$P_n = 1500Kw; I_n = 204A; V_n = 6000V$$

From the no-load condition, and three-phase short-circuit at its terminals.

Estimation of the results obtained, when using the techniques proposed above, was carried out by comparison with the appropriate calculations made by the use of algorithms based on numerical integrating the system of the differential Parc-Gorev equations. The frequency-response characteristics reflecting the dynamic properties of the AC machines being studied were obtained experimentally from the DC decay in the armature winding at standstill test (Canay, 1994; Satish and Saravanakumar, 2008; Dehkordi et al., 2005).

Computer programs realizing the above mentioned algorithms for calculating the electromechanical transients in AC machines were elaborated within the framework of the MathCAD 7.0.

The time-dependence of changing the generalized stator current vector and the electromagnetic running torque at connection the unexcited model generator to the network under the various initial rotor slips were carried out without the account and in view of changing the rotor speed at transient .The invariable rotor speed was simulated by way of setting the great value of the inertia constant (Bacalao et al., 1995).

As follows from comparison of the results obtained for the given slip values, equal to 0, 0.01, 0.03, 0.05 and 0.1 put, the changes in the time-dependence of the generalized stator current vector and electromagnetic torque practically does not differ from the analogous calculations made on the basis of the Parc-Gorev

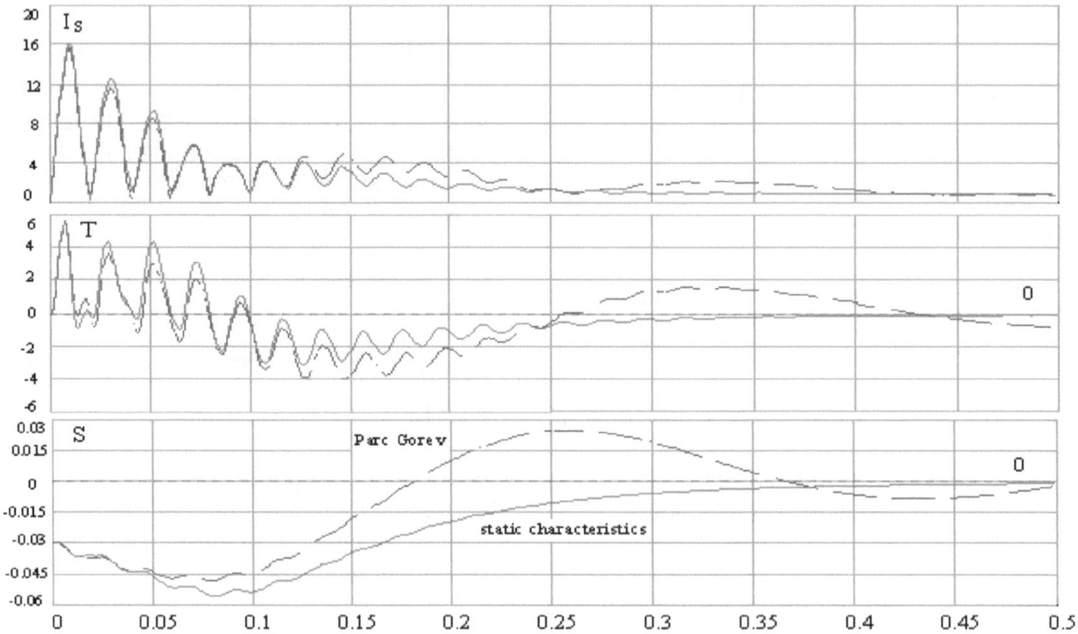

Figure 2. Connection to the network of the unexcited model turbo generator.

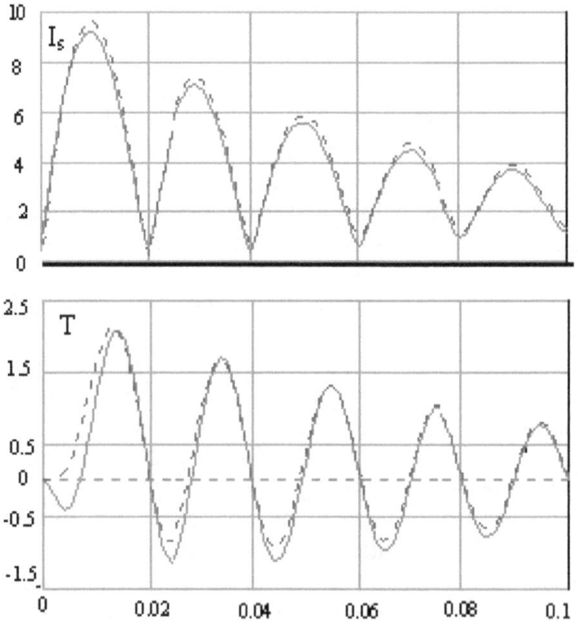

Figure 3. Short-circuit on the terminals of the induction motor.

equations. In these cases the difference in the maximum values of the similar operating variables being compared did not exceed 10.4%. The typical changes in the transients differ not at all. So, when making use of the static frequency-response characteristics, one can infer that the electromagnetic processes may be identified with a sufficiently high degree of accuracy.

The analysis of the transients calculated with taking into consideration the rotor speed changes, following the connection of the model generator, points to some differences in the time-dependent variables. For example, in the Figure 2 are shown the results of calculating the transients at connection the unexcited model machine to the network with the field winding short-circuited.

The calculations carried out in compliance with the system of Parc-Gorev equations (see dotted line) reflect the features connected with changes in the current , I_s ,and electromagnetic torque, T , with the rotor speed changes. The time dependence of the slip in the case under consideration has the oscillatory character. Mathematical simulation based on the static characteristics (see solid line) brings about the monotonous changes in the rotor slip under the transient process. Meanwhile, the resultant time of approaching the rotor speed to the synchronous one, being estimated at the instant a rotor slip for the second time passes through zero, practically agrees with the time being determined from the solid line obtained at simulating the transients by means of the method proposed.

Distinguishing features of the variables being considered are in close agreement; their maximum values appearing at the initial stage of the transient process correlate well with the data got without regard for speed changes of the rotor. In the Figure 3 are given the curves reflecting the changes in the variables at the

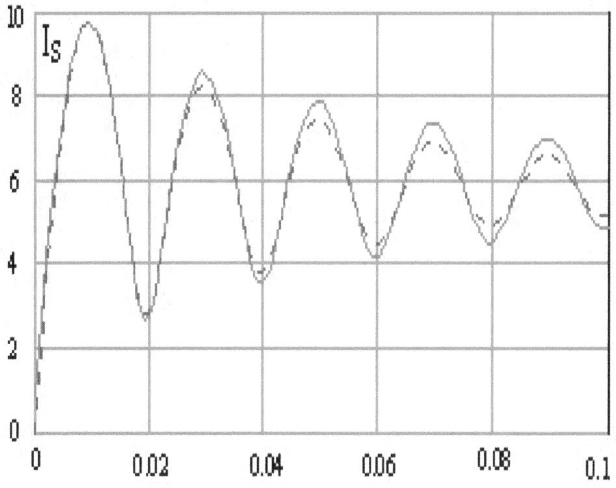

Figure 4. The time–dependence of the generalized vector of the stator current at connecting the induction motor.

short-circuit on the terminals of the induction motor ДАЗО-1914-10/12А type.

The quantities of the motor equivalent circuits synthesized in accordance with (Guha and Kar, 2006; Lam and Yee, 1998) having three parallel branches and the magnetizing one, separated in the manner as is shown in the Figure 1, are as follows (in per unit on machine base):

$$X_\delta + X_\gamma = 2.19; X_1 = 0.271; X_2 = 1.179$$

$$X_3 = 0.717 ; R_1 = 0.0055 ; R_2 = 0.1139$$

$$R_3 0.624$$

The comparative analysis of the results obtained by calculating the generalized stator current vector, I_s and electromagnetic torque, T , calculated by various methods points to their close agreement because of the maximum values of the mentioned variables differ less than 7,8%.

The analysis of the electromechanical transients at starting the non-loaded motor also indicates to the satisfactory coinciding of the results obtained by using the mentioned calculation techniques. In particular, the starting time determined by the technique proposed differs from the same parameter obtained through the use of the Parc Gorev equations less than 9, 2%.

As is seen from the Figure 4, the electromagnetic transients within the time interval from 0 up to 0.1 s correspond closely with the results obtained by the Parc Gorev equation (see dotted line).

The mentioned acceptable results are attributable to the fact that the change in the motor speed takes place at the small rotor acceleration. In this case, the application of the frequency-response characteristics of a machine does not introduce large errors into calculation of the transient processes. When the rotor speed is close to the rated value there are considerable deviations in the changes of the current and electromagnetic torque with time.

As may be inferred from the research, the mentioned deviations decrease with increasing the inertia constant, M, and the loading factor of the induction motor. The transients in this case are accompanied by the less acceleration of a rotor.

The investigation of the transients called forth by connection of the unexcited turbo generator ТГВ-200 type to the network was carried out with the use of the equivalent circuits containing five parallel branches in d- and q-axis [6]. It was ascertained that the errors being introduced in the transient processes by reducing the quantity of the circuit branches, describing the physical properties of the solid rotor, to three do not exceed the errors in a frequency domain equal to 11%.

Conclusion

In this paper, we presented a survey about the methods of frequency-response characteristics used for investigating and evaluating the transient conditions of the AC machines in electrical systems. In fact, a mathematical models of the asynchronous electrical machines based on the experimental frequency-response characteristics are presented. These models allow us to investigate the transients processes at short-circuits and the connection of the machines to the network without solution of the conventional differential equations. In order to lead to this task, we take into consideration the occurring speed changes of the AC machine rotor.

REFERENCES

Arjona LMA, MacDonald DC (1999). Characterising the d-axis machine model of a turbogenerator using finite elements, IEEE Transaction on Energy Conversion 14 (3): 340- 346.

Bacalao UNJ, de Arizon P, Sanchez LRO (1995). A model for the synchronous machine using frequency response measurements, IEEE Transactions on Power Systems, 10(1):457 -464.

Burakov A, Arkkio A (2007). Low-order parametric force model for eccentric-rotor electrical machine equipped with parallel stator windings and rotor cage, IET Electric Power Applications, 1 (4): 532-542.

Canay IM (1994). Advance calculation of the characteristic quantities of synchronous machines and comparison with measured values, IEE

Dehkordi AB, Gole AM, Maguire TL (2005). "Permanent Magnet Synchronous Machine Model for Real- Time Simulation", International Power System Transient Conference (IPST 2005), Montreal.

Guha S, Kar NC(2006). A New Method of Modeling Magnetic Saturation in Electrical Machines, Canadian Conference on Electrical and Computer Engineering, CCECE '06. pp.1094- 1097.

Houdouin, Gilles, Contribution à la modélisation de la machine asynchrone en présence de défauts rotoriques thése doctorat de l'université du Havre – 2004.

Khemliche M, Latreche S, Khellaf A (2004). Modelling and identification of the asynchronous machine, First International Symposium on Control, Communications and Signal Processing,. 815- 818.

Kirtley JL(1994). On turbine-generator rotor equivalent circuit structures for empirical modeling of turbine generators," IEEE Trans. on Energy Conversion, PWRS,9(1): 269-271.

Lam DM, Yee H (1998). A study of frequency responses of generator electrical torques for power system stabilizer design, IEEE Transactions on Power Systems, 13 (I):3 1136-1142.

Lamari A (2004). Simulation mathématique des régimes dynamiques des machines électriques à courant alternative à base des caractéristiques fréquentielles statique, thèse doctorat de l'université de Donetsk,

Lei Hao, Namuduri C (2009). Modeling of an alternator using Stand Still Frequency Response Test, IEEE Vehicle Power and Propulsion Conference, VPPC '09. 7(10):1541- 1546.

Liuchen C(1996). An improved FE inductance calculation for electrical machines, IEEE Transactions on Magnetics, 32 (4): 3237-3245. Proceedings Electric Power Applications, 141 (1): 13-18.

Ronkowski M (2008). Modelling of electrical machines using the Modelica Bond-Graph Library, 13th Power Electronics and Motion Control Conference, EPE-PEMC 2008. 1(3) :880- 886.

Satish L, Saravanakumar A (2008). Identification of Terminal Connection and System Function for Sensitive Frequency Response Measurement on Transformers, IEEE Transactions on Power Delivery, 23 (2): 742-750.

Shiqin Du, Yuejin Zhang, Jianzhong Jiang (2008). Research on a novel combined permanent magnet electrical machine, International Conference on Electrical Machines and Systems, 2008. ICEMS 17-(20) 3564-3567.

Slemon GR, Awad ML (1999). On equivalent circuit modeling for synchronous machines, IEEE Transaction on Energy Conversion, 14 (4):982- 988.

17

Predicting shelf life of dairy product by using artificial neural networks (ANN) and statistical computerized methods

Sumit Goyal* and Gyanendra Kumar Goyal

Dairy Technology Division, National Dairy Research Institute, Karnal-132001 (Haryana), India.

Artificial neural networks (ANN) have been developed as generalizations of mathematical models of biological nervous systems. Generalized regression (GR) and multiple linear regression (MLR) models for shelf life prediction of dairy product were developed. Results of both the models were evaluated with three types of prediction performance measures *viz.*, mean square error, root mean square error and coefficient of determination R^2, and compared with each other. Based on these results, regression equations were developed. From the study, it is concluded that ANN and statistical computerized methods can be employed for predicting shelf life of dairy products.

Key words: Artificial neural networks (ANN), shelf life, dairy product, prediction, generalized regression, multiple linear regression.

INTRODUCTION

Milky bars are popular Indian sweet made out of solidified, sweetened milk and cottage cheese. It owes its origin to the milk-rich *Braj* area of western Uttar Pradesh, India. It is a very popular sweetmeat (Wikipedia website, 2011). The human brain provides proof of the existence of massive neural networks that can succeed at those cognitive, perceptual, and control tasks in which humans are successful. The brain is capable of computationally demanding perceptual acts (for example, recognition of faces and speech) and control activities (for example, body movements and body functions). The advantage of the brain is its effective use of massive parallelism, the highly parallel computing structure, and the imprecise information-processing capability. The human brain is a collection of more than 10 billion interconnected neurons. Treelike networks of nerve fibers called dendrites are connected to the cell body or soma, where the cell nucleus is located. Extending from the cell body is a single long fiber called the axon, which eventually branches into strands and substrands, and is connected to other neurons through synaptic terminals or synapses. The transmission of signals from one neuron to another at synapses is a complex chemical process in which specific transmitter substances are released from the sending end of the junction. The effect is to raise or lower the electrical potential inside the body of the receiving cell. If the potential reaches a threshold, a pulse is sent down the axon and the cell is 'fired'. Artificial neural networks (ANN) have been developed as generalizations of mathematical models of biological nervous systems. A first wave of interest in neural networks (also known as connectionist models or parallel distributed processing) emerged after the introduction of simplified neurons by McCulloch and Pitts (1943). The basic processing elements of neural networks are called artificial neurons or simply neurons or nodes. In a simplified mathematical model of the neuron, the effects of the synapses are represented by connection weights that modulate the effect of the associated input signals, and the nonlinear characteristic exhibited by neurons is represented by a transfer function. The neuron impulse is then computed as the weighted sum of the input signals, transformed by the transfer function. The learning capability of an artificial neuron is achieved by adjusting the weights in

*Corresponding author. E-mail: thesumitgoyal@gmail.com.

accordance to the chosen learning algorithm. A neural network has to be configured such that the application of a set of inputs produces the desired set of outputs. Various methods to set the strengths of the connections exist. One way is to set the weights explicitly, using a priori knowledge. Another way is to train the neural network by feeding it teaching patterns and letting it change its weights according to some learning rule. The learning situations in neural networks may be classified into three distinct sorts. These are supervised learning, unsupervised learning and reinforcement learning. In supervised learning, an input vector is presented at the inputs together with a set of desired responses, one for each node, at the output layer. A forward pass is done, and the errors or discrepancies between the desired and actual response for each node in the output layer are found. These are then used to determine weight changes in the net according to the prevailing learning rule. The term supervised originates from the fact that the desired signals on individual output nodes are provided by an external teacher (Softcomputing website, 2011).

Generalized regression (GR) model

GR models are a kind of radial basis network that is used for function approximation.
Syntax: net = newgrnn (P, T, spread)
net = newgrnn(P,T,spread) takes three inputs,
P: R-by-Q matrix of Q input vectors
T: S-by-Q matrix of Q target class vectors

Spread: Spread of radial basis functions (default = 1.0) and returns a new GR model. To fit data very closely, use a spread smaller than the typical distance between input vectors. To fit the data more smoothly, use a larger spread; the larger the spread, the smoother the function approximation. Newgrnn creates a two-layer neural network. The first layer has radbas neurons in it and calculates weighted inputs with dist and net input with netprod. The second layer has purelin neurons, which calculates weighted input with normprod, and net inputs with netsum. Only the first layer has biases. newgrnn sets, the first layer weights to *P'*, and the first layer biases are all set to 0.8326/spread, resulting in radial basis functions that cross 0.5 at weighted inputs of +/- spread. The second layer weights *W2* are set to *T* (Mathworks. website, 2011).

Multiple linear regressions (MLR)

Regression reveals average relationship between two variables and makes possible to predict the yield. In mathematics, Y is called a function of X, but in statistics it is termed as regression which describes relationship. Hence, regression is the study of functional relationship between two variables of which one is dependent (Y) and other is independent (X). Regression analysis provides an estimate of values of the dependent variable from values of the independent variable. This estimation procedure is called the regression line. Regression analysis gives a measure of the error. With the help of regression coefficients, we can find the value of correlation coefficient. The multiple regression analysis gives the best linear prediction equation involving several independent variables. It also helps in finding the subset that gives the best prediction values of Y. The multiple regression equation describes the average relationship between dependent and independent variables which is used to predict the dependent variable. If Y depends partly on X1 and partly on X2, then the population regression equation is written as:

$$Y_R = \alpha - \beta_1 X_1 + \beta_2 X_2, \qquad (1)$$

β_1 measures the average change in Y when X_1 increases by 1 unit, X_2 remaining unchanged is called the partial regression coefficient of Y on X_1 and β_2 the partial regression coefficient of Y on X_2 which measures the average change in Y when X_2 increases by 1 unit, X_1 remaining unchanged. Thus, the regression model is:

$$Y = \alpha + \beta_1 X_1 + \beta_2 X_2 + \varepsilon, \qquad (2)$$

Where, $\varepsilon = N(0, \sigma^2)$ (Agarwal, 2010).

Goyal and Goyal (2011a) successfully applied artificial neural engineering and regressions models for forecasting shelf life of instant coffee drink. Goyal and Goyal (2011b) developed linear layer (design) and time-delay methods of intelligent computing expert system for shelf life prediction of soft mouth melting milk cakes and Kalakand (Goyal and Goyal, 2011c). Prediction of shelf life is important in order to achieve good quality of food products. As per government norms, it is mandatory to state expiry date on the package of food products. Factory owners, shopkeepers and restaurants do not have the facility of testing shelf life. So, they pay huge amount of money to the organizations that have the facility of testing shelf life in laboratory. Testing of shelf life in laboratory is a very time consuming activity. Hence, it would be relevant to develop such a model that could predict shelf life of milky bars at low cost and in less time.

METHODOLOGY

The models were tyrosine, moisture, free fatty acids, titratable acidity and peroxide value; and sensory score was output parameter, as shown in Figure 1. The dataset consisted of 60 live observations. Further, the dataset was divided into two subsets, that is, 48 data observations (80% of data observations) were used for training the network and 12 for testing (20% of data observations) the network. GR and MLR models were developed and compared with each other for shelf life prediction of milky bars. The network was trained with 100 epochs and number of neurons in single and double hidden layers varied from 1 to 30. Different

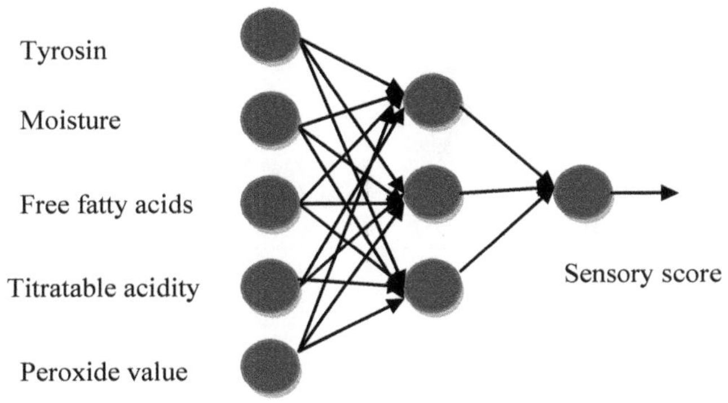

Figure 1. Design of neural network.

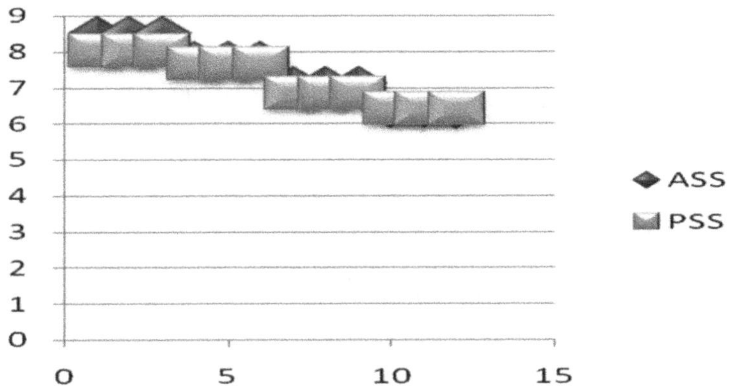

Figure 2. Graphical representation of actual and predicted sensory score for GR model.

combinations were tried and tested, as there is no predefined rule of achieving good results other than hit and trial method. The number of neurons increased as the training time. Two problems that were kept in mind while training the network were problem of overfitting and problem of underfitting. Overfitting means that the size of neurons used in training the network should not be large, as it is difficult for the network to train and underfitting means neurons should not be less as it is difficult for a neural network to get properly trained. Hence, balance must be maintained, while training the neural network. The neural network toolbox under MATLAB 7.0 software was used for development of artificial intelligence computing models.

Performance measures for prediction

$$MSE = \left[\sum_{1}^{N} \left(\frac{Q_{\exp} - Q_{cal}}{n} \right)^2 \right] \quad (3)$$

$$RMSE = \sqrt{\frac{1}{n} \left[\sum_{1}^{N} \left(\frac{Q_{\exp} - Q_{cal}}{Q_{\exp}} \right)^2 \right]} \quad (4)$$

$$R^2 = 1 - \left[\sum_{1}^{N} \left(\frac{Q_{\exp} - Q_{cal}}{Q_{\exp}^{2}} \right)^2 \right] \quad (5)$$

$Q_{\exp}$ = Observed value; Q_{cal} = predicted value; n = number of observations in dataset.

RESULTS AND DISCUSSION

The comparison of actual and predicted sensory score for ann models are illustrated in Figure 2 and Figure 3, respectively. Several experiments were carried out with GR and MLR models. Different combinations were tried, tested and compared with each other as shown in Tables 1 and Table 2. GR models best results with spread constant as 2 are MSE 0.001152787; RMSE: 0.033952711; R^2: 0.986166561. Statistical model of MLR was developed to compare the performance of artificial intelligence neural computing models. It displayed better results than GR model (MSE 0.000144005; RMSE:

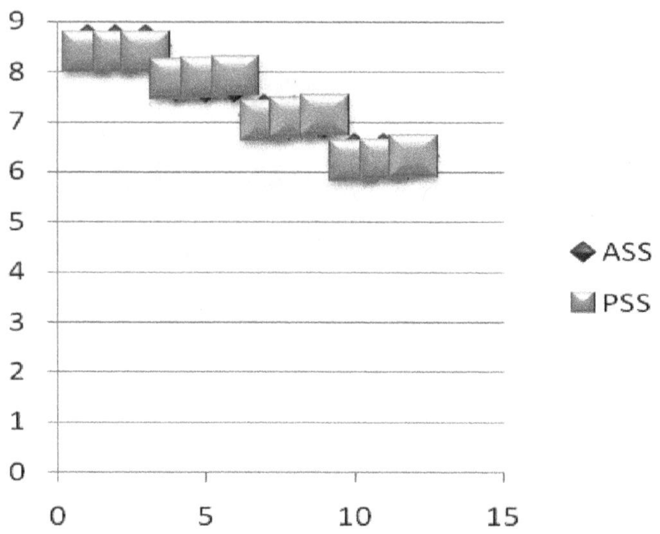

Figure 3. Graphical representation of actual and predicted sensory score for MLR model.

Table 1. Results of experiments for GR model.

Spread constant	MSE	RMSE	R^2
2	*0.001152787*	0.033952711	0.986166561
3	0.002836909	0.053262638	0.965957096
4	0.005046995	0.071042204	0.939436063
5	0.006850000	0.082764727	0.917799999
6	0.008135249	0.090195614	0.902377015
7	0.009032628	0.095040137	0.891608467
8	*0.009667907*	0.098325516	0.883985114
9	0.010129284	0.100644342	0.878448597
10	0.010471581	0.102330745	0.874341023
25	0.011789805	0.108580870	0.858522335
40	0.011952980	0.109329685	0.856564239

Table 2. Result of regression model.

Regression model	MSE	RMSE	R^2
MLR	*0.000144005*	0.0120002	0.998271839

0.0120002; R^2: 0.998271839) (Table 3). Our results are in agreement with the earlier findings of Goyal and Goyal (2011a). They developed artificial neural engineering and regression models for forecasting shelf life of instant coffee drink and concluded that MLR models are better than artificial neural engineering models in predicting shelf life instant coffee drink.

Based on the results, MLR model was selected for predicting shelf life of milky bars by building regressions equations based on sensory scores and constant came out as 8.516, regression coefficient as -0.041 and R^2 was found to be 99% as shown in Figure 4; after solving them 1.35 came as the output which was subtracted from the actual shelf life of the product *that is*, days. Hence, it was found 38.65 days.

Conclusion

The possibility of artificial intelligence neural network and statistical computing approach was investigated to predict shelf life of milky bars. GR model and statistical model of

Table 3. Displaying best results of different models.

Model	Best results
GR model	MSE 0.001152787; RMSE: 0.033952711; R^2: 0.986166561
MLR model	MSE 0.000144005; RMSE: 0.0120002; R^2: 0.998271839

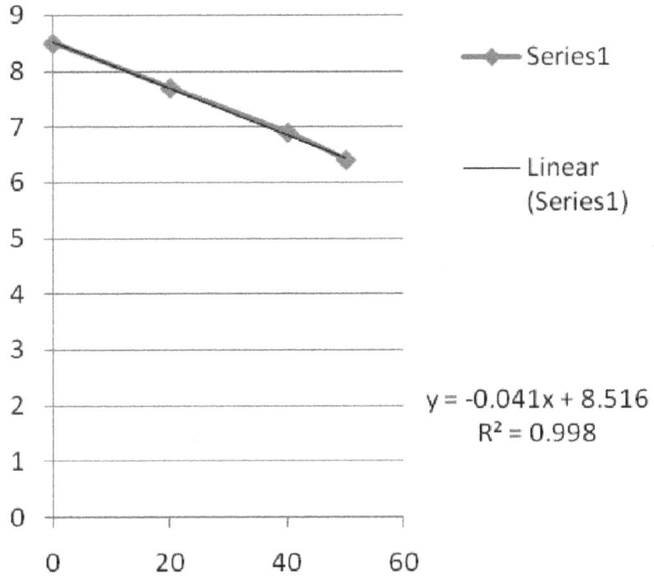

Figure 4. Displaying regression equations.

MLR was developed. From the results, it can be concluded that statistical computing model of MLR is superior over GR model in predicting shelf of milky bars stored at 6°C.

REFERENCES

Agarwal SB (2010). Manual on Statistical Methods for Agriculture and Animal Sciences. Published by National Dairy Research Institute (Deemed University), Karnal 132 001 (Haryana) India.

Goyal S, Goyal GK (2011a). Application of artificial neural engineering and regression models for forecasting shelf life of instant coffee drink. Int. J. Compt. Sci., 8(4): 320-324.

Goyal S, Goyal GK (2011b). Development of Intelligent Computing Expert System Models for Shelf Life Prediction of Soft Mouth Melting Milk Cakes. Int. J. Compt. Appl., 25(9): 41-44.

Goyal S, Goyal GK (2011c). Advanced Computing Research on Cascade Single and Double Hidden Layers for Detecting Shelf Life of Kalakand: An Artificial Neural Network Approach. Int. J. Compt. Sci. Emerging Technol., 2(5): 292-295.

Mathworks. Web-site accessed on 1.2.2011: "http://www.mathworks.com/help/toolbox/nnet/ref/newgrnn.html".

Softcomputing web-site accessed on 27.1.2011: "http://www.softcomputing.net/ann_chapter.pdf".

Wikipedia website accessed on 29.2.2011: "http://en.wikipedia.org/wiki/Kalakand"

Design and simulation of an SMS driven microcontroller for home automation using proteus software

Olusanya O. Olamide and Ayeni O. A. Joshua*

Computer Science Department, University of Lagos, Akoka, Lagos, Lagos State, Nigeria.

Technology has moved from a level at which a user is always present in a place before he/she can control or do anything at the place. Imagine what television used to be before the inception of remote control. With the inception of remote control, the television can be controlled while lying on the bed or sitting down on the chair. You do not have to move towards it and press the button on it before you can control it. Now envision how it will be, being able to control your entire home appliances automatically and even remotely. Different types of technology are available to do this but this paper looks at designing and simulating the usage of an SMS from mobile phone together with microcontroller (PIC16F876) in communicating with and controlling home appliances. The firmware is written in C language and translated into a Hexadecimal file using Custom Computer Services (CCS) Compiler. The translated Hexadecimal file is loaded into the microcontroller and the microcontroller is then interfaced with the mobile phone such that when this phone receives SMS, it gives the detail of the state of the home appliances remotely. SMS can be sent to instruct the system to do some specific tasks like switching on or off of any of the appliances in the home, switching on the pumping machine to pump water and monitor it. Anytime one feels like stopping an invoked action, it can be done remotely without being in the vicinity of the equipment.

Key words: Home automation, short message service, custom computer services compiler, simulation, microcontroller, general packet radio system networks, proteus software, firmware.

INTRODUCTION

The design and implementation of an embedded system using an SMS-driven microcontroller for home automation involves strong interrelationship of both hardware and software to produce what will perform simple, specific and repeatable tasks; often with little or no input from the user. Most experiments/tasks performed today normally require the physical presence of the operator in order to monitor and run the task. Imagine what it will be like to be able to perform other activities elsewhere while still carrying out and monitoring an important task where one is.

This work designs and simulates a system using Proteus software that will act as mobile interface between a machine and the user or operator such that simple, specific and repeatable task could be performed by users without being on the same location with the machine.

REVIEW OF PREVIOUS WORKS

Embedded computer

Barr (2001) says an embedded computer is frequently a computer that is implemented for a particular purpose. In contrast, an average personal computer (PC) usually serves a number of purposes: Checking email, surfing the internet, listening to music, word processing, programming different applications, etc. However,

*Corresponding author. E-mail: jayeni@unilag.edu.ng.

embedded systems usually only have a single task, or a very small number of related tasks that they are programmed to perform.

Real time operating system

From an implementation viewpoint, there is a major difference between a computer and an embedded system. Embedded systems are often required to provide real-time response. A real-time system is defined as a system whose correctness depends on the timeliness of its response. Barr (2001) gave examples of such systems: flight control systems of an aircraft, sensor systems in nuclear reactors and power plants. For these systems, delay in response is a fatal error. A more relaxed version of real-time systems is the one where timely response with small delay is acceptable. Example of such a system would be the Scheduling Display System on the railway platforms.

Programming embedded system using C programming language

Henbury (2001) emphasizes the fact that C programming language remains a very popular language for micro-controller developers due to the code efficiency and reduced overhead and development time. C offers low-level control and is considered more readable than assembly language.

Interfacing

The system is the combination of both hardware and software. And these two parts of the system have to be interfaced. Aula (2012) states that the hardware is an electronic circuit that matches with PC's port protocol signal, and the software is the programming of the PC to manage all input/output signals from its ports.

IEEE Live Project (2012) also presents the controlling of appliances through SMS. The usage of microcontroller was highlighted as a powerful element that provides a highly flexible and cost-effective solution to many embedded control applications. Sami (1998) recommends the use of both the internet and mobile communication devices in controlling home appliances.

METHODOLOGY

The design flow of the embedded system reported here begins with design/requirements specification, followed by hardware design. This is followed by the software (firmware) design in order to optimize design result and still satisfy the requirements. Hardware and software integration is done after hardware/software detail design. Finally, system testing is carried out.

Hardware used

The following, are the components and devices used in the circuit design and their functions:

- Transformer (TRAN-2P2S); it is a magnetic (inductive) device, it receives AC from power supply.
- Rectifier (2W005G); It converts AC to DC.
- Capacitor; Stores and releases electrical charge. It filters unwanted signals.
- Transistors; act like switches. It is used in general-purpose switching and amplification. The arrow in the NPN transistor symbol is on the emitter leg and points in the direction of the conventional current flow when the device is in forward active mode.
- Resistors; pass current in proportion to voltage.
- Diodes; conducts electricity easily in one direction.
- Crystal; a ceramics crystal used to generate precise frequencies. It filters high frequencies e.t.c.

Software used

The program used in controlling the system is written using C programming language. After the program has been written in C, it was compiled on Custom Computer Services (CCS) compiler in order to generate the microcontroller compatible HEX files. Figure 1 shows a portion of the HEX file generated by the CCS compiler; the compiler that provides a complete integrated tool suite for developing and debugging embedded applications running on Microchip PIC.

Theory of operation

The hardware was designed on the Proteus software. The Proteus is a simulation package tool that permits real time debugging of codes and circuit on the system. This Proteus VSM tool even permits the real interface of the mobile station / modem with the computer system, permitting all necessary tests to be performed. The circuit was drawn on the Proteus and the HEX file generated from the code compilation on CCS compiler (Figure 1), is written into the microcontroller in the circuit (Figure 2). This microcontroller is embedded in the circuit designed on the Proteus simulation package.

The mobile station (phone) is interfaced with the computer via Bluetooth in order to communicate with the microcontroller embedded in the circuit and the port number on the UART port is changed to the COM port number on the phone. The message (instruction command) is sent from the remote phone to the phone, interfaced with the computer system and the running button on the simulation package is pressed to start the simulation. The microcontroller fetches the SMS from phone, decodes it, recognizes the phone number and switches on the relays that are responsible for controlling the appliances. The microcontroller also sends back the report to the remote phone through an SMS.

RESULTS AND DISCUSSION

Figure 2 shows the circuit before the simulation is carried out. The pumping machine is not working, it is in its OFF state. The temperature sensor is also not working as well as the LEDs that indicate whether the devices (home appliances) are in ON or OFF state. In order to test the functionality of this system, there are two mobile stations

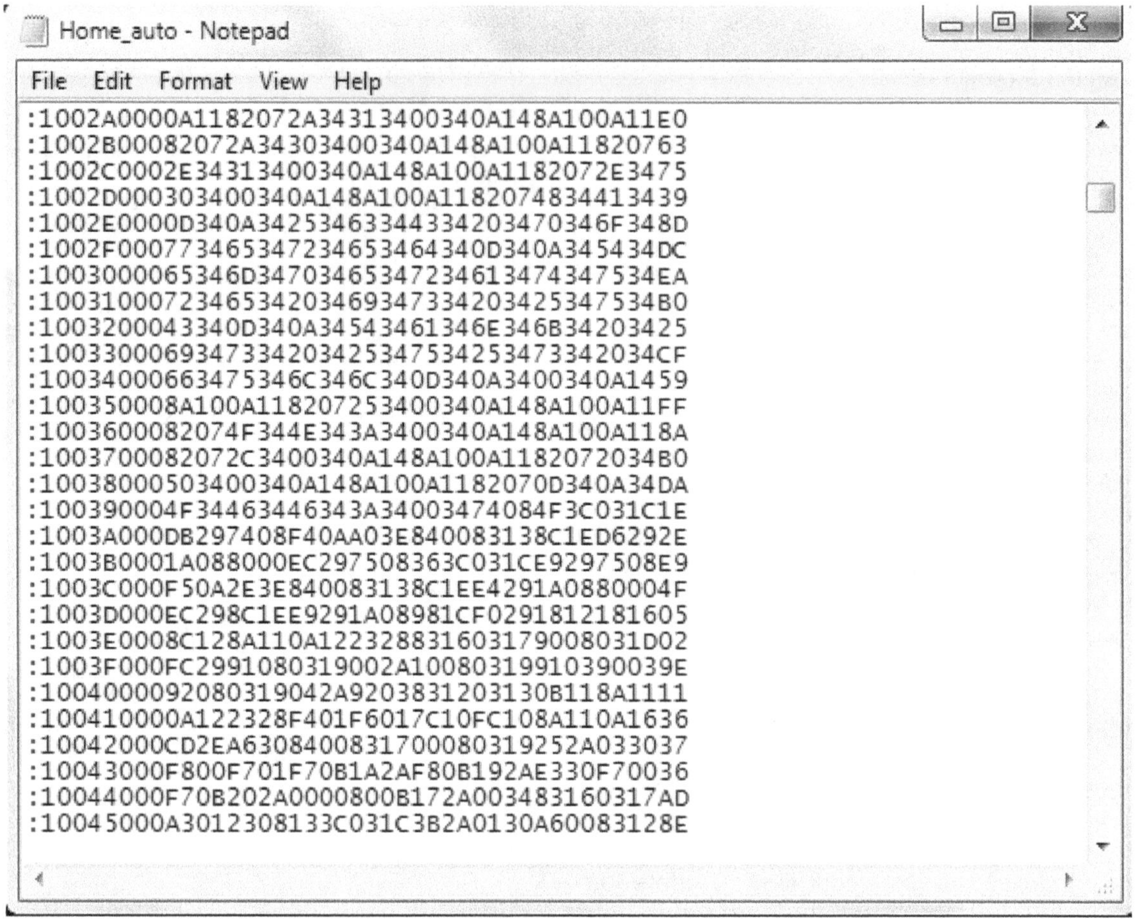

Figure 1. A portion of the HEX file generated by the CCS compiler.

(phones): the remote one, that sends command and the one that is interfaced with the system, that recieves the command. After the connection between the mobile station and the computer system has been established, the simulation button is triggered on and the simulation starts. Then the mobile station from a remote area is used to send the instructions(commands) to the mobile station connected with the system. The command is either to turn ON or OFF the home appliances. If it is to turn ON the home appliances, the command is like this:

HA
D.1*1.2*1.3*1.4*1
P.1
R.1#.

The command could also be to turn OFF those appliances and if it is to turn them OFF, the command goes thus:

HA
D.1*0.2*0.3*0.4*0
P.1
R.1#.

There are two virtual terminals that appear on the surface of the Proteus showing the way the two mobile stations and the microcontroller on the circuit are communicating. One of these virtual terminals is for the microcontroller in the circuit and the other virtual terminal is for the mobile station that is interfaced with the system. These two virtual terminals show how the instruction received by the phone interfaced with the system from the remote phone is read and carried out by the microcontroller in the circuit. The two of them communicated well and they both carried out the instructions given to them. The terminals are shown in Figures 3a and b and each of the command generated is discussed one after the other:

- The "at" shown on the microcontroller virtual terminal is attention command to call the attention of the mobile phone interfaced with the system (something like handshake).
- The "at+cmgf =0" command is talking about how to read the command sent whether it will be read on text mode or protocol data unit mode (PDU). In PDU mode, all SMS

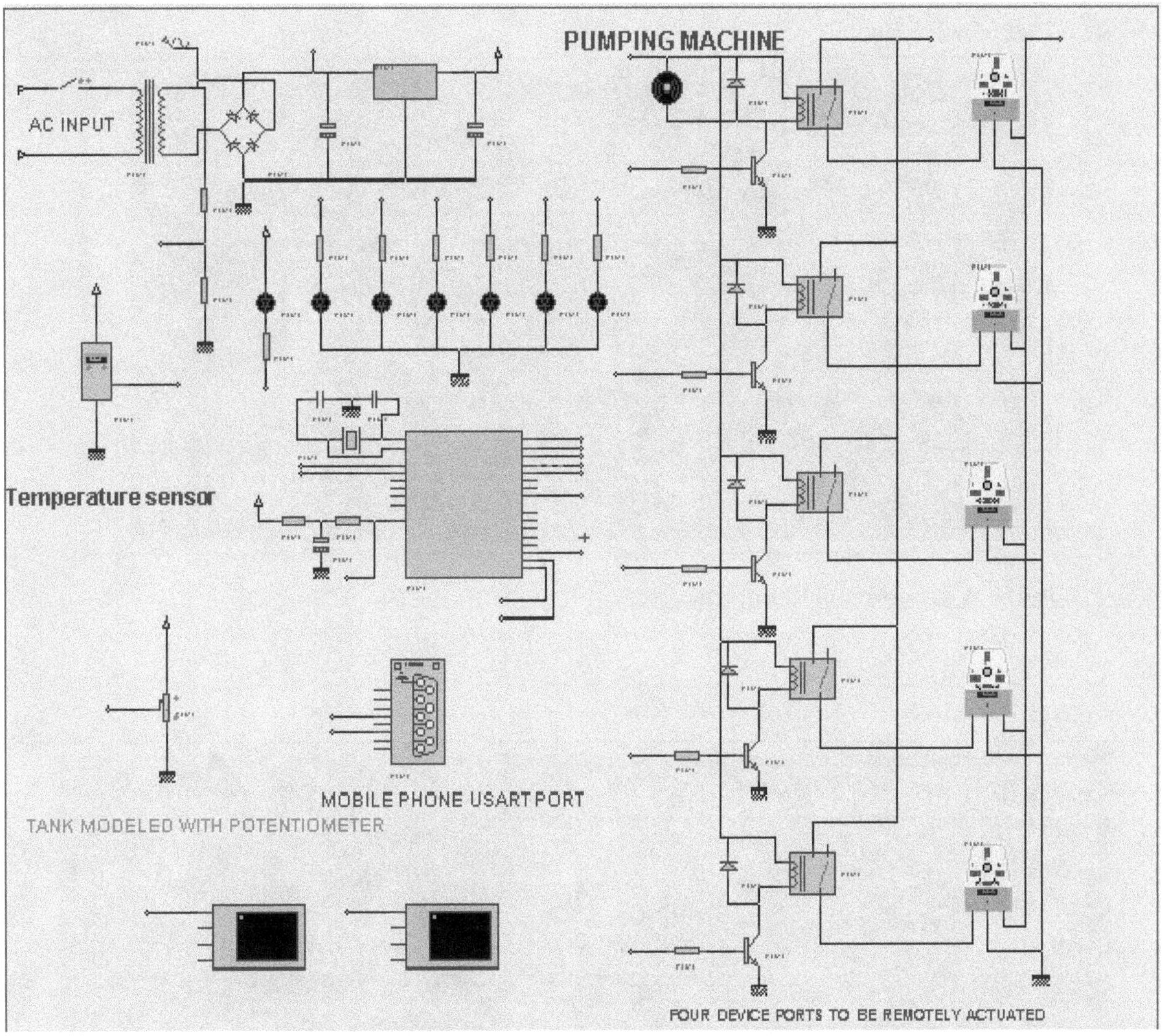

Figure 2. Diagram of the circuit on Proteus software before the simulation is carried out.

messages are represented as binary strings encoded in hexadecimal character; like, while in text mode, SMS messages are represented as readable text. If the data is to be read on text mode, the command will be "at+cmgf =1" and if it is in PDU mode, the command is "at+cmgf =0". The phone connected to the system can only read the message in PDU mode, that is why the microcontroller gave the aforementioned command; that is, " at+cmgf =0".

- The "at+ cmps =ME,ME,ME" tells the controller to read either from phone memory or SIM memory. The first ME means saving, the second one means reading and the third one means deleting.
- The "at+ cmgr =1" means the controller is reading the SMS (short message service) sent remotely to the mobile station connected to it from memory location 1 of the phone.
- The "at+ cmgr =2" means the controller is reading the SMS sent remotely to the mobile station connected to it from memory location 2 of the phone.
- The "at+ cmgs = "08057418758"" command on the controller virtual terminal is telling the mobile station connected to it that it should send the message shown subsequently to the remote mobile station in order to tell the state of the appliances at home.

"HA
AC Powered
Temperature is 53°C
Tank is 70% full
ON: P.1.2.3.4
OFF: "

- The HA means Home Automation.

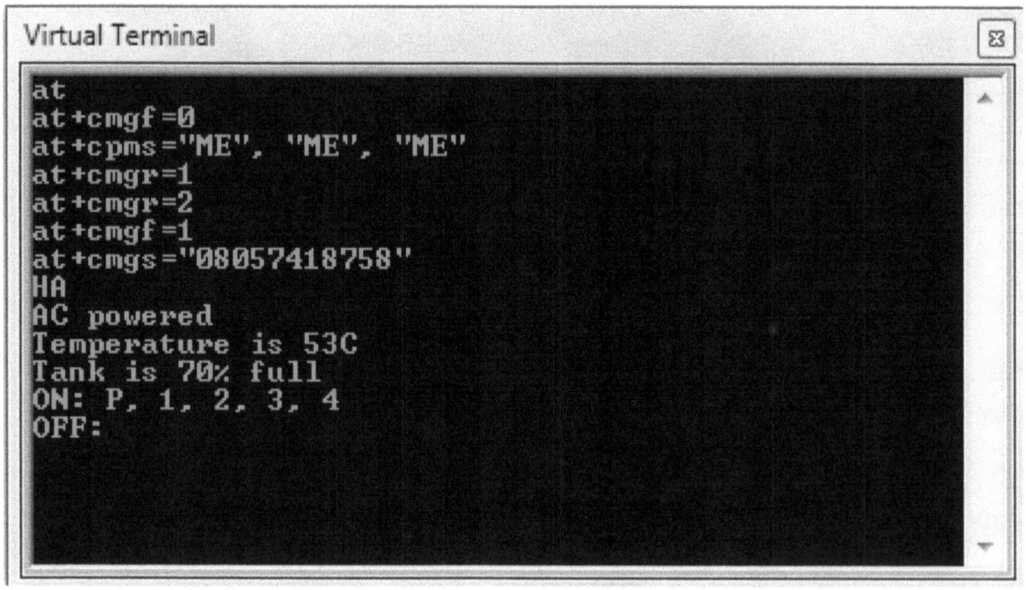

Figure 3a. Virtual terminal for microcontroller.

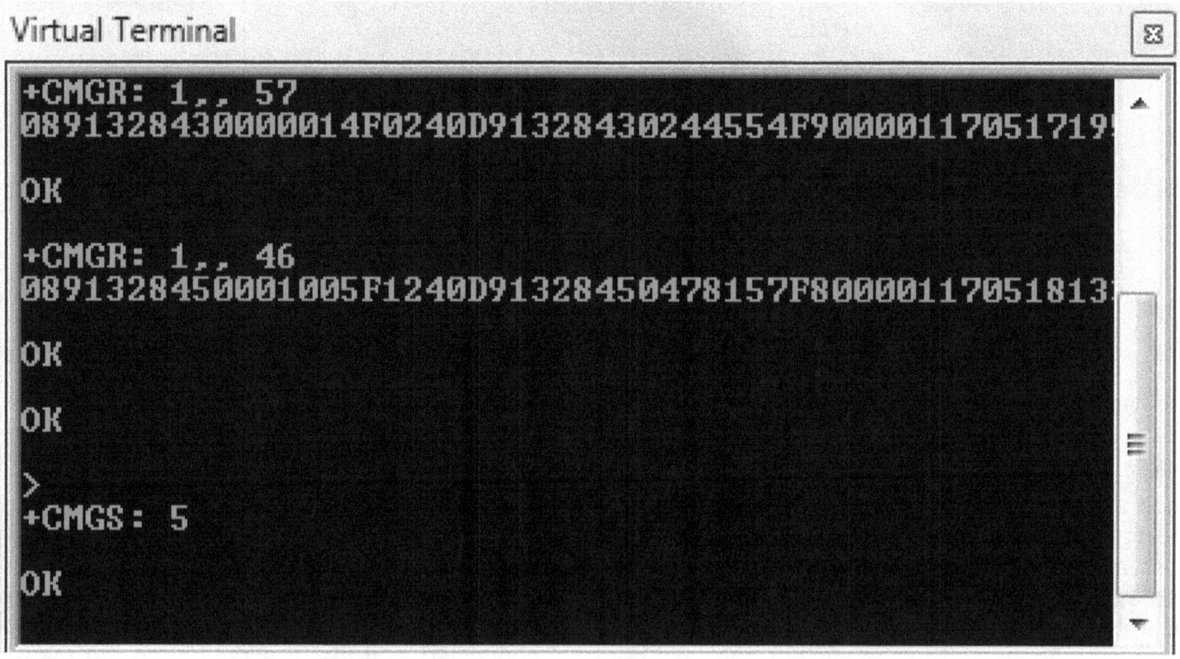

Figure 3b. Virtual terminal for mobile station connected to the system.

- AC Powered means the system is using AC power supply.
- Temperature is 53°C means the house temperature is 53°C. If the temperature is too high for you and you are about coming home from work, you can send an SMS to the machine to turn on the AC at home before you get home.
- Tank is 70% full means the level of water in the tank is 70%, so the pumping machine has to be turned on in order to pump water into the water tank; but if the water level is about 95%, the controller will turn off the pumping machine immediately because the water level has reached its maximum level.
- ON: P.1.2.3.4 means the pumping machine is on, the devices connected to the sockets 1, 2, 3 and 4 are also on.

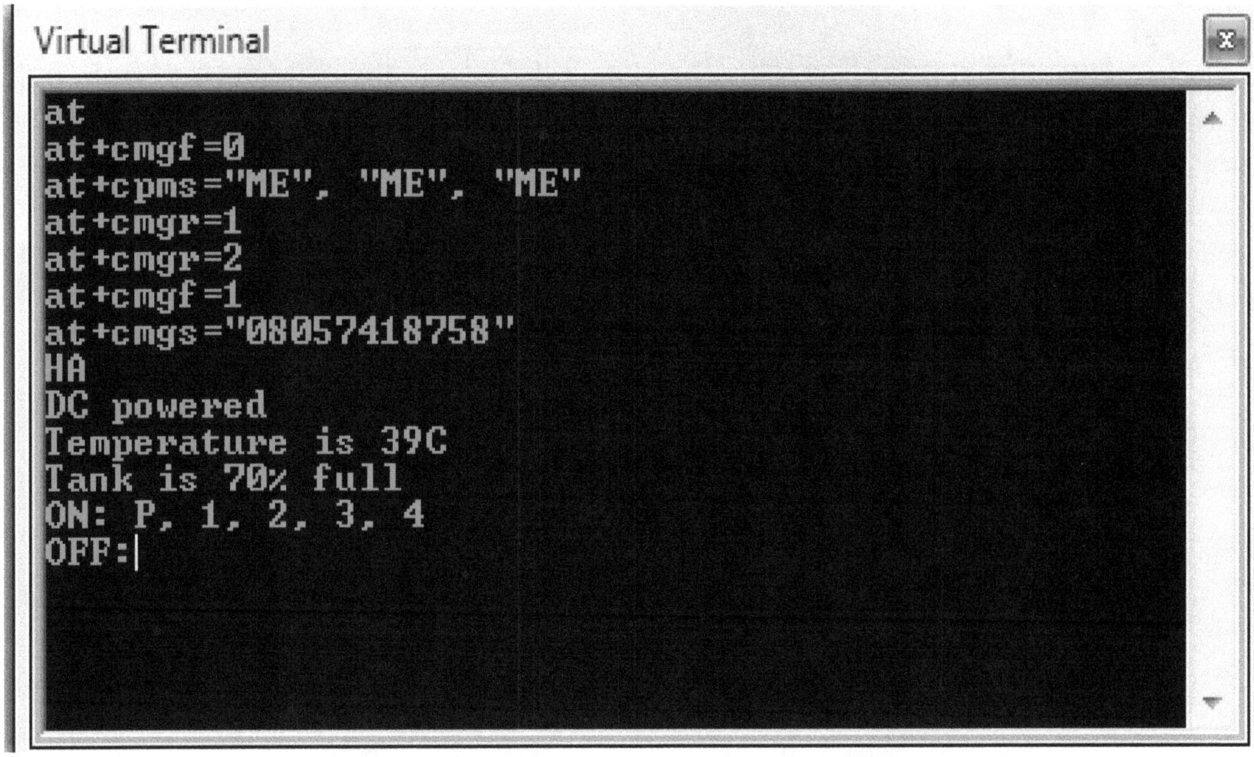

Figure 4. Microcontroller virtual terminal showing that the system is being powered by DC power supply.

- OFF: means no device is turned off.

The following are the commands shown on the mobile station virtual terminal:

"OK
+CMGR: 1, , 57
089132843000001............
OK
+CMGR: 1, , 46
089132843000001............
OK
+CMGS: 5"

- The OK is responding to the controller that it has been connected.
- +CMGR: 1, , 57 means the SMS was read from the memory location 1 of the remote mobile station and the phone still have about 57 capacity to hold SMS.
- 089132843000001............: this is telling us the first number that remotely sent the command.
- +CMGR: 1, , 46 means the SMS was read from the memory location 1 of the second remote mobile station and the phone still has about 46 memory capacity to hold SMS.
- +CMGR: 5" is telling the phone to send the reply (message on its memory location 5) to the remote mobile station.

The power supply can be from DC supply also because of the battery connected in parallel to the rectifier, as shown in Figure 4. This battery is being charged when the AC supply is powering the system and automatically switches over to the DC supply when there is power outage. Even though the DC supply cannot trigger the appliances to work but the SMS sent will be stored in the memory of the controller so that when the AC supply comes up, the system continues from where it stopped.
The command sent remotely through the mobile station to turn on some of the home appliances actually turns them on and the snap shot of it is shown in Figure 5. The pumping machine and the LEDs indicating the aplliances were turned ON after the command has been sent to the mobile station, these are the blue colour shown on pumping machine and red colours shown on the LEDs. The MS sent the read SMS to the microcontroller and the microcontroller carried out the instruction accordingly by turning ON the appliances. The appliances can be turned OFF as well by sending the instruction to do that. The green light on one of the LEDs shows the phone is connected to the controller.

DISCUSSION

The operation of the system is confirmed (tested) by sending an SMS from the sending MS (Mobile Station) to

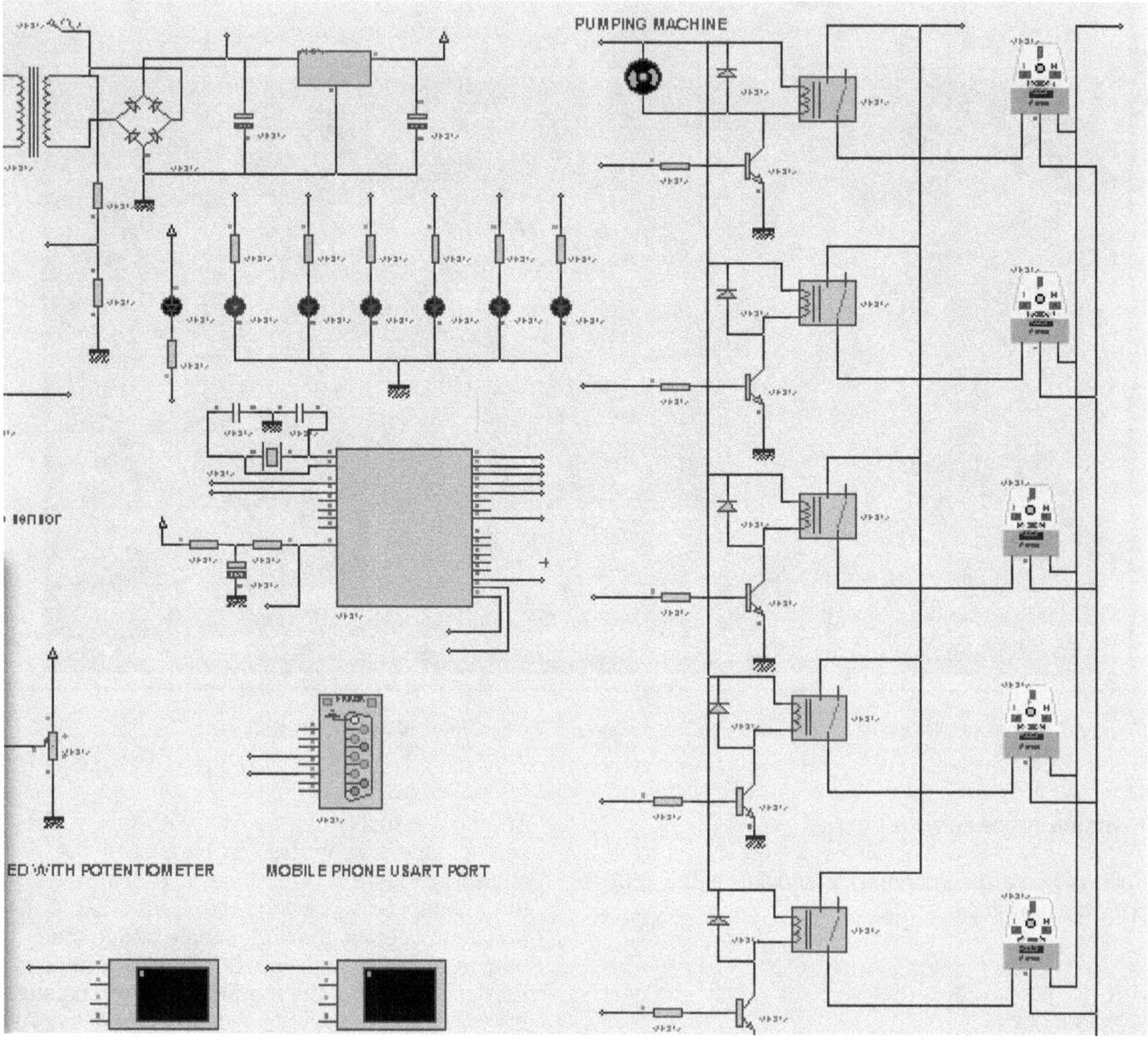

Figure 5. Diagram showing how the command sent remotely turned on the appliances.

trigger and to stop the operation of the appliance. The use of mobile communication system has the advantage of controlling the appliances remotely and it also makes life easy for the user. For example, the user can get alerts anywhere through the GSM technology thus making the system location independent.

Also, an SMS driven microcontroller for home automation is cost effective because you do not have to spend so much before you can control your appliances remotely. Once you have enough credit on your mobile system that can allow you to send the instructions to the mobile phone, connected to the system and the phone interfaced with the system also has credit that can allow it to send you back the reply.

A lot of people have used similar methodology to control appliances, but this work does not only control the appliances, it also monitors the appliances. For example, the system monitors the level of water in the tank in order to know when to turn ON or OFF the pumping machine and monitors the home temperature, so that it will know when to switch on an Air Conditioner or not.

Conclusion

In this work, the possibility of minimizing the stress of wanting to be physically present at home while one is at work or elsewhere before being able to control and monitor what is going on in the home is looked into. A system is designed that allows one to send message remotely and get the instructions carried out. In achieving this goal, some design steps were followed and the implementation of the system was carried out. The system was validated through testing and found to be working perfectly well.

REFERENCES

Aula FT (2012). Retrieved from http://www.emo.org.tr/ekler/8808cfb5939be38_ek.pdf. Accessed on 21/03/2012.

Barr M (2001). "Memory Types," Embedded Systems Programming, May 2001. Retrieved from http://www.netrino.com.

Henbury C (2001). Embedded System- Tooling up for Tomorrows World, Revised October 2001. Retrieved from http://www.cheshirehenbury.com/embedded/index.html.

IEEE Live Project (2012). http://1000projects.org/appliances-control-through-sms-electronics-pr... - India. Accessed on 21-03-2012.

Sami L (1998). Mobile Home Automation, 1998. Retrieved from http://www.lababidi.com/mobileAutomation.

New Holder-type inequalities for the Tracy-Singh and Khatri-Rao products of positive matrices

Zeyad AL-Zhour

Department of Basic Sciences and Humanities, College of Engineering, University of Dammam, Kingdom of Saudi Arabia (KSA).

Recently, authors established a number of inequalities involving Khatri-Rao product of two positive matrices. Here, in this paper, the results are established in three ways. First, we find new Holder-type inequalities for Tracy-Singh and Khatri-Rao products of positive semi-definite matrices. Secondly, the results are extended to provide estimates of sums of the Khatri-Rao and Tracy-Singh products of any finite number of positive semi-definite matrices. Finally, the results lead to inequalities involving the Hadamard and Kronecker products, as a special case.

Key words: Tracy-Singh products, Khatri-Rao products, positive (semi) definite matrices, Holder inequalities.

INTRODUCTION

Consider matrices $A = [a_{ij}], C = [c_{ij}] \in M_{m,n}$ and $B = [b_{kl}] \in M_{p,q}$. Let A and B be partitioned as $A = [A_{ij}]$ and $B = [B_{kl}]$ $(1 \le i \le t, 1 \le j \le c)$, where A_{ij} is an $m_i \times n_j$ matrix and B_{kl} is a $p_k \times q_l$ matrix $(m = \sum_{i=1}^{t} m_i, n = \sum_{j=1}^{c} n_j, p = \sum_{i=1}^{t} p_i, q = \sum_{j=1}^{c} q_j)$. Let $A \otimes B$, $A \circ C$, $A\Theta B$ and $A * B$ be the Kronecker, Hadamard, Tracy-Singh and Khatri-Rao products, respectively. The definitions of the mentioned four matrix products are given by Al-Zhour and Kilicman (2007); Al-Zhour and Kilicman (2006a); Al-Zhour and Kilicman (2006b); Cao et al. (2002); Liu (2002); Mond and Pecaric (2000) and Visick (2000).

$$A \otimes B = \left(a_{ij}B\right)_{ij} \; ; \; A \circ C = \left(a_{ij}c_{ij}\right)_{ij} \; ; \tag{1}$$

$$A * B = \left(A_{ij} \otimes B_{ij}\right)_{ij} \; ; \; A\Theta B = \left(A_{ij}\Theta B\right)_{ij} = \left(\left(A_{ij} \otimes B_{kl}\right)_{kl}\right)_{ij}. \tag{2}$$

Additionally, the Khatri-Rao product can be viewed as a generalized Hadamard product and the Tracy-Singh product as a generalized Kronecker product, that is, for a non-partitioned matrix A and B, their $A\Theta B$ is $A \otimes B$ and $A * B$ is $A \circ B$. For any compatibly partitioned matrices A, B, C, D, we shall make frequent use the following properties of the Tracy-Singh product (Al-Zhour and Kilicman, 2007; Al-Zhour and Kilicman, 2006a and b; Cao et al., 2002; Liu, 2002):

$$(A\Theta B)(C\Theta D) = (AC)\Theta(BD); \tag{3}$$

$$(A\Theta B)^* = A^*\Theta B^*. \tag{4}$$

The Hermitian matrix A is called positive semi-definite (Written $A \ge 0$) if $\langle Ax, x\rangle \ge 0$ for any vector x and positive definite (Written $A > 0$) if $\langle Ax, x\rangle > 0$ for any non-zero vector x. For Hermitian matrices A and B, the relations $A \ge B$ mean that $A - B \ge 0$ is a positive semi-definite. Given a positive semi-definite matrix A and $k \ge 1$ be a given integer, then there exists a unique positive semi-definite matrix B such that $A = B^k$, written as $B = A^{1/k}$. Denote H_n^+ be the set of all positive definite

*Corresponding author. E-mail: zeyad1968@yahoo.com.

$n \times n$ matrices. If $A \in H_n^+$, then the spectral decomposition of A assures that there exists a unitary matrix U such that (Zhang, 1999):

$$A = U^* D\, U = U^* diag(\lambda_i) U \;,\; U^* U = I_m \;.$$

Here, $D = diag(\lambda_i) = diag(\lambda_1, \cdots, \lambda_m)$ is the diagonal matrix with diagonal entries λ_i (λ_i are the positive eigen values of A). For any real number r, A^r is defined by:

$$A^r = U^* D^r U = U^* diag(\lambda_i^r) U \;. \tag{5}$$

Now we present the following basic results (Al-Zhour and Kilicman, 2007; Al-Zhour and Kilicman, 2006b; Cao et al., 2002; Rao and Rao 1998).

Lemma 1

Let $A_i \in M_{m(i),n(i)}$ $(1 \le i \le k \;, k \ge 2)$ be compatibly partitioned matrices ($m = \prod_{i=1}^{k} m(i)$, $n = \prod_{i=1}^{k} n(i)$, $r = \sum_{j=1}^{t}\prod_{i=1}^{k} m_j(i)$, $s = \sum_{j=1}^{c}\prod_{i=1}^{k} n_j(i)$, $m(i) = \sum_{j=1}^{t} m_j(i)$, $n(i) = \sum_{j=1}^{c} n_j(i)$). Then there exists two real matrices Z_1 of order $m \times r$ and Z_2 of order $n \times s$ such that $Z_1^T Z_1 = I_1$, $Z_2^T Z_2 = I_2$ and:

$$\prod_{i=1}^{k} * A_i = Z_1^T \left(\prod_{i=1}^{k} \Theta A_i \right) Z_2 \,. \tag{6}$$

Here, I_1 and I_2 are identity matrices of order $r \times r$ and $s \times s$, respectively.

Lemma 2

Let a_i and b_i $(1 \le i \le k)$ be positive scalars. If $1 \le p, q < \infty$ satisfy $(1/p) + (1/q) = 1$. Then the scalar Holder inequality is given by:

$$\sum_{i=1}^{k} a_i b_i \le \left(\sum_{i=1}^{k} a_i^p \right)^{1/p} \left(\sum_{i=1}^{k} b_i^q \right)^{1/q} . \tag{7}$$

Corollary 1

Let a_i and b_i $(1 \le i \le k)$ be positive scalars. If $0 < p < \infty$ and $0 < q < 1$ satisfy $(1/q) - (1/p) = 1$. Then:

$$\sum_{i=1}^{k} a_i b_i \ge \left(\sum_{i=1}^{k} a_i^{-p} \right)^{-1/p} \left(\sum_{i=1}^{k} b_i^q \right)^{1/q} \tag{8}$$

Proof: The condition $(1/q) - (1/p) = 1$ can be rewritten as $\dfrac{1}{(p/q)} + \dfrac{1}{(1/q)} = 1$.

Since $1 \le \dfrac{p}{q} < \infty$ and $1 \le \dfrac{1}{q} < \infty$, then by Lemma 2 we have:

$$\sum_{i=1}^{k} (b_i)^q = \sum_{i=1}^{k} a_i^{-q} (a_i b_i)^q \le \left(\sum_{i=1}^{k} \left((a_i)^{-q} \right)^{p/q} \right)^{q/p} \left(\sum_{i=1}^{k} \left((a_i b_i)^q \right)^{1/q} \right)$$

$$= \left(\sum_{i=1}^{k} (a_i)^{-p} \right)^{q/p} \left(\sum_{i=1}^{k} (a_i b_i) \right)^q .$$

hence

$$\sum_{i=1}^{k} a_i b_i \ge \left(\sum_{i=1}^{k} a_i^{-p} \right)^{-1/p} \left(\sum_{i=1}^{k} b_i^q \right)^{1/q} .$$

This completes the proof of Corollary 1. ϒ

The problem may occur that we cannot find Holder-type inequalities for usual product of positive semi definite matrices, but here, we can find new Holder-type inequalities for the Tracy-Singh, Khatri-Rao, Kronecker and Hadamard products of positive matrices which are very important for applications to establish new inequalities involving these products. Since it is sometimes difficult to compute, for example, ranks, determinants, eigen values, norms of large matrices, it is of great importance to provide estimates of sums of these products of any finite number of matrices by applying Holder-type inequalities of positive matrices.

MAIN RESULTS

Based on the aforementioned basic results, and the general connection between the Khatri-Rao and Tracy-Singh products in Lemma 1, we derive some inequalities with respect to the Tracy-Singh and Khatri-Rao products and extend these results to any finite number of matrices. These results lead to inequalities involving Kronecker and Hadamard products, as a special case.

Theorem 1

Let $A_i \in H_n^+$ and $B_i \in H_m^+$ be partitioned matrices ($1 \le i \le k$). If $1 \le p,q < \infty$ satisfy $(1/p)+(1/q)=1$. Then:

$$\sum_{i=1}^{k} A_i \Theta B_i \le \left(\sum_{i=1}^{k} A_i^p\right)^{1/p} \Theta \left(\sum_{i=1}^{k} B_i^q\right)^{1/q}. \quad (9)$$

Proof: By assumption there exist a unitary matrix $U \in M_n$ and a unitary matrix $V \in M_m$ such that $A_i = U^* D_i U$ with $D_i = diag(d_{i1},\cdots,d_{in})$ and $B_i = V^* T_i V$ with $T_i = diag(t_{i1},\cdots,t_{im})$, where d_{ij}, t_{ij} are nonnegative real numbers for all i and j. It follows that:

$$A_i \Theta B_i = \left(U^* D_i U\right)\Theta\left(V^* T_i V\right) = \left(U^* \Theta V^*\right)\left(D_i \Theta T_i\right)\left(U \Theta V\right)$$
$$= \left(U\Theta V\right)^* diag(d_{i1}t_{i1},\cdots,d_{i1}t_{im},\cdots,d_{in}t_{i1},\cdots,d_{in}t_{im})\left(U\Theta V\right)$$

So, by using Lemma 2, we have:

$$\sum_{i=1}^{k} A_i \Theta B_i =$$
$$\left(U\Theta V\right)^* diag\left(\sum_{i=1}^{k} d_{i1}t_{i1},\cdots,\sum_{i=1}^{k} d_{i1}t_{im},\cdots,\sum_{i=1}^{k} d_{in}t_{i1},\cdots,\sum_{i=1}^{k} d_{in}t_{im}\right)\left(U\Theta V\right)$$

$$\le \left(U\Theta V\right)^* diag\left[\left(\sum_{i=1}^{k} d_{i1}^p\right)^{1/p}\left(\sum_{i=1}^{k} t_{i1}^q\right)^{1/q},\cdots,\left(\sum_{i=1}^{k} d_{i1}^p\right)^{1/p}\left(\sum_{i=1}^{k} t_{im}^q\right)^{1/q},\cdots,\left(\sum_{i=1}^{k} d_{in}^p\right)^{1/p}\right.$$
$$\left.\left(\sum_{i=1}^{k} t_{i1}^q\right)^{1/q},\cdots,\left(\sum_{i=1}^{k} d_{in}^p\right)^{1/p}\left(\sum_{l=1}^{k} t_{im}^q\right)^{1/q}\right]\left(U\Theta V\right)$$

$$= \left(U\Theta V\right)^*\left\{diag\left[\left(\sum_{i=1}^{k} d_{i1}^p\right)^{1/p},\cdots,\left(\sum_{i=1}^{k} d_{in}^p\right)^{1/p}\right]\right.$$
$$\left.\Theta diag\left[\left(\sum_{i=1}^{k} t_{i1}^q\right)^{1/q},\cdots,\left(\sum_{i=1}^{k} t_{im}^q\right)^{1/q}\right]\right\}\left(U\Theta V\right)$$

$$= \left(U^*\Theta V^*\right)\left\{\left(\sum_{i=1}^{k} D_i^p\right)^{1/p}\Theta\left(\sum_{i=1}^{k} T_i^q\right)^{1/q}\right\}\left(U\Theta V\right)$$

$$= \left\{\left(U^*\left(\sum_{i=1}^{k} D_i^p\right)^{1/p} U\right)\Theta\left(V^*\left(\sum_{i=1}^{k} T_i^q\right)^{1/q} V\right)\right\}$$

$$= \left(\sum_{i=1}^{k} A_i^p\right)^{1/p}\Theta\left(\sum_{i=1}^{k} B_i^q\right)^{1/q}. \Upsilon$$

Corollary 2

Let $A_i \in H_n^+$ and $B_i \in H_m^+$ be partitioned matrices ($1 \le i \le k$). If $1 \le p,q < \infty$ satisfy $(1/p)+(1/q)=1$. Then:

$$\sum_{i=1}^{k} A_i * B_i \le \left(\sum_{i=1}^{k} A_i^p\right)^{1/p} * \left(\sum_{i=1}^{k} B_i^q\right)^{1/q}. \quad (10)$$

Proof: Follows immediately by applying Lemma 1 and Theorem 1.. Υ

Corollary 3

Let $A_i^{(j)} \in H_{n^{(j)}}^+$ $(1 \le i \le k)$ be partitioned $n^{(j)} \times n^{(j)}$ matrices, $(1 \le j \le r)$. Let $1 \le \left\{p^{(j)}\right\}_{j=1}^{r} < \infty$ satisfy $\sum_{j=1}^{r}(1/p^{(j)}) = 1$. Then:

$$\sum_{i=1}^{k}\left(\prod_{j=1}^{r}\Theta A_i^{(j)}\right) \le \prod_{j=1}^{r}\Theta\left(\sum_{i=1}^{k}(A_i^{(j)})^{p^{(j)}}\right)^{1/p^{(j)}}. \quad (11)$$

Proof: Using Theorem 1, the corollary follows by induction on k. Υ

Corollary 4

Let $A_i^{(j)} \in H_{n^{(j)}}^+$ $(1 \le i \le k)$ be commutative partitioned $n^{(j)} \times n^{(j)}$ matrices, $(1 \le j \le r)$. Let $1 \le \left\{p^{(j)}\right\}_{j=1}^{r} < \infty$ satisfy $\sum_{j=1}^{r}(1/p^{(j)}) = 1$. Then:

$$\sum_{i=1}^{k}\left(\prod_{j=1}^{r} * A_i^{(j)}\right) \le \prod_{j=1}^{r} *\left(\sum_{i=1}^{k}(A_i^{(j)})^{p^{(j)}}\right)^{1/p^{(j)}}. \quad (12)$$

Proof: Using Corollary 3 and Lemma 1, the corollary follows by induction on k .Υ

We give an example using products of three matrices ($r = 3$). Let $A_i^{(j)}$ $(1 \le i \le k)$ be $n \times n$ positive definite partitioned matrices, $(1 \le j \le 3)$. Let $1 \le \left\{p^{(j)}\right\}_{j=1}^{3} < \infty$ satisfy $(1/p^{(1)}) + .(1/p^{(2)}) + (1/p^{(3)}) = 1$. Then:

(i)

$$\sum_{i=1}^{k} A_i^{(1)} \Theta A_i^{(2)} \Theta A_i^{(3)} \le \left(\sum_{i=1}^{k} A_i^{p^{(1)}}\right)^{1/p^{(1)}} \Theta \left(\sum_{i=1}^{k} A_i^{p^{(2)}}\right)^{1/p^{(2)}} \Theta \left(\sum_{i=1}^{k} A_i^{p^{(3)}}\right)^{1/p^{(3)}}. \quad (13)$$

(ii)

$$\sum_{i=1}^{k} A_i^{(1)} * A_i^{(2)} * A_i^{(3)} \le \left(\sum_{i=1}^{k} A_i^{p^{(1)}}\right)^{1/p^{(1)}} * \left(\sum_{i=1}^{k} A_i^{p^{(2)}}\right)^{1/p^{(2)}} * \left(\sum_{i=1}^{k} A_i^{p^{(3)}}\right)^{1/p^{(3)}}. \quad (14)$$

Theorem 2

Let $A_i \in H_n^+$ and $B_i \in H_m^+$ be partitioned matrices $(1 \le i \le k)$. If $0 < p < \infty$ and $0 < q < 1$ satisfy $(1/q) - (1/p) = 1$. Then:

$$\sum_{i=1}^{k} A_i \Theta B_i \ge \left(\sum_{i=1}^{k} A_i^{-p}\right)^{-1/p} \Theta \left(\sum_{i=1}^{k} B_i^{q}\right)^{1/q} \quad (15)$$

Proof: By assumption there exist a unitary matrix $U \in M_n$ and a unitary matrix $V \in M_m$ such that $A_i = U^* D_i U$ with $D_i = diag(d_{i1},\cdots,d_{in})$ and $B_i = V^* T_i V$ with $T_i = diag(t_{i1},\cdots,t_{im})$, where d_{ij}, t_{ij} are nonnegative real numbers for all i and j. It follows that:

$$A_i \Theta B_i = \left(U^* D_i U\right)\Theta\left(V^* T_i U\right) = \left(U^* \Theta V^*\right)\left(D_i \Theta T_i\right)\left(U \Theta V\right)$$
$$= \left(U\Theta V\right)^* diag(d_{i1}t_{i1},\cdots,d_{i1}t_{im},\cdots,d_{in}t_{i1},\cdots,d_{in}t_{im})\left(U\Theta V\right)$$

So, by using Corollary 1, we have:

$$\sum_{i=1}^{k} A_i \Theta B_i =$$
$$\left(U\Theta V\right)^* diag\left(\sum_{i=1}^{k} d_{i1}t_{i1},\cdots,\sum_{i=1}^{k} d_{i1}t_{im},\cdots,\sum_{i=1}^{k} d_{in}t_{i1},\cdots,\sum_{i=1}^{k} d_{in}t_{im}\right)\left(U\Theta V\right)$$
$$\ge \left(U\Theta V\right)^* diag\left[\left(\sum_{i=1}^{k} d_{i1}^{-p}\right)^{-1/p}\left(\sum_{i=1}^{k} t_{i1}^{q}\right)^{1/q},\cdots,\left(\sum_{i=1}^{k} d_{i1}^{-p}\right)^{-1/p}\left(\sum_{i=1}^{k} t_{im}^{q}\right)^{1/q},\right.$$
$$,\cdots,\left(\sum_{i=1}^{k} d_{in}^{-p}\right)^{-1/p}\left(\sum_{i=1}^{k} t_{i1}^{q}\right)^{1/q}$$
$$\left.,\cdots,\left(\sum_{i=1}^{k} d_{in}^{-p}\right)^{-1/p}\left(\sum_{i=1}^{k} t_{im}^{q}\right)^{1/q}\right]\left(U\Theta V\right)$$
$$= \left(U\Theta V\right)^* \left\{ diag\left[\left(\sum_{i=1}^{k} d_{i1}^{-p}\right)^{-1/p},\cdots,\left(\sum_{i=1}^{k} d_{in}^{-p}\right)^{-1/p}\right]\right.$$
$$\left.\Theta diag\left[\left(\sum_{i=1}^{k} t_{i1}^{q}\right)^{1/q},\cdots,\left(\sum_{i=1}^{k} t_{im}^{q}\right)^{1/q}\right]\right\}\left(U\Theta V\right)$$
$$= \left(U^*\Theta V^*\right)\left\{\left(\sum_{i=1}^{k} D_i^{-p}\right)^{-1/p}\Theta\left(\sum_{i=1}^{k} T_i^{q}\right)^{1/q}\right\}\left(U\Theta V\right)$$
$$= \left\{\left(U^*\left(\sum_{i=1}^{k} D_i^{-p}\right)^{-1/p} U\right)\Theta\left(V^*\left(\sum_{i=1}^{k} T_i^{q}\right)^{1/q} V\right)\right\}$$
$$= \left(\sum_{i=1}^{k} A_i^{-p}\right)^{-1/p}\Theta\left(\sum_{i=1}^{k} B_i^{q}\right)^{1/q}. \Upsilon$$

Corollary 5

Let $A_i \in H_n^+$ and $B_i \in H_m^+$ be partitioned matrices $(1 \le i \le k)$. If $0 < p < \infty$ and $0 < q < 1$ satisfy $(1/q) - (1/p) = 1$. Then:

$$\sum_{i=1}^{k} A_i * B_i \ge \left(\sum_{i=1}^{k} A_i^{-p}\right)^{-1/p} * \left(\sum_{i=1}^{k} B_i^{q}\right)^{1/q} \quad (16)$$

Proof: Follows immediately by Lemma 1 and Theorem 2. Υ

Remark: The results obtained in this section are quite general. Now, as a special case, consider if the matrices in the main result are non-partitioned, we then have Holder type inequalities involving Kronecker and Hadamard products by replacing Θ by $\otimes$ and $*$ by $\circ$.

Conclusion

The problem may occur that we can't find Holder-type inequalities for usual product of positive (semi) definite matrices, but we established some Holder-type inequalities for the Tracy-Singh, Khatri-Rao, Kronecker and Hadamard products of positive semi-definite matrices which are very important for applications. How to extend the use of Holder-type inequalities in the main result for estimating, for example, ranks, determinants, eigen values, norms of sums of the mentioned four matrix products of finite number of large positive semi-definite matrices, requires further research.

ACKNOWLEDGMENTS

The author expresses his sincere thanks to referee(s) for careful reading of the manuscript and several helpful suggestions. The author also gratefully acknowledges that this research was partially supported by Deanship of Scientific Research, University of Dammam, Kingdom of Saudi Arabia, under the grant number: 2012152.

REFERENCES

Al-Zhour Z, Kilicman A (2007). Some New Connections between Matrix Products for Partitioned and Non-Partitioned Matrices, Comput. Math. Appl., 54(6): 763-784.

Al-Zhour Z, Kilicman A (2006a). Matrix Equalities and Inequalities Involving Khatri-Rao and Tracy-Singh Sums. J. Ineq. Pure Appl. Math., 7(1): 496-513.

Al-Zhour Z, Kilicman A (2006b). Extensions and Generalization Inequalities Involving, The Khatri-Rao Product of Several Positive Matrices. J. Ineq. Appl., doi: 10.1155/JIA/80878, p. 21.

Cao C, Zhang X, Yang Z (2002). Some Inequalities for the Khatri-Rao Product of Matrices". Elect. J. Linear Algebra, ISSN 1081-3810, 9: 276-281.

Liu S (2002). Several Inequalities Involving Khatri-Rao Products of Positive Semi definite Matrices. Linear. Algebra Appl., 354:175-186.

Mond B, Pecaric JE (2000). On Inequalities Involving the Hadamard Product of Matrices. Elect. J. Linear Algebra., 6: 56-61.

Visick G (2000). A quantitative Version of the Observation that the Hadamard Product is A principle Submatrix of the Kronecker Product", Linear. Algebra. Appl., 304: 45-68.

Zhang F (1999). Matrix Theory: Basic Results and Techniques, (Springer- Verlag, NewYork ,Inc.

Rao CR, Rao MB (1998). Matrix Algebra and its Applications to Statistics and Econometrics, World Scientific publishing Co. Pte. Ltd.

High performance efficiency of distributed optical fiber Raman amplifiers for different pumping configurations in different fiber cable schemes

Abd El–Naser A. Mohamed, Ahmed Nabih Zaki Rashed* and Mahmoud M. A. Eid

Department of Electronics and Electrical Communication Engineering, Faculty of Electronic Engineering, Menouf 32951, Menoufia University, Egypt.

Fiber Raman amplifiers (FRAs) are attractive for ultra wide dense wavelength division multiplexing (UW-DWDM) transmission systems due to their advantages of broad amplification bandwidth and flexible central wavelength. With recent developments of optical pump sources with high power near 1.4 μm wavelength and highly nonlinear fiber having a peak effective Raman gain coefficient, more than ten times that of conventional single mode fiber, distributed FRAs (DFRAs) are emerging as a practical optical amplifier technology, especially for opening new wavelength windows such as the short and ultra long wavelength bands. Optical pump powers required for Raman amplification were significantly higher than that for erbium-doped fiber amplifier (EDFA), and the pump laser technology could not reliably deliver the required powers. However, with the improvement of pump laser technology, Raman amplification is now an important means of expanding span transmission reach and capacity. In the present paper, we have deeply investigated the proposed model for optical DFRAs in the transmission signal power and pump power within Raman amplification technique in co-pumped, counter-pumped and bi-directional pumping direction configurations through different types of fiber cable media. The validity of this model was confirmed by using experimental data and numerical simulations.

Key words: Distributed fiber Raman amplifier, signal power, pumping power, forward pumping, different fiber media, backward pumping, bidirectional pumping configuration.

INTRODUCTION

The first fiber optical telecommunication systems emerged with the engineering of low loss optical fiber (Maan et al., 2009). Even though the complexity of the system has increased, the basic elements remain the same. They consist of an optical source, a means of modulating the source, the transmission medium (that is, the optical fiber), and a detector at the output end of the fiber. Fiber loss is one limitation to the transmission distance of this system. In the early days of fiber-optic communications, the loss of the fiber was compensated for in long spans by using electrical regenerators. As their name implies, these devices detected the signal, converted it to an electrical signal, and using a new laser transmitted a new version of the signal. Electrical regenerators were expensive and also limited the rate at which data could be transmitted as time for the much slower electrical processing to occur had to be built into the system. In order to overcome the limitations imposed by electrical regeneration, a means of optical amplification was sought. Two competing technologies emerged: the first was erbium-doped fiber amplifiers (EDFA) (Raghavendra and Vara, 2010; Abd El-Naser and Ahmed, 2010) and the second Raman amplification (Ming-Jun and Daniel, 2008). In the first deployed systems, EDFA emerged as the preferred approach. One reason was that the optical pump powers required for

*Corresponding author. E-mail: ahmed_733@yahoo.com

Raman amplification were significantly higher than that for EDFA, and the pump laser technology could not reliably deliver the required powers. However, with the improvement of pump laser technology, Raman amplification is now an important means of expanding span transmission reach and capacity (Abd El-Naser et al., 2009).

In a multiple wavelength telecom system, it is important that all signal wavelengths have similar optical powers. The variation in the gain provided to different wavelengths after passing through an amplifier is referred to as the gain flatness. If the signal at one wavelength is disproportionately amplified, as it passes through several amplifiers, it will grow super linearly relative to the other channels reducing the gain to other channels (ITU-T Recommendation G.652, 2009). The system, however, will still be limited by the channel with the lowest gain. As a result, after each amplifier the gain spectrum generally is flattened. One approach is to insert wavelength-dependent lossy elements, within the amplifier, with the appropriate spectral profile. Raman amplification offers the ability to achieve this without lossy elements. In Raman amplification, a flat spectral profile can be obtained by using multiple pump wavelengths (Abd El-Naser et al., 2009; Shahi et al., 2009). For a given fiber, the location of the Raman gain is only dependent on the wavelength of the pump, the magnitude of the gain is proportional to the pump power, and the shape of the gain curve is independent of the pump wavelength. Therefore, if multiple pumps are used a flat spectral gain profile can be obtained (Banerjee, 2009). The required pump wavelengths and the gain required at each wavelength can be predicted by summing the logarithmic gain profiles at the individual pump wavelengths (Abd El-Naser and Ahmed, 2009).

In the present study, we have deeply analyzed the signal power, pumping power, rate of change of signal, pumping powers with respect to transmission distance under the variations of signal, pump powers and signal and pump wavelengths for different fiber link media in different pumping direction configurations (forward, backward, and bidirectional) over wide range of the operating parameters.

DEVICE MODELING ANALYSIS

Signals fad with distance when they traveling through any type of media. As the optical signal moves along a SMF, it gets attenuated along the fiber. The signal power when it travels through the distance z without any amplification, P_{sWNA} can be expressed as follows:

$$P_{sWNA}(z) = P_{so} \exp(-\alpha_{Ls} z) \quad (1)$$

Systems avoid this problem by amplifying signals along the way. So there is a need for using optical fiber amplifiers. The evolution of the input signal power (P_s) and the input pump power (P_p) propagating along the single mode optical fiber in watt, can be quantitatively described by different equations called propagation equations. The rate of change of signal and pump power with the distance z, can be expressed as mentioned in Makoui et al. (2009):

$$\frac{dP_p}{dz} = -\alpha_{Lp} P_p(z) - \frac{\lambda_s}{\lambda_p} g_{\mathrm{Re}ff} P_s(z) P_p(z) \quad (2)$$

$$\frac{dP_s}{dz} = -\alpha_{Ls} P_s(z) + \frac{\lambda_s}{\lambda_p} g_{\mathrm{Re}ff} P_s(z) P_p(z) \quad (3)$$

Where λ_s and λ_p are the signal and pump wavelengths in μm, respectively, z is the distance in km from z=0 to z=L, α_{Ls} and α_{Lp} are the linear attenuation coefficient of the signal and pump power in the optical fiber in km^{-1}, respectively, The linear attenuation, α_L can be expressed as follows:

$$\alpha_L = \alpha / 4.343 \quad (4)$$

Where α is the attenuation coefficient in dB/km. g_{Reff} is the Raman gain efficiency in $W^{-1}km^{-1}$ of the fiber cable length, L in km, which is a critical design issue and is given by the equation as follows:

$$g_{\mathrm{Reff}} = \frac{g_R}{A_{eff} \times 10^{-18}} \quad (5)$$

Where g_R is the maximum Raman gain in km W^{-1}, A_{eff} is the effective area of the fiber cable used in the amplification in μm^2. Equation 1 can be solved when both sides of the equation are integrated. When using forward pumping, the pump power can be expressed as follows (El Mashade, et al., 2009):

$$P_{PF}(z) = P_{poF} \exp(-\alpha_{Lp} z) \quad (6)$$

Where P_{PoF} , is the input pump power in the forward direction in watt at z=0.

In the backward pumping, the pump power is given by Abd El Naser et al. (2009):

$$P_{PB}(z) = P_{poB} \exp\left[-\alpha_{Lp}(L - z)\right] \quad (7)$$

Where P_{PoB} , is the input pump power in the backward direction in watt at z=L.

In the case of bidirectional pump, both of the pump can be equal or different in the used wavelength or the used amount of power, therefore, in this case, the following equation can be used to calculate the pump power at point z (Raghuawansh et al., 2006):

Table 1. Typical values of operating parameters in proposed model.

Operating parameter	Symbol	Value			
Operating signal wavelength	λ_s	$1.45 \le \lambda_s$, μm ≤ 1.65			
Operating pump wavelength	λ_p	$1.40 \le \lambda_p$, μm ≤ 1.44			
Input signal power	P_{so}	$0.002 \le P_{so}$, W ≤ 0.02			
Input pump power	P_{po}	$0.165 \le P_{po}$, W ≤ 0.365			
Percentage of power launched in forward direction	r_f	0.5			
Attenuation of the signal power in silica-doped fiber	α_S	0.25 dB/km			
Attenuation of the pump power in silica-doped fiber	α_P	0.3 dB/km			
Types of fiber cable media		True wave reach fiber	LEAF (NZ-DSF)	SMF-28 (NDSF)	Unit
Effective area	A_{eff}	55	72	84.95	$(\mu m)^2$
Raman gain efficiency	g_{Reff}	0.6	0.45	0.38	$(W.km)^{-1}$

$$P_{PFB}(z) = (rf)P_{poF}\exp(-\alpha_{Lp}\, z) + (1-rf)P_{poB}\exp[-\alpha_{Lp}(L-z)] \qquad (8)$$

Where r_f is the percentage of pump power launched in the forward direction. If the values of P_P are substituted in differential Equation 2, and is integrated from z=0 to z=L for the signal power in the forward and the backward pumping, the result mathematical equation can be written as mentioned in Abd El Naser et al. (2009):

$$P_S(z) = P_{so}\exp\left[\left(\frac{g_R}{A_{eff}}\right)P_{po}L_{eff} - \alpha_{Ls}z\right] \qquad (9)$$

Where P_{so} and P_{po} denotes to the input signal and pump power, respectively. This means that $P_{po}= P_{poF}$ in case of forward pump and $P_{po}=P_{poB}$ in case of backward pump, and L_{eff}, is the effective length in km, over which the nonlinearities still holds or SRS occurs in the fiber and is defined as (de Matos et al., 2003):

$$L_{eff} = \frac{1-\exp(-\alpha_{Lp}\, z)}{\alpha_{Lp}} \qquad (10)$$

Recently, there have been many efforts to utilize fiber Raman amplifier (FRA) in long-distance, high capacity wavelength division multiplexing (WDM) systems. This is mainly because FRA can improve the optical signal to noise ratio (OSNR) and reduce the impacts of fiber nonlinearities (Son et al., 2005).

SIMULATION RESULTS AND PERFORMANCE ANALYSIS

In the present study, the optical distributed Raman amplifiers have been modeled and have been parametrically investigated, based on the coupled differential equations of first order, and also based on the set of the assumed of affecting operating parameters on the system model. In fact, the employed software computed the variables under the following operating parameters as shown in Table 1.

The following points of discussion will cover the entire operating design parameters of multiplexing/demultiplexing based optical distributed Raman amplifier device, such as, input signal power, input pumping power, operating signal wavelength, operating pump wavelength, and different fiber link media. Then, based on the basic model analysis and the set of series of the figures shown in this study, the following facts can be obtained:

Variations of the output pumping power, P_p

Variation of the output pumping power, P_p is investigated against variations of the controlling set of parameters as shown in Figures 1 to 4. Figures 1 to 4 clarify the results as follows:

A) In case of forward direction:

1) As distance z increases, the output pumping power decreases exponentially.
2) For certain value of distance z, with increasing the initial pumping power, the output pumping power also will increase.

B) In case of backward direction:

1) As distance z increases, the output pumping power increases exponentially.
2) For certain value of distance z, with increasing the

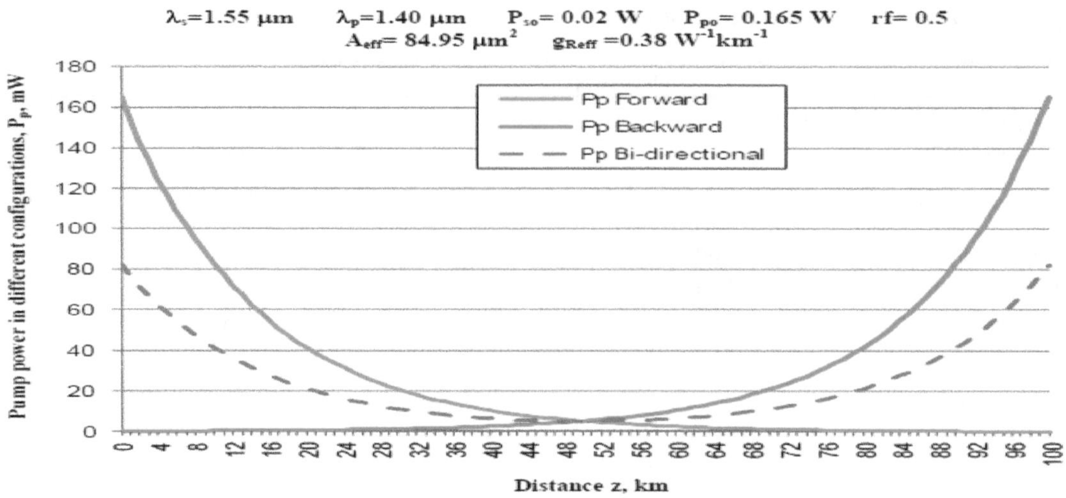

Figure 1. Variations of pump power in different configurations against variations of distance at the assumed set of the operating parameters.

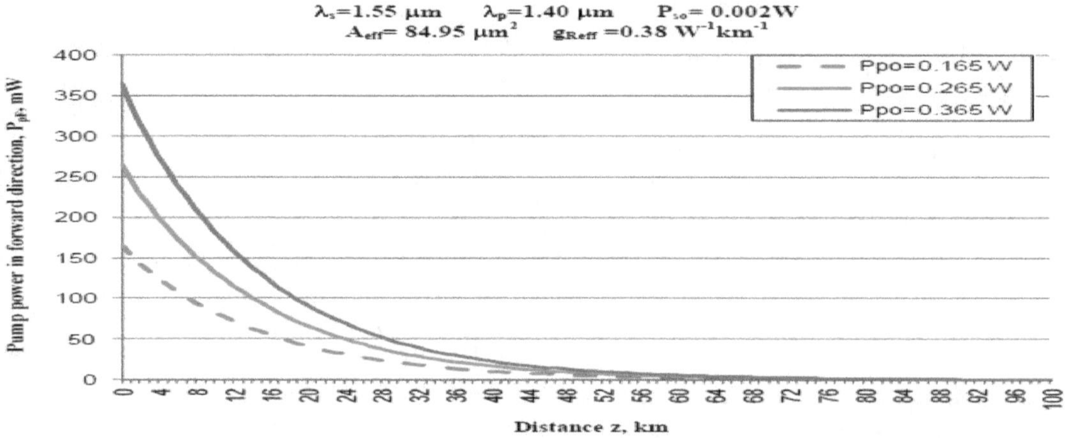

Figure 2. Variations of pump power in forward direction against variations of distance z at the assumed set of the operating parameters.

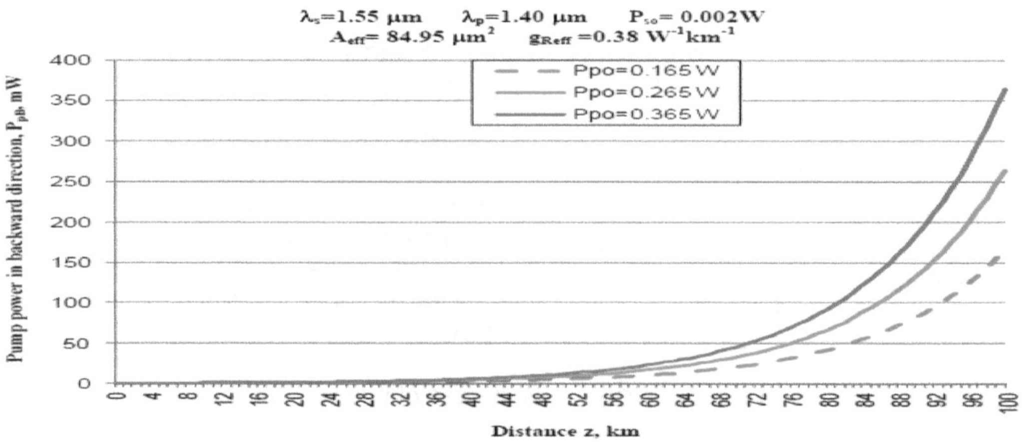

Figure 3. Variations of pump power in backward direction against variations of distance z at the assumed set of the operating parameters.

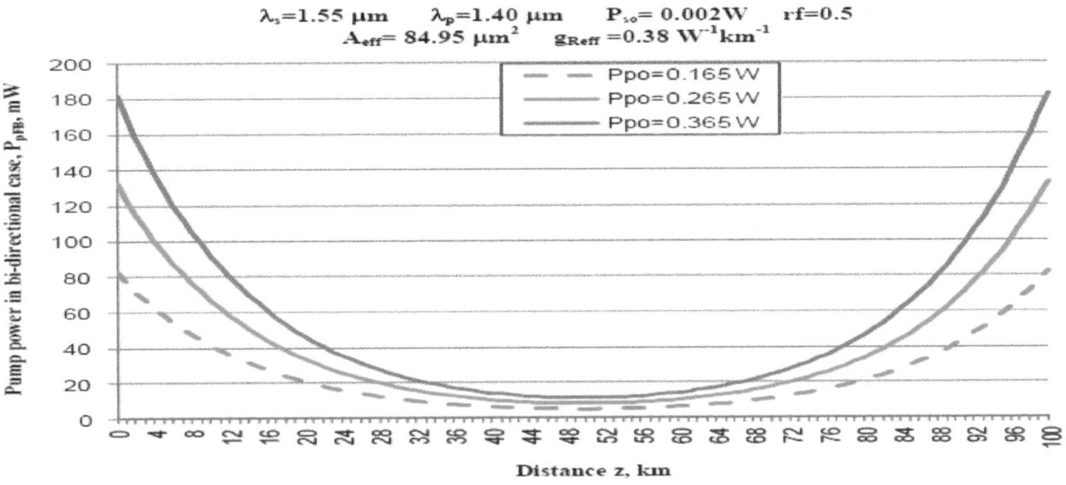

Figure 4. Variations of pump power in bi-directional case against variations of distance z at the assumed set of the operating parameters.

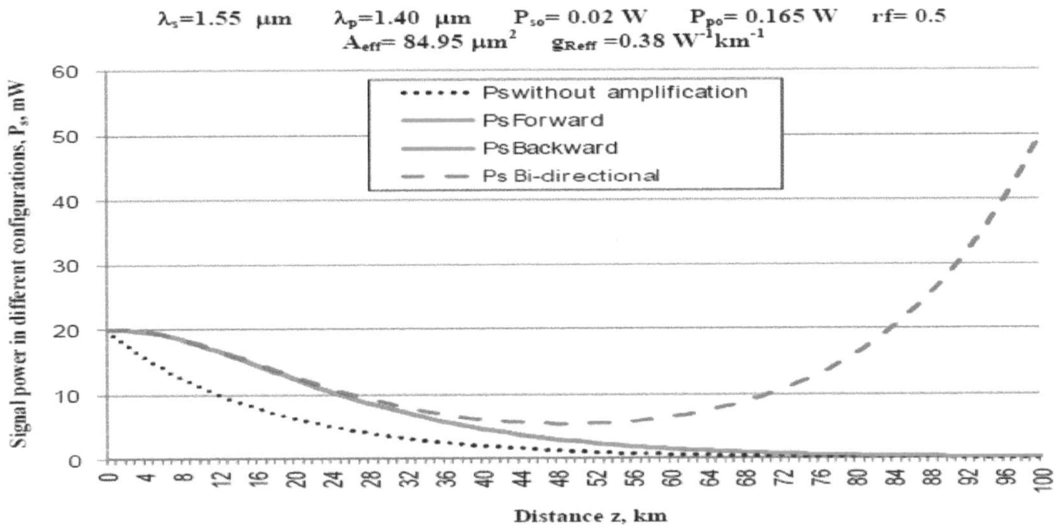

Figure 5. Variations of signal power in different configurations against variations of distance z at the assumed set of the operating parameters.

initial pumping power, the output pumping power also will increase.

C) In case of bidirectional:

1) For z ≤ 50 km, the output pumping power decreases exponentially, and for z ≥ 50 km, P_{pFB} increases exponentially.

2) For certain value of distance z, with increasing the initial pumping power, the output pumping power also will increase.

Variations of the output signal power, P_s

Variation of the output signal power, P_s is investigated against variations of the controlling set of parameters as shown in Figures 5 to 11. Figures 5 to 11 clarify the results as follows:

A) Without any amplification: with increasing distance, z, the output signal power decreases exponentially.

B) In case of forward direction:

1) For certain value of initial pumping power:

i) Initial pumping power = 0.165 mW, for distance z ≤ 2 km, the output signal power increases exponentially, and for z ≥ 2 km, the output signal power decreases exponentially.

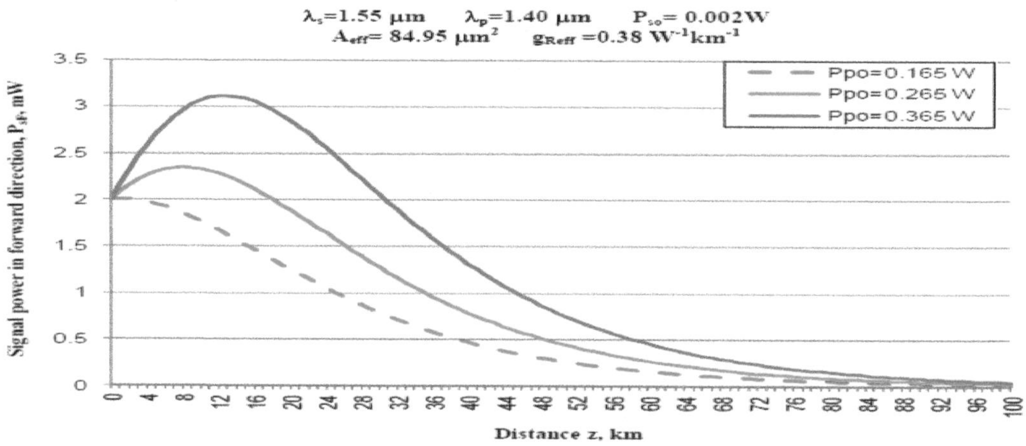

Figure 6. Variations of signal power in forward direction against variations of distance z at the assumed set of the operating parameters.

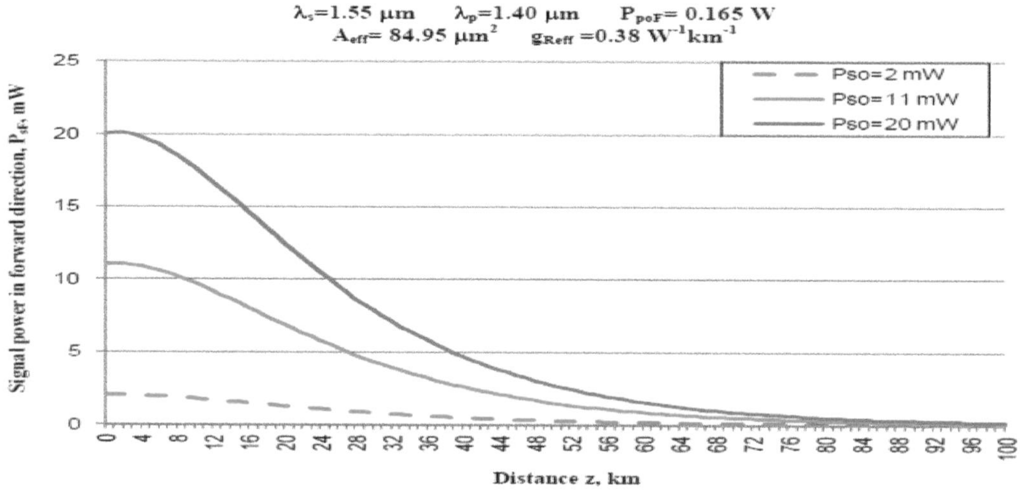

Figure 7. Variations of signal power in forward direction against variations of distance z at the assumed set of the operating parameters.

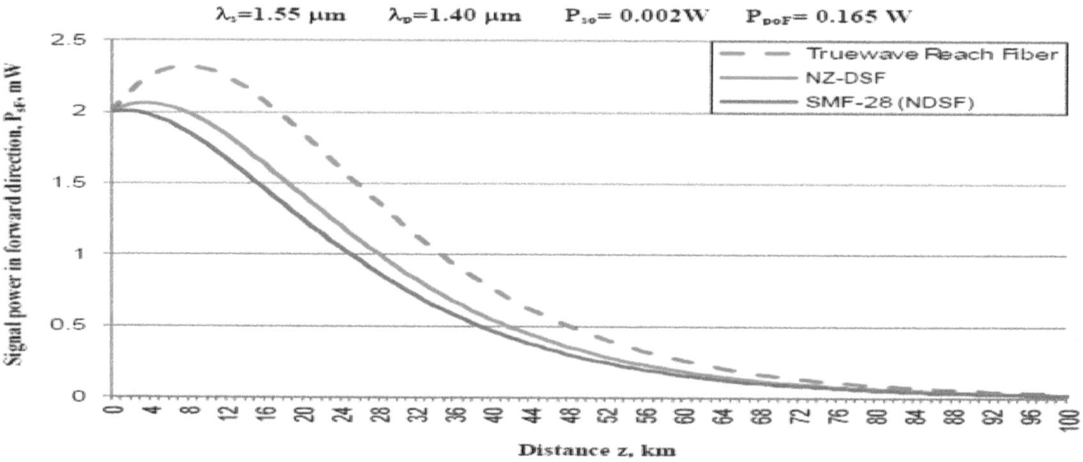

Figure 8. Variations of signal power in forward direction against variations of distance z at the assumed set of the operating parameters.

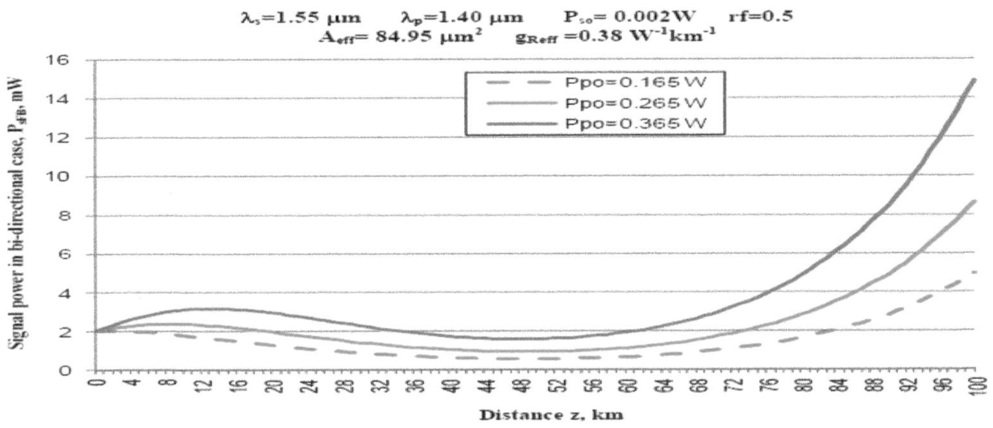

Figure 9. Variations of signal power in bi-directional case against variations of distance z at the assumed set of the operating parameters.

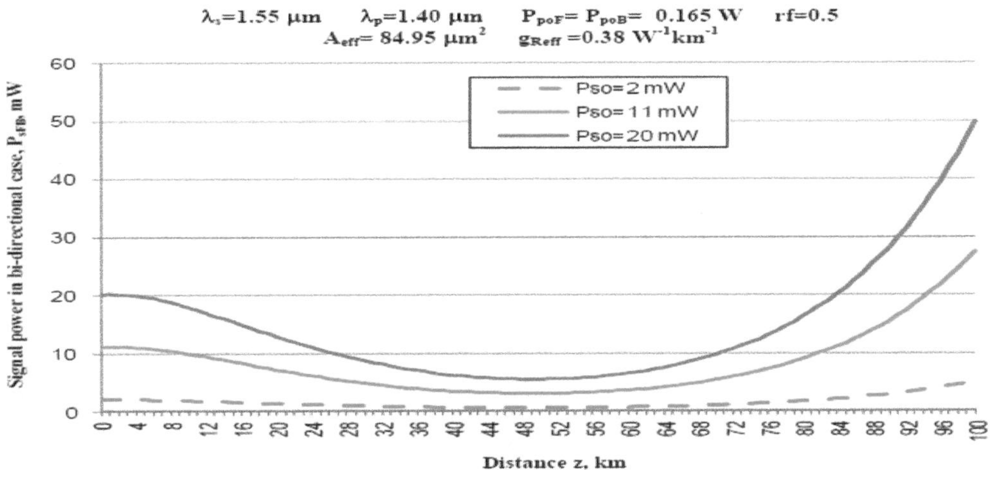

Figure 10. Variations of signal power in case of bi-directional case against variations of distance z at the assumed set of the operating parameters.

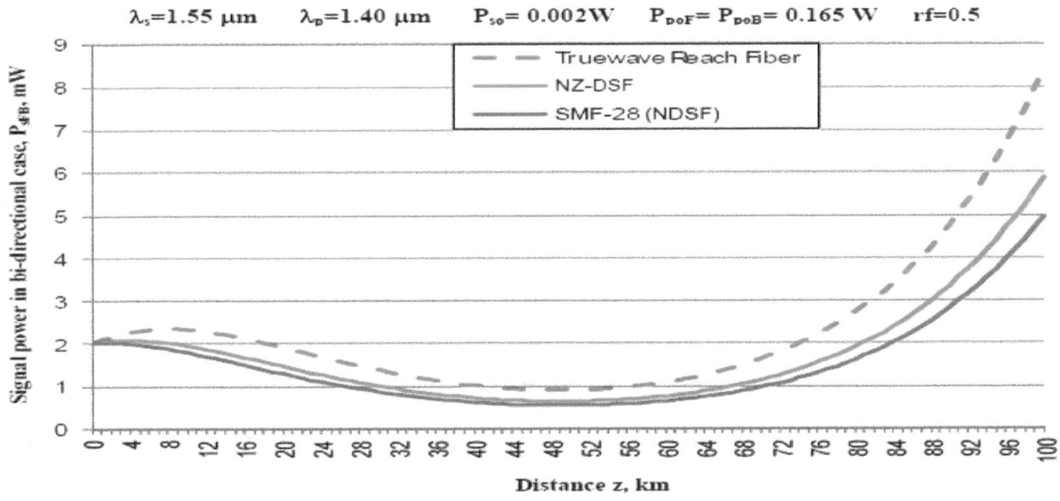

Figure 11. Variations of signal power in bi-directional case against variations of distance z at the assumed set of the operating parameters.

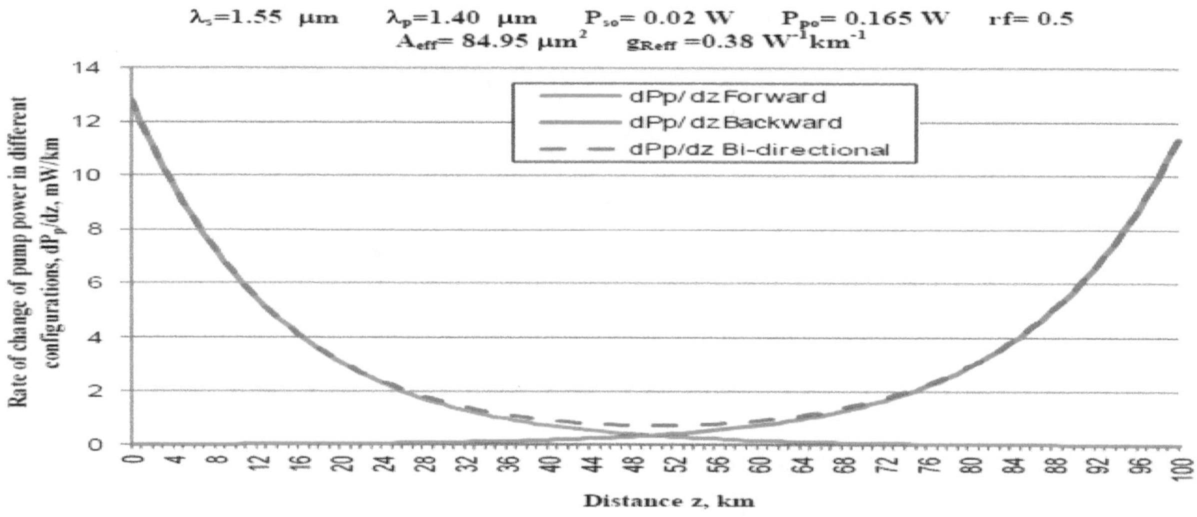

Figure 12. Variations of rate of change of pump power in different configurations against variations of distance z at the assumed set of the operating parameters.

ii) Initial pumping power = 0.265 mW, for distance z ≤ 8 km, the output signal power increases exponentially, and for z ≥ 8 km, the output signal power decreases exponentially.
iii) Initial pumping power = 0.365 mW, for distance z ≤ 13 km, the output signal power increases exponentially, and for z ≥ 13 km, the output signal power decreases exponentially.
2) For certain value of distance z:

i) With increasing the initial pumping power, the output signal power also will increase.
ii) With increasing the initial signal power, the output signal power also will increase.
3) After using different media of optical fiber cable, it is indicated that the true wave reach fiber presented the best results.
C) In case of backward direction:

The results are the same as in case of forward direction.
D) In case of bidirectional:

1) For certain value of initial pumping power:

i) Initial pumping power = 0.165 W, for distance z ≤ 1 km, the output signal power increases exponentially, for 1 ≤ z, km ≤ 50 the output signal power decreases exponentially, and for z ≥ 50 km, the output signal power increases exponentially again.
ii) Initial pumping power = 0.265 W, for distance z ≤ 8 km, the output signal power increases exponentially, for 8 ≤ z, km ≤ 49 the output signal power decreases exponentially, and for z ≥ 49 km, the output signal power increases exponentially again.
iii) Initial pumping power = 0.365 W, for distance z ≤ 13 km, the output signal power increases exponentially, for 13 ≤ z, km ≤ 48 the output signal power decreases exponentially, and for z ≥ 48 km, the output signal power increases exponentially again.
2) For certain value of distance z:

i) With increasing the initial signal power, the output signal power also will increase.
ii) With increasing the initial pumping power, the output signal power also will increase.
3) After using different media of optical fiber cable, it is indicated that the true wave reach fiber presented the best results.

Variations of rate of change of pump power, dP_p/dz

Variation of the rate of change of pump power in different configurations; dP_p/dz is investigated against variations of the controlling set of parameters as shown in Figures 12 to 17. Figures 12 to 17 clarify the results as follows:

A) In case of forward direction:

1) As distance z increases, dP_{pF}/dz decreases exponentially.
2) For certain value of distance z, with increasing the initial pumping power, dP_{pF}/dz also will increase.
3) For certain value of distance z, with increasing the initial signal power, dP_{pF}/dz also will increase
B) In case of backward direction:

1) As distance z increases, dP_{pB}/dz increases exponentially.
2) For certain value of distance z, with increasing the initial pumping power, dP_{pB}/dz also will increase.
C) In case of bidirectional:

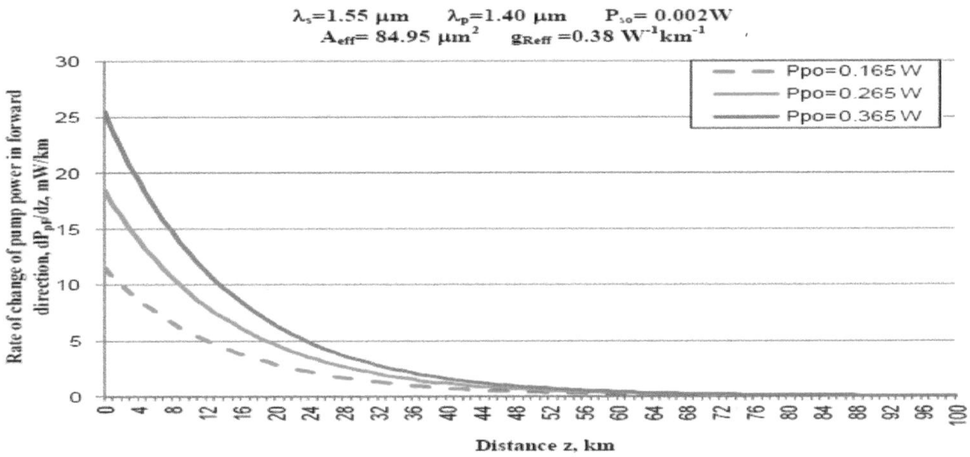

Figure 13. Variations of rate of change of pump power in forward direction against variations of distance z at the assumed set of the operating parameters.

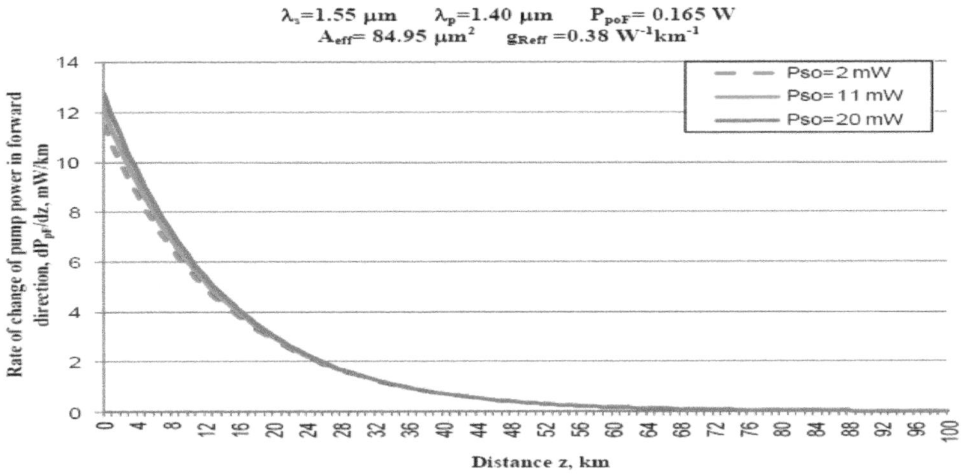

Figure 14. Variations of rate of change of pump power in forward direction against variations of distance z at the assumed set of the operating parameters.

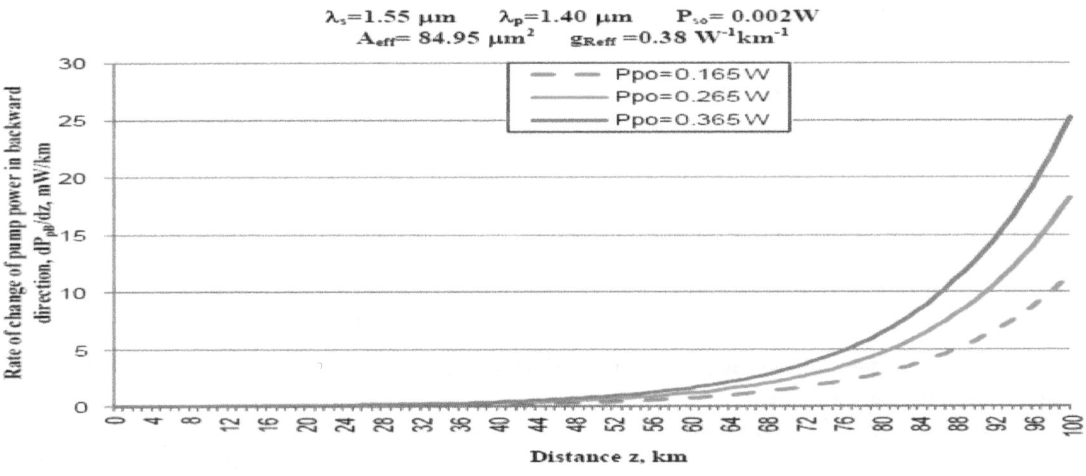

Figure 15. Variations of rate of change of pump power in backward direction against variations of distance z at the assumed set of the operating parameters.

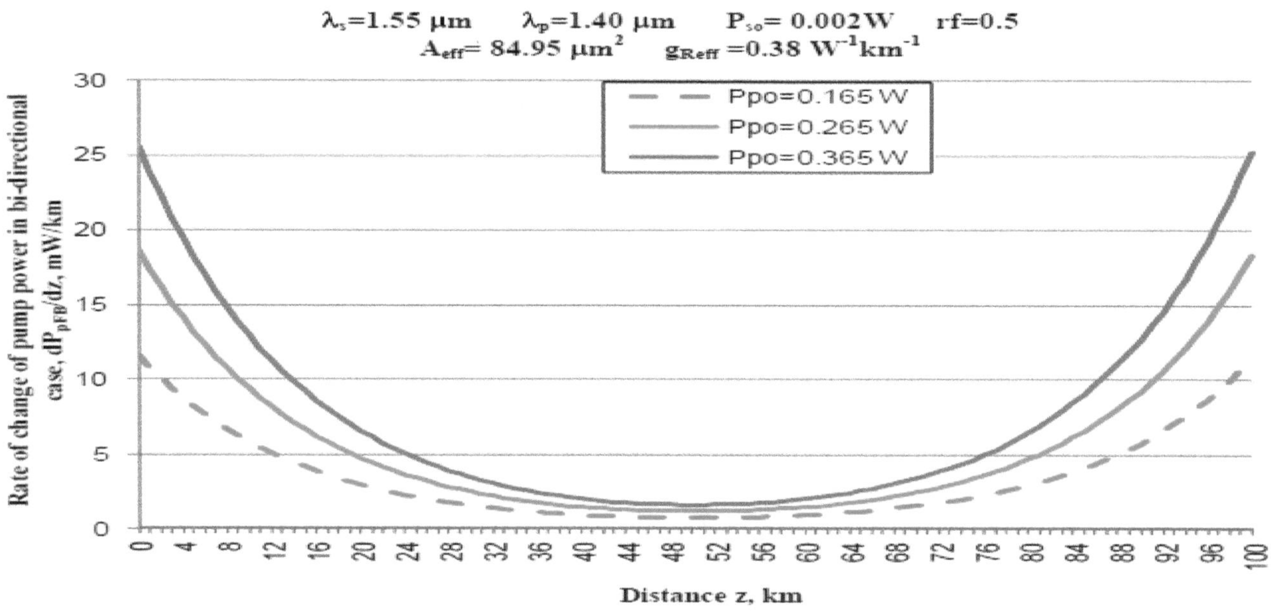

Figure 16. Variations of rate of change of pump power in bi-directional case against variations of distance z at the assumed set of the operating parameters.

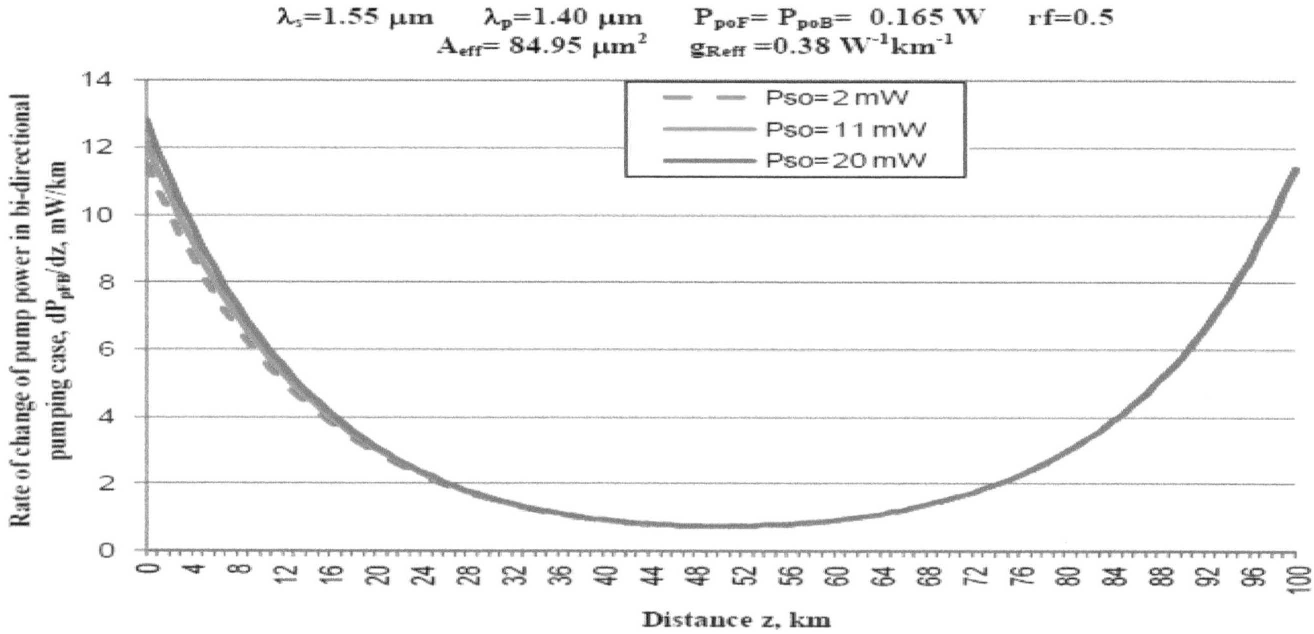

Figure 17. Variations of rate of change of pump power in bi-directional pumping case against variations of distance z at the assumed set of the operating parameters

1) For $z \leq 50$ km, dP_{pFB}/dz decreases exponentially, and for $z \geq 50$ km, dP_{pFB}/dz increases exponentially.
2) For certain value of distance z, with increasing the initial pumping power, dP_{pFB}/dz also will increase.
3) For certain value of distance z, with increasing the initial signal power, dP_{pFB}/dz also will increase.

Variations of rate of change of signal power, dP_s/dz

Variation of the rate of change of signal power in different configurations; dP_s/dz is investigated against variations of the controlling set of parameters as shown in Figures 18 to 31. Figures 18 to 31 clarify the results as follows:

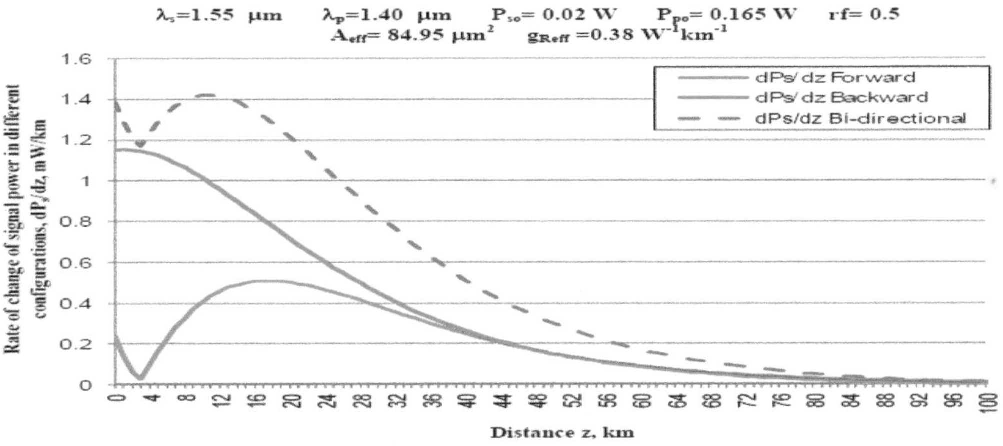

Figure 18. Variations of rate of change of signal power in different configurations against variations of distance z at the assumed set of the operating parameters.

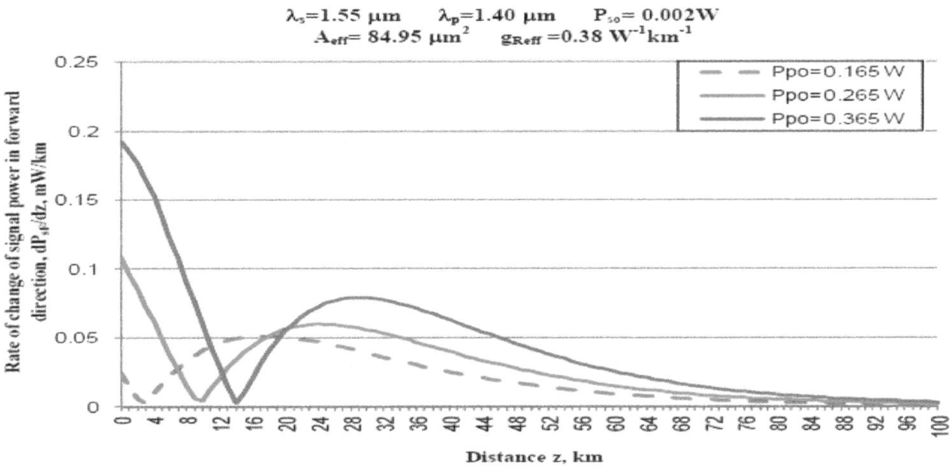

Figure 19. Variations of rate of change of signal power in forward direction against variations of distance z at the assumed set of the operating parameters.

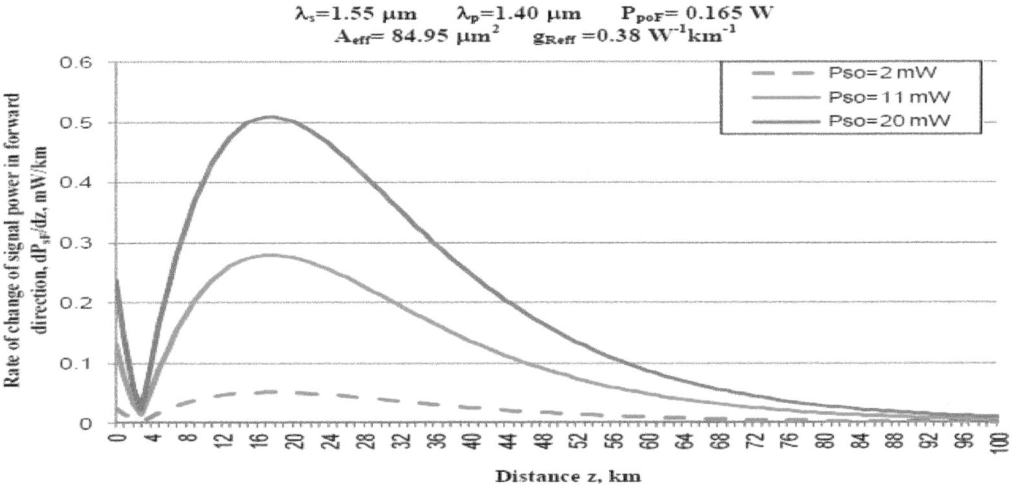

Figure 20. Variations of rate of change of signal power in forward direction against variations of distance z at the assumed set of the operating parameters.

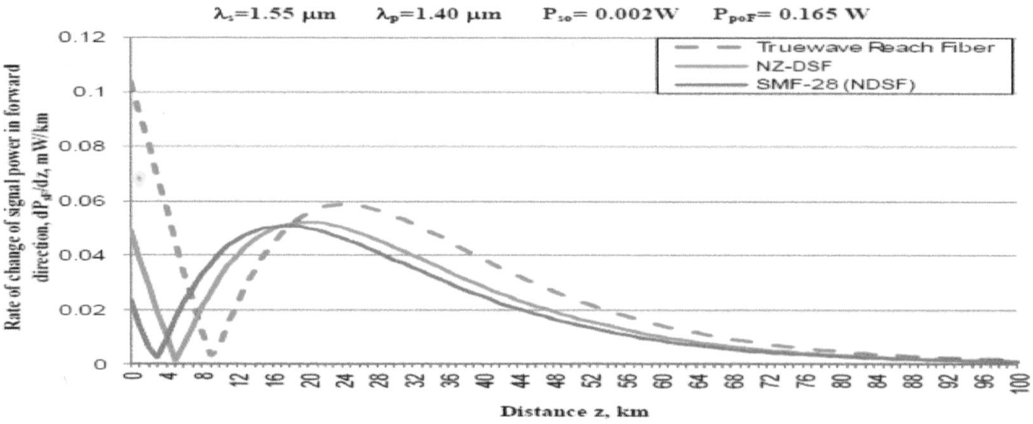

Figure 21. Variations of rate of change of signal power in forward direction against variations of distance z at the assumed set of the operating parameters.

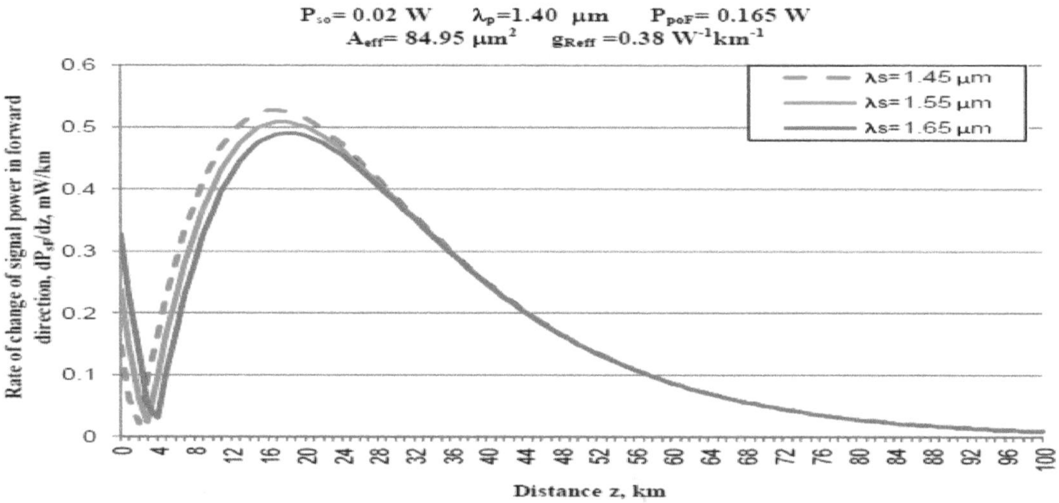

Figure 22. Variations of rate of change of signal power in forward direction against variations of distance z at the assumed set of the operating parameters.

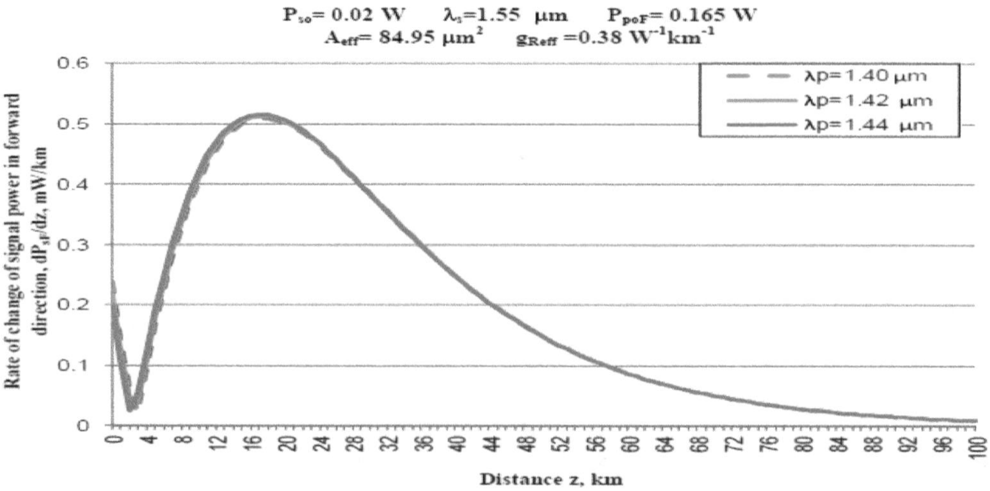

Figure 23. Variations of rate of change of signal power in forward direction against variations of distance z at the assumed set of the operating parameters

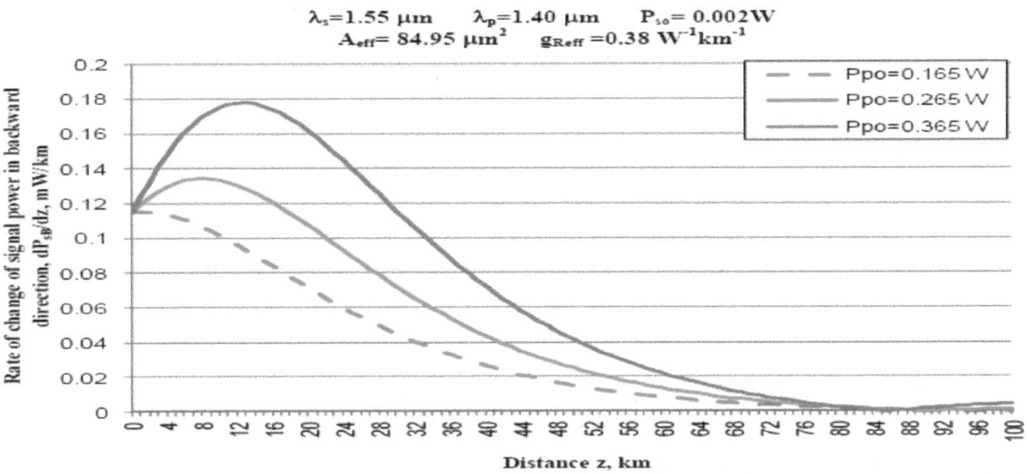

Figure 24. Variations of rate of change of signal power in backward direction against variations of distance z at the assumed set of the operating parameters.

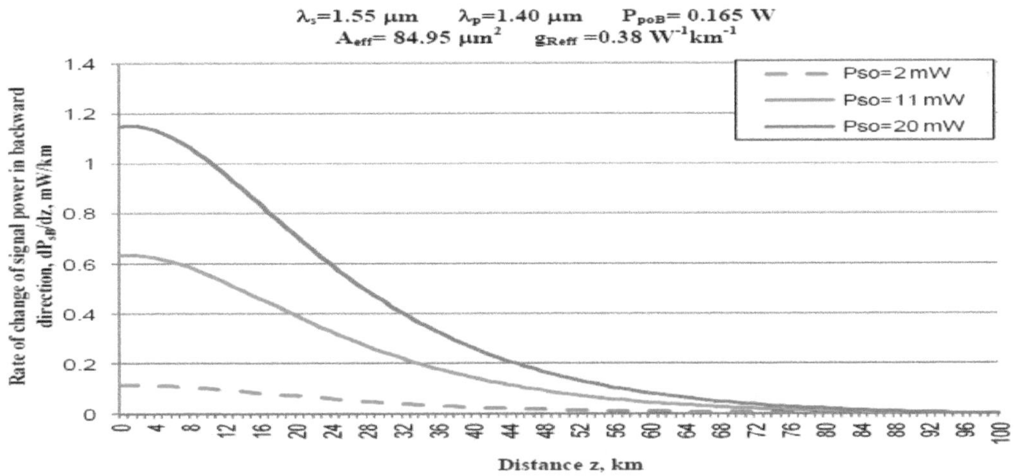

Figure 25. Variations of rate of change of signal power in backward direction against variations of distance z at the assumed set of the operating parameters.

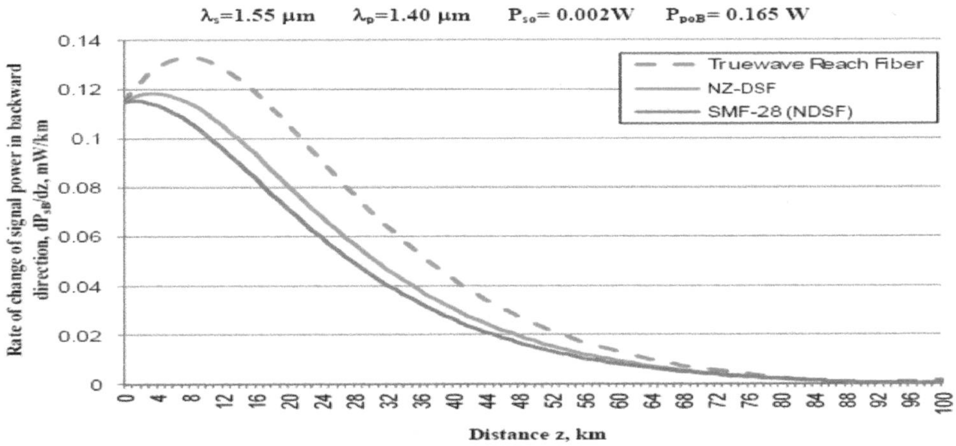

Figure 26. Variations of rate of change of signal power in backward direction against variations of distance z at the assumed set of the operating parameters.

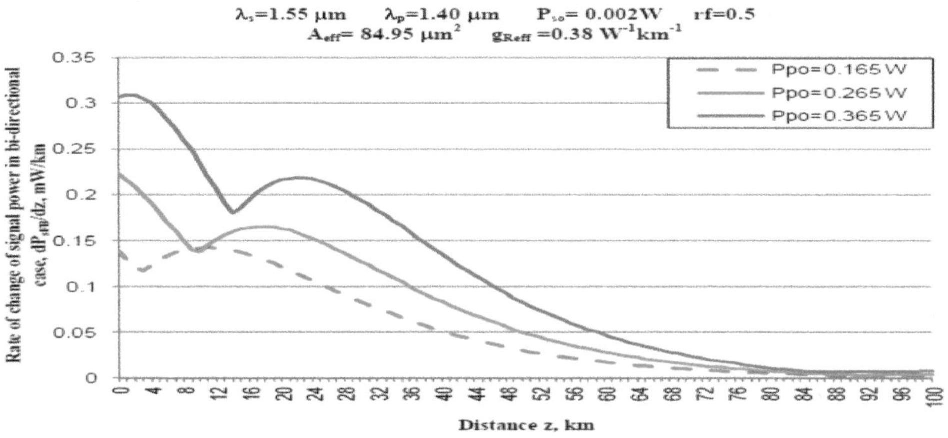

Figure 27. Variations of rate of change of signal power in bi-directional case against variations of distance z at the assumed set of the operating parameters.

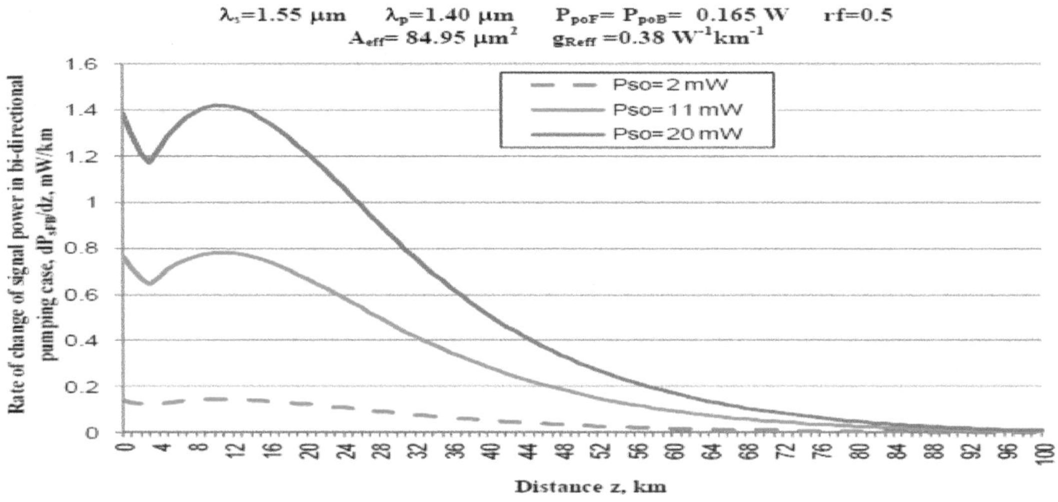

Figure 28. Variations of rate of change of signal power in bi-directional pumping case against variations of distance z at the assumed set of the operating parameters.

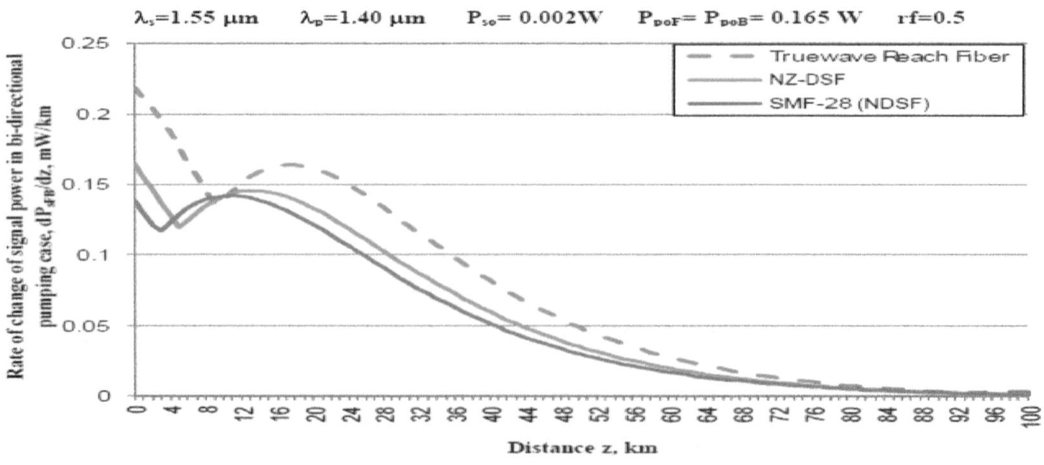

Figure 29. Variations of rate of change of signal power in bi-directional pumping case against variations of distance z at the assumed set of the operating parameters.

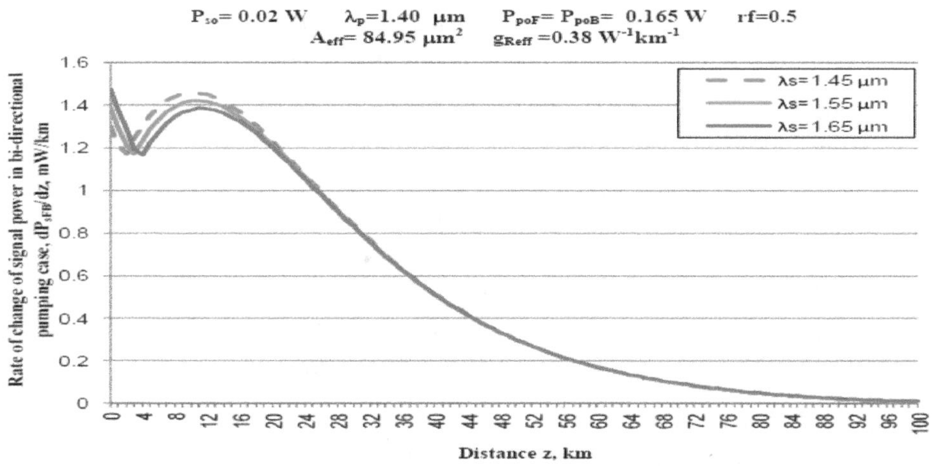

Figure 30. Variations of rate of change of signal power in bi-directional pumping case against variations of distance z at the assumed set of the operating parameters.

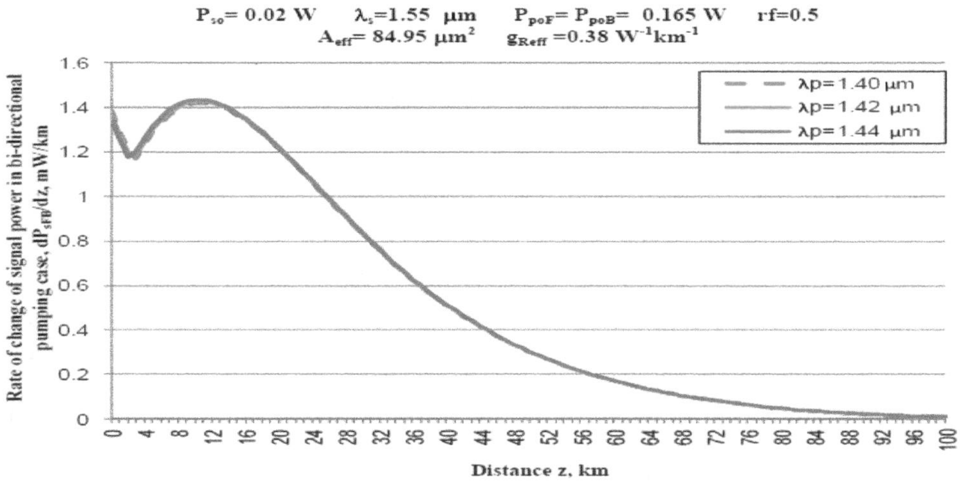

Figure 31. Variations of rate of change of signal power in bi-directional pumping case against variations of distance z at the assumed set of the operating parameters.

A) In case of forward direction:
1) For certain value of initial pumping power:

i) Initial pumping power = 0.165 W, for 0 ≤ z, km ≤ 3, dP_{sF}/dz decreases linearly, for 3 ≤ z, km ≤ 18, dP_{sF}/dz increases exponentially, and for z ≥ 18 km, dP_{sF}/dz decreases exponentially.
ii) Initial pumping power = 0.265 W, for 0 ≤ z, km ≤ 10, dP_{sF}/dz decreases linearly, for 10 ≤ z, km ≤ 24, dP_{sF}/dz increases exponentially, for z ≥ 24 km, dP_{sF}/dz decreases exponentially.
iii) Initial pumping power = 0.365 W, for 0 ≤ z, km ≤ 14, dP_{sF}/dz decreases linearly, for 14 ≤ z, km ≤ 29, dP_{sF}/dz increases exponentially, for z ≥ 29 km, dP_{sF}/dz decreases exponentially.

2) For any value of initial signal power: for 0 ≤ z, km ≤ 3, dP_{sF}/dz decreases linearly, for 3 ≤ z, km ≤ 18, dP_{sF}/dz increases exponentially, and for z ≥ 18 km, dP_{sF}/dz decreases exponentially.
3) For certain value of distance, z:

i) With increasing the initial signal power, dP_{pF}/dz also will increase.
ii) With increasing the initial pumping power, dP_{pF}/dz also will increase.
4) For certain value operating signal wavelength, λ_s:

i) λ_s = 1.45 μm, for 0 ≤ z, km ≤ 2, dPs_F/dz decreases linearly, for 2 ≤ z, km ≤ 17, dPsF/dz increases exponentially, and for z ≥ 17 km, dPs_F/dz decreases exponentially.
ii) λ_s = 1.55 μm, for 0 ≤ z, km ≤ 3, dPs_F/dz decreases linearly, for 3 ≤ z, km ≤ 18, dPsF/dz increases

exponentially, and for z ≥ 18 km, dPs_F/dz decreases exponentially.
iii) λ_s = 1.65 µm for 0 ≤ z, km ≤ 4, dPs_F/dz decreases linearly, for 4 ≤ z, km ≤ 19, dPsF/dz increases exponentially, and for z ≥ 19 km, dPs_F/dz decreases exponentially.
5) At the beginning with increasing the operating signal wavelength, λ_s dP_{sF}/dz also will increase, after that dP_{sF}/dz decreases with increasing the operating signal wavelength, λ_s.
6) For certain value operating pump wavelength, λ_p:

i) λ_p = 1.40 µm, for 0 ≤ z, km ≤ 3, dPs_F/dz decreases linearly, for 3 ≤ z, km ≤ 18, dPsF/dz increases exponentially, and for z ≥ 18 km, dPs_F/dz decreases exponentially.
ii) λ_p = 1.42 µm, for 0 ≤ z, km ≤ 2, dPs_F/dz decreases linearly, for 2 ≤ z, km ≤ 17, dPsF/dz increases exponentially, and for z ≥ 17 km, dPs_F/dz decreases exponentially.
iii) λ_p = 1.44 µm for 0 ≤ z, km ≤ 1, dPs_F/dz decreases linearly, for 1 ≤ z, km ≤ 16, dPsF/dz increases exponentially, and for z ≥ 16 km, dPs_F/dz decreases exponentially.
7) After using different media of optical fiber cable, it is indicated that the true wave reach fiber presented the best results.
B) In case of backward direction:

1) For certain value of initial pumping power:

i) Initial pumping power = 0.165 mW, for distance z ≤ 2 km, dP_{sB}/dz increases exponentially, and for z ≥ 2 km, dP_{sB}/dz decreases exponentially.
ii) Initial pumping power = 0.265 mW, for distance z ≤ 8 km, dP_{sB}/dz increases exponentially, and for z ≥ 8 km, dP_{sB}/dz decreases exponentially.
iii) Initial pumping power = 0.365 mW, for distance z ≤ 13 km, dP_{sB}/dz increases exponentially, and for z ≥ 13 km, dP_{sB}/dz decreases exponentially.
2) For certain value of distance z:

i) With increasing the initial pumping power, dP_{sB}/dz also will increase.
Ii) With increasing the initial signal power, dP_{sB}/dz also will increase.
3) After using different media of optical fiber cable, it is indicated that the true wave reach fiber presented the best results.
C) In case of bi-directional:

1) For certain value of initial pumping power:

i) Initial pumping power = 0.165 W, for 0 ≤ z, km ≤ 3, dP_{sFB}/dz decreases linearly, for 3 ≤ z, km ≤ 11, dP_{sFB}/dz increases exponentially, and for z ≥ 11 km, dP_{sFB}/dz decreases exponentially.
ii) Initial pumping power = 0.265 W, for 0 ≤ z, km ≤ 10, dP_{sFB}/dz decreases linearly, for 10 ≤ z, km ≤ 18, dP_{sFB}/dz increases exponentially, for z ≥ 18 km, dP_{sFB}/dz decreases exponentially.
iii) Initial pumping power = 0.365 W, for 0 ≤ z, km ≤ 14, dP_{sFB}/dz decreases linearly, for 14 ≤ z, km ≤ 22, dP_{sFB}/dz increases exponentially, for z ≥ 22 km, dP_{sFB}/dzs decreases exponentially.
2) For any value of initial signal power: for 0 ≤ z, km ≤ 3, dP_{sFB}/dz decreases linearly, for 3 ≤ z, km ≤ 11, dP_{sFB}/dz increases exponentially, and for z ≥ 11 km, dP_{sFB}/dz decreases exponentially.
3) For certain value of distance, z:

i) With increasing the initial signal power, dP_{sFB}/dz also will increase.
ii) With increasing the initial pumping power, dP_{sFB}/dz also will increase.
4) For certain value operating signal wavelength, λ_s:

i) λ_s = 1.45 µm, for 0 ≤ z, km ≤ 2, dP_{sFB}/dz decreases linearly, for 2 ≤ z, km ≤ 10, dP_{sFB}/dz increases exponentially, and for z ≥ 10 km, dP_{sFB}/dz decreases exponentially.
ii) λ_s = 1.55 µm, for 0 ≤ z, km ≤ 3, dP_{sFB}/dz decreases linearly, for 3 ≤ z, km ≤ 11, dP_{sFB}/dz increases exponentially, and for z ≥ 11 km, dP_{sFB}/dz decreases exponentially.
iii) λ_s = 1.65 µm for 0 ≤ z, km ≤ 4, dP_{sFB}/dz decreases linearly, for 4 ≤ z, km ≤ 12, dP_{sFB}/dz increases exponentially, and for z ≥ 12 km, dP_{sFB}/dz decreases exponentially.
5) At the beginning with increasing the operating signal wavelength, λ_s dPs_{FB}/dz also will increase, after that dPs_{FB}/dz decreases with increasing the operating signal wavelength, λ_s.
6) For certain value operating pump wavelength, λ_p:

i) λ_p = 1.40 µm, for 0 ≤ z, km ≤ 3, dP_{sFB}/dz decreases linearly, for 3 ≤ z, km ≤ 11, dP_{sFB}/dz increases exponentially, and for z ≥ 11 km, dP_{sFB}/dz decreases exponentially.
ii) λ_p = 1.42 µm, for 0 ≤ z, km ≤ 2, dP_{sFB}/dz decreases linearly, for 2 ≤ z, km ≤ 11, dP_{sFB}/dz increases exponentially, and for z ≥ 11 km, dP_{sFB}/dz decreases exponentially.
iii) λ_p = 1.44 µm for 0 ≤ z, km ≤ 1, dP_{sFB}/dz decreases linearly, for 1 ≤ z, km ≤ 11, dP_{sFB}/dz increases exponentially, and for z ≥ 11 km, dP_{sFB}/dz decreases exponentially. After using different media of optical fiber cable, it is indicated that the true wave reach fiber presented the best results.

Conclusions

The points of discussion indicated all the operating

design parameters of multiplexing/demultiplexing based distributed optical FRA device, such as input signal power, input pumping power, operating signal wavelength, operating pump wavelength and different fiber link media. Therefore, we have deeply investigated multiplexing/demultiplexing based distributed optical FRA over wide range of the affecting parameters. As well as we have taken into account signal power, pumping power, and the rate of change of both signal power and pumping power along the transmission distance within the variety of operating signal wavelength, operation pumping wavelength, input signal power, input pumping power, different fiber link media, and finally Raman gain efficiency for all pumping direction configurations such as forward, backward and bidirectional pumping. The effects of the verity of these parameters were previously mentioned in details. After using different media of optical fiber cable, it is indicated that the true wave reach fiber presented the best candidate media for the highest signal transmission performance efficiency.

REFERENCES

Abd El Naser AM, Mohamed M, Ahmed NZR, Mahmoud MAE (2009). Distributed Optical Raman Amplifiers in Ultra High Speed Long Haul Transmission Optical Fiber Telecommunication Networks, Int. J. Compt. and Network Security (IJCNS), 1(1): 1-8.

Abd El-Naser AM, Abd El-Fattah AS, Ahmed NZR, Mahomud ME (2009). Characteristics of Multi-Pumped Raman Amplifiers in Dense Wavelength Division Multiplexing (DWDM) Optical Access Networks, IJCSNS Int. J. Compt Sci. and Network Security., 9(2): 277-284.

Abd El-Naser AM, Ahmed NZR (2009). Ultra Wide Band (UWB) of Optical Fiber Raman Amplifiers in Advanced Optical Communication Networks, J. Media and Communication Studies (IJMCS), 1(4): 56-78.

Abd El-Naser AM, Ahmed NZR (2010). Comparison Performance Evolution of Different Transmission Techniques With Bi-directional Distributed Raman Gain Amplification Technique in High Capacity Optical Networks, Int.J. Phy. Sci., 5(5): 484-495.

Abd El-Naser AM, Gaber ESME, Abd El-Fattah AS, Ahmed NZR (2009). Applications of Conventional and A thermal Arrayed Waveguide Grating (AWG) Module in Active and Passive Optical Networks (PONs), Int. J. Compt. Theory Engin., 1(3): 290-298.

Banerjee A (2009). New Approach to Design Digitally Tunable Optical Fiber System for Wavelength Selective Switching Based Optical Networks, Progress In Electromagnetics Research Letters, 9(2): 93-100.

de Matos CJS, Hansen KP, Taylor JR (2003). Experimental Characterization of Raman Gain Efficiency of Holey Fiber, Electronics Lett., 39(5): 424.

El Mashade MBM, Abdel Aleem MN (2009). Analysis of Ultra Short Pulse Propagation in Nonlinear Optical Fiber, Progress In Electromagnetics Research B, 12(3): 219-241.

ITU-T Recommendation G.652 (2009). Characteristics of Single Mode Optical Fiber and Cable, ITU-T Study Group, pp. 1-14.

Maan MS, Mahmood SM, Raid WD (2009). Functioning the Intelligent Programming to find Minimum Dispersion Wavelengths," Wseas Transactions on Communications, 8(2): 237-248.

Makoui SMS, Rostami A, Koozehkanani ZD (2009). Dispersion Flattened Optical Fiber Design for Large Bandwidth and High Speed Optical Communications Using Optimization Technique, Progress In Electromagnetics Research B, 13(3): 21-40.

Ming-Jun L, Daniel AN (2008). Optical Transmission Fiber Design Evolution, J. Lightwave Technol., 26(9): 1079-1092.

Raghavendra MV, Vara PPLH (2010). Estimation of Optical Link Length for Multi Haul Applications, Int. J. Engin. Sci. Technol., 2(6): 1485-1491.

Raghuawansh SVG, Denesh V, Talabattula S (2006). Bi-directional Optical Fiber Transmission Scheme Through Raman Amplification: Effect of Pump Depletion, J. Indian Instit. Sci., 5(2): 655-665.

Shahi S, Harun SW, Dimyati K, Ahmad H (2009). Brillouin Fiber Laser With Significantly Reduced Gain Medium Length Operating in L Band Region, Progress In Electromagnetics Research Letters, 8(3): 143-149.

Son ES, Lee JH, Chung YC (2005). Statistics of Polarization-Dependent Gain in Fiber Raman Amplifiers, J. Lightwave Technol., 23(3): 1219-1226.

Real-time operating system (RTOS) with application to play models

Hiba Shahid[1] , Wadee Alhalabi[2] and John Reif[3]

[1]Department of Electrical and Computer Engineering, Effat University, Jeddah, Saudi Arabia.
[2]Faculty of Computing and Information Technology (FCIT), King Abdulaziz University (KAU), Jeddah, Kingdom of Saudi Arabia.
[3]Department of Computer Science, Duke University, Durham, NC 27707 USA and Adjunct Faculty of Computing and Information Technology (FCIT), King Abdulaziz University (KAU), Jeddah, Kingdom of Saudi Arabia.

It is very important to improve the design of the real-time operating system (RTOS) especially if we want to use it in some special devices. Numerous researches have accepted conventional RTOS as being the customary approach for designing devices used by children. This is because these are able to facilitate the implementation different criteria such as clustering, stability and alternate programs. In this paper, numerous publications have been analyzed to observe the performance of the RTOS when it is subjected to varied constraints. The study focuses on a review of RTOS in relation to play models to analyze their capabilities on various computing platforms and OSs. The publications which we have collected have been sorted out to comprehensively review thereby leading to the configuration of several factors affecting the features within the system. Likewise, statistics and results have facilitated adoption of a more focused approach towards the development of RTOS. While this program ranks clustering and performance as being the highest RTOS criteria for all applications, alternate programs considered this to be the least important. Thus, criteria choice becomes an important issue to address.

Key words: Operating system (OS), play model, real-time, real-time operating system (RTOS) performance, RTOS criteria.

INTRODUCTION

In 1984, a book was published on a reviewing operating system (OS) design, and dealing with OS interface, processes and services along with various important topics (Watson, 1983). An overview on the anomalies frequently experienced by OSs along with proposal for self- management strategies at OS level was presented by Momeni et al. (2008). A survey was conducted on by Romman (2009) to establish a reliable OS for multimedia files and applications and compare it with three of its existing counterparts. Nevertheless, a systematic review on real-time operating system (RTOS) with play model for children as being one of its applications has never been published at least to our knowledge. Owing to this, it has become essential to observe previous and ongoing research results on optimal OS for play models.

The aim of this paper is to investigate the tradeoffs that occur between certain factors that impact the functionality of the OSs. Since the intention underlying this review is to delicately delve into the possibility of finding a suitable OS for children, it would surely pave the way for development of more reliable and sophisticated RTOS.

LITERATURE REVIEW

An OS is the necessary part of every technical arena because it enables the user to access documents and files and also governs the functioning of all other programs within the system. Examples of some well-known OSs are Mac OS, Unix, Microsoft Windows and Linux all of which have been tested and certified on the basis of various factors throughout their areas of functionality. Therefore, maintaining an acute vigilance is a necessity, while deciding on an apposite resource for technical utility and this in turn is based on several factors compiled bearing in mind the existing market conditions. Once the answer to selecting the best criteria has been identified, it would be easier to judge whether the OSs found in children's toys provide inevitable support within as claimed. Numerous techniques for the selection of an OS have been devised and subsequently categorized in general under the areas of hardware, software, interface, security and virtualization.

A RTOS is an OS that serves real-time application requests, with the ability to process data as it is input, without significant buffering delays. Examples of RTOS are OS for scientific instruments, for machinery control, and industrial control systems.

The jitter of a RTOS is the variability in the time required by the OS to accept and process an application request. A RTOS with low jitter is termed a hard RTOS, and a RTOS with high jitter is termed a soft RTOS.

In addition to time to process data and jitter, there are a number of key potential properties of OS which include:

1) **Reliability and Stability**: The likelihood that the OS is not in failure or crash mode.
2) **Scalability:** This is the ability of the OS to improve in performance as further resources are added.
3) **Availability**: This is the likelihood that OS is actively processing requests, and not either in crash-mode or being updated.
4) **Usability**: This is the degree the OS has been demonstrated in the market.
5) **Security**: This is the degree that the OS is not susceptible to external attack.
6) **Portability and clustering**: This is the ability of the OS to migrate and/or distribute is operations among cluster of computers.
7) **User-Interface:** The ability of the OS to interact with the user.
8) **Certification**: Whether the OS has been demonstrated to provide certain properties.

A RTOS generally has high reliability, availability, but often has limited user-interface. Other OS have different combinations of properties.

Studies undertaken by Swift et al. (2004) described the importance of reliability of any system and hence seek to enhance this factor by isolating the system from driver failures. Reliability factor has been taken into account courtesy of numerous incidences of driver-caused crashes within the system where there has been little or no change in existing driver or system code. It is due to this that system reliability has been described as an important but impenetrable area under discussion (Patterson et al., 2002; Segal and Frieder, 1989). Another fact that has also been noted is that whilst the outlay of high-end computing continues to decline, the failure outlay has been rising ever since. These failures include the unnecessary lay-offs on e-commerce server which result in delay of numerous activities that are performed by the work force for help desk overhaul within the working environment. Furthermore, the emerging segment of daily-use technical appliances based on hardware and software augments the need for reliability since efforts are underway to make these appliances as diminutive, user friendly and automotive as possible (Lin and Chang, 2013).

According to Baier et al. (2012), a particularly crucial development has been the construction of scalable OSs so that the existing system is more robust and shows an improvement in performance when new hardware resources have been added. Basically, this calls for improving the resources of computer system in order to accommodate the rising functionality demand, while at the same time economizing the cost. Some of the factors on which these dimensions depend on are size of processor, memory, software and heterogeneity. Software scalability assumes importance as subject of inspection particularly when one node is shared between a system featuring multiple processor connections and a symmetric multiprocessor with single memory location from where availability plays a vital role in terms of system performance.

Availability is a crucial criterion when choosing an OS since it is an important determinant of all ongoing activities including the execution of instructions by the processor. In such a situation, it is important to have an OS that would allow application of software updates and patches without any downtime or loss of service (Baumann and Appavoo, 2005). Even rebooting or restarting could be deferred without losing the ability to apply security fixes or enhance functionality through software updates provided the system is available at all times. The resolve for availability has been strengthened even more due to the fact that computing infrastructures have been targets of unplanned down-time which has even caused the potential overlay of scheduled down-time to increase significantly. For instance, the processing system for Visa transaction goes through a routine update of approximately 20,000 times per year, however, it tolerates down-time of less than 0.5% (Gillen and Kusnetzky, 2002). Quite a few techniques to minimize down-times and increase availability have been devised such as dynamic update (Tushman and Newman, 2004) which could enable the running of software update application without interrupting service which in turn amplifies the usability of the system.

According to Zhu et al. (2001), usability or market proven factor is one of the most reliable criteria for selecting an OS. OSs which have been in market for more than 10 to 15 years have been employed in many safety-critical applications and tested (or used) by customers for a long time. Over the years, users have stumbled upon numerous inaccuracies within the framework which have been rectified by formulating updated versions. These avatars of OSs include pSOSystem, VxWorks and VRTX. According to a survey published by StaCounter covering the time period from January, 2009 to January, 2013 on the market share held by OSs in the United States, the usability of Windows 7 was 44.02% in March 2012 and dramatically increased to over 50% to gain the top spot in January, 2013. This is chiefly attributed to the efficient usage of Windows Vista alongside the effective marketing strategies of Windows 7 (Swift et al., 2007) and system security.

Yang (2001) addressed one of the fundamental subjects of concern namely security of OSs. This is the foremost cause of apprehension amongst end-users since OS is the core software which executes instructions from configured devices, servers, desktop and other parts. Thus, lack of security could result in unwanted attacks or break-in from one application to the next. According to "DOD Trusted Computer System Evaluation Criteria" (1985), of US government, most OSs available for purchase have C2 level of security which requires Discretionary Access Control (DAC) protection that is particularly supportive of and protects environment in which multiple applications are running simultaneously. Numerous endeavours have been made to develop OS model with utmost security. Studies conducted by Spencer et al. (1999) were made available along with HP-LX (Dalton and Choo, 2001) and Trusted Solaris and these might be an indication that the underlying security of OSs is responsible for the overall security of applications.

Other factors dwell upon portability and clustering. Clustering is basically used to distribute the load over a number of machines. If one machine fails, it could be sent for maintenance without interrupting the running of other services. This is basically determined by the number of machines connected together (Bekman and Cholet, 2003). As per Zhu et al. (2001), some of the criteria entail selecting OS based on certification and OSs which have been developed from scratch using a formally defined semantic specification and were subjected to a rigorous method of testing. Equally, difficult is the proposition of acquiring alternate programs and interface support as also of getting a device driver for a non-supported device while working with an OS (Smith, 2000).

METHODOLOGY

Categorizing OS

OSs can be categorized into distinct categories by the clustering OSs by the various properties we have listed above.

The problem of clustering OSs by the various properties can be reduced to the problem of clustering a set of data, consisting of n distinct d dimensional vectors, into m clusters, so that the Euclidian distance of each element of each cluster from the median of each cluster is minimized. There are a number of algorithms for efficiently determining a near-optimal clustering of multidimensional vectors (Shore and Gray, 1982), for example vector quantization (Gray, 1984; Gersho and Gray, 1992). In our case, the number n of OSs is very large, but the intended number of OS clusters is just 6, so our work was manageable.

OSs is partitioned into six categories in order to estimate the number of devices under each OS so that some estimate of efficiency and usability of each O. This categorization was done particularly for play models. Linux OS comprised of publications related to disability that has been well-known since an early age (Huber et al., 2008), RC products for children cars experiment using the Internet (Aoto et al., 2005) and Bluetooth toy car control (Cai et al., 2011) were found as examples of devices using Linux as well. For variants of Windows, toy plane (Tanguay, 2000), musical computer games (Hämäläinen et al., 2004) and controllers for simulated car racing (Togelius and Lucas, 1906-1919) were found. Many robot toys were found for assisting and playing with severely disabled children featured an underlying core of Unix OS (Kronreif, 2005) and hence pertaining to specific disabilities, certain special purpose OSs were built which limited system's portability.

There were special purpose OSs built specifically for particular applications that included interactive C, the core of certain low cost vehicles for simple reactive behaviours (Capozzo, 1999), Robot C was the OS for a monoball robot based on LEGO Mindstorms which focused on educating children in elementary school (Prieto et al., 2012). Strifeshadow Fantasy OS was used for a multi-player online game (Chan and Chang, 2004). Designing of UAV helicopter also required special purpose OS (Cai et al., 2005) along with a personalized R-Learning system which operated on Robot Software Platform (Ko et al., 2010). Another multiplayer computer game named Amaze used V-System, Distributed OS (Berglund and Cheriton, 1985). Publications related to embedded systems were also reviewed which included LEGO Mindstorms NXT concepts aimed at developing technical skills in students (Sharad, 2007). CELL processor was used in scientific computing on PlayStation 3 (Buttari et al., 2007) and Intel Microcontroller was found at the core of ESoccer Robot Toy developed as an educational play model (Vial et al., 2007).

It was observed that Windows OS was used for several devices as compared to other OSs. This raised the question as to what

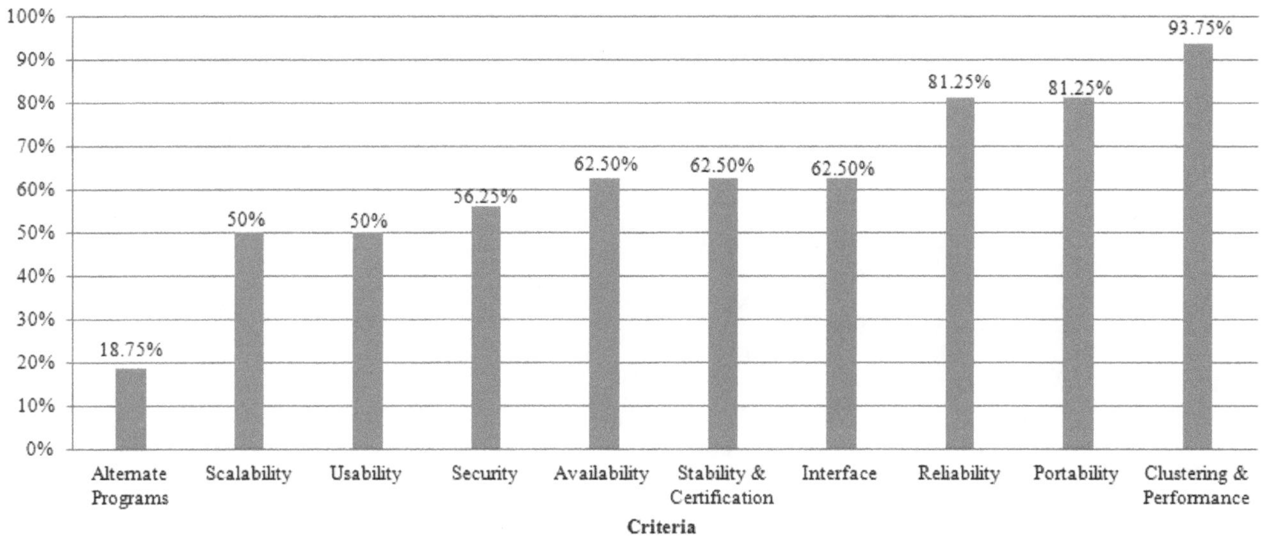

Figure 1. Criteria in RTOS used in play models publication.

could be the reason behind its popularity and hence journal articles known to discuss appropriate criteria for choosing an OS were reviewed in depth.

Some of the most commonly used parameters that were selected as forming the basis on which an OS should be chosen are reliability, scalability, availability, usability, security, portability, clustering and performance, stability and certification, alternate programs and interface. The reason behind the presence of each criteria within publications reviewed were determined and the findings were numerically analyzed. In order to carry out numerical analysis, literatures in agreement to achieving particular criteria were selected. It must be noted that numerical values to show the concurrence were not mentioned as far as the studies related to criteria are concerned and hence the criteria tends to agree as a whole numerically. However, data were given in few literatures which presented the percentage of criteria with respect to percentage of limitations within RTOS. Hence, the given data was summed up with the rest of literatures in agreement to criteria from which the percentage was discerned. Accordingly, the graph depicting the percentage of criteria present in literature related to play model for children reviewed was plotted as shown in Figure 1. It was observed that clustering and performance measure of OS is the highest that is, 93.75% in all the devices except one. Likewise, it was also revealed that the OS run on various devices could not appropriately run applications from other OSs that is, 18.75%.

These findings were compared with RTOS for other applications which included medicine, supercomputing, natural disaster recovery scheme, cloud computing, automobile, manufacturing industry and underwater devices. The objective was to compare the performance of OSs within toys with the performance of the same OS within other applications.

Similar behaviour is observed in Figure 3 which shows the percentage of criteria present in each publication in relation with all applications except play models in which the clustering and performance criteria was highest that is, 96%. However, the criteria pertaining to alternate programs was the lowest that is, 8% which implies the applications built ranging from medicine to underwater devices are mostly specific to certain OS and hence could not operate on different OSs. Hence, it could be sufficiently concluded that the performance of OSs within toys and the performance of the same OS within other applications is almost similar.

DISCUSSION

Outcomes with respect to applications

Play models with respect to criteria and vice versa were analyzed and their values were recorded based on numerical facts provided within publications. These data were plotted in Figure 2 in order to individually observe the performance of each application with respect to OS and vice versa.

Outcomes with respect to criteria

It is highly deemed for the system to be reliable in the context of operating large parallel jobs successfully over long period of time. It basically aims at reducing the mean time between job failures thus affecting reliability and usually aims at improving resiliency of the system thus enhancing the security feature which responded to 95% alongside reliability. Hence, this application displays high response for clustering and performance criteria alongside usability that is, 97%, as shown in Figure 4 which has been improved with the newly proposed high performance computing option which provides accelerated data processing of large orders of magnitude over single-processor systems and few others. Availability and scalability criteria were fairly stable to about 77 and 67% on average, while portability and interface were below average that is, 33% which reflects the size for most RTOS used for this application. The graph took hit the lowest for alternate programs criteria

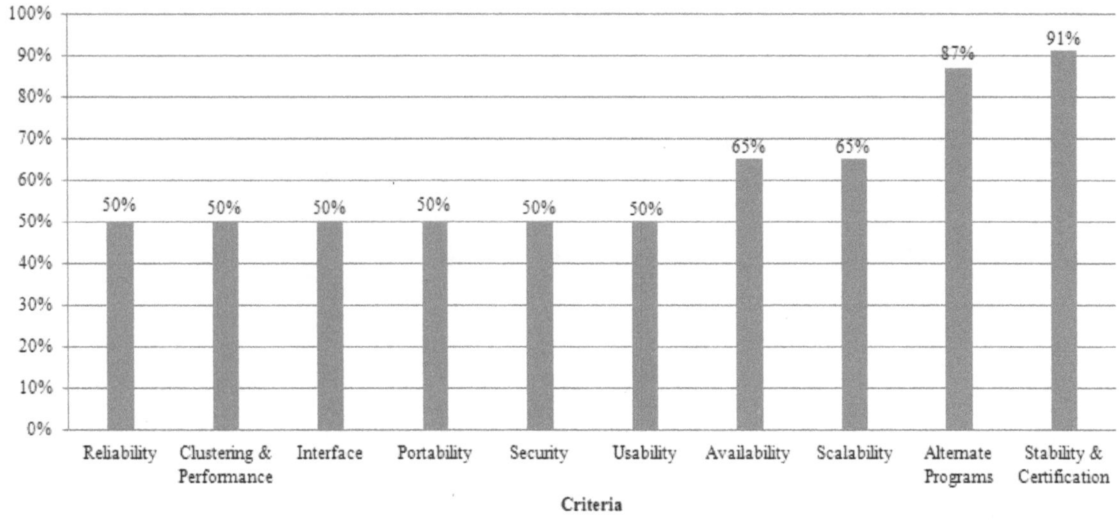

Figure 2. Criteria in RTOS used in manufacturing industry.

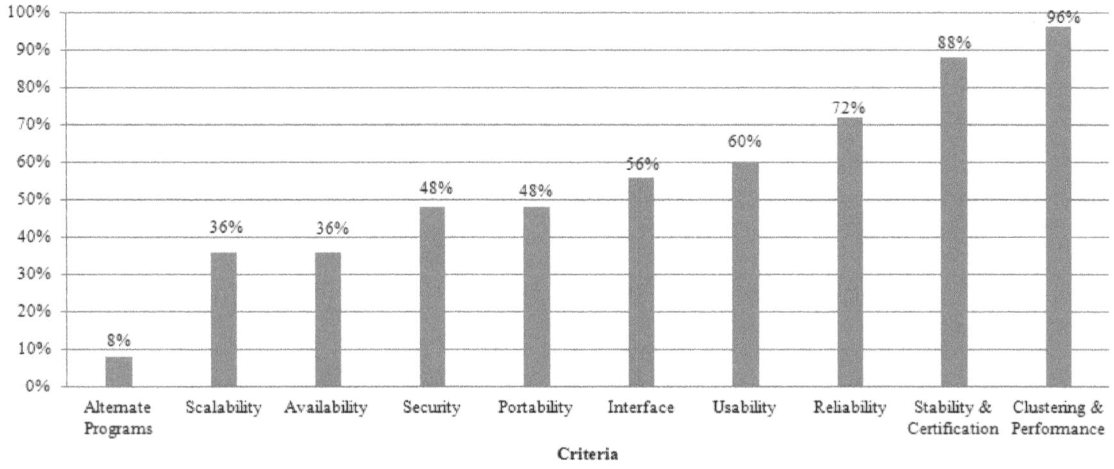

Figure 3. Criteria in RTOS used in other applications.

that is, 13% which implies that the built applications are specific to particular OS and hence could not run on different platform most of the time without making major modifications. On the other hand, manufacturing industry showed relatively stable response of all criteria where the least score was 50% pertaining to reliability, performance, interface, portability, security and usability. Literatures analyzed related to manufacturing industry implied the use of basic OS design over various production lines that is, the load of machine has to be shared by multiple production lines in most frequent cases. Even more specific scenario has been presented by Lin and Chang in case of tile manufacturing system were a similar product has been generated by two different production lines in which the functionality of the machines are the same. However, one generated compact product type with certain machines, while the other produces regular product types with all machines and hence the load of machine is common to both the production types (Lin and Chang, 2013). Without going much into details of performance of machine with respect to each production line, several other literatures have been assessed which shows fairly similar pattern for most of the criteria related to manufacturing industries. Security and usability responded to 65% which was much closer to former criteria, while alternate programs responded to 87%. This pattern implies that the application could easily run from one OS to the next which was expected given a common platform for all the production lines. However, stability and certification peaked up to 91% which was the highest thus reflecting the overall behavioural pattern and compatibility.

Figure 5 displays criteria performance with respect to different applications in which supercomputing and

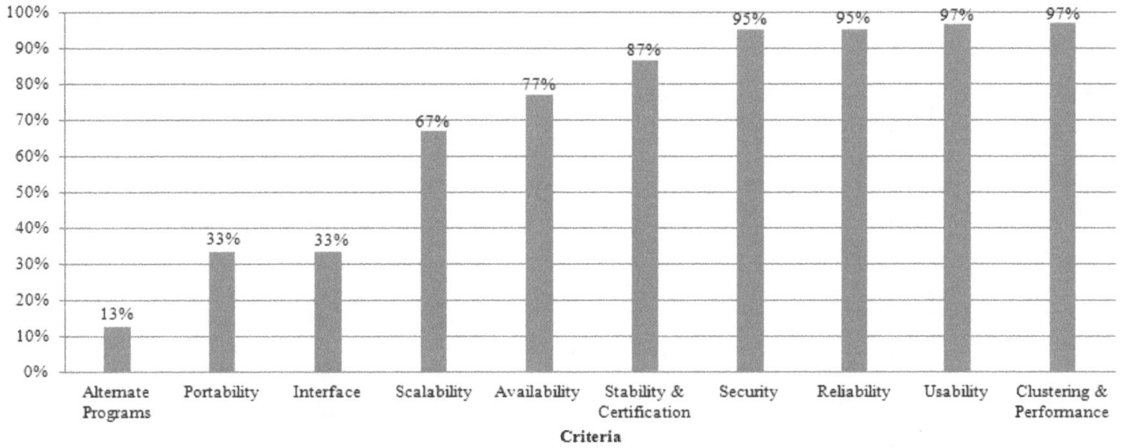

Figure 4. Criteria in RTOS used in supercomputing.

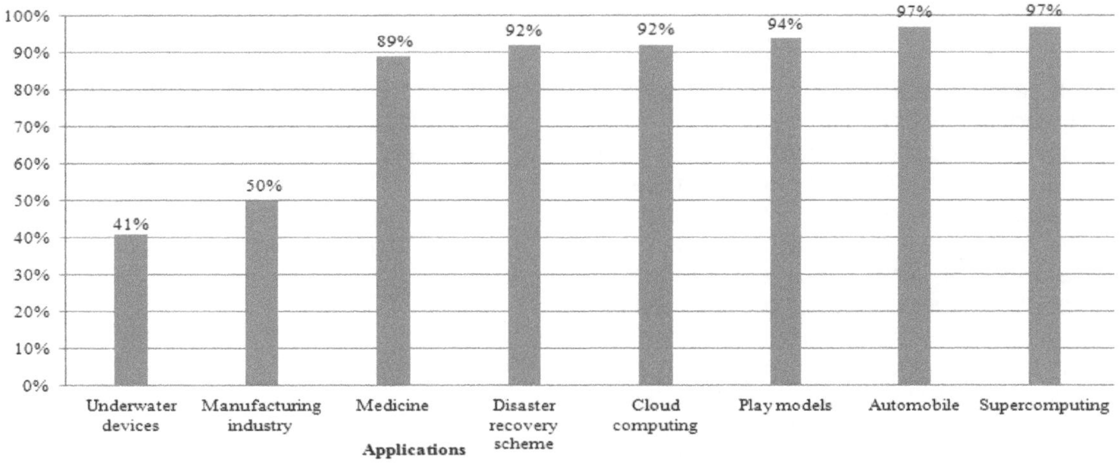

Figure 5. Clustering and performance in different applications.

automobile reaches the highest point that is, 97%. Performance of the system is of critical concern of automotive manufacturers in designing increasingly complex software. Furthermore, the issue of security could be seen in two folds within the design of automobile as well as supercomputers, while reliability and usability are traditional key concerns in the context of mechanical, electrical and software systems (Broy et al., 2007). Play models for children responded to 94% in which the software design for most of the learning systems was separated for the purpose of enhancing the performance and security. For instance, UAV helicopter was based on special purpose OS which was highly clustered into different technical sub areas which in turn reduces the load of all operations on one area thus enhancing the security feature thereby escalating its performance. Disaster recovery schemes and cloud computing displayed fairly stable response of 92% in terms of performance. Quite differently, cloud computing reaches high performance measure by replacing clustering since they are geographically distributed unlike clusters which are tightly coupled connections within small-scale. This is followed by medicine which includes the medical equipment controllers that has responded to 89% on average, while manufacturing industry has reached a response of 50%, underwater devices were quite closer to it that is, 41%. This has been followed by the reason that, in general, the mean time between job failures escalates as the devices goes deeper at lower levels of the ocean. Numerous techniques have been developed to enhance the operation of these devices which has been successful in terms of their performance but this area has not been able to escalate its performance as compared to the rest of applications. Alternate programs were observed to be the least satisfying criteria within applications. As shown

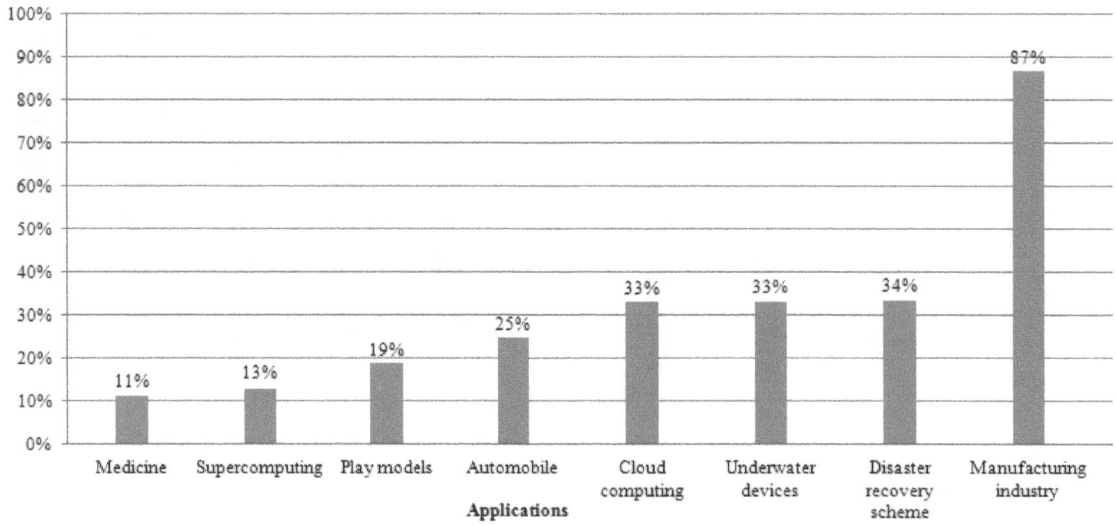

Figure 6. Alternate programs in different application.

in Figure 6, it reached the highest point at 87% for manufacturing industry where software design within products belonging to distinct production lines which includes similar basic design with few modifications according to product requirements. The criteria goes down to 33% for cloud computing and underwater devices since most of time, these applications are specific to the OS alongside disaster recovery scheme with 34% response. Due to the nature of conditions under which these applications are used, the complex designs are built restricted to a single RTOS model. The response for automobile and play models deescalates to 25 and 19%, respectively while supercomputing responded by 13%, medicine marks the lowest point at 11%. The response rate merely reflects the competition between various organizations in development of applications along with the importance laid on the application itself on nature of condition under which it is used. In terms of OS usage, Unix OS was used the maximum especially because it showed greater potential for security and performance. It is also characterized with good load balancing feature which makes it robust against crashes.

PUBLICATION SCREENING AND INCLUSION

Publications were selected on the based on a common point where the abstract and title reflected that the publication deals with OS being applied effectively to play model for children. These publications were sorted out after carefully scanning the OSs used within the information published. This number was condensed to include criteria which were thoroughly reviewed as well as their data were included for analysis. The article sources were taken from IEEE Transactions, Elsevier and ACM Database. Exclusion criteria included patents since they mainly focused on hardware side of the system and representative samples and articles were the ones which showed a participant response rate of 50% or more. Longitudinal study design was followed with the units of analysis being type of OS, applications and criteria.

Conclusions

The paper provided a review of RTOS for use for play models, analyze their capabilities on various computing platforms and OSs. We partitioned OSs into six categories in order to estimate the number of devices under each OS so that some estimate of efficiency and usability of each OS could be formed.

Conflict of Interest

The author(s) have not declared any conflict of interest.

AKNOWLEDGEMENTS

We wish to acknowledge support to both co-authors by King Abdulaziz University (KAU) as well as support to John H Reif NSF CCF-1141847, NSF CCF- 1217457, and NSF CCF-1320360.

REFERENCES

Aoto K, Inoue M, Nagshio T, Kida T (2005) Nonlinear control experiment of RC car using internet. Control Applications. Proceedings of IEEE Conference.

Christel B, Marcus D, Benjamin E, Hermann H, Joachim K, Sascha K, Steffen M, Hendrik T, Marcus V (2012). Chiefly symmetric: Results on the scalability of probabilistic model checking for operating-system code. Systems Software Verification Conference, Sydney, Australia.

Baumann A, Appavoo J (2005). Improving dynamic update for operating systems. In Proceedings of the 20th ACM Symposium on OS Principles, Work-in-Progress Session, Brighton, UK. Bekman S, Cholet E (2003). Practical Mod Perl. Beijing : Sebastopol, CA: O'Reilly.

Berglund EJ, Cheriton DR (1985). Amaze: A Multiplayer Computer Game. 2(3):30-39.

Broy M, Grünbauer J, Hoare T (2007). Software System Reliability and Security, IOS Press.

Cai J, Wu J, Wu M, Huo M (2011). A bluetooth toy car control realization by android equipment. Transportation, Mechanical, and Electrical Engineering (TMEE), International Conference

Capozzo L, Attolico G, Cicirelli C (1999). Building low cost vehicles for simple reactive behaviors. Systems, Man, and Cybernetics. IEEE SMC Conference Proceedings. IEEE International Conference, 6:675-680.

Chan HT, Chang RKC (2004). Strifeshadow Fantasy: a massive multi-player online game. Consumer Communications and Networking Conference. First IEEE, pp. 557-562

DOD 5200.28-STD (1985). DOD Trusted Computer System Evaluation Criteria (Orange Book). http://www.radium.ncsc.mil/tpep/library/rainbow/5200.28-STD.pdf.

Dalton C, Choo TH (2001). An Operating System Approach to Securing E-Services. Communications of the ACM, 44(2):58.

Gillen A, Kusnetzky D, McLaron S (2002). The role of Linux in reducing the cost of enterprise computing. IDC white paper.

Hämäläinen P, Mäki-Patola T, Pulkki V, Airas M (2004). Musical Computer Games Played by Singing. In Proc. of the 7th Int. Conference on Digital Audio Effects (DAFX-04), Naples, Italy, October 5-8.

Huber M, Rabin B, Docan C, Burdea G, Nwosu ME, AbdelBaky M, Golomb MR (2008). PlayStation 3-based tele-rehabilitation for children with hemiplegia, Virtual Rehabilitation.

Ko WH, Lee SM, Nam KT, Shon WH, Ji SH (2010). Design of a personalized r-learning system for children. Intelligent Robots and Systems (IROS), IEEE/RSJ Int. Conf. pp. 3893-3898.

Kronreif G, Prazak B, Mina S, Kornfeld M, Meindl M, Fürst M (2005). Playrob - robot-assisted playing for children with severe physical disabilities. Presented at IEEE, 9th International Conference on Rehabilitation Robotics, Chicago, IL, USA.

Lin YK, Chang PC (2013). Graphical-based reliability evaluation of multiple distinct production lines. J. Syst. Sci. Syst. Eng. 22(1):73-92.

Momeni H, Kashefi O, Sharifi H (2008). How to Realize Self-Healing Operating Systems? Information and Communication Technologies: From Theory to Applications. 3rd International Conference.

Patterson D, Brown A, Broadwell P, Candea G, Chen M, Cutler J, Enriquez P, Fox A, Kıcıman E, Merzbacher M, Oppenheimer D, Sastry N, Tetzlaff W, Traupman J, Treuhaft N (2002). Recovery Oriented Computing (ROC): Motivation, definition, techniques, and case studies. Technical Report CSD-02-1175, UC Berkeley Computer Science.

Prieto SS, Navarro TA, Plaza MG, Polo OR (2012). A Monoball Robot Based on LEGO Mindstorms. Control Systems, IEEE, 32(2):71-83.

Rumman NA (2009). Operating system support for multimedia: Survey. Computer Science and Information Technology-Spring Conference. International Association.

Segal ME, Frieder O (1989). Dynamic Program Updating: A Software Maintenance Technique for Minimizing Software Downtime. J. Software Maintenance, 1(1):59-79.

Sharad S (2007). Introducing Embedded Design Concepts to Freshmen and Sophomore Engineering Students with LEGO MINDSTORMS NXT. Microelectronic Systems Education. IEEE Int. Conf. pp. 119-120.

Smith RW (2000). Linux Hardware Handbook: [selecting, Installing, and Configuring the Right Components for Your Linux System ...]. Indianapolis, IN: Sams.

Spencer R, Smalley S, Loscocco P, Hibler M, Andersen D, Lepreau J (1999). The Flask security architecture: System support for diverse security policies. In Proc. of the 8th Usenix Security Symposium, pp.123-139.

Swift MM, Bershad BN, Levy HM (2003). Improving the Reliability of Commodity Operating Systems, in Proceedings of the 19th ACM Symposium on Operating Systems Principles, Bolton Landing, NY.

Swift MM, Bershad BN, Levy HM (2004). Improving the Reliability of Commodity Operating Systems, ACM Transact. Comp. Syst. 22(4).

Tanguay D (2000). Flying Toy Plane. Computer Vision and Pattern Recognition. Proceedings. IEEE Conference, 2:231-238.

Tushman ML, Newman WH, Romanelli E (2004). Convergence and upheaval: managing the unsteady pace of organizational evolution. Tushman, M.L. and Anderson, P. (Eds.), Managing Strategic Innovation and Change: A Collection of Readings, pp. 530-540. New York: Oxford University Press.

Vial PJ, Serafini G, Raad I (2007). Soccer RoBot Toy within an Educational Environment. The First IEEE International Workshop on Digital Game and Intelligent Toy Enhanced Learning, Jhongli, Taiwan, March 26-28 2007, 215-217. Copyright IEEE 2007

Watson DJ (1983). Book Review: Operating System Concepts. 3:2.

Yang CQ (2001). Operating System Security and Secure Operating Systems. V. 1.4b, Option 1 for GSEC.

Zhu MY, Luo L, Xiong GZ (2001). A Provably Correct Operating System. ACM SIGOPS Operating Systems Review 35(1):17-33. Print.

The comparison of time division multiple access (TDMA) (global system for mobile communication, GSM) and wideband-code division multiple access (W-CDMA) (third generation, 3G) system based on their modulation techniques

Olusanya Olamide O.[1] and Ogunseye Abiodun A.[2]

Department of Electrical and Electronic Engineering, College of Engineering, Bells University of Technology, Ota, Ogun State. Nigeria.

Mobile network communication system offers the users with seamless communication and this has caused wireless communication to increasingly become the preferred method of carrying multimedia traffic or messages such as voice, video, images, and data files. Time division multiple access (TDMA) is the multiple access scheme used in global system for mobile communication (GSM), while third generation (3G) system uses wideband-code division multiple access (W-CDMA). The former is designed majorly for voice and a little of data. Due to the increase in number of phone users and the services enjoyed by the users, there is higher demand for non-voice services, mobile extensions to fixed-line services and richer mobile content. This has caused the network operators to develop 3G system with the goal of providing a network infrastructure that can support a much broader range of services than existing systems in which its penetration level has reached market saturation. This paper presents a comparison of the two wireless systems performance based on their modulation techniques. From the constellation gotten, the two systems were analyzed and the analysis shows that W-CDMA (that is, 3G) provides a network infrastructure that can support a much broader range of services than existing systems (GSM) because the main forces behind development of the 3G have been driven by the second generation systems' low performance data services, incompatible service in different parts of the world, and lack of capacity.

Key words: Time division multiple access (TDMA), wideband-code division multiple access (W-CDMA), call drop rate, call set-up success rate (CSSR), handover rate, constellation.

INTRODUCTION

In recent years, cellular communication has experienced exponential growth, and the growth continues unabated worldwide, with cell phone users numbering billions. It presents the users with seamless communication where

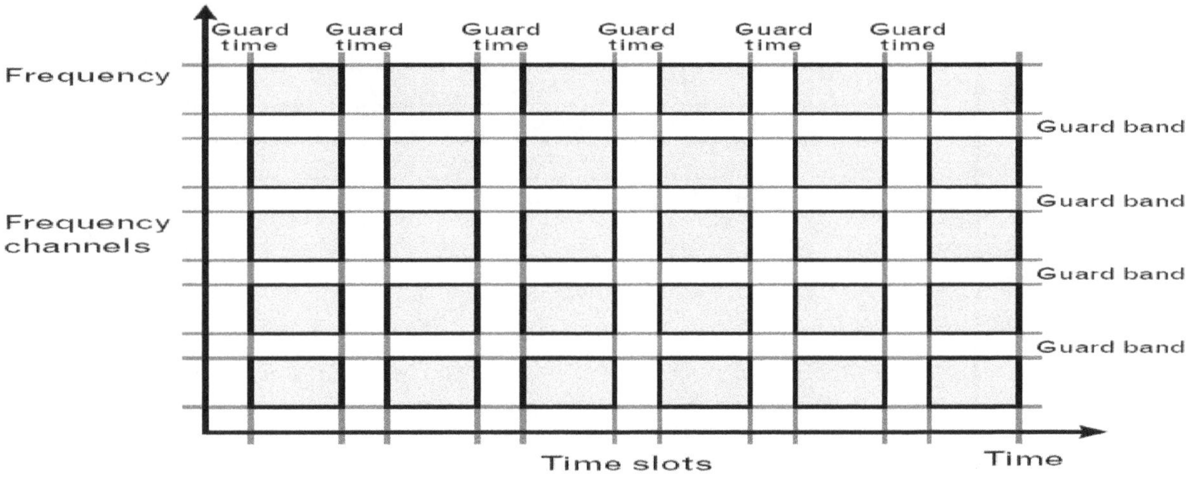

Figure 1. Hybrid frequency division multiple access/ time division multiple access (FDMA/TDMA) system. Korhonen (2003).

possible end-to-end. As more wireless solutions become available, it becomes more important to understand the strength and capabilities of each technology.

The third generation (3G) system is now the generally accepted term used to describe the latest wave of mobile networks and services. The previous wave, 2G system, arrived in the late 1980s and moved towards a digital solution which gave the added benefit of allowing the transfer of data and provision of other non-voice services.

Of these, the global system for mobile communication (GSM) has been the most successful, with its global roaming model (Jeffrey et al., 2004). 3G leverages on the developments in cellular to date, and combines them with complementary developments in both the fixed-line telecom networks and the world of the internet.

The result is the development of a more general purpose network, which offers the flexibility to provide and support access to any service, regardless of location. These services can be voice, video or data and combinations thereof, but, as already stated, the emphasis is on the service provision as opposed to the previous technology.

REVIEW OF PREVIOUS WORKS

The concept of multiple access

According to Miceli (2003), cellular system would not be very practical if it only allows one call per system at a time. Thus, cellular designers need to implement methods of multiple accesses (that is, allowing multiple conversations simultaneously).

Today's digital systems use a combination of frequency division multiple access (FDMA) with another multiple access technique, time division multiple access (TDMA). TDMA involves separating users into different timeslots and then adding at different frequencies these "time-divided".

In a TDMA system, the used system bandwidth is usually divided into smaller frequency channels. So in that sense GSM is actually a hybrid FDMA/TDMA system (Figure 1), as are most other 2G systems. In a TDMA system, all users can use the entire channel bandwidth and are distinguished by allocating short and distinct time slots to each user. In this system, a physical channel is defined as a time slot with a time slot number in a sequence of TDMA frame (Poonam et al., 2007)

In code divisional multiple access (CDMA), all users are allowed to use the entire system bandwidth all the time. The signals of users are distinguished by assigning different spreading codes (Poonam et al., 2007). Figure 2 shows how the signals are separated from each other by means of special codes.

Radio-channel access schemes

The usage of radio spectrum must be carefully controlled because it is a scarce resource. Mobile cellular systems use various techniques to allow multiple users to access the same radio spectrum at the same time. In fact, many systems employ several techniques simultaneously (Korhonen, 2003).

Modulation techniques

Freeman (2005) defined modulation as the process of putting useful information on a carrier that can be transmitted from one point to another. This information can be voice, data or signaling data. Data modulation is

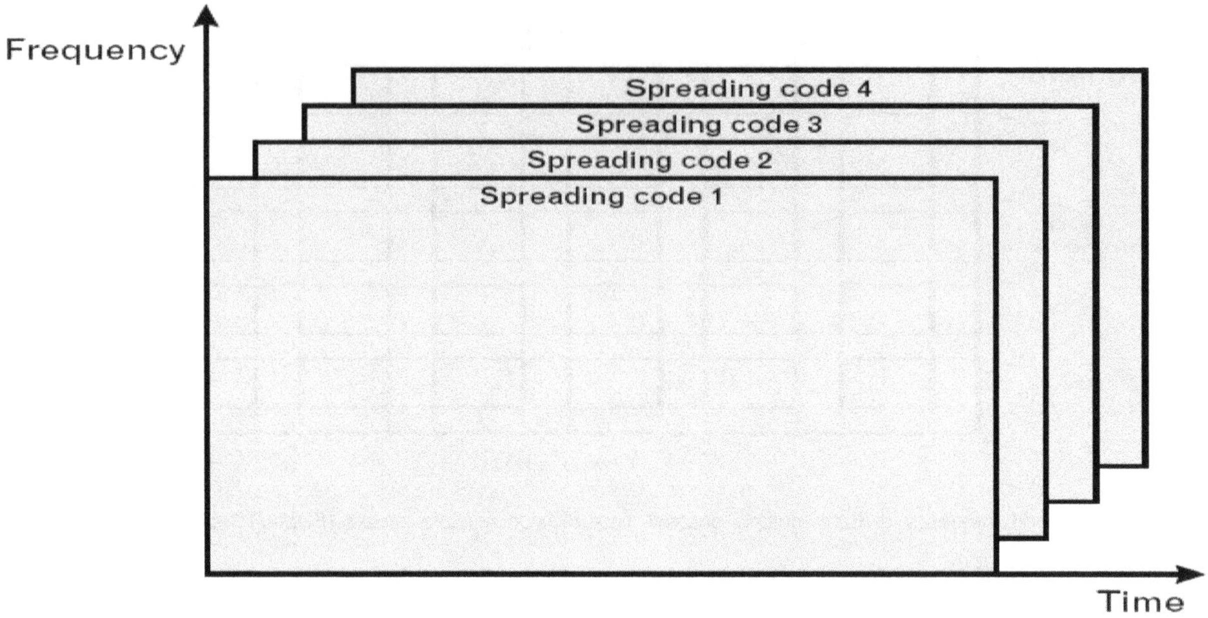

Figure 2. CDMA system: all users occupy the same frequency at the same time, but their signals are separated from each other by means of special codes. Korhonen (2003).

always in digital sense. Modulation techniques used in GSM and 3G were reviewed.

Digital modulation consists of mapping bit sequences into waveforms for transmission over the channel. The main considerations in choosing a particular digital modulation technique are:

1) High data rate
2) High spectral efficiency (minimum bandwidth occupancy)
3) High power efficiency (minimum required transmit power)
4) Robustness to channel impairments (minimum probability of bit error)
5) Low power/cost implementation.

Modulation in 3G

According to Jeffrey et al. (2004), Universal mobile telecommunication system (UMTS) defines the use of quadrature phase shift keying (QPSK) modulation for the air interface. With a QPSK modulation scheme, the complex signal that results from the spreading function is split by a serial to parallel converter into a real and an imaginary branch, each of which is multiplied with an oscillator signal. However, the imaginary branch is 90° out of phase with the real branch. When summed, the resulting signal can have four possible phase angles, each of which represents two data bits.

Figure 3 illustrates the general principle. QPSK modulation is specified for use in both the uplink and the downlink; however, the use of the QPSK modulation scheme does present some difficulties in the uplink. Consider that the amplifier is at a maximum output power and needs to change its signal by 180°. This consumes a considerable amount of power in the amplifier to retain the linearity of the signal, particularly across such a wide frequency band, and most of this power ends up wasted as heat. This is not so difficult a problem at the BTS, but is quite impractical at the UE, where cost, power consumption, battery life and heat dissipation are all significant issues. A common solution to this problem is to use offset QPSK in the uplink instead. With offset QPSK, there is a delay introduced into the imaginary branch to offset the phase shifting of this branch relative to the real branch. The result is that when 180° phase shift is required, the shift is performed in two steps of 90°. QPSK modulation provides a one-to-one relationship between the bit rate of an unmodulated signal and the symbol rate after modulation. In practice, this means that a 3.84 Mcps spread signal entering the modulator will emerge as a 3.84 MHz signal. In the course of the modulation process, pulse shaping is also performed. Wideband-code division multiple access (W-CDMA) uses a root-raised cosine filter with a roll-off of 0.22. A modulated signal with this roll off, plus the provision of a guard band between neighboring frequencies, equates to the 5 MHz of spectrum allocated per W-CDMA carrier. For frequencies licensed to the same operator, there can be less than 5 MHz spacing between carriers. However, the centre frequency must lie on a 200 kHz raster (Jeffrey et al., 2004).

Pulse shaping is a spectral processing technique by

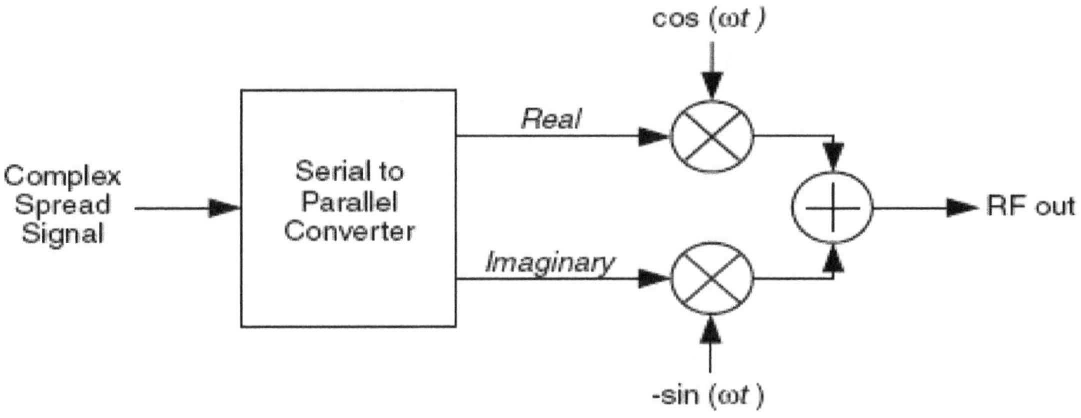

Figure 3. QPSK modulation principle. This modulation technique is used in 3G system. Jeffrey et al. (2004)

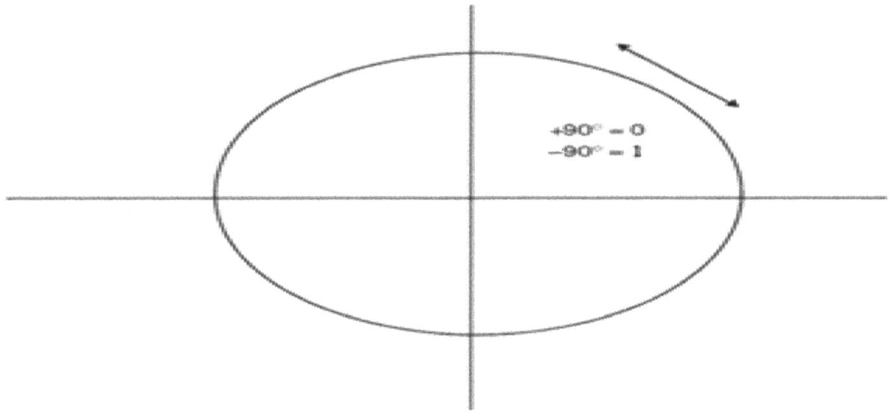

Figure 4. GSM uses GMSK modulation. Amplitude remains constant during phase shifts of ±90. The constellation of a GSM signal thus resembles a circle. Andrew (2003).

which fractional out of band power is reduced for low cost, reliable, power and spectrally efficient mobile radio communication systems. It is clear that the pulse shaping filter not only reduces inter-symbol interference (ISI), but it also reduces adjacent channel interference (Kang and Sharma, 2011).

Modulation in GSM

Masud et al. (2010) stated that GSM uses a modulation format called Gaussian minimum shift Keying (GMSK) (Figure 4). The transmit rate of the GSM system is 270.833 Kbps, while the bandwidth of the signal is 200 kHz. Thus, the modulation efficiency of GSM (data rate divided by bandwidth) is 1.35 bps/Hz. This is a lower efficiency than North American (NA)-TDMA (1.6 bps/Hz).

One of the trade-offs for the lower modulation efficiency is that GSM uses a constant signal envelope, which means less battery drain and more robustness in the presence of interfering signals. In having a constant signal envelope, the constellation diagram of a GSM signal is a circle, and, thus, unlike NA-TDMA and CDMA, constellation analysis will not tell a technician very much about the quality of modulation.

Another important difference between GSM and NA-TDMA pertains to the downlink transmission. In NA-TDMA, the base station transmitted all slots.

This GMSK modulation can only transmit data rate of 1 bit per symbol. So it is quite sure that this kind of modulation scheme is not suitable for the 3G communication system (Masud et al., 2010). So, there is a need to study the performance of new modulation technique that could deliver higher data rate effectively in a multipath fading channel.

However, the implementation of high data rate modulation techniques that have good bandwidth efficiency in W-CDMA cellular communication requires perfect modulators, demodulators, filter and transmission path that are difficult to achieve in practical radio environment. Modulation schemes which are capable of delivering more bits per symbol are more immune to

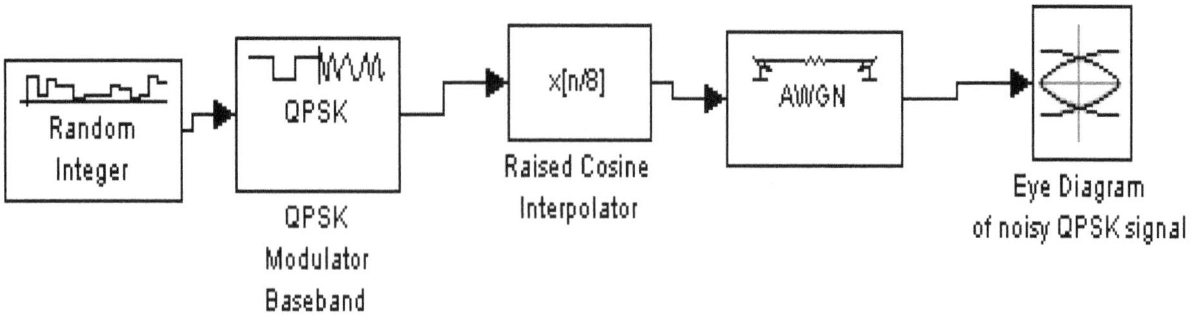

Figure 5. Block diagram of QPSK transmitter. The quadrature form of modulating using I and Q channel.

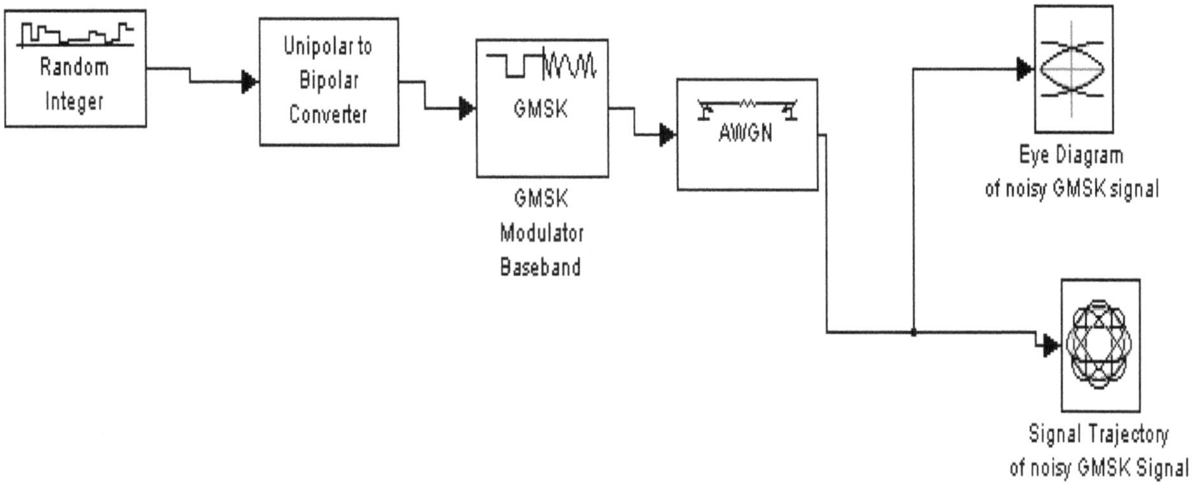

Figure 6. A GMSK modulator implemented.

errors caused by noise and interference in the channel. Moreover, errors can be easily produced as the number of users is increased and the mobile terminal is subjected to mobility (Masud et al., 2010).

Tomislav et al. (2009) emphasized the fact that it is important for base-band signals to be heavily band limited before modulation and that can be achieved by pulse shaping of rectangular bits.

National Instruments RF Projects (2013) also presents these two important requirements: generation of band limited channels, and reduction of ISI from multi-path signal reflections as pulse shaping filter fundamentals on wireless communication system

METHODOLOGY

Simulation of modulation techniques

Simulation of their modulation techniques using MATLAB was carried out. Simulation is programs often quite complex that mimic the dynamic behavior of the model system over time. This method was chosen because simulation is of particular interest during system design, when real life hardware is not available for measurement and in situations where a reasonable accurate analytical model of a system is not mathematically tractable. W-CDMA uses QPSK modulation, while GSM uses GMSK as its own modulation technique.

The circuit diagram for W-CDMA modulation is shown in Figure 5. In the simulation environment, the following outlines were followed:

1) Random number generation (1000).
2) Those numbers were shaped using a square root raised cosine filter.
3) Modulation of the output in ii above was done using QPSK.
4) Constellation plot was carried out.

The circuit diagram for TDMA modulation is also shown in Figure 6. In the simulation environment, the following outlines were also followed for GMSK modulation:

1) Random number generation (1000).
2) Those numbers were shaped using a Guassian low pass filter.
3) Modulation of the output in ii above was done using FSK.
4) Constellation plot was carried out.

SIMULATION RESULTS AND DISCUSSION

Figure 7 shows the Gaussian pulse-shaping filter used in GMSK modulation technique. It is used to smooth the

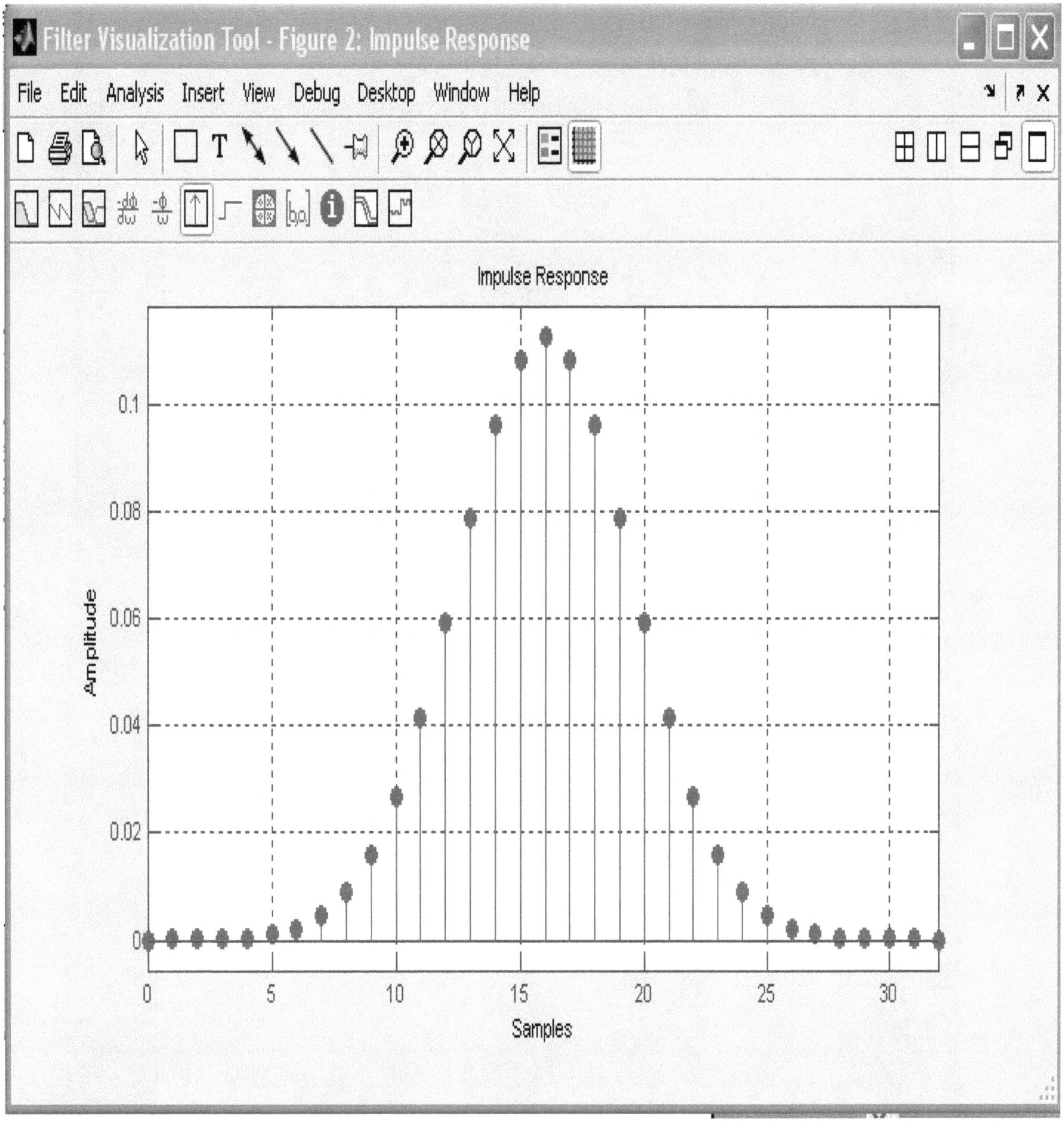

Figure 7. Gaussian pulse-shaping Filter used in GMSK modulation technique.

phase transitions of the modulated signal and also to effectively eliminate spectral leakage, reducing channel width, and reduction of interference from adjacent symbols (ISI) (Tomislav et al., 2009).

Figure 8 represents the GMSK constellation. From the figure it can be seen that the signals were separated among phase state by 45°. This causes the system not to be resilient to noise and this has caused it to be more exposed to interference. All these accounted to its high drop call rate, poor CSSR, poor handing over e.t.c. This kind of modulation scheme is not suitable for the 3G communication system and will not be able to deliver higher data rate effectively in a multipath fading channel.

From Figure 9, the type of filter used in QPSK modulation can be seen (square root raised cosine filter). The amplitude steps in a digital chip stream are the cause for high-frequency spectral components. Since the signal is transmitted on a bandwidth-limited channel,

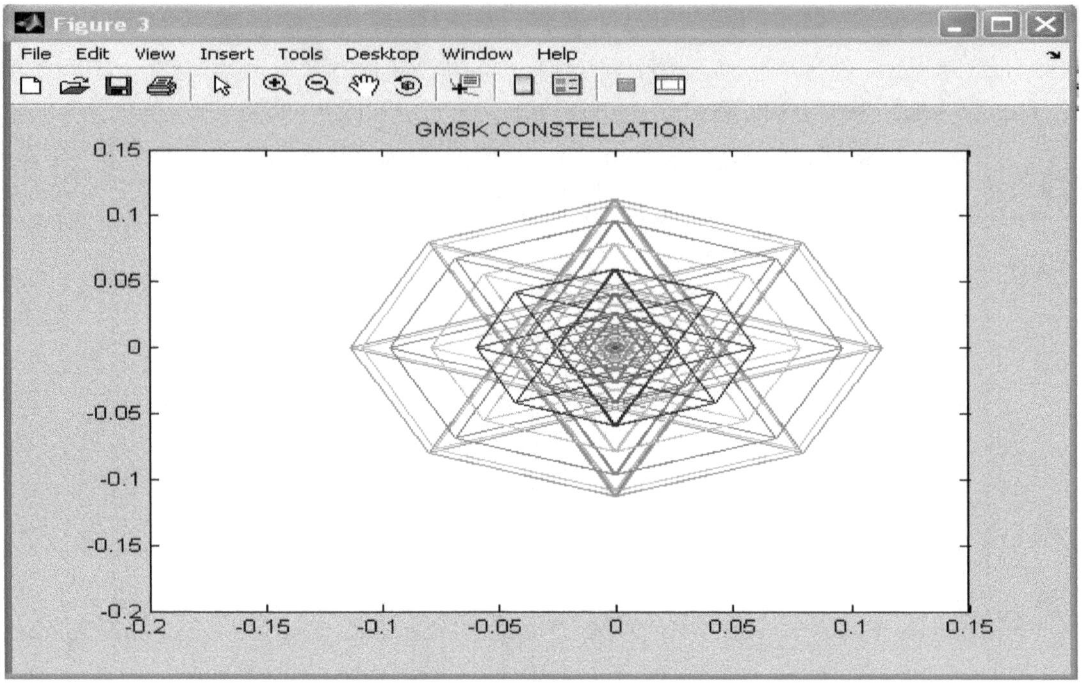

Figure 8. GMSK constellation plot.

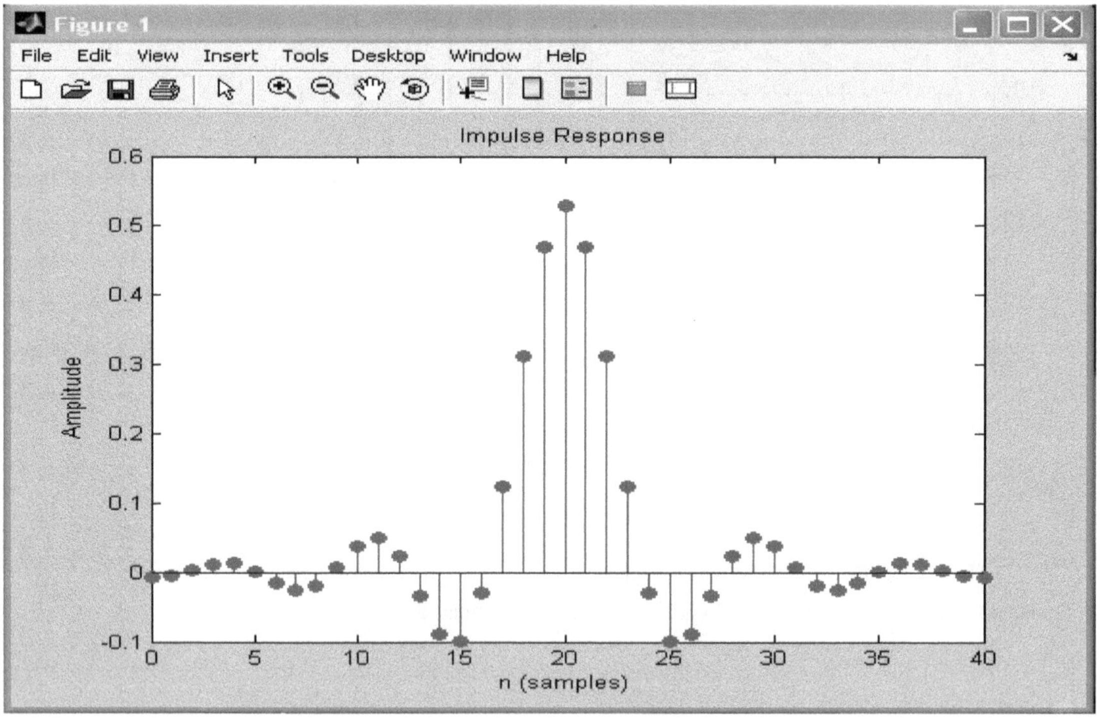

Figure 9. Square root raised cosine filter used in QPSK modulation technique.

smearing of adjacent symbols may happen, known as ISI. In order to avoid such interference, the signal is low-pass filtered using square root raised cosine filter and this accounts for its high performance (Joost, 2010).

Also, Figure 10 shows the QPSK constellation plot. In it the signals were separated among phase states by 90° and this helps it to be:

i) Resilient to noise
ii) More efficient in bandwidth usage

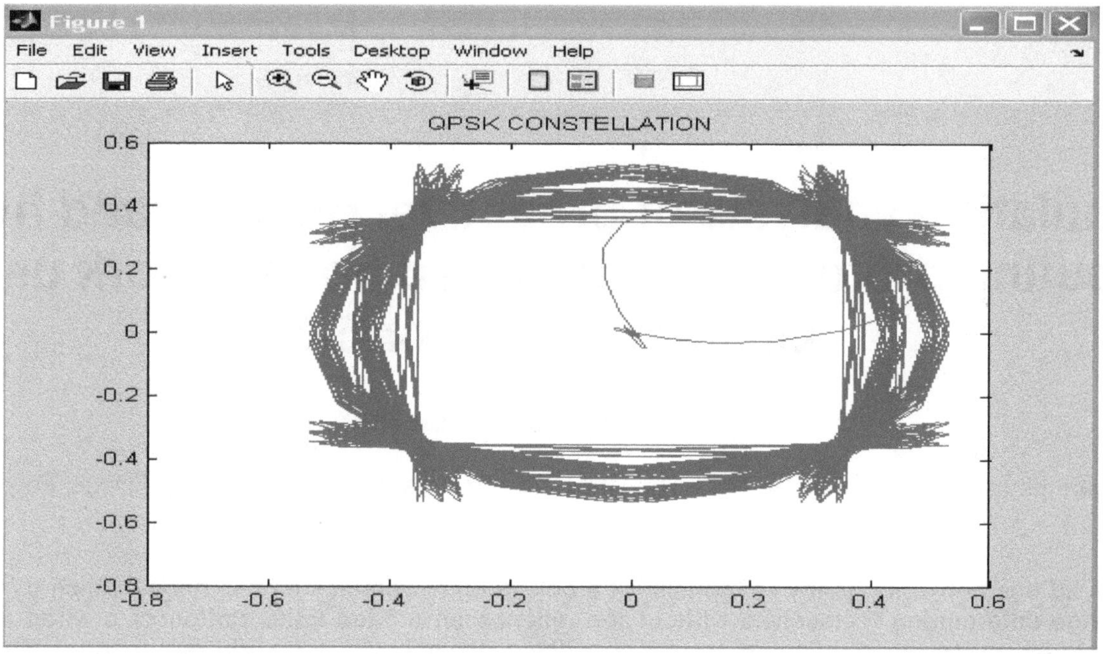

Figure 10. QPSK constellation plot.

iii) Better in data communication speed, because 3G system uses 3 of GSM E1 - is like a frame inside a Radio base station (RBS). RBS is responsible for all the call we make. Each E1 is 2 MBit/s and is divided into 32 time slots.

On the E1, after the slot in the location 0 and 15 have been allocated to framing and signaling, it remains 30 time slots. Each time slot is further divided into 8, which means in an E1, about 240 people can make use of it on time slot basis.

Therefore, in GSM system, about 240 people can use it on time slot basis, while in 3G system, about 720 people use it on time slot basis since it uses 3 of GSM E1 (6 MBit/s).

3G systems also have higher security compared to GSM system because all signals are separated from each other by means of special code since they all used the same frequency channel at the same time.

Conclusions

In this paper, we have evaluated the two systems (W-CDMA and TDMA) based on their modulation techniques. An examination of the two systems (W-CDMA and TDMA) revealed that W-CDMA system renders more general purpose network, which offers the flexibility to provide and support access to any service, regardless of location. These services can be voice, video or data and combinations thereof due to the characteristics and features embedded in it. The features include fast power control, soft handover, efficiency in bandwidth usage, resilient to noise, rake receiving and a lot more.

Conflict of Interest

The authors have not declared any conflict of interest.

REFERENCES

Freeman RL (2005). Fundamentals of Telecommunications. Second Edition. John Wiley & Sons, Inc., Hoboken, New Jersey. Canada.

Jeffrey B, Paul M, Coope S (2004). Convergence technologies For 3G networks IP, UMTS, EGPRS and ATM. England. John Wiley & Sons Ltd.

Joost M (2010). Theory of Root-Raised Cosine Filter. Research and Development, 47829 Krefeld, Germany, EU.

Kang AS, Sharma V (2011). Pulse Shape Filtering in Wireless Communication-A Critical Analysis. Int. J. Adv. Comp. Sci. Appl. (IJACSA) 2(3).

Korhonen J (2003). Introduction to 3G mobile communications-2nd (Artech House mobile communications series). 685 Canton Street Norwood

Masud MA, Samsuzzaman M, Rahman MA (2010). Bit Error Rate Performance Analysis on Modulation Techniques of Wideband CodeDivision Multiple Access, J. Telecomm. 1(2).

Miceli A (2003). Wireless technician's handbook/Andrew Miceli.—2nd ed. (Artech House mobile communications series) 685 Canton Street Norwood.

National Instruments RF projects (2013). Pulse-Shape Filtering in Communications Systems. Aug 14, 2013.

Tomislav Š, Marijan H, Tomislav M (2009). A Simple Signal Shaper for GMSK/GFSK and MSK Modulator Based on Sigma-Delta Look-up Table. Radio Eng. 18(2).

23

Simulation analysis of proactive, reactive and hybrid routing protocols in mobile ad hoc network using Qualnet simulator 5.0.2

Nitin Arora* and Suresh Kumar

Department of Computer Science and Engineering, Govind Ballabh Pant Engineering College, Pauri, India.

Mobile ad hoc networks (MANETs) consist of a collection of wireless mobile nodes which dynamically exchange data among themselves without the reliance on a fixed base station or a wired backbone network. All nodes are mobile and can be connected dynamically in an arbitrary manner. There is no static infrastructure such as base station. All nodes of these networks behave as routers and take part in discovery and maintenance of routes to other nodes in the network. There are various protocols for handling the routing problem in the ad hoc wireless network environment. In this paper, focus is given on studying the performance evaluation of various routing protocols using Qualnet simulator 5.0.2. The performance of the proactive, reactive and hybrid protocols are analyzed with different node densities for stationary nodes. The metrics used for the performance evaluation include throughput, packet delivery ratio and average end to end delay.

Key words: Proactive, reactive, hybrid, performance evaluation, Qualnet, end-to-end delay, throughput, packets delivery ratio.

INTRODUCTION

Wireless networks are an emerging new technology that will allow users to access information and services electronically, regardless of their geographic position. Wireless networks can be classified in two types:

1. Infrastructure Network and
2. Infrastructure less (ad hoc) Networks

Infrastructure Network consists of a network with fixed and wired gateways. A mobile host communicates with a bridge in the network or called base station within its communication radius. The mobile unit can move geographically while it is communicating. When it goes out of range of one base station, it connects with new base station and starts communicating through it.

A mobile ad hoc network (MANET) (Siva and Manoj, 2011) group has been formed within IETF (Internet Engineering Task Force). The goal of IETF is to support mobile ad hoc networks with hundreds of routers and solve challenges. MANET is a self-configuring infrastructure, with small network of mobile devices connected by wireless links. Each device in a MANET is free to move independently in any direction, and will therefore change its links to other devices frequently. An ad hoc network is a collection of mobile computers or mobile nodes that cooperate to forward packets for each other to extend the limited transmission range of each node's wireless network interface. Each node must forward traffic unrelated to its own use, and therefore be a router. The primary challenge in building a MANET is equipping each device to continuously maintain the information required to properly route traffic. Such networks may operate by themselves or may be connected to the larger Internet. Active research work for mobile ad hoc networks is currently done mainly in the fields of Medium Access Control (MAC), routing, resource management, power control, and security. Because of the importance of routing protocols in dynamic multi hop networks, a lot of mobile ad hoc network routing protocols have been proposed in the last few years. Table 1 shows some of

*Corresponding author. E-mail: nitinarora47@gmail.com.

Table 1. Some routing protocols for MANETs.

Pro-active routing or table-driven protocols	DSDV, FSR, OLSR
Reactive routing or On-demand routing protocols	AODV, DSR
Hybrid (pro-active/reactive)	ZRP

the routing protocols for MANETs.

In this work performance evaluation of various routing protocols like Optimized Link State Routing (OLSR), Ad hoc On-demand Distance Vector routing (AODV), Dynamic Source Routing (DSR) and Zone Routing Protocol (ZRP) are studied using Qualnet 5.0.2 network simulator (www.scalable-networks.com) for 25, 50 and 100 stationary nodes.

Various routing techniques

Proactive routing technique (Table driven protocols)

Optimized link state routing (OLSR): It is a proactive routing protocol where the routes are always available when needed. OLSR is an optimized version of a pure link state protocol. The topological changes cause the flooding of the topological information to all available hosts in the network. To reduce the possible overhead in the network protocol multipoint relays (MPR) are used. Reducing the time interval for the control messages transmission brings more reactivity to the topological changes (Philippe et al., 2001).

OLSR uses two kinds of the control messages namely hello and topology control. Hello messages are used for finding the information about the link status and the host's neighbours. Topology control messages are used for broadcasting information about its own advertised neighbours, which includes at least the MPR selector list (Philippe et al., 2001).

Reactive routing technique (on-demand routing protocols)

Ad hoc on-demand distance vector (AODV): The Ad hoc on-demand Distance Vector (AODV) routing protocol (Baccala, 1997) is a reactive MANET routing protocol. Similar to DSR, AODV broadcasts a route request to discover a route in a reactive mode. The difference is that in AODV, a field of the number of hops is used in the route record, instead of a list of intermediate router addresses. Each intermediate router sets up a temporary reverse link in the process of a route discovery. This link points to the router that forwarded the request. Hence, the reply messages can find its way back to the initiator when a route is discovered. When intermediate routers receive the reply, they can also set up corresponding forward routing entries. To prevent old routing information being used as a reply to the latest request, a destination sequence number is used in the route discovery packet and the route reply packet. A higher sequence number implies a more recent route request. Route maintenance in AODV is similar to that in DSR (Boukerche, 2001).

One advantage of AODV is that AODV is loop-free due to the destination sequence numbers associated with routes. The algorithm avoids the Bellman-Ford "count to infinity" problem (Haas et al., 2002).

Therefore, it offers quick convergence when the ad hoc net-work topology changes which, typically, occurs when a node moves in the network (Haas et al., 2002). Similar to DSR, poor scalability is disadvantage of AODV (Aron and Gupta, 2001).

We use the example topology shown in Figure 1 to illustrate the discovery procedure of AODV. Note that Routers A and C are disconnected from each other while both of them connect to B. When Router A starts a route discovery to C, a route request is broadcast. The request packet contains the requested destination sequence number, which is 1 greater than the one currently kept at A. For example, assume that the destination sequence number for C at A is 0x00000000, then the destination sequence number in the route discovery packet is 0x00000001. The intermediate routers reply to the source if they know the route to that destination with the same or higher destination sequence number. We assume that B does not have a record for a route to C. Therefore, B first sets up a temporary link pointing back to A. In the second step, it increases the number of hops by 1 and rebroadcasts the request. When C receives that request, it creates a new destination sequence number. A route reply with that new sequence number is sent by C. The initiator and all intermediate routers build routing entries associated with this new sequence number when they receive the reply. The number of hop values can be used to find a shorter path if a router receives two replies with the same destination sequence number. AODV uses a similar scheme as DSR to handle unreliable transmission of control messages.

Dynamic source routing (DSR): When a node generates a packet to a certain destination and it does not have a known route to that destination, this node starts a route discovery procedure. Therefore, DSR is a reactive protocol. One advantage of DSR is that no periodic routing packets are required. DSR also has the capability to handle unidirectional links. Since DSR

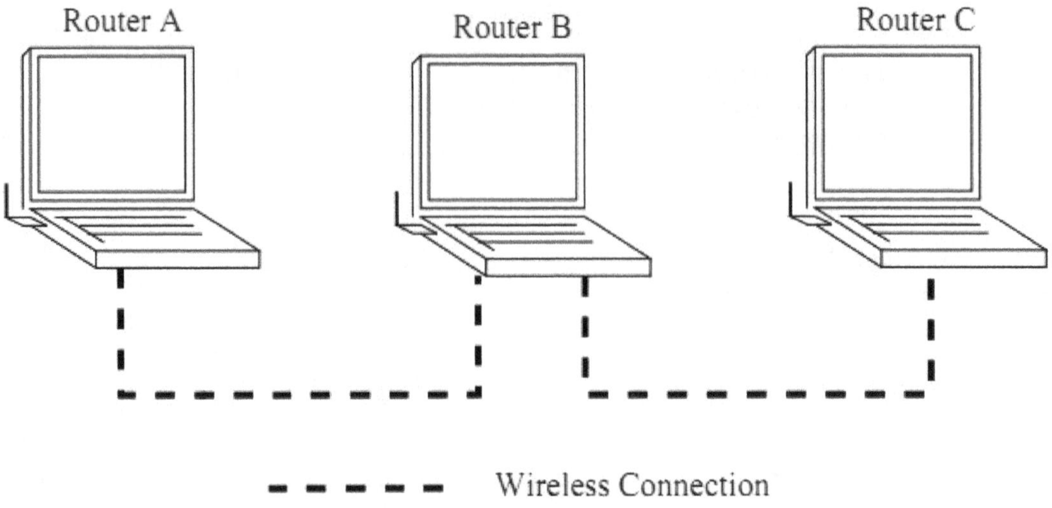

Figure 1. Example of DSR and AODV routing protocols.

discovers routes on-demand, it may have poor performance in terms of control overhead in networks with high mobility and heavy traffic loads. Scalability is said to be another disadvantage of DSR (Aron and Gupta, 2001), because DSR relies on blind broadcasts to discover routes.

There are two main operations in DSR, route discovery and route maintenance. Figure 1 shows a simple example for DSR. Routers A, B, and C form a MANET. Routers A and C are disconnected, while both of them connect to router B. Assume that at the beginning, the route caches that memorize previous routes in the routers are empty. When Router A wants to send a packet to Router C, it broadcasts a route request to start the corresponding route discovery procedure. Router B receives the request since it is within the radio range of A. Router C is the destination in the request and B does not have a route entry to C in its cache at this time. Hence, Router B appends its own ID to the list of intermediate router IDs in the request and rebroadcasts it. When C receives the broadcast route request message originated by B, it determines that the destination ID matches its own ID. Thus, the route from A to C is found. To help the initiator and all intermediate routers construct proper routing entries, Router C sends a reply back to A using source routing if links are bi-directional. This procedure is feasible because all intermediate routers are in the ID list of the corresponding route request. Intermediate routers construct proper routing tables when they receive the reply originated from C. Thus, a route from A to C is built. During the route discovery procedure, routers maintain ID lists of the recently seen requests to avoid repeatedly processing the same route request. Requests are discarded if they were processed recently since they are assumed to be duplicates. If a router receives a request and detects that the request contains its own ID in the list of intermediate routers, this router discards the request to avoid loops. The route maintenance procedure is used when routes become invalid due to the unpredictable movement of routers. Each router monitors the links that it uses to forward packets. Once a link is down, a route error packet is immediately sent to the initiator of the associated route. Therefore, the invalid route is quickly discarded (Boukerche, 2001).

Hybrid routing technique

Hybrid Routing Protocols combines the merits of proactive and reactive routing protocols by overcoming their demerits. In this section some light on hybrid routing protocol is given.

Zone routing protocol (ZRP): The Zone Routing Protocol (ZRP) is a prototype routing protocol. ZRP is formed by two sub-protocols, the Intra zone Routing Protocol (IARP) and the Inter zone Routing Protocol (IERP). IARP is “a limited scope proactive routing protocol used to improve the performance of existing globally reactive routing protocols” (Haas et al., 2002). It relies on the service of a certain neighbor discovery protocol (NDP) to provide neighbor information. IARP may use a scheme based on the time-to-live (TTL) field in IP packets to control the zone range. (When a broadcast packet passes a router, the value of TTL is decremented by one before it is rebroadcast, and when TTL equals to zero, the packet is not rebroadcast). IERP is the reactive routing component of ZRP (Haas et al., 2002). This scheme is responsible for finding a global path. It avoids global queries for destinations that would be sent to surrounding r-hop neighbors. When global queries are required, “the routing zone based broadcast service can be used to efficiently guide route queries outward, rather

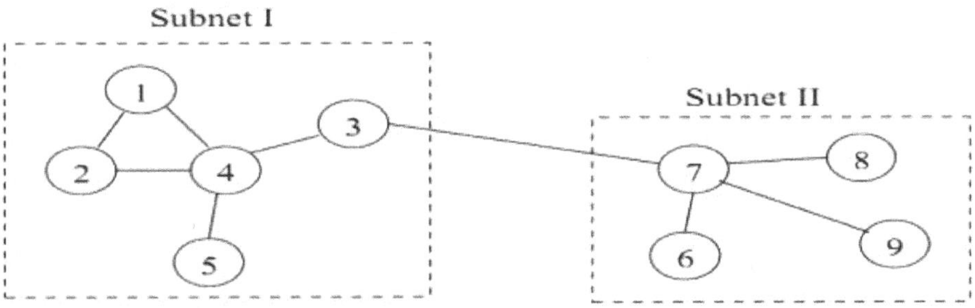

Figure 2. Example of ZRP.

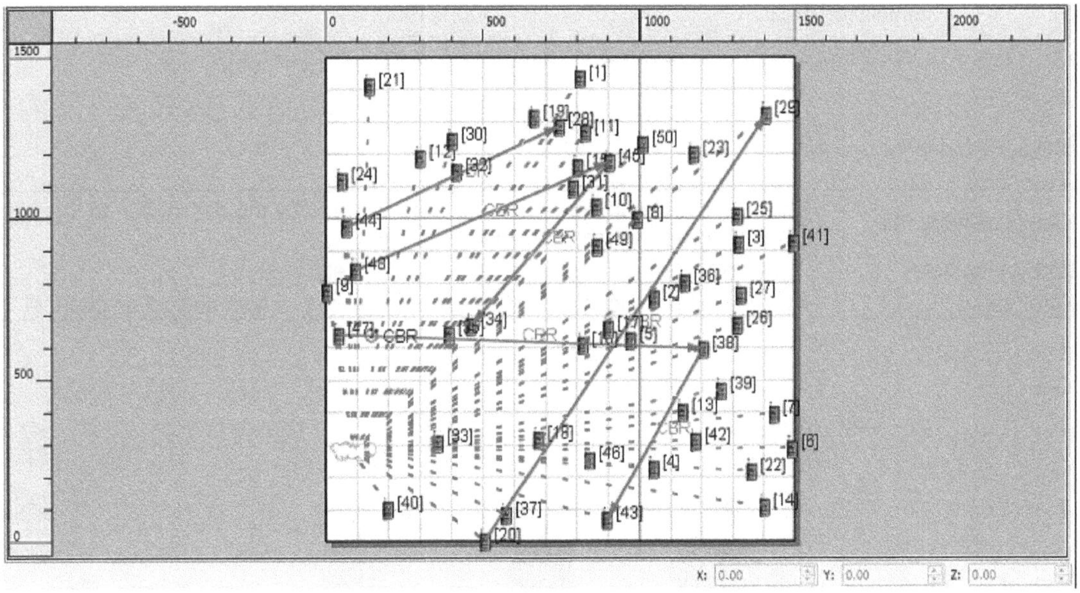

Figure 3. Node placement scenario.

than blindly relaying queries from neighbor to neighbor" (Haas et al., 2002). ZRP tries to combine the advantages of reactive and proactive routing protocols. The potential disadvantage is the lack of route optimization. We use the example network in Figure 2 to briefly show the concept of ZRP. The range of the zone is set to one. So routers in Subnets I and II use proactive IARP to find routes to other routers in the same subnet. For routes to the other subnet, reactive IERP is used.

The performance of the routing protocols OLSR, AODV, DSR and ZRP are compared using Qualnet 5.0.2 Network Simulator with the metrics like throughput, end-to-end delay and packets delivery ratio.

METHODS

Node placement scenario and simulation environment

Qualnet 5.0.2 network simulator (www.scalablenetworks.com/products/Qualnet/download.php#docs) has been used to evaluate the performance of OLSR, AODV, DSR and ZRP routing protocols of mobile ad hoc networks. The physical medium used is 802.11 PHY with a data rate of 2 Mbps. The MAC protocol used is the 802.11 MAC protocol, configured for MANET mode. The simulations are carried out for network densities of 25, 50 and 100 nodes respectively. The area considered for the above network densities are 1500 m × 1500 m for stationary nodes. Simulations are configured for the performance evaluation of different routing protocols with the metrics like packet delivery ratio, end to end delay and throughput. Figure 3 shows the node placement scenario for the 50 nodes. Network environment is described in Table 2.

Performance metrics

We compared the performance of OLSR, AODV, DSR and ZRP under 25, 50 and 100 stationary nodes. We evaluate the performance according to the following metrics as shown in the Table 3.

RESULTS

The variation of PDR of various routing protocols for

Table 2. Scenario parameter.

Routing protocols	OLSR, AODV, DSR, ZRP
Radio type	802.11b
No. of channels	1
Channel frequency	2.4 GHz
Mobility	Stationary
Path loss model	Two way
Energy model	Mica Motes
Shadowing model	Constant
Pause time	30 s
Simulation time	300 s
Battery model	Linear Model
Simulation area	1500 × 1500
Number of nodes	25, 50, 100

Table 3. Performance matrices.

Packet delivery ratio	The ratio of the number of data packets received by the destination to the number of data packets sent by the source.
End-to-end delay	The average end-to-end latency of data packets.
Throughput	Average rate of successful message delivery over a communication channel.

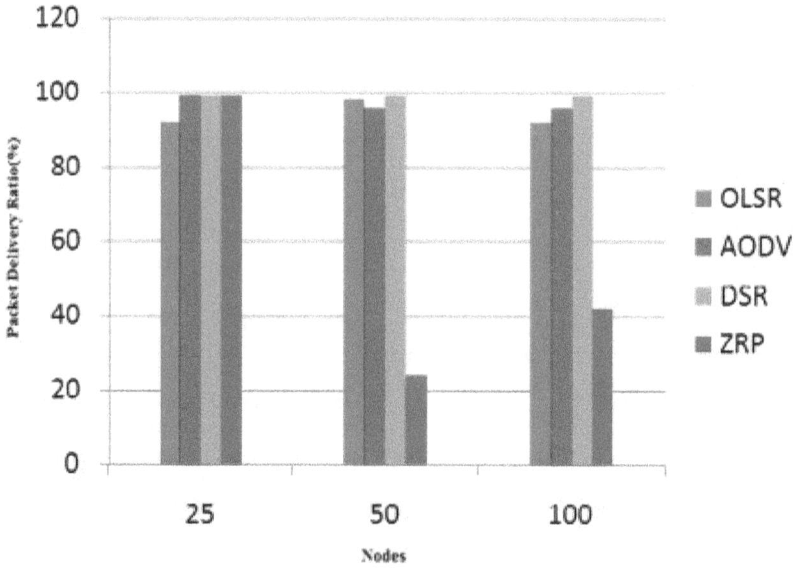

Figure 4. Plot of packet deliver ratio (%) vs node.

stationary nodes with respect to node densities 25, 50 and 100 nodes is given in Figure 4.

Figure 5 shows the variation in end-to-end delay for stationary nodes with respect to node densities 25, 50 and 100 nodes.

Figure 6 shows the variation in throughput of various routing protocols considered for stationary nodes with respect to node densities 25, 50 and 100 nodes.

Conclusion

The performance evaluation of proactive (OLSR), reactive (AODV, DSR) and hybrid (ZRP) routing protocols for stationary nodes are studied by varying the node density (25, 50 and 100) using Qualnet 5.0.2 network simulator. From the results it can be observed that reactive routing protocols AODV and DSR are suited for

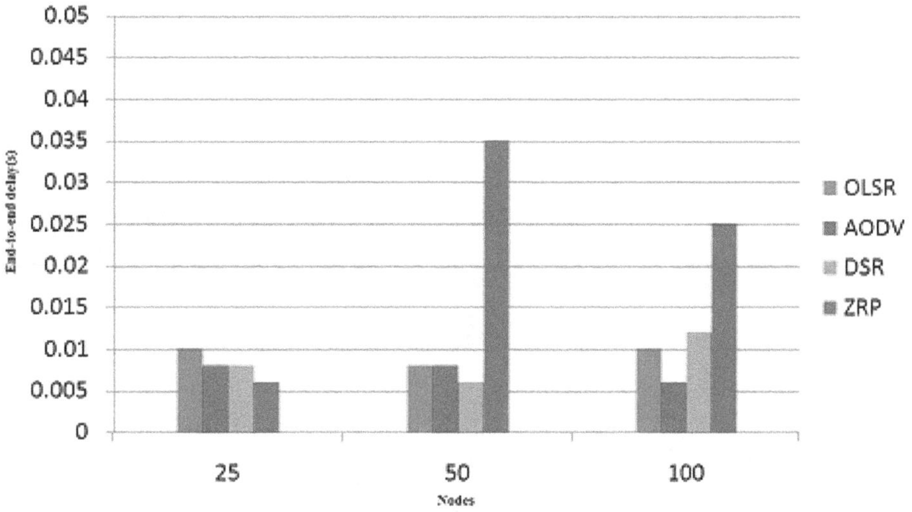

Figure 5. End-to-end-delay(s) vs nodes

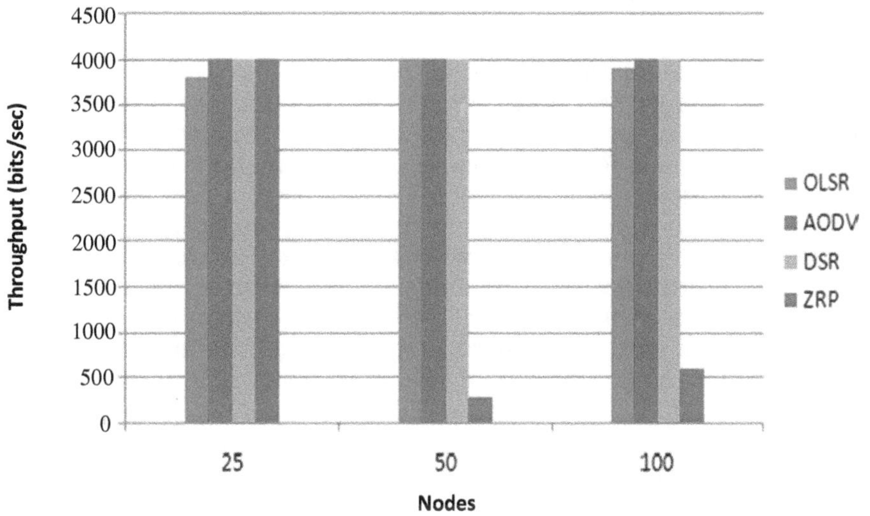

Figure 6. Throughput (bits/sec) vs nodes.

applications where throughput are very critical. ZRP and OLSR being the location based protocols need sufficient time to establish route discovery and route maintenance; hence for large range mobile applications they are best suited.

REFERENCES

Aron ID, Gupta SKS (2001). On the scalability of on-demand routing protocols for mobile ad hoc networks: an analytical study,". J. Interconnect. Networks., 2(1): 5-29.

Baccala B (1997). Editor, Link State Routing Protocols, Connected: An Internet Encyclopedia, Available at http://www.freesoft.org/CIE/index.htm.

Boukerche A (2001). Performance comparison and analysis of ad hoc routing algorithms, in Proc. of IEEE International Conference on Performance, Computing, and Communications, pp. 171-178.

Force (IETF) draft, Avail-able at http://www.ietf.org/internet-drafts/draft-ietf-manet-zone-ierp-02.txt.

Haas ZJ, Pearlman MR, Samar P (2002). The Interzone Routing Protocol (IERP) for Ad Hoc Networks," Internet Engineering Task.

Haas ZJ, Pearlman MR, Samar P (2002). The Intrazone Routing Protocol (IARP) for Ad Hoc Networks," Internet Engineering Task Force (IETF) draft, Available at http://www.ietf.org/internet-drafts/draft-ietf-manet-zone-iarp-02.txt.

Philippe JPM, Amir Q (2001). Optimized Link State Routing Protocol, IETF Draft, http://www.ietf.org/internet-drafts/draft-ietf-manet-olsr-06.txt.

QualNet documentation, QualNet 5.0 Model Library: Advanced Wireless; http://www.scalablenetworks.com/products/Qualnet/download.php#docs.

QualNet Network Simulator; Available: http://www.scalable-networks.com.

Siva RC, Manoj BS (2011). Ad hoc wireless networks architectures and protocols. Pearson Education, pp. 85-89.

24

An open source Geographic Information System (GIS) approach to water supply management, distribution and billing

David Ndegwa Kuria[1]*, Douglas Engoke Musiega[2], Moses Murimi Ngigi[2] and Simon Kibue Ngugi[2]

[1]Department of Geomatic Engineering and Geospatial Information Science, Kimathi University College of Technology, Nyeri, Kenya.

[2]Department of Geomatic Engineering and Geospatial Information Systems, Jomo Kenyatta University of Agriculture and Technology, Nairobi, Kenya.

In this work a comprehensive solution for the Gatanga Water Trust (GWT) has been developed to assist it in managing its water supply and distribution. The solution comprises two subcomponents: a mapping component and a billing component which are tightly coupled together. The proposed system uses stable open source products for the mapping component and the database. At present the GWT uses outdated maps and sketches for design and installation of a new water supply infrastructure. A billing system is in place which is used to manage client accounts, record meter readings, prepare bills and record payments made. This presents a somewhat disjointed approach to management of the water supply and its attendant infrastructure. The database that stores the account information is very different (softcopy) from that storing the spatial information (hardcopy/paper based). In the proposed solution, a single database is used, centralized or distributed. The mapping component provides an interface through which preliminary design of new and planned infrastructure can be done. After installation, these are reflected in the database and the information becomes available as soon as it is stored. The billing component uses the same database to manage account information. Since the information is managed in one system, there is a streamlined and orderly flow from data collection to the final products from the system. The proposed solution leverages advancement in technology by providing two approaches - a desktop application for users within the Trust's intranet and a web mapping application for users utilizing the wider internet.

Key words: Open source, Geographic Information Systems (GIS), water supply, billing, distribution.

INTRODUCTION

Progress made in information technology has greatly opened up the number of opportunities supporting data analyses and communications in the recent years. Geographic Information Systems (GIS) have provided new and exciting ways of acquiring natural resource data and are also providing efficient means of processing, managing and integrating this data (Opadeyi, 2007). A Geographic Information System (GIS) in a narrow sense is a computer system for the input, manipulation, storage and output of digital spatial data (Konecny, 2003). The more encompassing definition considers it to be a digital system for the acquisition, management, analysis, and visualization of spatial data for the purposes of planning, administering and monitoring in the natural and socio-economic environment (Konecny, 2003).

A Geographic Information System allows one to create and manage spatially referenced data which is useful for any field or situation that utilizes spatial information (Longley et al., 2005). In the recent past GIS has been mainstreamed, since every conceivable field can

*Corresponding author. E-mail: dn.kuria@gmail.com.

potentially be enriched by using GIS technology to manage the location based information, that is, education (Kuria et al., 2011), water resource management (Kuria et al., 2012), among a host of others. There are a number of GIS products that can be used – proprietary (closed source) and open source. Commercial products while possessing powerful analysis features are expensive and for most clients, such solutions may not be fully utilized when procured. On the other hand, while open source products may not have the same level of complexity, they have features that can be used to answer some simple analyses. In some cases though, they are excellent alternatives since some have advanced analysis features.

With the advent of internet and associated technologies such as mobile and wireless technology, internet based applications have proliferated, greatly lowering costs to the end consumers who do not need to procure expensive software to realize solutions to their problems. On the other hand, desktop applications are able to utilize the full power of the host computing infrastructure. They are less likely to be targeted for attacks since they are not easily reachable and hence present a level of security that internet applications do not have.

For planning and design, the GWT uses outdated topographical maps and sketches drawn when pipes are laid out. At present it does not have any softcopy spatial management system in place. This approach implies that it is very difficult to visualize this information in real-time incorporating proposed designs and new infrastructure installations. There is an electronic billing system in place which the management says is fraught with some inconsistencies. Since this system is not connected with the spatial management system, it is not easy for employees to visually connect between client accounts and their locations in space. This current approach is thus very limited and the Trust is not able to leverage technological advances to improve the management of the water trust.

This work sought to develop an open source geocomputing solution to assist the Gatanga Water Trust manage its water supply infrastructure and distribution network. This solution comprises a desktop mapping and billing solution targeted for the intranet user and a web mapping and billing solution for both internet and intranet users.

To realize this, the following specific objectives were formulated: (i) determine current and future system needs for the Trust, (ii) formulate a desktop GIS strategy to solve the needs, (iii) formulate a web based GIS strategy for internet users, (iv) combine the two solutions (strategies) into one overall solution for the Trust.

Study area

The Gatanga Water Trust (GWT) forms part of the original Kandara water project which was constructed in the early seventies. The project was a community initiative with the then local leaders spearheading the sourcing for funds (Figure 1).

GWT was formed as a result of the water sector reforms initiated in 2002. It is run by a board of trustees drawn from Gatanga District representing individual locations. The distribution system in the scheme is wholly gravity serving a rural set up. It is served by two water intakes constructed inside the Kimakia Forest. The intakes draw water from the Kimakia and Thika Rivers. Initially the GWT had 2000 active connections but since the injection of the funds the number rose to 4000. The current water production stands at 7000 m^3 per day. It is serving approximately 9000 active consumers of which 4000 have been metered. The core functions of the GWT are sourcing of water, treatment and conservation of water, distribution of water, billing and revenue collection.

The scheme has two subsystems which are independent of each other. They are referred to as North and South of Kiama. The North of Kiama River system gets its water from the old intake constructed on the Thika River. It serves Kigoro, Mukarara, Kiriaini and Kihumbuini locations. The laid pipeline stretches from the forest edge (Kimakia) to Wanyaga – Kimandi – Ndakaini – Ndunyu chege – Mukarara, Gitiri – Mukurwe – Jasho. The South of Kiama River system gets water from the newly constructed intake on the Kimakia River. It serves Kariara, Gatanga and Mugumoni locations. The pipe network stretches from Kinguri –Gatura – Chomo – Kirwara – Kigio and Gatunyu. Gatanga Water Company (GWC) was formed in 2004 mandated to manage the GWT, and was registered as a licensed water provider with Athi Water services board. The company headquarters are situated at the Gatanga divisional headquarters in Mabanda (Gatanga Constituency, 2010).

METHODOLOGY

Planning is crucial to the successful implementation of the GIS supported solution as recommended by Tomlinson, (2007). The work was undertaken in a two pronged fashion; fieldwork coupled with system development, and the eventual system deployment and subsequent maintenance scheduling. Field data collection was done using Global Positioning System (GPS) receivers. Details picked were decided after the user needs assessment analysis.

The composite system uses two design approaches geared at coming up with (i) an internet application and (ii) a desktop application.

Figure 2 captures this design viewpoint where two types of users are anticipated: the intranet user and the internet user. The intranet user is a staff member of the Trust while the internet user is thought of as (i) an account holder or (ii) a general internet visitor or (iii) a staff member working from home or office. For this purpose two application approaches have been adopted, with the desktop solution addressing the needs of the intranet user, while the web mapping application addresses the needs of the internet users. The composite system uses the same underlying database server to manage the information. The desktop application connects and communicates with the database server but does not make use of the map server. On the other hand, the internet application

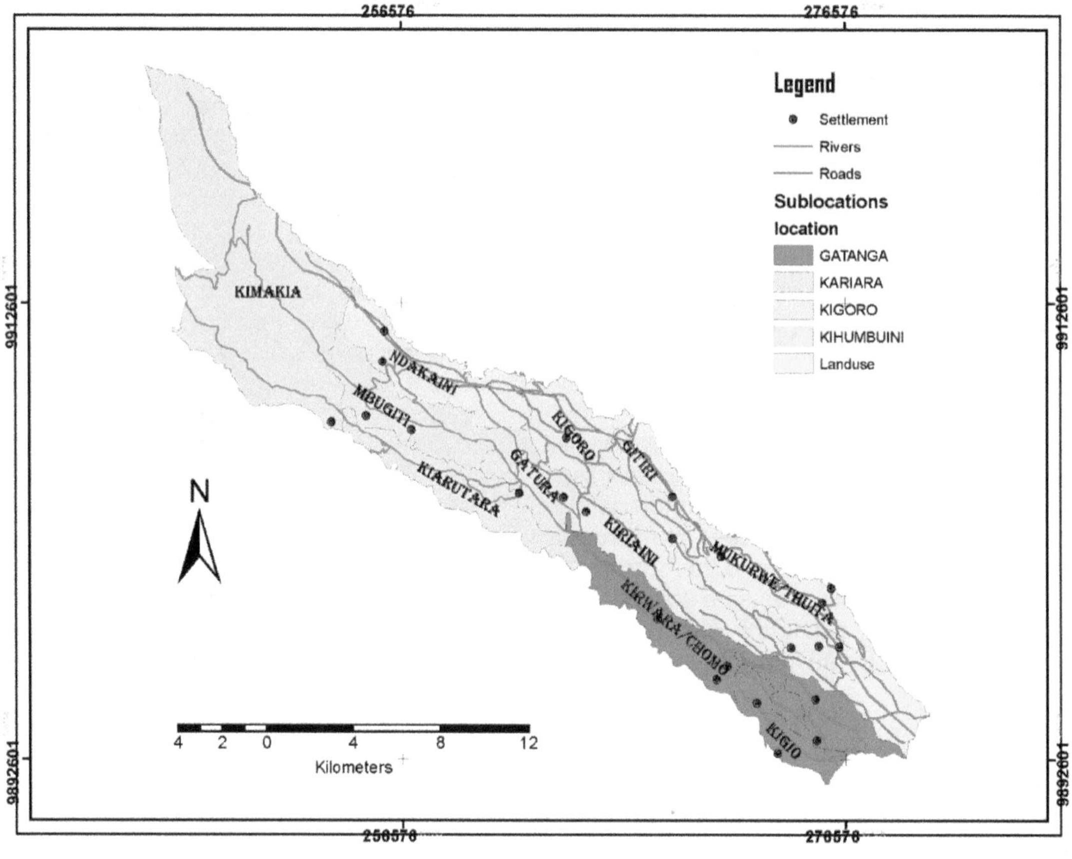

Figure 1. The study area.

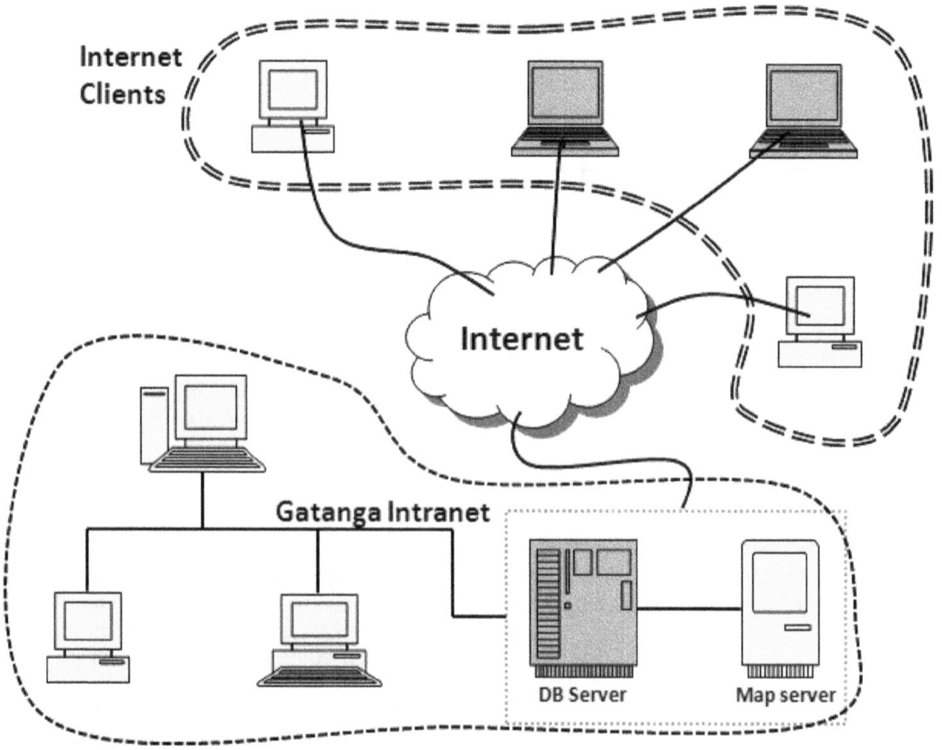

Figure 2. The envisaged system infrastructure.

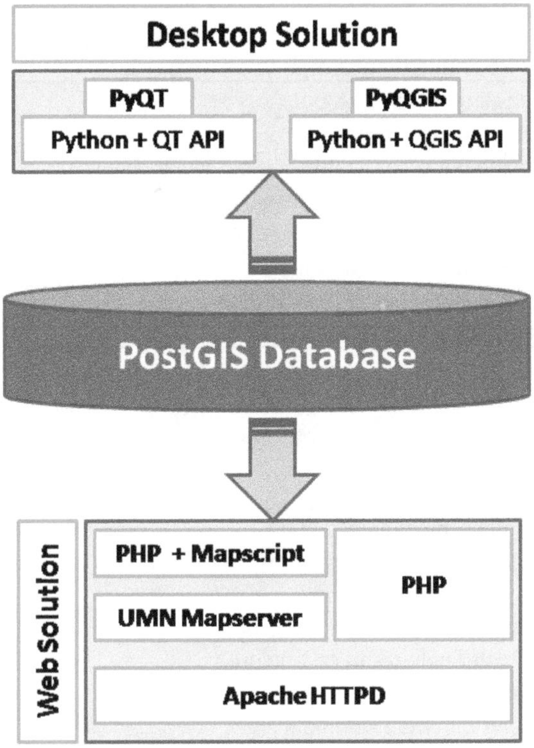

Figure 3. Open source tools used.

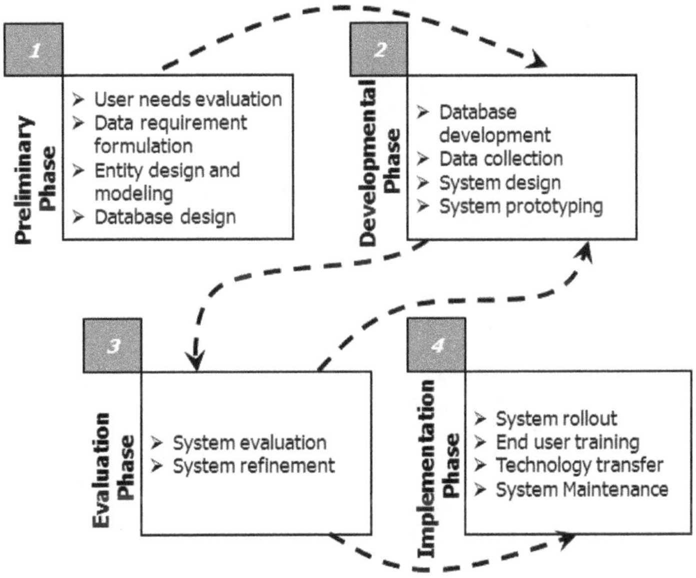

Figure 4. Project workflow.

connects to the database via the map server. In this case the map server serves as a proxy and as a rendering engine to prepare the maps for onward transmission to the internet client.

Figure 3 shows the various open source tools used in the solution development. For the desktop solution, a standalone application was developed using Python and the Python bindings for QT (PyQT version 4) and QGIS (PyQGIS) allowing access to the respective Application Programming Interfaces (APIs). The web solution uses P. Mapper framework, which is a custom PHP Mapscript application that utilizes PHP Mapscript and University of Minesota Mapserver as the map rendering interface, with billing implemented using PHP and extending the P. Mapper based application. Both systems utilize a PostGIS database which is a spatially aware PostgreSQL database.

Figure 4 captures the flow of activities that were undertaken to realize this research. It comprises four phases (i) a preliminary

Table 1. Clients' needs analysis.

S/N	Functionality/Feature	Average rank
1.	Indicating meter location	3
2.	Interaction with map	3
3.	Finding out billing status of a particular client	2
4.	Confirming client's meter reading	1
5.	Should the WSP information be accessible online?	1
6.	Access to internet enabled devices	3
7.	Specialized views with map data	4
8.	Reporting problems on the system	2

Table 2. WSPs staff expected functionalities ranking.

S/N	Feature/Functionality	Average rank
1.	Receiving bill payments	1
2.	Recording meter readings	1
3.	Adding new meters/accounts	1
4.	Indicating new/old meter locations	2
5.	Editing water network infrastructure	2
6.	Being able to work on the system remotely	2
7.	Interacting with map elements	3
8.	Identifying leakages on the infrastructure	3
9.	Performing zone summaries and statistics	3
10.	Reducing non-revenue water	2
11.	Scheduling meter reading outings	2
12.	Maintaining a journaling system	3
13.	Use free and open source approaches	3
14.	Consider commercial approaches	4

(conceptualization) phase, (ii) a development phase, (iii) an evaluation and assessment phase and, (iv) an implementation phase.

During conceptualization phase, a detailed inventory of the current and anticipated future needs was carried out based on interviews. This yielded information on the data required to address those needs. In this phase all entities that needed to be stored in the database and their relationships were identified. 300 questionnaires were distributed to the clients in the catchment region of the WSP. Of these 102 responses were collected back and used to draw up a list of features they desired to have offered. Table 1 illustrates the relative importance of features that the clients would want implemented. The ranking was done on a scale of 1 to 5 with 1 being the most significant and 5 being the least significant. From the analysis, clients expect the system to be able to support querying of billing status, meter reading and report incidences occurring on their metered accounts. There was consensus that the WSP needs to embrace Internet approaches in disseminating and allowing clients interrogate the database.

To determine the level of functionality to support for the WSPs staff, 60 questionnaires were distributed to these staff members. 45 questionnaires were collected. The ranking adopted was similar to that for the clients. Table 2 illustrates the importance of the features that the staff desired to be implemented.

During the developmental phase, the necessary database schema for the entities identified was implemented. In parallel, all necessary data was collected and aggregated into this database. The entire system was designed identifying the various features and functionalities that needed to be implemented to answer all (or most) of the user needs. In this phase a prototype of the whole system was made available incorporating as many of the features as possible. The system was developed following the Object Oriented Programming concepts due to the advantages the paradigm possesses (Gamma et al., 1995).

Table 3 shows the main entities, their attributes and methods following the OO model. These main entities are pipelines, customers, meters, bill payment, meter reading and users.

The evaluation phase was used for rigorously testing all the implemented features of the prototype, carefully assessing how well the proposed system was able to address all the needs of the end users. In this phase any refinements required were be undertaken. In case of major refinements, these were developed and incorporated in the prototype and reevaluated. Hence the development and evaluation phases fed back and forward until a stable prototype was achieved. It is during this phase that user manuals and system documentation were written.

At the implementation phase, the prototype was migrated to the Trust's network, installed and configured for daily usage. To ensure proper use of the solution, end user training was conducted. This training served as a means to transfer knowledge about the underlying technologies to the Trust. A maintenance schedule is currently being discussed with a view of keeping the system up-to-date and incorporating new ideas and needs.

After the roll out of the implementation, some problems inherited

Table 3. Main objects identified with their associated properties and methods.

Entity (Object)	Properties (Attibutes)	Methods
Pipelines	ID, diameter, material, date installed, geometry, status	addPipe(), removePipe(), getProperties(), getStatus(), updatePipeline()
Customers	Last name, First Name, customer id, meter no, date connected, address	addCustomer(), updateCustomer(), removeCustomer(), disconnect(), reconnect(), connect()
Meter	Meterno, user type, zone, date installed, sewered, geometry	addMeter(), replaceMeter(), updateMeter(), checkLeakage()
Users	Name, username, password, department	addUser(), removeUser(), updateUser(), login()
Meter reading	Meterno, date read, reading, reader	readMeter(), updateReading()
Bill payment	Meterno, amount, date paid,	payBill(), updatePayment()

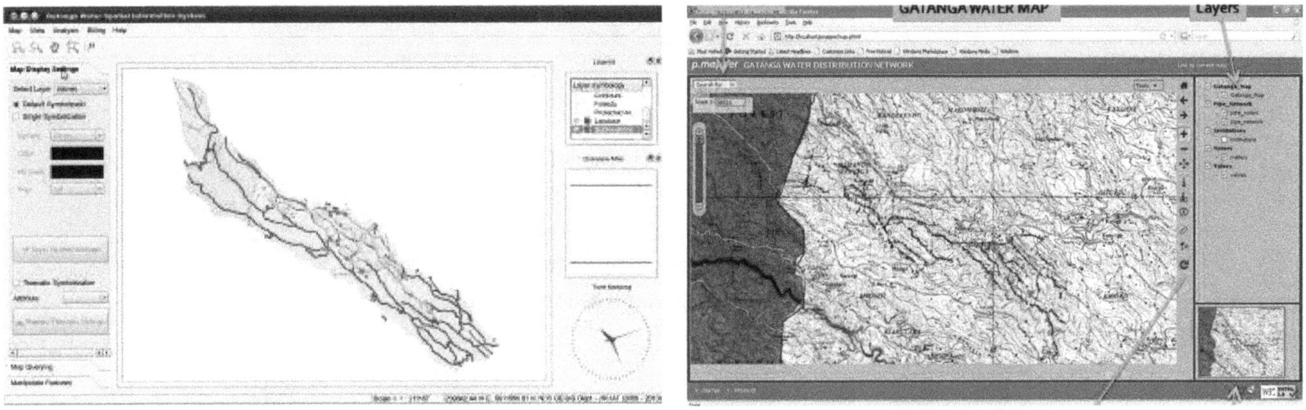

(a) (b)

Figure 5. The main interface for (a) the desktop solution and (b) the web-based solution.

from the database held by the WSP were revealed. These include duplicated meters, illegal connections and logistical challenges in pinpointing leakages in the system. This system was able to identify 298 duplicated meters which were subsequently cleaned; and highlight illegal connections collected from the GPS field collection exercise.

RESULTS AND DISCUSSION

The following mapping features were included in the solution: (i) interface with a map window with tools that allow users to zoom in/out, pan, zoom to full extent or zoom to a window of interest, (ii) tools to allow turning on/off of data layers in the window, (iii) tools to allow users to interrogate the map displayed to retrieve non spatial attribute information for the point under a cursor, (iv) tools that allow the users to display a layer using default symbolization (using symbols from the Gatanga) or allow the user to use other symbolization, display a thematic display of the layer using any of the available attributes, (v) allow the users to perform attribute querying using available attributes, (vi) tools to allow entering of GPS coordinates for new features and their attributes, (vii) tools for deleting data that may need to be removed. Figure 5 show the main interfaces to the system. To access this interface the user has to log into the system using credentials that allow tracking in case there are changes made and therefore can assign responsibility for any actions made.

On the billing front, the following features were implemented: (i) tools to allow addition of new clients, edit client details, delete former clients, (ii) tools to record meter readings, edit or delete erroneous meter readings and printing out of meter reading forms, (iii) tools to process account billing, allowing printing of receipts. These tools are a sampling of the collection of tools that were developed in this project venture. Figures 6 and 7 show some of the interfaces exposing these functionalities.

The total client based was pegged at 9350 members

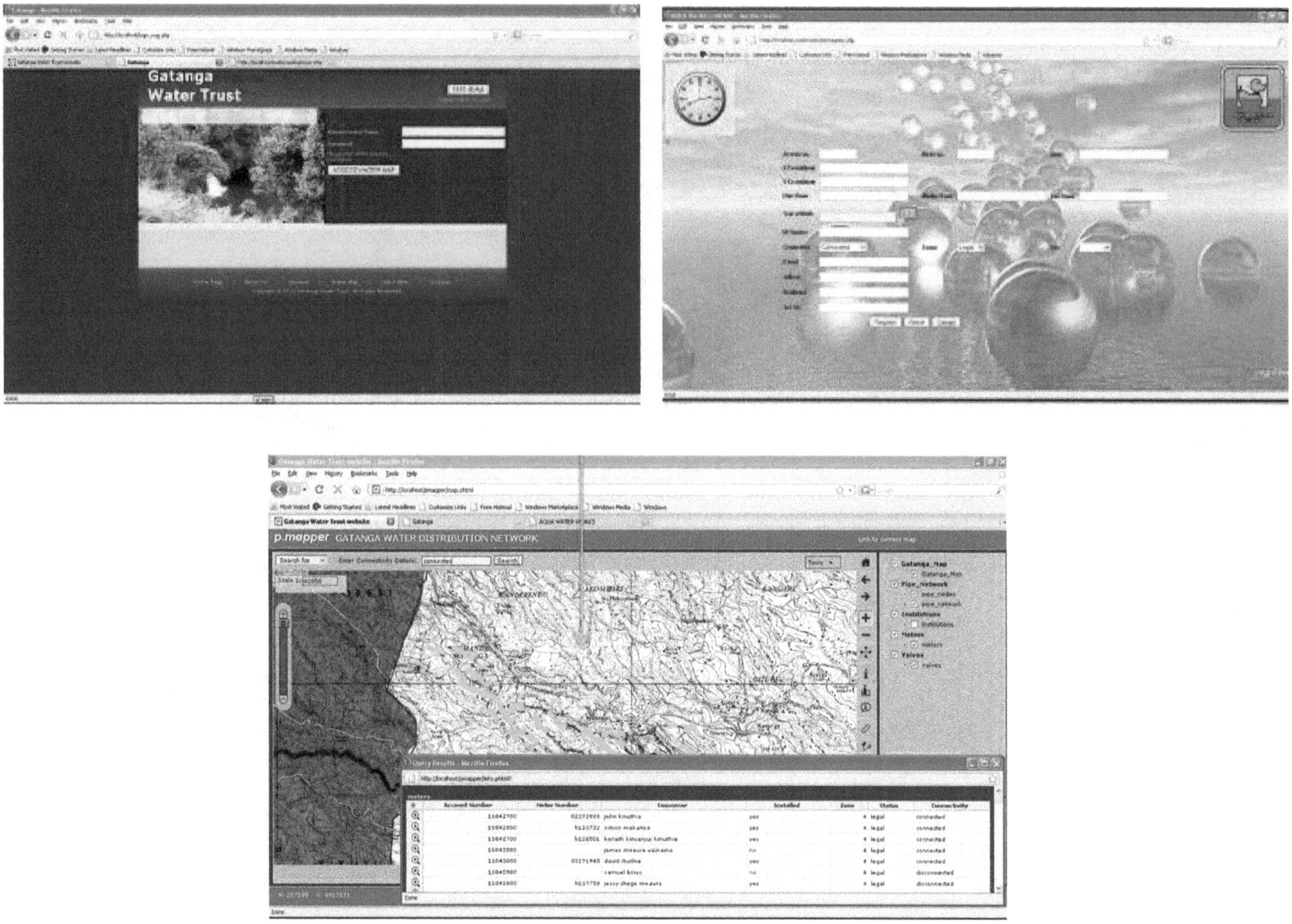

Figure 6. The web-based interfaces to the functionalities.

Table 4. Improvement in Revenue Collection (in Million KSh).

Month	Collection in 2009 (Prior)	Collection in 2010 (After)
January	1.49	1.94
February	1.35	1.97
March	1.34	1.98
April	1.42	2.01
May	1.39	2.07
June	1.50	2.14

spread across the 9 zones. Within the first six months that the system was in use in the WSP, there was marked increase in revenue collection while streamlined workflows can now be generated.

Table 4 shows the improvement in revenue collection over a similar period prior to the onset of the project. Over this period, there was no significant increase in connections and thus the improved revenue collections can be attributed to ability to rope in illegal connections and reductions in non-revenue water.

Conclusion

The proposed system has been demonstrated as meeting the objectives set out. The following products have been delivered: (i) an open source desktop geocomputing application featuring GIS tools and a billing system, (ii) an open source web mapping solution featuring scaled down GIS tools and billing capabilities. To support this system, (iii) a spatially aware database system with the Gatanga water infrastructure database.

This system has already been deployed on the Gatanga Water Trust's offices and is currently being evaluated and used before it can be fully rolled out. It is therefore recommended that the system once satisfactory be cascaded to other water service providers. This solution has also demonstrated the utility of open source GIS software and the coupling of systems to enhance infrastructure and asset management.

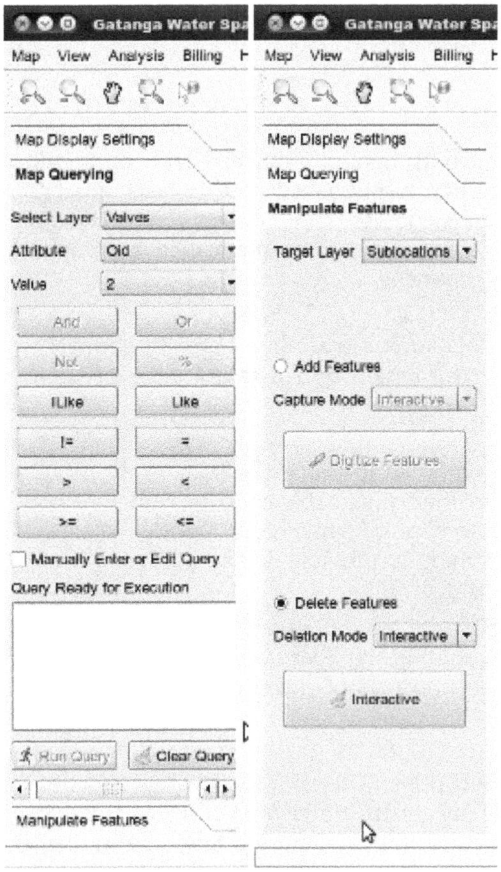

(a) Map querying functionalities

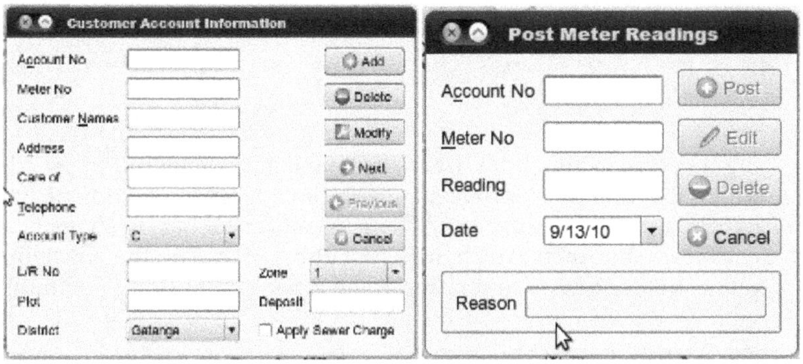

(b) Some data entry functionalities

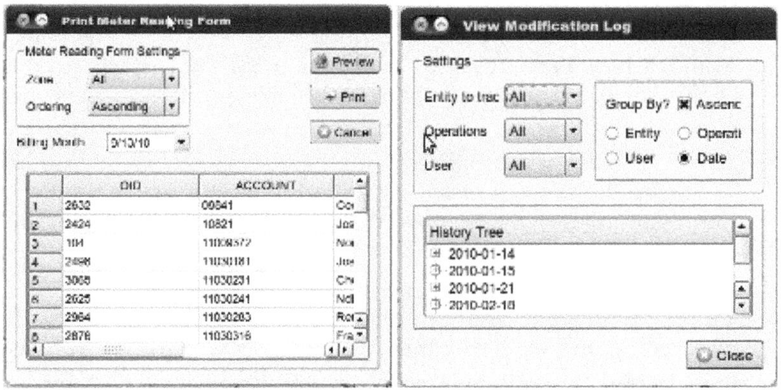

(c) Printing functionalities

Figure 7. Some of the implemented functionalities in the desktop application.

ACKNOWLEDGEMENTS

The authors wish to thank the Jomo Kenyatta University of Agriculture and Technology for providing resources to support this research work and Gatanga Water Trust for their cooperation during data capture and evaluation phases.

REFERENCES

Gamma E, Helm R, Johnson R, Vlissides J (1995). Design Patterns: Elements of Reusable Object-Oriented Software. Addison-Wesley Professional, Boston.

Gatanga Constituency (2010). Development Projects Overview. Gatanga Constituency. http://www.gatanga.com/projects/20.html. (Accessed 10th October 2012).

Kuria DN, Gachari MK, Macharia MW, Mungai E (2012). Mapping groundwater potential in Kitui District using geospatial technologies. Int. J Water Resour. Environ. Eng. 4(1):15–22.

Kuria DN, Ngigi MM, Wanjiku JW, Kasumuni RK (2011). Managing distribution of national examinations using geospatial technologies: A case study of Pumwani and Central divisions. Int. J. Comput. Eng. Res. 2(5):82–92.

Konecny G (2003). Geoinformation: Remote Sensing, Photogrammetry and Geographic Information Systems. Taylor & Francis, London.

Longley PA, Goodchild MF, Maguire DJ, Rhind DW (2005). Geographic Information Systems and Science. John Wiley & Sons Ltd, Chichester.

Opadeyi J (2007). Road Map Towards Effective Mainstreaming of GIS for Watershed Management in the Caribbean. Caribbean Environmental Health Institute, The Morne, St. Lucia. http://www.cep.unep.org/events-and-meetings/13th-igm-1/IWCAM-2en.pdf. (Accessed 17th April 2011).

Tomlinson R (2007). Thinking about GIS: Geographic Information System Planning for Managers (Third ed.). ESRI Presss, California.

Permissions

All chapters in this book were first published in IJCER, by Academic Journals; hereby published with permission under the Creative Commons Attribution License or equivalent. Every chapter published in this book has been scrutinized by our experts. Their significance has been extensively debated. The topics covered herein carry significant findings which will fuel the growth of the discipline. They may even be implemented as practical applications or may be referred to as a beginning point for another development.

The contributors of this book come from diverse backgrounds, making this book a truly international effort. This book will bring forth new frontiers with its revolutionizing research information and detailed analysis of the nascent developments around the world.

We would like to thank all the contributing authors for lending their expertise to make the book truly unique. They have played a crucial role in the development of this book. Without their invaluable contributions this book wouldn't have been possible. They have made vital efforts to compile up to date information on the varied aspects of this subject to make this book a valuable addition to the collection of many professionals and students.

This book was conceptualized with the vision of imparting up-to-date information and advanced data in this field. To ensure the same, a matchless editorial board was set up. Every individual on the board went through rigorous rounds of assessment to prove their worth. After which they invested a large part of their time researching and compiling the most relevant data for our readers.

The editorial board has been involved in producing this book since its inception. They have spent rigorous hours researching and exploring the diverse topics which have resulted in the successful publishing of this book. They have passed on their knowledge of decades through this book. To expedite this challenging task, the publisher supported the team at every step. A small team of assistant editors was also appointed to further simplify the editing procedure and attain best results for the readers.

Apart from the editorial board, the designing team has also invested a significant amount of their time in understanding the subject and creating the most relevant covers. They scrutinized every image to scout for the most suitable representation of the subject and create an appropriate cover for the book.

The publishing team has been an ardent support to the editorial, designing and production team. Their endless efforts to recruit the best for this project, has resulted in the accomplishment of this book. They are a veteran in the field of academics and their pool of knowledge is as vast as their experience in printing. Their expertise and guidance has proved useful at every step. Their uncompromising quality standards have made this book an exceptional effort. Their encouragement from time to time has been an inspiration for everyone.

The publisher and the editorial board hope that this book will prove to be a valuable piece of knowledge for researchers, students, practitioners and scholars across the globe.

List of Contributors

Mohamed Najeh Lakhoua
High Institute of Applied Sciences and Technology (ISSAT), Laboratory ACS (Analysis and Command of Systems), Route de Tabarka 7030, Mateur, Tunisia

Taieb Ben Jouida
High Institute of Applied Sciences and Technology (ISSAT), SEPE (Systemic, Energetic, Productique and Environnement), Route de Tabarka 7030, Mateur, Tunisia

Khandaker Abir Rahman
Department of Computer Science and Engineering, University of Dhaka, Dhaka-1000, Bangladesh

Shafaeat Hossain
Department of Computer Science and Engineering, University of Dhaka, Dhaka-1000, Bangladesh

Al-Amin Bhuiyan
Department of Electronics and Computer Science, Jahangirnagar University, Savar, Bangladesh

Tao Zhang
Department of Automation, Tsinghua University, Beijing, China

Md.Hasanuzzaman
Department of Computer Science and Engineering, University of Dhaka, Dhaka-1000, Bangladesh

H. Ueno
National Institute of Informatics (NII), Tokyo, Japan

Medhat H. A. Awadalla
Department of Communication, Electronics and Computers, Faculty of Engineering, University of Helwan, Egypt

Rania R. Darwish
Department of Mechatronics, Faculty of Engineering, University of Helwan, Egypt

O. Zohreh Akbari
Department of Information and Communication Technology, Faculty of Engineering, Payame Noor University, Tehran, Iran

M. B. Mutanga
Department of Computer Science, University of Zululand, KwaDlangezwa, South Africa

P. Mudali
Department of Computer Science, University of Zululand, KwaDlangezwa, South Africa

M. O. Adigun
Department of Computer Science, University of Zululand, KwaDlangezwa, South Africa

M. N. Lakhoua
Department of Electronics, ISSAT Mateur, Laboratory of Analysis and Command of Systems, ENIT Tunisia

A. F. Alajmi
Communication and Electronics Department, Faculty of Engineering, Helwan University, Egypt

E. M. Saad
Communication and Electronics Department, Faculty of Engineering, Helwan University, Egypt

M. H. Awadalla
Communication and Electronics Department, Faculty of Engineering, Helwan University, Egypt

Hakan Koyuncu
Computer Science Department, Loughborough University, Loughborough, United Kingdom

Shuang Hua Yang
Computer Science Department, Loughborough University, Loughborough, United Kingdom

S. S. Patil
Rajarambapu Institute of Technology Rajaramnagar/CSE, Sangli, India

GU Feng
ZheJiang Technical Institute of Economics, Hangzhou, China

M.EL-Sayed Waheed
Department of Mathematics, Faculty of science, Zagzig University, Egypt

Osama Abdo Mohamed
Department of Mathematics, Faculty of science, Zagzig University, Egypt

M.E. Abd El-Aziz
Department of Mathematics, Faculty of science, Zagzig University, Egypt

Aran Nayebi
727 Moreno Avenue, Palo Alto, California, United States of America

David Ndegwa Kuria
Department of Geomatic Engineering and Geospatial Information Science, Kimathi University College of Technology, P. O. Box 657 - 10100, Nyeri, Kenya

Moses Murimi Ngigi
Department of Geomatic Engineering and Geospatial Information Systems, Jomo Kenyatta University of Agriculture and Technology, P. O. Box 62000 - 00200, Nairobi, Kenya

Josephine Wanjiru Wanjiku
Department of Geomatic Engineering and Geospatial Information Science, Kimathi University College of Technology, P. O. Box 657 - 10100, Nyeri, Kenya

Rachel Kavutha Kasumuni
Department of Geomatic Engineering and Geospatial Information Systems, Jomo Kenyatta University of Agriculture and Technology, P. O. Box 62000 - 00200, Nairobi, Kenya

Ravneet Kaur
Department of Computer science and Engineering, Beant College of Engineering and Technology, Gurdaspur Punjab, India

Fuad .M. Alkoot
HITN-PAAET P. O. Box 4575, Alsalmia, 22046, Kuwait

Abdesslem Lamari
High Institute of Applied Sciences and Technology (ISSAT), Department of Electronics, Route de Tabarka 7030, Mateur, Tunisia

Sumit Goyal
Dairy Technology Division, National Dairy Research Institute, Karnal-132001 (Haryana), India

Gyanendra Kumar Goyal
Dairy Technology Division, National Dairy Research Institute, Karnal-132001 (Haryana), India

Olusanya O. Olamide
Computer Science Department, University of Lagos, Akoka, Lagos, Lagos State, Nigeria

Ayeni O. A. Joshua
Computer Science Department, University of Lagos, Akoka, Lagos, Lagos State, Nigeria

Zeyad AL-Zhour
Department of Basic Sciences and Humanities, College of Engineering, University of Dammam, Kingdom of Saudi Arabia (KSA)

Abd El-Naser A. Mohamed
Department of Electronics and Electrical Communication Engineering, Faculty of Electronic Engineering, Menouf 32951, Menoufia University, Egypt

Ahmed Nabih Zaki Rashed
Department of Electronics and Electrical Communication Engineering, Faculty of Electronic Engineering, Menouf 32951, Menoufia University, Egypt

Mahmoud M. A. Eid
Department of Electronics and Electrical Communication Engineering, Faculty of Electronic Engineering, Menouf 32951, Menoufia University, Egypt

Hiba Shahid
Department of Electrical and Computer Engineering, Effat University, Jeddah, Saudi Arabia

Wadee Alhalabi
Faculty of Computing and Information Technology (FCIT), King Abdulaziz University (KAU), Jeddah, Kingdom of Saudi Arabia

John Reif
Department of Computer Science, Duke University, Durham, NC 27707 USA and Adjunct Faculty of Computing and Information Technology (FCIT), King Abdulaziz University (KAU), Jeddah, Kingdom of Saudi Arabia

O. Olusanya Olamide
Department of Electrical and Electronic Engineering, College of Engineering, Bells University of Technology, Ota, Ogun State. Nigeria

A. Ogunseye Abiodun
Department of Electrical and Electronic Engineering, College of Engineering, Bells University of Technology, Ota, Ogun State. Nigeria

Nitin Arora
Department of Computer Science and Engineering, Govind Ballabh Pant Engineering College, Pauri, India

Suresh Kumar
Department of Computer Science and Engineering, Govind Ballabh Pant Engineering College, Pauri, India

David Ndegwa Kuria
Department of Geomatic Engineering and Geospatial Information Science, Kimathi University College of Technology, Nyeri, Kenya

Douglas Engoke Musiega
Department of Geomatic Engineering and Geospatial Information Systems, Jomo Kenyatta University of Agriculture and Technology, Nairobi, Kenya

Moses Murimi Ngigi
Department of Geomatic Engineering and Geospatial Information Systems, Jomo Kenyatta University of Agriculture and Technology, Nairobi, Kenya

Simon Kibue Ngugi
Department of Geomatic Engineering and Geospatial Information Systems, Jomo Kenyatta University of Agriculture and Technology, Nairobi, Kenya

Printed in the USA
CPSIA information can be obtained
at www.ICGtesting.com
JSHW051437221024
72173JS00006B/1501

9 781682 851005